EPIC ROMANCE

To my parents

'The debt immense of endless gratitude'
(*Paradise Lost*, IV. 52)

EPIC ROMANCE

Homer to Milton

COLIN BURROW

CLARENDON PRESS · OXFORD

Oxford University Press, Walton Street, Oxford OX2 6DP
Oxford New York
Athens Auckland Bangkok Bombay
Calcutta Cape Town Dar es Salaam Delhi
Florence Hong Kong Istanbul Karachi
Kuala Lumpur Madras Madrid Melbourne
Mexico City Nairobi Paris Singapore
Taipei Tokyo Toronto
and associated companies in
Berlin Ibadan

Oxford is a trade mark of Oxford University Press

Published in the United States
by Oxford University Press Inc., New York

First Published 1993

British Library Cataloguing in Publication Data
Data available

Library of Congress Cataloging in Publication Data
Burrow, Colin.
Epic romance: Homer to Milton/ Colin Burrow.
Includes bibliographical references and index.
1. English poetry—Early modern, 1500-1700—History and criticism.
2. Epic poetry, English—Classical influences. 3. Spenser, Edmund.
1552?-1599—Knowledge—Literature. 4. Milton, John, 1608-1674—
Knowledge—Literature. 5. Influence (Literary, artistic, etc.)
6. Epic poetry—History and criticism. 7. Romances—History and
criticism. 8. Homer—Influence. I. Title.
PR539.E64B87 1993
809.1'32—dc20   92-45882
ISBN 0-19-811794-9

3 5 7 9 10 8 6 4 2

Printed in Great Britain
on acid-free paper by
Ipswich Book Co Ltd.

Acknowledgements

MANY people have read and commented on parts of this book at many stages, and have complained about many of its errors, some of which no doubt remain, because I either like them or have failed to see them. It began life as a D.Phil. thesis called 'The English Humanist Epic 1580–1614' (Oxford, 1988). I would like to thank my supervisor, Emrys Jones, for encouraging me to follow my instincts into comparative literature. Without his encouragement this would have been a much narrower book. All of the following have also offered indispensable advice. Several of them have also given me lunch: Gavin Alexander, J. A. Burrow, J. P. Casey, P. B. Diffley, John Gould, Jill Gould, Jasper Griffin, Diana Wynne Jones, Jill Mann, Charles Martindale, Tony Nuttall, J. B. Trapp. The Master and Fellows of Gonville and Caius College have provided employment and conversations which have been vital for its production. Parts of Chapter 5 appeared as 'Original Fictions: Metamorphoses in *The Faerie Queene*', in Charles Martindale (ed.), *Ovid Renewed: Ovidian Influences on Literature and Art from the Middle Ages to the Twentieth Century* (Cambridge, 1988). I am grateful to the Cambridge University Press for permission to reprint in a metamorphosed form.

I would not have written it at all, had I not read C. S. Lewis, *The Allegory of Love*, Hans-Georg Gadamer, *Truth and Method*, Frank Kermode, *The Classic*, Erich Auerbach, *Mimesis*, and Gerard Genette, *Narrative Discourse*. It may be influenced too by Harold Bloom, *The Anxiety of Influence*; but I'm sure that if it were I should not want to say so.

Contents

Note on Spelling and Abbreviations

Suspensions and abbreviations have been silently expanded in quotations from early printed sources. Modern English usage has been adopted for i/j and u/v, except in the case of quotations from Spenser. Since the book makes no attempt to play Homer on original instruments, all Greek names have been anglicized. On the whole references to classical texts have been made compatible with the Loeb Classical Library editions, simply for ease of reference and comparison. These references have been checked against appropriate early printed editions, and more dependable modern editions, although the results of my collation are not indicated unless there is a particular textual point at stake. All translations are my own, unless otherwise indicated.

The following abbreviations have been used:

Aen.   The *Aeneid*, in Virgil, *Opera*, ed. R. A. B. Mynors (Oxford, 1969).

BW   The *Barons Warres*, in Michael Drayton, *The Works*, ed. J. W. Hebel *et al.*, 5 vols. (Oxford, 1931–41).

CPW   *The Complete Prose Works of John Milton*, ed. Don M. Wolfe, 8 vols. (New Haven, Conn., 1953–82).

CW   *The Civil Wars*, in *The Complete Works of Samuel Daniel in Verse and Prose*, ed. A. B. Grosart, 5 vols. (London, 1885–96).

FQ   Edmund Spenser, *The Faerie Queene*, in *The Works of Edmund Spenser: A Variorum Edition*, ed. Edwin Greenlaw *et al.*, 10 vols. (Baltimore, 1932–49).

GL   Torquato Tasso, *Gerusalemme liberata*, ed. Lanfranco Caretti (Turin, 1971).

Il.   Homer, *The Iliad*, ed. with a translation by A. T. Murray, Loeb Classical Library, 2 vols. (Cambridge, Mass., and London, 1924–5).

Har.   *Ludovico Ariosto's Orlando furioso translated into English Heroical Verse by Sir John Harington (1591)*, ed. Robert McNulty (Oxford, 1972).

Met.   Ovid, *The Metamorphoses*, ed. with a translation by Frank Justus Miller, Loeb Classical Library, 2 vols. (Cambridge, Mass., and London, 1916).

Od.   Homer, *The Odyssey*, ed. with a translation by A. T. Murray,

Loeb Classical Library, 2 vols. (Cambridge, Mass., and London, 1919).

OF   Ludovico Ariosto, *Orlando furioso*, ed. Emilio Bigi, 2 vols. (Milan, 1982).

Phars.   Lucan, *The Civil War (Pharsalia)*, ed. with a translation by J. D. Duff, Loeb Classical Library (Cambridge, Mass., and London, 1928).

PL   *Paradise Lost*, in *The Poems of John Milton*, ed. John Carey and Alastair Fowler (London, 1968).

'Hail Muse! etcetera'

'Epic', in popular usage, tends these days to mean 'vast'. It may also be used to suggest that readers will find much to endure in the works so described (with sometimes, as in a recent advertisement, 'Buying a Used Car Need not be an Epic Experience', a suggestion that the whole protracted business is likely to end in a swindle). Even in its literary applications the word often seems unattractive. Most people would regard 'epic' as a unified and purposive mode of writing, which grows from, and celebrates, the values of a society simple enough to regard some people as heroes. This view is an offshoot of a very pervasive critical mythology which has grown up around the epic form, a mythology which has its roots in a bizarre mixture of composts. Neoclassical literary theory has, since at least the mid-sixteenth century, celebrated epic as a form unified by plot, by canons of decorum, and by subject-matter. And since at least the middle of the last century those influenced by romantic aesthetics have praised the epic as a manifestation of the primal, unsophisticated values of the 'heroic' societies which are supposed to be able to produce distinctively 'epic' works.[1] The combination of these two folk-beliefs has produced the current instinctive presumption that the genre is stiff, perhaps bloodily primitive, and tedious at length. Several recent theorists have perpetuated this view of the genre. For Bakhtin, 'epic' discourse is a single, monoglot, past-centred opposite to the delightsome plurality of the novelistic mode. His most damning remark on the genre, that it is 'congealed and half-moribund',[2] evokes long-dead meat still twitching with the spasms of life. Not all readers would put their dislike so colourfully; but for most 'epic' connotes everything which they would not be predisposed to like: eulogy, heroism, unity, dull officialdom, maleness.

Several critics have, in recent years, attempted to improve the image of the genre through reappraisals of its chief exemplars. It has been argued with a predictable frequency over the past half-century that the

---

[1] G. W. F. Hegel, *Aesthetics: Lectures on Fine Art*, trans. T. M. Knox, 2 vols. (Oxford, 1975), ii. 1045: 'In epic proper the childlike consciousness of a people is expressed for the first time in poetic form. A genuine epic poem therefore falls into that middle period in which a people has awakened out of torpidity, and its spirit has been so far strengthened as to be able to produce its own world and feel itself at home in it, while conversely everything that later becomes firm religious dogma or civil and moral law still remains a living attitude of mind from which no individual separated himself, and as yet there is no separation between feeling and will.'

[2] M. M. Bakhtin, *The Dialogic Imagination: Four Essays*, trans. C. Emerson and M. Holquist (Austin, Tex., and London, 1981), 14.

main epic poems are not as unified, or as simply committed to their apparent heroic values, as might appear. Critics of Virgil, for example, are now very keen to detect in the *Aeneid* 'other', or 'further', and perhaps will even discover 'yet more', voices in the epic, which are opposed to the purposive empire-building of the hero.[3] These developments make the epic form seem less grimly purposive than it appears to be for earlier critics; but these new approaches are still parasitic on earlier traditions. Critics in the 'further voices' school would confess (some, perhaps, under protest) that the central voice in the *Aeneid* is still a public one, of duty, sacrifice, heroism; its 'other' elements are other indeed, the odd minor and regretful squeak from the piccolos of selfhood, which try vainly to make themselves heard over the bass drums, the full strings, and strident brass of a driving heroic melody.

These lines of criticism have led to the current impression that 'romance' is something very different from epic. 'Romance' is now often stressed on the first syllable, and is often used to mean Barbara Cartland. 'Romance', outside the rarefied atmosphere of Northrop Frye's works, means sex, travel, social aspiration, swooning heroines, rakish heroes, a touch of class, a trace of scandal, and, above all, wish-fulfilment. It has become a term which is antithetical to 'epic'. The creation of this antithesis goes back a long way, and is intricately entangled in the reception history of epic. It derives ultimately from a determination to see the two Homeric poems as rootedly distinct from each other: the *Iliad* shows fighting, and heroic goings-on, so it is epic; the *Odyssey* relates wanderings, magical adventures abroad, and a final comic reunion in the return of the hero to his wife and home, so it is a romance. The roving and amorous heroes of the Greek prose romances of Heliodorus and Achilles Tatius (among others) helped to heighten the distinction between the loving vagrancy of the *Odyssey* and the fierce wars of the *Iliad*.[4] European literature has never been entirely comfortable since with the idea that the Homeric poems might have much more in common than a shared tradition, the odd epithet, and innumerable stylistic tics. More recently (although still, perhaps, in the regions of literary folk-memory), W. P. Ker's remarkably wide-ranging and brilliant book *Epic and Romance* used the implicitly disjunctive 'and' of its title to powerful effect. Ker frequently turns 'epic'

---

[3] See Adam Parry, 'The Two Voices of Virgil's *Aeneid*', *Arion*, 2: 4 (1963), 66–80; R. O. A. M. Lyne, *Further Voices in Virgil's Aeneid* (Oxford, 1987).

[4] The most stimulating general accounts of romance are Northrop Frye, *The Secular Scripture: A Study of the Structure of Romance* (Cambridge Mass., and London, 1976), and Gillian Beer, *The Romance*, The Critical Idiom, 10 (London, 1970). Efforts to describe the distinctive character of Greek prose romance include Ben Edwin Perry, *The Ancient Romances: A Literary-Historical Account of their Origins*, Sather Classical Lectures, 37 (Berkeley and Los Angeles, 1967) and B. P. Reardon, *The Form of Greek Romances* (Princeton, NJ, 1991).

and 'romance' into two principles at war with one another, and makes it quite clear which side he is on, as when he remarks: 'The French epics are full of omens of the coming victory of romance, though they have not yet given way.' There are moments, indeed, when Ker adopts a *Howard's End* view of literary history: the solid old values of epic, sustained by 'the ideal of the old-fashioned Northern gentleman, who was accustomed to consideration and respect from the freeman', yields reluctantly to the *nouveau riche* romances.[5] His book creates the impression that there is something wrong with calling a book *Epic Romance*, that there might even be something scandalous in suggesting that 'epic' and 'romance' might interpenetrate, coalesce, or even be facets of the same texts.

I have struggled in this book to think myself outside these traditionally established antitheses, and to formulate an alternative way of looking at the tradition of epic poems deriving from Homer. I have remained trapped to a degree by the polarity of the two main terms of my title, partly (although not, I fear, only) because many of the writers I discuss were involved in one way or another with manufacturing or exploiting the opposition of the two modes. I sometimes oppose 'epic' austerity and purpose to 'romance' vagrancy and pity, when this reflects what the writers under discussion appear to think. But I have always tried to bear in mind that *epos* originally means 'word, song, story': it originally encompasses all forms of discourse. And it is with this vastness in mind, and with a conviction that epic emanates a multiplicity of blended voices to the future, that I relate the whole tradition of epic romance back to the Homeric poems—both of them. The core notion of this book is that the *Iliad* and the *Odyssey* present a structure of emotion which is extremely hard to grasp; that they are both—with differing emphases, certainly, and with different priorities of representation—concerned with the nature of sympathy, and its relation to complex social rituals such as guest-friendship and supplication. Homeric pity has a multiplicity of aspects; at one moment a character pities another because of some perceived analogy between his or her condition and that of the sufferer, while at another, pity arises from a sense that there is a contingent affinity between two characters, that the pitiers know that they could be like the pitied at some future time, or that both parties share their subjection to death. There are also extraordinary moments in the *Iliad* when pity becomes a

---

[5] *Epic and Romance: Essays on Medieval Literature*, 2nd edn. (London, 1926), 57, 58. Charles Rowan Beye, *Epic and Romance in the 'Argonautica' of Apollonius* (Carbondale, Ill., 1982), 71 also adopts a political tone in opposing epic and romance, but is inclined to the freer fare provided by romance: 'Epic is a product of a closed society, conservative, conventional, with established beliefs, whereas an open society which is centrifugal and questing, without fixed beliefs or set answers—a problematical society—produces romance.'

motive for fighting, and generates a 'ruthless' sense (as it were) that all people live under death, and that one should consequently do nothing to help a sufferer. This complex body of concerns (it is nothing so simple as a single 'passion' or a unified 'emotion') has preoccupied many classicists over the past twenty or so years, and I have drawn heavily, though no doubt at times inaccurately, on their work. This complex attitude, however, lies ultimately behind the whole line of epic romance described here. Writers in this tradition struggle repeatedly to comprehend this many-sided experience.

Most do so through the medium of Virgil, who shows a repeated tendency to *oppose* something like pity to something like imperial duty; but he also attempts, through the ambiguous and multi-valent term *pietas*, to replicate something of the range of experience related in the Homeric poems. Sixteenth-century writers in the vernacular approach Virgil through a web of Christian values, and through a significant manifestation of those values: the widespread European tendency for *pietas* to shift and soften in meaning towards our word 'pity'. This semantic change, and the changes in mentality to which it testifies, effectively invents romance as a genre. Pitiful heroes do not go in straight lines towards their duty. They delay, they pursue attractive and pitiable ladies endlessly, they desire. Their narratives do not follow straight lines: they exfoliate, digress, and endlessly ramify. This shift in the meaning of terms makes two modes of behaviour which in Homer could be related back to the same way of feeling—killing and sparing a victim—near antitheses, and gives to each a narrative structure which is potentially at odds with that of the other: the pitiful hero spares his adversary, and wanders on; the martial hero kills his victim, and proceeds on in a ruthlessly linear progression towards his destiny.

My particular interest lies in the later phases of this history, when writers begin to try to work their way back into the mental structures of Virgilian *pietas*, by curbing their pitiful heroes' declinations from whatever imperial or dynastic goals they are set. There are signs in the later stages of the *Orlando furioso*—which marks the point at which many of the features which interest me begin to emerge—that Ariosto is starting to attack his own creation, to check his own amorous reading of classical epic, and, in the process, to encounter strange forms of feeling which he cannot fully understand. This phase in the story of epic marks the emergence of a mode that could be called 'epic romance'. 'Epic' here implies not just an effort on the part of heroes to enact some imperial or dynastic purpose; it also implies an effort on the part of the author to comprehend and to embrace alien forms of feeling. Sixteenth-century epic romance is underwritten by an urge to fight back to Virgil, and to unwrite prevalent readings of the *Aeneid*. Ariosto's battle with himself (and, *pace* Harold Bloom's model of literary influence, it is a battle with himself, and with received modes of understanding epic, rather than with a Virgilian father-figure) sets up a dynamic of enquiry into the motive structures of classical epic, which runs through the rest of the sixteenth century. Ariosto's endeavour to reform his own earlier pitiful transformation of the *Aeneid* leads to Tasso's and Spenser's efforts to make a mode of writing (both a narrative structure and a way of describing the experiences of their heroes and heroines) which would resolve the increasingly antagonistic elements of epic romance. Underlying the work of all these writers is a perplexed sense that their language will not quite permit the coalescences of pity and piety, sympathy and combat, which shape classical epic.

The book ends with Milton, and is partly an attempt to explore the genealogy of *Paradise Lost*. It includes two quite detailed chapters on the English epic between Spenser and Milton—the subjects of which may be on the dry side for the taste of many readers—partly in order to give some neglected writings a critical airing, but also in order to show that there lies a whole history of emerging, changing, and hardening attitudes towards classical epic between the two poets. Although I fear that reasons of space have made the literary tradition presented here look as narrowly canonical as that of Harold Bloom, none the less I am committed to the belief that responding to the texts of the past is a mediated activity. Generations of writers, who range from dullards to minor geniuses, construct the medium through which major authors perceive classical texts. The rebellions of these great figures against their predecessors are not patriarchal gigantomachies, as a poet-hero struggles for mastery over a Great Name from the past. They are revolutions of discourse, which consist in rejecting the established mechanisms and stylistic mannerisms by which past texts had previously been assimilated. Milton did not fight with Homer and Virgil; he fought for them and against himself, against the accreted (and, as I suggest, politically loaded) medium through which earlier English epic poets had read and imitated them.

Since I am travelling towards Milton, this book is in danger of having the narrative structure of a *nostos*, or homecoming; it might appear from the structure of the book—running from Homer to Milton—that I wish to claim that *Paradise Lost* marks the ultimate and only revival of the 'true shape' of Homeric compassion. I have tried to lessen the hold of this narrative form on my imagination, but it must become deeply seated in the mind and narrative structures of any student of epic romance, and especially in the minds of those concerned with the revivals and reversals of classical models in the sixteenth and seventeenth centuries. The last

chapter does not, however, suggest that Milton revived a Homeric form
of sympathy. It argues, rather, that he broke out of many of the clichés
of the romance tradition, in a way that enabled him constructively to
transform Homer. When Adam falls, Milton makes him willingly choose
to be able to feel a kind of Homeric fellow-feeling for Eve, which is
founded on a shared mortality. This is indeed the ultimate over-going of
Homer: his central motive is not simply accepted as a necessary consequence of being mortal; it is chosen by a Christian hero. The form of
mortal sympathy that runs through Homer's poems is consequently made
to appear as though it is enabled by the pivotal action of Milton's poem.
This is, though, no simple revival of Homer, nor is it a simple conquest
of his territory by the very straightforward means of staking a prior claim
to it. *Paradise Lost*—a poem in which almost every episode is reflected
and refracted by at least one other moment in itself or in its models—is
preoccupied with sameness and difference, with obligations to an ultimate
creator, and with the dangers and difficulties of imitating either God or
prior literary creations. These concerns, which unstably run through the
human story of the loving relation between Adam and Eve, and which
permeate Milton's own continuing interest in debts to, obligations towards,
and refractions of his own literary predecessors, make the entire character
of the poem rootedly secondary. *Paradise Lost* is continually engaged with
the difficulties which arise from not being the first maker in, or indeed
of, the world. These features make it hard to sustain a belief that *Paradise
Lost* marks a grand home-coming for the epic to the shores of Homeric
Truth, after centuries when it ranged in the forests of Error—though
Milton, no doubt, would have some sneaking desire that his poem should
be thought of in this way.

As well as having a suppressed structure of a home-coming, this book
also has a rather more entrenched teleological shape. Hayden White has
drawn attention to the ways in which histories participate in the structures
of fiction.[6] This has caused some flurries in the academy, and has led
many critical historians to attempt to break out of the accepted tyrannies
of narrative form, and to present, as Terence Cave does in his non-
historical history of recognitions, 'a repertory of instances disguised as a
sequence',[7] rather than unified histories. This is an odd tendency in
literary history. If it is accepted that histories necessarily participate in
fictional forms, then it is very strange to endeavour to break out of such
forms. The argument for doing so is that to rupture—nay, deconstruct—
these forms shows how arbitrary they are, and so demystifies the whole

---

[6] *Tropics of Discourse: Essays in Cultural Criticism* (Baltimore, 1978).
[7] *Recognitions: A Study in Poetics* (Oxford, 1988), 490.

process of telling histories. But this argument implies an ambition which is at odds with its chief premiss: if all histories are governed by forms, then it is, surely, impossible ever to evade the tropes of formalism, anti-formalism, post-formalism, or whatever. Some readers may wish that I had encoded more breaks, ruptures, and uncertainties into my history in order to signify that I do not think I am relating an immutably true story, and that post-modernism has not passed me by. Others might note significant lacunae in my history. (Where is Apollonius Rhodius? Euripides? The scholiasts? And what about Ronsard's *Franciade*?) The tendency in recent literary histories to pretend very hard that they have no wish to present a complete story testifies to genuine and well-founded anxieties about the adequacy of historical representation. But this tendency also makes them harder to read than old-fashioned teleological histories, often without offering compensatory benefits to a reader, or the sat-isfactions of a story told. I hope my readers will accept that the genre of this book *is* teleological history, a history going towards an end, and read, as all readers must, with a sense of the decorums and dangers of such a genre. It is a partial account, in both chief senses of 'partial': it is not complete, and it is motivated by my interests.

Right from the start I gear my readings of Homer and Virgil to what comes next, and this inevitably creates teleological distortions. Classicists and Italianists may well feel that I have trespassed incautiously upon, or even that I have unscrupulously shifted the boundaries of their proper fields. I am, though, attempting a conceptually impossible task, which explains many, though I am sure not all, of the oddities in emphasis in the following chapters. I wish to give a sense of what texts came to mean to their successors (and *how* they came to have that meaning), at the same time as giving an inkling of how those subsequent readings do not encompass every aspect of their originals. Sometimes—particularly in the case of Homer—I stress the alienness of my proto-texts in order to show that they do not have to be read as subsequent authors did in fact read them. I am not sure that there are any grounds upon which I could claim to know that my reading is any more 'accurate' than those of the literary reinterpreters, except, perhaps, that I have to construct some critical and ethical ideas that do not come readily to me in order to describe what I see in those earlier texts. But since the history must move forward, and must be related from the point of view of its ending, I have usually emphasized the emergent elements of a particular text, rather than aspects which seem—at present, at any rate—interestingly to go nowhere.

Underlying the whole book is a prolonged worry about how we know the past, and how much we can ever hope to know about it. My conclusion, such as it is, is that Renaissance writers conceived the past as being not-present. This maxim sounds tautological and obscure; but it reveals one central aspect of the poetics engendered by Renaissance humanism. The first stage in acknowledging that there have been other modes of thinking is to recognize that there are minds which are not your own. This entails acknowledging the existence of strangeness. Establishing some tentative impression of what goes on in those other minds, or of how those minds are habitually articulated, is a secondary process, which depends upon this primary acknowledgement. Writers of Renaissance epic often begin either with more or less contented assimilations of classical epic to post-classical norms, or with deliberately provocative revisions of their classical sources. Many of them go on to alter, revise, extend, or mutilate their poems. Often these revisions and alterations indicate an awareness that past epic is different, strange, and other. The influence of these strange texts is apparent in the ways in which, and the extent to which, writers depart from or modify their own practices, and those of their contemporaries. In the case of Tasso, this process of self-alteration led to the wholesale revision and ruination of his epic romance; but many other writers, including Ariosto, and several minor late sixteenth-century English epic poets, changed or expanded their poems after publication, in order to erode the modernity of their texts. These revisions and modifications are sometimes responses to changing critical ideas, some-times responses to changing political circumstances, and sometimes responses to direct criticisms of the works concerned. But very often they mark an effort to acknowledge the difference of past writing, by a deliberate alteration of the present writer's idiom. This can produce some strained and unconvinced writing, as Renaissance poets strive to unmake their own idiom in order to arrive at a rapprochement with some idea of what constitutes the past. It can also produce some further, but rather different, simplifications of classical epic. It is, for example, a central tenet of many epic poets in the Renaissance that classical epic deals in anger and war. This conviction can lead them to change their heroes from people who, at the start of their poems, are unreflectively subject to pity, into people who are, at their ends, unreflectively subject to anger. It would be strange to say that this idiom was any closer to the conceptual structures of classical epic than the idiom it supersedes. But in their restless revisions, and in their repeated reiterations and modifications of episodes from classical poems, Renaissance writers acknowledge the otherness of the past: the past is—in a powerful sense, in a way that creates uncertainty, a sense of lack, of failure to correspond, and even a measure of guilt—not-present.[8] The most powerful of these poets bring

---

[8] On the growing sense of anachronism in Renaissance dealings with past literatures, see Thomas

about revolutions in the inherited idiom of the epic tradition as a result of continuing and continuingly incomplete processes of engagement with the difference of the past. The past is not-present; to enter into dialogue with it is to attempt to forgo, or to attempt to transfigure, some significant aspect of the language of that present.

Understanding the past is a process of approximation and revision. It means a continual questioning and modification of present modes of expression, and entails the creation of mind-bending notions in order to evade some of the more glaring differences between the language of the past and that of the present. This method of hesitant, self-consciously anachronistic approximation creates Renaissance epic romance. The exploration—and the glorification—of this process of tentative and revisionary reading is the ultimate polemical purpose behind this book. It is as much a genealogical account of a mode of reading as a teleological account of a genre. The idea that literature invites a meeting of minds is a central tenet of some forms of unregenerate twentieth-century literary humanism. This book is in part a historical investigation of this mode of reading. It attempts to historicize the simple and, to my mind, untenable belief that literature creates affinities between unchanging human hearts across the barriers of years. I aim to give a historical account of how different periods have varied in their conceptions of what is involved in such sympathetic recognition of self in the other. The book relates a history of sympathy; and in order to tell a story of how different periods have differently understood what it is to feel for another, it engages with the varying ways in which different periods have conceived analogies and correspondences between the past and the present. Changing ideas of sympathy accompany changing attitudes to the past. This book is in that sense caught up in a project that might broadly be termed 'humanism'. But it is not on a search for the final or resolvable meanings of past texts, nor is it founded on the belief that we can talk unmediatedly, without fear of being at cross-purposes, with the past. There will always be occasions when present concerns seem to dominate the voice of the past. There will always be a restless sense accompanying any attempt to explicate past thought structures that something has been lost, that something is still to be changed before the past and the present could meet. This sense of disparity, of lack, of anachronism, in our negotiations with the past is our most intimate and persistent legacy from the Renaissance. It is intensely valuable: a sense of never quite having arrived at the past testifies to a belief in its difference, and generates a desire to

M. Greene, *The Light in Troy: Imitation and Discovery in Renaissance Poetry* (New Haven, Conn., and London, 1982).

change in response to it. This book, in its efforts to give a historical account of how minds meet, and of the halts and starts that impede their meeting, attempts to contribute to a kind of new humanism in literary study, a kind of humanism which is driven by a wish to converse with the past, but which is critically aware of the genealogy of its own modes of reading.

I

Homer

Homer is hard not to read as a unified and intelligible author. Yet it is difficult to avoid feeling at the same time that the Homeric poems are, to some degree, falling apart. Similar phrases and epithets keep recurring in different places with slightly new emphases, and narrative elements in the poems seem often shadily to repeat one another. Achilles is often swift of foot; Hector is very often called 'horse-taming'; encounters between warriors seem often to be governed by flexible but discernible laws. These features—which modern scholars would attribute to the oral composition of the poems[1]—give the impression that the *Iliad* and the *Odyssey* stem from a unified vision, since many of the new turns of phrase which one encounters read like variant versions of idioms which one has already met, and several narrative episodes—say council scenes—seem like revisions of ones which have gone before. Epithets which attach themselves to particular names, entire speeches, and whole scenes reflect and recall each other across different books. But, although these features make the Homeric poems seem more of a piece the more one reads them, they also give one the impression of being able to see the mortar flaking between the building blocks of the Homeric narrative. They make it appear that the author is generating a fiction by recombining old material in new ways, and that the material recombined in this manner remains partially undigested. Homer's stories, and the local effects of Homeric verse, develop as though a mind is using special techniques to make itself say new things through familiar words; and those familiar words resist total absorption into the texture of the action.

The narrative style of the poems often appears, similarly, to present fragments which are in the process of coagulating into a unified structure. One might start off reading Homer with the idea that epics are unified things; but one then rapidly discovers that his narratives are full of jolts, shifts of time, tense, or subject-matter which are often not prepared for, nor readily interpretable. Why—to take one striking instance—once Odysseus has supplicated Circe to be allowed to leave her and go home, does his magical mistress tell him that he must visit the house of the

---

[1] On this vast area—the detail of which need not concern a student of the reception of Homer— see e.g. Adam Parry, *The Making of Homeric Verse* (Oxford, 1971); G. S. Kirk, *The Songs of Homer* (Cambridge, 1962); J. B. Hainsworth, *The Flexibility of the Homeric Formula* (Oxford, 1968).

dead and consult Teiresias before he can return to Ithaca?[2] The command
seems abrupt and inexplicable.

It is just these moments of inexplicable abruptness that have made the
Homeric poems central to Western fiction. They invite explanation.
Writers wordlessly show how they feel the world fits together through
transitions of place, tense, and subject; and subsequent readers build up
their new visions by interpreting and imposing new motives on such
moments. Modern critics might respond to Circe's apparent non-sequitur
by saying, 'This shows "Homer" roughly editing in another episode from
the traditional repertoire of stories about Odysseus'; or, 'It is a typical
folk-tale motif to make the hero undergo a symbolic death before returning
home.' These sorts of interpretation have strong claims to authority in
the present critical environment, but they are very unlike the kinds of
assimilative interpretation to which Homer has been subjected by his
literary followers. A lot of Western fiction has been created by writers
who have worried over, and attempted to motivate, the sudden jolts in
the Homeric narrative.[3] For Virgil, the visit to the house of the dead
becomes a pivotal movement, in which Aeneas begins to transform the
experience of past defeats into an imperial future. It is motivated by a
desire to see his father, mingled with a sense of imperial destiny. These
are perhaps the most distinctive motives in the *Aeneid*, and they fill in
and explain the space left by one of Homer's inexplicable jolts. Through
Dante (and right up to Seamus Heaney's *Station Island*) the trip to the
land of the dead has become an increasingly self-conscious means of
exploring how writers encounter, absorb, or transcend their literary
predecessors. Generations of writers have scratched and puzzled over the
sudden shifts and inexplicable transitions in the Homeric poems, as they
attempt to produce a composed assimilation of Homer. The Homeric
poems are generously capacious: they leave later writers space to invent
motives.

The notes to Alexander Pope's translation of Homer are one small
instance of the widespread need among later writers to invent forces by
means of which to hold Homer together. They are driven by a desire—
which is often comically exacting—to impose a consistent sense, emotional
or thematic, on even the most abrupt transition. The chief gelling agent
applied by Pope's annotator to the Homeric poems is love. When Circe
sends Odysseus to Hades, it is in order to avoid telling him herself how
he will die: 'Her love for Ulysses induces her not to make the discovery

---

[2] *Od.* 10. 483–95.
[3] On the way in which such rough moments in a text generate histories of reception, see Wolfgang
Iser, *The Act of Reading: A Theory of Aesthetic Response* (Baltimore and London, 1978), 197–8.

herself.'[4] The notes also often sternly categorize some feature of the narrative as an abrupt transition, when the poem has simply failed to provide the kind of loving unity which the author of the notes expects from it. At the moment when Odysseus and Penelope are finally united, the couple, rather than falling into each other's arms, at once lay plans for a fake wedding celebration, in order to prevent the relatives of the dead wooers from realizing that their kin have been killed. This abrupt piece of pragmatism scandalizes the annotator, who wants some tenderness:

I must confess, that here may seem to be an unseasonable transition: *Homer* brings *Ulysses* and *Penelope* together, raises our expectations to see a warm and tender description at the discovery of the husband to the wife, and all of a sudden he starts from the subject, and leaves us under an uncertainty equal to that of *Penelope*.[5]

This note springs from a desire to read the *Odyssey* as a poem of domestic sympathy, and so it regards the abrupt shift to tactical planning as an 'unseasonable transition'. But it manages to assimilate this abrupt change of subject: this 'unseasonable transition', the note implies, brings readers closer to the action than any description of tearful joy would, since by it we are made to share Penelope's uncertainty.

The way Odysseus and Penelope suddenly shift tack from joy to plotting could, though, be read in a number of ways. It might be taken as expressing the character of the hero, as the anticipated delightful meeting of man and wife is compulsively transformed by the tricksy Odysseus into a plot. It could also be seen as a species of sublimation: a fake marriage replaces a real reunion. The episode could alternatively be taken as indicating a rough edit to another element in the inherited tradition of stories about Odysseus. The change of subject—if that is what it is—might make it seem as though another author has stepped in, and has twisted the tale away from fulfilment. But, whichever of these explanations one is inclined towards, the unseasonable transition is fraught with possible motives. The poem might be a mass of unformed story elements, sometimes roughly edited together; but—partly because entrenched habits of reading make it necessary to interpret sequences, rather than neutrally to accept them—its transitions suggest meanings.

All origins have two aspects: they are just new, abrupt, and full of potential when considered in themselves; but they are also subsequently limited and defined by the things to which they give rise. Homer, as effectively the origin of Western fiction, is both a fragmentary amalgam

[4] *The Odyssey of Homer*, in *The Twickenham Edition of the Poems of Alexander Pope*, ix, ed. Maynard Mack (New Haven, Conn., and London, 1967), 370.
[5] Ibid. x. 325.

of disparate elements, raw materials waiting for a multiplicity of interpretations, and a writer whom it is not possible to read without some received
sense of the unified structures which later writers imposed upon his text.
The poems seem almost to be aware of, and to be seeking from their
readers, this combination of wonder and familiarity. They, as it were,
assimilate and familiarize themselves. The *Odyssey* describes many
moments of contact with the absolutely strange, when a Cyclops, or a
Siren, or an unfamiliar human being, is overcome by a hero who knows
how to operate on the boundaries of the known. Through its reiteration
of such moments, the poem invites a response of mingled familiarity and
wonder to these miraculous meetings between man and supermen. When
the naked and shipwrecked Odysseus encounters the Phaeacian princess
Nausicaa, he asks her flatteringly if she is a goddess. This episode is
evoked a little later in Odysseus's story, when he meets an unidentified
shepherdess on the sea-shore of Ithaca. The second encounter (when
Odysseus is marvelling at the strange shape of his own defamiliarized but
familiar coastline) is in fact supernatural, since the shepherdess is Athene
in disguise;[6] but it is made to seem like the reiteration of something
familiar. The goddess blends into the figure of the mortal Nausicaa, and
Nausicaa acquires retrospective vestiges of the divine. The actions related
in the *Odyssey* are never either simply familiar or unrelentingly supernatural: the poem gradually makes the two overlap and meld unstably
into each other.

   This oscillation between wonder and familiarity is a central element in
the Homeric style. It is also primary to the way in which the whole
tradition of epic romance has absorbed and familiarized its predecessors.
One generation of poets produces a work which breaks strangely into
marvellous encounters with the unexpected, or shifts subject-matter with
apparent arbitrariness; the next generation seeks to assimilate, normalize,
or interpret these moments of release. This process can become strongly
assimilative, as an interpretation turns by gradual stages into a rigid
decoding of earlier epic; but, periodically, new authors shift, fragment, or
discard their predecessors' view of the forces which shape earlier epic
narrative. They are moved by an encounter with the past text to break
down some of the received wisdom about it, and so make a new and
strange phase in the history. A purposive oscillation between wonder and
assimilation—which is driven by a desire to make sense of the strange,
but checked by repeated, over-ready assimilations of that strangeness—
makes up the history of epic. This is the process described, and to a
certain extent performed, by this book. The chapter on Homer which

---

[6] *Od.* 13. 221–351; *Od.* 6. 149–55.

follows aims to show that many of the strange transitions in the Homeric poems can be related to the peculiar nature of Homeric sympathy. This is unashamedly part of a project to assimilate Homer into the tradition of epic romance, in which pity comes to be the chief motive emotion felt by heroes and heroines. But as well as attempting to show how the poems give rise to what comes after them, the following chapter also tries to convey the deep strangeness of their prototypical versions of sympathy, and with it the way Homer resists comfortably final assimilation. His poems radiate possibilities: any number of alternative narratives of Western literature could have emerged from them. This book, however, is, sadly perhaps, limited to one of them.

THE *ILIAD*

Several recent accounts of the *Iliad* see it as a tragic poem, which explores the contrasts between life and death, and the nature of sympathy.[7] What tends to get lost from even the best of such grave interpretations is the way that, when reading the poem, one can never be quite sure what is going to happen next. In the midst of battle a god might intervene, a warrior might be whisked away and replaced by a *doppelgänger*, or a hero might be attacked by a natural force such as a river. The *Iliad* is not confined to the battlefield, nor is it limited to a single time or subject. Very often, before or during an encounter between two warriors, the narrative, or one of the combatants himself, digresses to the past and relates events which happened years before (and occasionally years after) the events of the literal present. These digressions create a poem which is not by any means solely focused on war: the *Iliad* is repeatedly drawn to ways in which fighting is interrupted by events sometimes magical, sometimes pathetic, and sometimes strikingly irrelevant.

In the early stages of the poem it is chiefly the gods who interrupt battles, and often they do so with little apparent motive. The first fight in the *Iliad*, appropriately enough, is between Paris and Menelaus, the two instigators of the whole war. When Paris is in danger of being killed, Aphrodite seizes him up and sets him down in a bedchamber. The shift of setting from battlefield to bedchamber is magically swift, and there is no direct account of Aphrodite's motive for her action: 'But Aphrodite snatched him up, with the great ease of a god, and shrouded him in a

---

[7] See e.g. Jasper Griffin, *Homer on Life and Death* (Oxford, 1980); Colin MacLeod, *Collected Essays* (Oxford, 1983), 1–15, and his edition of *The Iliad Book XXIV* (Cambridge, 1982); R. B. Rutherford, 'Tragic Form and Feeling in the *Iliad*', *Journal of Hellenic Studies*, 102 (1982), 145–60.

thick mist, and set him down in his perfumed, vaulted chamber, and went herself to call Helen.'[8] This magical transition might be read as a coded euphemism: if the goddess of love whisks a warrior off the battlefield, then, perhaps, Homer is delicately implying that Paris bolted back to Helen, his love, at the first sign of danger.[9] The episode could also be less drastically interpreted by supplying some sort of motive for it: Aphrodite feels for and so rescues Paris. The sudden shift of setting could be read as indicating the power of *eros* and sympathy to deflect a story away from war and death. This way of assimilating the rapid shift of place does seem particularly appropriate in the light of what follows. Aphrodite continues to break the inevitable movement from wounds to death, when Diomedes strikes Aeneas on the thigh with a stone:

and crushed the cup-bone, and broke both sinews. The jagged stone tore the skin away. Then the hero fell on his knees, still, and leaned with his strong hand on the earth. And dark night enfolded his eyes. And now the king of men, Aeneas, would have died, had not the daughter of Zeus, Aphrodite, been quick to notice him. She was his mother, and had become pregnant with him by Anchises as he tended his herd.[10]

That line 'And dark night enfolded his eyes' is a variant of one of the most frequent Homeric formulae for death.[11] Aeneas's story might well end here,[12] since there is little room in the *Iliad* for terminally wounded warriors.[13] The poem is rarely drawn to liminal moments between life and death, where the story could follow one of two potential directions, since a guiding principle of its style is the ruthless closure of episodes, and with them lives. But this is an exception: Aeneas does not die. Aphrodite arrives, and introduces a protracted break in the fighting: she begins to carry her son away from the battlefield, until Diomedes wounds

[8] *Il.* 3. 380–3. All translations are my own unless otherwise indicated.

[9] See the note to Pope's *Iliad*: 'This Machine is Allegorical, and means no more than the Power of *Love* triumphing over all the Considerations of *Honour*, *Ease*, and *Safety*.' *Twickenham Pope*, viii. 214. A desire to allegorize Aphrodite persists among commentators. See G. S. Kirk, *The Iliad 1–4: A Commentary* (Cambridge, 1985), 323.

[10] *Il.* 5. 305–13.

[11] Cf. *Il.* 6. 11. See also G. S. Kirk, *The Iliad 5–8: A Commentary* (Cambridge, 1990), ad loc. 92.

[12] Bernard Fenik, *Typical Battle Scenes in the 'Iliad': Studies in the Narrative Technique of Homeric Battle Description*, *Hermes*, 21 (Wiesbaden, 1968), 35, notes, however, that Aeneas's 'killing' is associated with other elements (a man who descends from a chariot; a man shouts loudly; a man throws a stone, etc.) which are elsewhere associated with a recovery: e.g. *Il.* 8. 323–34. He does also note, p. 39, 'It happens frequently in the *Iliad* that a god prevents something that both the poem, and, apparently, the tradition forbade.'

[13] Cf. *Il.* 5. 683–98; 16. 477–505, which show Sarpedon is something of a special case; *Il.* 16. 843–54, in which Patroclus, another important character, delays his death by a speech; *Il.* 22. 337–63 describes the protracted last moments of Hector. These are all exceptions to a general rule established by Fenik, *Battle Scenes*, 69.

her, whereupon she drops Aeneas and flees to Olympus. Apollo then
snatches up Aeneas, carries him off to Pergamos, and cures him, while
leaving a mimic shape of his corpse on the battlefield. No other episode
in the *Iliad* is so full of space. Characters fly off in all directions from the
battlefield, as though once they have escaped the mess of fighting they
can move through the world as swift as thought. The fights in the *Iliad*
are surrounded by a magically easy world; and the point of entry into
this magical ease is the kind of compassionate care felt by parents for
their children. What starts and prompts the long departure from war is
the reminder that Aphrodite is Aeneas's mother. And the end result of
this familial link between men and gods is to turn death into a fantasy.
The real Aeneas later re-enters the battle; his corpse is just a spirit made
by Apollo. This urge to bifurcate reality, to allow a magically resurrected
warrior to live at the same time as satisfying the push of battle towards
death by providing a fantasmic corpse, came to be a vital technique in
Renaissance epic romance. Where the logic of a story leads to death, and
the participants in it want to avert that death, epic romances often
either shift location suddenly or split the characters in two in order to
accommodate both needs. This is a technique used repeatedly by Spenser,
Ariosto, and Tasso; but it originates in Homer, where the feelings of the
gods for their mortal relations lead to sudden shifts of location, and the
doubling of bodies.

The Aphrodite episodes are unusual in the *Iliad*, and have seldom been
treated warmly by scholars. But they illustrate how the often unspoken
compassion of the gods can pull the narrative to a new geographical
location, and so break down even the most absolute of limits on human
life imposed by the poem's style.[14] When the poem itself pauses over a
death, however, it usually shifts tense as well as place, introducing an
abrupt flashback into the utterly different past of the warrior who has
died:

Then Telamonian Ajax struck Anthemion's son, a vigorous young man called
Simoeisius, whom his mother bore by the banks of the Simois, as she travelled
down from Ida, following her parents to see their flocks. For this reason they
called him Simoeisius; but he did not repay the price of his upbringing to his
parents, and his life was short: he was struck down by the spear of great-souled
Ajax.[15]

This flashback has some features in common with the brief cameo
narrative, quoted in the previous extract, of how Aphrodite conceived
Aeneas. But, because the narrative of Simoeisius's past is not tied in with

[14] On the compassion of the Homeric gods, see Griffin, *Life and Death*, 87, 195-8.
[15] *Il.* 4. 473-9.

the emotions of a god, it has no influence on what happens in the main story. It is just a separate plane of time, about which the killer, Ajax, knows—and does—nothing. The text places the birth and death of Simoeisius side by side. The two pockets of time are simply juxtaposed, without causal connection, and without narrative consequences.[16] A story about a warrior's birth need only delay a death when a god is involved.

Things are rather different, however, when it is not simply the narrator, but a warrior within the text who relates a tale of the past to an opposing warrior. Such a narrative of the past can create a tie between two warriors sufficient to prevent a fight. After the chaotic and digressive interventions of the gods in Books 3–5, Book 6 is occupied mainly by human actors who follow their own instincts. These instincts appear pretty grim in the first fifty or so lines (they sound grimmer in Loeb English: 'And Polypoetes staunch in fight slew Astyalus, and Odysseus with his spear of bronze laid low Pidytes of Percote, and Teucer goodly Aretaon'[17]), which produce a body count of around one every three lines. But the remainder of the book dwells protractedly on the various combinations of rituals, feelings, and forms of story-telling which make people stop fights. The first of these interrupting mechanisms to be invoked in Book 6 is supplication. This is a ritual act in which the suppliant grasps the knees, and possibly also the chin, of the supplicated in a ritual display of powerlessness, and begs either for his life on the battlefield, or for guest-friendship if he is wandering in a strange land.[18] Adrastus duly grasps the knees of Menelaus, and promises many rewards if he will take him alive. Menelaus decides to grant his request; but Agamemnon, his brother, intervenes and kills the suppliant, saying there is no bond of *philia* between the two houses of Atreus and Troy.[19] Agamemnon is called by his patronymic, Atreides, when he kills the suppliant, which emphasizes the kinship between the two brothers. This first attempt by men to interrupt fighting does not generate another ghostly *doppelgänger*, like the mimic shape of Aeneas, but it does lead to the division of narrative possibilities between two people. It is again as though the poet wants his story to go in two directions at once, and gives each of these potential directions a body. The two brothers split between them the two options open to warriors on the battlefield, to kill or spare.

The next interruption of the fighting in Book 6, however, does not

---

[16] On Homer's 'objective' pathos, see Griffin, *Life and Death*, 109–19.

[17] *Il.* 6. 29–31; *The Iliad*, trans. A. T. Murray, Loeb Classical Library, 2 vols. (Cambridge, Mass. and London, 1924–5).

[18] See John Gould, 'Hiketeia', *Journal of Hellenic Studies*, 93 (1973), 74–103, and its derivative, Agathe Thornton, *Homer's Iliad: Its Composition and the Motif of Supplication*, Hypomnemata, 81 (Göttingen, 1984), esp. 113–47.

[19] *Il.* 6. 37–65.

lead to death. Diomedes and Glaucus step forward to fight. Diomedes asks who his opponent is, fearing he might be a god. Glaucus replies:

Great-souled son of Tydeus, why do you ask about my family tree? The generations of men are like those of leaves, some of which the wind scatters on the earth; but the budding forest produces more when springtime comes. Even so one generation of men grows up as the other passes away. However, if you wish, hear this story, so that you will know my lineage. There is a city Ephyre in the middle of Argos, that pasture-land of horses, and there lived Sisyphus the most cunning man alive, Sisyphus son of Aeolus; and he had a son Glaucus, and Glaucus bore peerless Bellerophon . . .[20]

The story that follows—a pause of about seventy lines in the sequence of deaths which precedes it—continues to tell of the past, how Bellerophon was tricked, and nearly killed, as a result of his king's wife's desire for him. The story is a huge digression in time and subject-matter from the business of war (it begins with frustrated erotic passion, though it returns rapidly to the heroic activities of the speaker's ancestor, which do have a bearing on his likely prowess). The time spent narrating it makes the battle pause, as though the warriors are frozen mid-combat. And the result of this narrative about the birth and genealogy of Glaucus is to break off the intended encounter between narrator and listener. Diomedes realizes that he is linked to Glaucus by guest-friendship, since his father entertained Bellerophon. This one fact stops the fight. Glaucus's whole speech juxtaposes a doublet of values which resonates through the entire poem. A belief in the shared mortality of men, that generations pass away like leaves, is not grounds for attempting to arrest the process by sparing an enemy; but knowledge of a tie in the past, to do with guest-friendship, can be sufficient to break off a battle.[21]

These values, and the deflections of the narrative time sequence away from the present with which they are generally accompanied in Homer, shape the next major episode in Book 6, the departure of Hector from his wife Andromache in order to go into battle. The episode has often been regarded (as it was by Dryden in 'The Last Parting of Hector and Andromache') as a vehicle for pathos, in which, as so rarely in Homer, pity is invoked as a force which might stop warriors fighting. Andromache does indeed begin with a protracted appeal for pity, in which she recoils

[20] *Il.* 6. 145–55. Kirk, ad loc. 'The whole episode is inorganic.'
[21] On Homer's temporal digressions, see Norman Austin, 'The Function of Digressions in the *Iliad*', in John Wright (ed.), *Essays on the Iliad: Selected Modern Criticism* (Bloomington, Ind., and London, 1978), 70–84. He notes that they often occur at moments of intensity, and often in a context of supplication. He perhaps underestimates the affective role of such digressions. See also Julia Haig Gaisser, 'A Structural Analysis of the Digressions in the *Iliad* and the *Odyssey*', *Harvard Studies in Classical Philology*, 73 (1969), 1–43.

into the past at length in order to describe how Achilles has killed her father, mother, and brothers: 'Come, have pity and remain here on the wall', she urges. But Hector's reply generates a form of pity which is far from being a motive opposed to fighting, as it was to become for later writers in the romance tradition. He tells her that he would be ashamed if he were to skulk away from the battle, and then produces the most remarkable disruption of the time sequence in the whole poem:

For I know this well in my heart and mind: the day shall come when sacred Ilios will be destroyed, together with Priam, and the people of Priam with their fine ash spears. But not the future grief of the Trojans, nor Hecuba's grief, nor Priam's grief, nor that of my many and brave brothers who then shall fall in the dust at the hands of their enemies, move me as much as your grief, when some brass-studded Achaean will lead you weeping away, and take from you your time of freedom. Then, perhaps, in Argos you will weave at another's command, or carry water from Messeis or Hypereia, utterly against your will. And you will be subject to compulsion. And then some man shall say as he sees you weep: 'Look, there's the quondam wife of Hector, who outfought all the other horse-taming Trojans, when men fought around Ilios.' So someone shall say; and it will bring you a grief renewed by your lack of a man like me to ward off the day of captivity. But let me be dead, and lie under a solid mass of earth, before I hear your cries as they drag you into servitude.[22]

This passage evokes a kind of pity which could intelligibly lead to, rather than prevent, Hector's return to battle. It creates a highly abstract, almost aesthetic version of the emotion: Hector says he fights, partly through a sense of shame, but chiefly because he cannot bear to share her future grief. Andromache had sought to elicit a backward-looking pity when she related how all the familial ties she has lost have become ties with Hector; Hector constructs a rival version of compassion in reply, a compassion which is founded on a consciousness of future suffering. Pity is tied into stories about the past and the future. And this is why Hector apparently prophesies: he constructs a rival narrative, which transforms pity into an attitude founded, not on the past, but on future contingencies, on knowing that one will share the future emotions of another. The shift into the future in a way *is* sympathy: it establishes that the couple share the same attitudes to what will happen, even while he goes out and she stays behind.

There is, underlying the speech, a suggestion that pity is founded on consciously sharing the condition of the sufferer; and the way most fully to share the condition of the sufferer is not to attempt in an active way to alleviate it, but to accept that it is the case for you too. This is why

---

[22] *Il.* 6. 447–65.

his pity, paradoxically, is not opposed to his departure, and why, indeed, he leaves through pity:

Saying these things he laid his child in his dear wife's arms, and she embraced him in her scented bosom, and wept smilingly. Her husband pitied this sight, and he caressed her, saying: 'Dear wife, do not grieve too much: no one shall send me to Hades before my due time. But no one, I say, has escaped his fate once he has been born, whether he is brave or a coward.'[23]

This most abstract phase of his parting address follows the warmest moment in the poem, when Astyanax, their son, winces away from his father's crested helmet, and both parents laugh. Hector prays for a great future for the boy, and then he pities. Hector's pity here has a strangely abstract foundation: it involves accepting that each of the two has a separate story which operates within similar constraints, but it does not lead him to alter his way of acting because of that recognition. This has its own logic: he cannot change the conditions within which their respective stories operate, and at the same time keep the sympathy which depends on those shared conditions: 'I know the limits on your life, and my knowing this leads me to leave you, since I acknowledge the limits on your life most fully when I live with the limits on mine.' This attitude could not result in anyone's attempting to stay with or console a sufferer; instead it leads one to reaffirm the constraining circumstances on one's own life, while acknowledging their analogy with the circumstances which restrict the life of another. Separation is the consequence of this type of pity—if pity it is.

This form of feeling runs through the Homeric poems. Sympathetic tears do not involve melting into the condition of the other, but rather lead to the reaffirmation of one's own grounds for sorrow. The strangest (and even perhaps deliberately down-market) form of this strange type of grief occurs when Achilles's slave-girls grieve for the death of Patroclus: 'The women groaned, apparently for Patroclus, but in fact each grieved for her own sorrow.'[24] At the climactic moment of the poem, when Achilles is supplicated by Priam for the return of Hector's body, there is a similar movement of memory behind the sympathetic union of the two enemies: Priam asks Achilles not just to pity him, but also to remember his own father. When Achilles weeps for his suppliant it is 'For his father and now too for Patroclus'.[25] This kind of simultaneous but separate grief

[23] *Il.* 6. 483–9.
[24] *Il.* 19. 301–2.
[25] *Il.* 24. 511–12. Michael M. Nagler, *Spontaneity and Tradition: A Study in the Oral Art of Homer* (Berkeley and Los Angeles, 1974), 189–91 notes the way that Priam's request and Achilles's response reflect each other's structure, which amplifies the effect of a union between different modes of experience. On this form of sympathy, see Rutherford, 'Tragic Form', 158–9; MacLeod, *Iliad XXIV*, 8–16.

re-emphasizes, rather than resolves, differences between the content of people's experience, although it often also acknowledges—as Hector does with Andromache, and as Achilles eventually does with Priam—a general similarity between their conditions of life. But the re-emphasis of difference explains why moments of sympathetic contact between people so often rupture the flow of the narrative: since Homeric sympathy involves memory and a sense of one's own separateness, it pulls the fiction away from simple linear temporal sequence. It might make the sympathizer recall his own analogous past, or the future which he will share with the sufferer. Alternatively the narrative voice itself might recoil to relate the past of the person who is suffering. This form of sympathy shapes itself naturally to the Homeric narrative style. When Homer, or a character in the text, interjects long units of retrospective narrative, which seem at first unconnected with the context in which they occur, these separable but resonant retrospects often attempt to establish the analogous separateness of two people's experience. These inset narratives—and especially the story which Phoenix relates to Achilles in Book 11 as part of the Achaeans' supplication of the hero—have often been regarded by scholars as either spurious or irrelevant; but they serve an affective purpose: they are the narrative form of Homeric sympathy.

Homeric sympathy is generally founded on memory of one's own suffering, and a sense that it is analogous to the suffering of the other. The ultimate point of such an analogy between the material conditions of two people's lives is death. So when the poet resounds a repeated formula to describe the death of a warrior, this is a deeply significant accident of style: it creates a final underlying similarity between the endings of a variety of stories. At the same time it signals a profound difference between the kind of sympathy explored in the Homeric poems and the forms of that emotion evoked in most post-Christian literature. Its sense of the inescapable similarity between mortal experiences associates Homeric pity not with the desire to save, cherish, and regenerate, but with death. You can kill someone through Homeric pity, not because you want to put him out of his misery, but because you accept the fact of your mortality in his death. When warriors in the *Iliad* pity a dead comrade, they rarely pause in fighting to tend their wounds. They go straight on and kill.[26] This is usually more than revenge, or is at least an

---

[26] Hector does not pause to help the wounded Sarpedon, but rushes past to kill more Achaeans, *Il.* 5. 689–91. Cf. 4. 127–219, the wounding of Menelaus, when Agamemnon prophesies Troy's utter destruction (anticipating Hector), and has to be reminded by his wounded brother that he could be cured. Again imposing death on an enemy is the natural response to the death of a friend. Warriors do more often, however, feel anger or sorrow at the death of a friend before they avenge them; e.g. *Il.* 13. 402–23; 14. 458. See Martin Mueller, *The Iliad* (London, 1984), 100. Pity motivates revenge at *Il.* 5. 561, 610.

unusually complex form of revenge: it is more like an activation of mortality, a recognition that things must die, which leads to an urge to universalize that recognition. The most dazzlingly alien feature of Homeric sympathy is its close kinship with death, and its intimate relation to fighting. As the exchange between Glaucus and Diomedes illustrates, a recognition of kinship or guest-friendship can stop a battle, but a sense of shared fragility ('The generations of men are like those of leaves, some of which the wind scatters on the earth; but the budding forest brings forth others when springtime comes') is, not precisely a motive of, but a condition of fighting. Sympathy of this kind, the kind that recognizes death, turns back into something which it is tempting to call ruthlessness.

This aspect of Homeric sympathy is subjected to a terrifying scrutiny through the figure of Achilles. When the Greeks supplicate him to rejoin the fighting he makes no response, but Patroclus (who is described as *meilikos*, honey-mild, and is the only character in the poem to be called *enēes*, amiable[27]) goes out in his place, pitying the Greeks, and so fighting for them. He is disguised as Achilles. Once more a moment associated with sympathy pulls the narrative into two strands, which are followed by two alternative versions of a single character. While Patroclus goes out to fight—moved to do so by pity—Achilles remains, unmoved by supplication. He is often regarded, partly because of his resistance to this appeal from the Greeks, as being stonily resistant to the forms of behaviour and feeling which throughout the poem are associated with being human. But this is not entirely true. Once Patroclus, his surrogate and friend, is dead, he re-enters the battle, and becomes Homeric sympathy militant. The notion that the highest form of sympathy lies in the shared consciousness of death has a mirror image: the willingness to kill, the wish to affirm this shared mortality by bringing death.

And this version of sympathy motivates Achilles's ruthless *aristeia*, which follows the death of Patroclus. With almost systematic rigour, he disrupts the forces which earlier deflected the course of war. He first encounters Aeneas, who gives a protracted narration of his genealogy. This story, unlike its chief predecessor, the narrative of Glaucus to Diomedes, has no point of contact with the history of Achilles; it merely postpones the encounter by the time it takes to relate it.[28] Achilles turns the rest of the poem strange. In the battle which follows, Aeneas looks (once more) as though he is about to be killed and is (once more) the beneficiary of a magical intervention by the gods. This time Poseidon

[27] *Il.* 17. 204; 21. 96; 23. 252, 648. See Seth L. Schein, *The Mortal Hero: An Introduction to Homer's Iliad* (Berkeley and London, 1984), 35.
[28] *Il.* 20. 200–58.

saves him by catapulting him to another part of the battlefield.[29] The gods can still relocate their favourites, but mortal methods of salvation, of the kind explored through Book 6, start to crack under the strain of accommodating Achilles. Soon after the miraculous salvation of Aeneas, Tros approaches to supplicate him, hoping 'he might pity me, being of like age' (*homelikiēn eleēsas*).[30] Achilles kills him before he can grasp his knees, and continues to fill the River Xanthus with slaughter. He then encounters Lycaon, a son of Priam whom he had already captured once, and whom he had previously allowed to live. Lycaon grasps Achilles's knees, and utters the line which is repeated with ritual frequency by suppliants: *gounoumai s', Achilleu; su de m' aideo kai m' eleēson*, 'I supplicate you Achilles; honour and pity me'.[31] In a frenzied rush he relates his story, how he has eaten with and been sold by Achilles, as he struggles desperately to establish a claim to guest-friendship with his antagonist. The language of Achilles elsewhere in the poem has been shown to be a distorted and disrupted version of the common idiom of the other characters in the poem.[32] His response to Lycaon is similar: it creates a distorted version of, a mirror image of, the kind of sympathy founded on the belief that all must die:

Fool, do not offer me ransom, and do not argue with me. Until Patroclus met his last day, I preferred to spare the Trojans: I took many and sold them abroad. But now none of those whom the god shall deliver to me before the walls of Troy shall escape death. No, not a single Trojan, least of all the sons of Priam. No, friend [*philos*], you die too. Why do you grieve like this? Patroclus died, who was much better than you. Look what a great and powerful man I am. My father was a fine man, and a goddess bore me. But death, and certain fate, loom over me. One dawn or evening or noon someone shall take my life too in battle, whether with a blow from a spear or an arrow from a bow.[33]

Where sympathy ceases to be the conscious relation of particular sorrows to particular sorrows, and becomes a sense of general and universal fragility, then the mortality of another person becomes identifiable with one's own, with one's friend's, with that of any sufferer. This attitude is simultaneously a kind of universal sympathy and a form of despair, which blurs suicidal and homicidal desire into a deadly composite. It is an

---

[29] Fenik, *Battle Scenes*, 39, notes Aeneas's association 'with the weird and supernatural'.

[30] *Il.* 20. 465.

[31] *Il.* 21. 74.

[32] Adam Parry, 'The Language of Achilles', *Transactions of the American Philological Association*, 87 (1956), 6: 'Achilles has no language with which to express his disillusionment. Yet he expresses it, and in a remarkable way. He does it by misusing the language he disposes of.' Fenik, *Battle Scenes*, 230, notes how often Book 21, Achilles's *aristeia*, shows deviations from the typical forms of battle.

[33] *Il.* 21. 99–113.

attitude which colours Hector's sense of shared fragility with Andromache, and which emerges in Glaucus's first words to Diomedes; but in both these earlier episodes the universal and deadly form of sympathy is qualified by a sense of some particular tie of kinship. Achilles here expresses a view that is repeatedly almost emergent in the *Iliad*, and is repeatedly checked, qualified, and overlaid with other forms of feeling. The horror of his ruthless *aristeia* is not that it is inhumane; in a way it is so super-humane that it presses the poem's own recurrent sense of shared fragility into horror: why, if death is universal, should it not be *made* to be universal?

Achilles continues to kill; and it is with this uneasy and unanswered question—why should a warrior not make death universal?—that the *Iliad* breaks off his *aristeia* with another magical intervention. The River Scamander rises up in rage at being choked with bodies, and fights Achilles. This episode has frequently been suspected of being an interpolation. But a strange rationale may underlie it. Compassion is an inherently magical emotion in its Homeric form: it is associated with some measure of disruption in the straightforward linear flow of events through time, or of wounds to death. Anti-compassion is even more magical: Achilles's recognition that he can sympathetically kill a 'friend', someone with whom he acknowledges kinship, is a terrifying, blown-apart version of the main heroic ethos of the poem. It can only be prevented from destroying the poem's whole set of attitudes through some huge and unexpected intervention by external forces: the unseasonable, magical intervention of the river asserts by a magical incongruity something which the poem has no other means to establish: that sympathy may be double-edged, and may be surrounded by a consciousness of death, but that consciousness of death must stop somewhere.

The poem eventually contains and tames Achilles when he finally receives Priam, who is magically transported in a mist into his enemy's hut, and who, in a scene fraught with danger, establishes a kinship between his experience and that of his enemy. To receive a suppliant and feel with him is the final end of the wrath of Achilles: his tears *with* Priam, but *for* Patroclus, contain and control the inversion of Homeric sympathy which drove him to kill Lycaon. But Achilles's *aristeia* in Book 21 shows the magical distortions of the world which can result from passing beyond the safe bounds established by supplication and sympathy. And this is the territory through which Odysseus wanders.

THE *ODYSSEY*

Supplication in Homer is not only a means of requesting one's life or the
return of one's body on the battlefield; it is also a way of gaining
recognition as a person and material assistance in a foreign land.[34] This
brings it to the heart of the *Odyssey*, in which a key index of civility is
the willingness to accept and assist wandering suppliants: such people
could turn out to be disguised gods,[35] or lost heroes. Because it marks
the boundary between being an alien and a friend, the rite of supplication
is skirted by magic and danger of the kind released in the *Iliad* when
Achilles rejects Lycaon's appeal. The *Odyssey* is so full of parahuman,
unpredictably magical beings because it is drawn repeatedly to the edges
of the known, to moments where familiar and integrating rituals confront
beings who do not accept their conventions. Strange rites translate in
fiction into strange shapes.

Odysseus needs to be tricksy in order to operate in this world beyond
the margins of the known, since it is out of kilter with normal expectations,
and he needs to be able to withhold his identity and to lie in order to
survive in a world where the rite for establishing one's claim to be part
of society often fails.[36] Early on in his journey he is too bound by
orthodoxy and the expectations it creates to avoid danger. Polyphemus
the Cyclops shows his otherness in customs as in physical form when he
responds to Odysseus's suppliant request for *xenia* (the gifts due to a
stranger) by bashing the brains out of two of his companions.[37] Supplicating Polyphemus is like offering a Martian a cup of tea: a touchingly
stupid act by someone who is sure that the rituals for greeting strangers
work their magic in all areas. Odysseus's bolshiest shipmate, Eurylochus,
does not allow him to forget this failure to anticipate the foreign a little
later on, when the hero invites his companions back to receive hospitality
from another parahuman, Circe. But this time Odysseus has ensured that
the bond of supplication has been made before he takes any risks. He
attacks Circe—in a gestural parody of Iliadic heroism—so that she
supplicates *him*.[38] He then extracts an oath that she will not harm him,
to be quite sure that she will not prove another Polyphemus. Once these

---

[34] See Gould, 'Hiketeia', 90–4.
[35] As occurs at e.g. *Od.* 14. 57–8; 17. 483–7. See further Douglas J. Stewart, *The Disguised Guest:
Rank, Role, and Identity in the Odyssey* (Lewisburg, Pa., and London, 1976), 17–27.
[36] See Sheila Murnaghan, *Disguise and Recognition in the Odyssey* (Princeton, NJ, 1987), 5.
[37] *Od.* 9. 259–71. On 'guest-friendship' and the importance for a stranger of establishing a *xenos*
(friend/guest) to ensure survival abroad, see M. I. Finley, *The World of Odysseus*, 2nd edn. (London,
1977), 99–103. On the inhospitality of Polyphemus, see ibid. 101.
[38] *Od.* 10. 321–435. For the echoes of the *Iliad*, see A. Heubeck (ed.), *A Commentary on Homer's
Odyssey*, ii. *IX–XVI* (Oxford, 1989), 61, note on *Od.* 10. 321–4. On the reciprocality of the suppliant
relationship, see Gould, 'Hiketeia', 93.

bonds of civility are established, Circe proves the perfect hostess for a year, and becomes sufficiently human to provide food and to be slept with. Then Odysseus supplicates her to be allowed to leave.[39] Circe, initially an alien creature who turns Odysseus's crew into pigs, has been drawn far enough inside the conventions of civility to grant his request— although a tincture of her magical otherness remains as she follows her acceptance of his departure by that strange moment when she tells him he must visit Hades before he can arrive home. But successful supplication is the means by which Odysseus gets away from her: it is the means of re-entry into the familiar.

He ensures his ultimate return home, however, by winning over the eminently civilized Phaeacian princess Nausicaa on the shore of Scheria. His way of approaching her shows how, in the later phases of Odysseus's story, supplication is turning from a rule-bound ritual into a locus for a number of convergent and eminently manipulable forces. Nausicaa has been primed by Athene to be thinking about marriage when Odysseus appears naked before her on the shore. His address to her combines tricksy manipulation of a stranger who may not understand the principles of *philoxenia* with a strategic deployment of supplication:

I supplicate you, princess. Are you a goddess or a mortal? If you are a goddess, one of those who live in broad heaven, I think you are most like Artemis, the daughter of Zeus, in beauty, shape, and form. But if you are an earth-dwelling mortal, then your father, your mother, and your family are thrice blessed.[40]

There is an element of real uncertainty mingled with the flattery, since in the *Odyssey* it is virtually impossible to tell who is mortal and who a god.[41] And the flattery is a vital complement to his plea, since Odysseus cannot be quite sure of success with Nausicaa even if she accepts the conventions of supplication. In its purest form the act depends on establishing physical contact with the supplicated, and this might, in the circumstances, be misconstrued.[42] Odysseus is a naked man and Nausicaa a girl without male protection. He winningly converts his genuine bemusement into smooth talk, and transforms *hiketeia* into a performative utterance: 'I supplicate you', literally *gounoumai se*, 'I beg you by your knees'.[43] The ritual is softening into something like a means of entering

---

[39] See Heubeck's note, p. 68, on *Od.* 10. 483–6: 'She has formally recognized the Greeks as guest-friends, and this act implies an obligation to facilitate the next phase of their journey.'

[40] *Od.* 6. 149–55.

[41] In the analogous scene of Odysseus's eventual arrival at Ithaca the equivalent to Nausicaa is Athene in disguise, *Od.* 13. 221–351.

[42] See A. Heubeck (ed.), *A Commentary on Homer's Odyssey*, i. *I–VIII* (Oxford, 1988), 300, note on *Od.* 1. 110–250 and ad loc.; and Gould, 'Hiketeia', 75–7.

[43] On the kinship between speech and action in the *Odyssey*, see Tzvetan Todorov, *The Poetics of Prose*, trans. R. Howard (Oxford, 1977), 56–7.

into a strange society through its milder members, and takes on the faintest tincture of the erotic. Odysseus asks Polyphemus to revere the gods (especially Zeus, the god of strangers and suppliants) by taking in travellers;[44] but when he supplicates Nausicaa he does not tie his appeal so mechanically to the requirements of justice—nor does he adopt the menacing undertone with which he tells Polyphemus that he is on the way home from the wars.[45] Big brutes should toughly be asked for what the order of the world requires them to give, but sweet young things can safely be asked only for a rag and to 'have pity'—and charm will do the rest.[46]

Throughout the poem supplication tends to succeed more with women than with men.[47] Even Calypso, who is prompted to release Odysseus by the gods rather than by supplication, likes to pretend that she let him go because she has soft feelings, pity among them.[48] Athene also tells Odysseus that his successful supplication of Arete will depend on her being taken with him: 'If she thinks friendly thoughts about you in her mind, then there is hope that you will see your friends and return to your high-roofed house and to your native land'.[49] The precise nuance of *ei ken toi keinē ge phila phroneēs' eni thumo* is hard to judge, but it does suggest that more is involved in supplication than simply succeeding in a ritual. Athene herself has just been asked to 'have pity' by Odysseus, which introduces a passionate affection into the composite of forces which helps Odysseus to get home. Girolamo Bacelli, the sixteenth-century Italian translator of the *Odyssey*, had no doubt that Odysseus's return depended on his eliciting pity from his hostess:

> E s'ella à te pietosa gl'occhi volge
> Con l'alma amica, e del tuo mal le 'ncresce
> Ben puoi sperar di riveder gl'amici
> Tosto, e tornare alle tue case amate.[50]

And if she turns her eyes towards you, pitiful, with a friendly spirit, and if she learns of your suffering, you can safely hope that you will see your friends again, and return to your beloved estate.

---

[44] *Od.* 9. 269–71.
[45] *Od.* 9. 259–66.
[46] *alla, anass', eleaire*, 'but, princess, have pity'; *Od.* 6. 175.
[47] Gould argues that *hiketeia* 'is a mime of aggressive symbolic significance, directed at what must be kept inviolate, but a mime whose aggressive implications are contradicted by the inversion of normal competitive behaviour patterns.' 'Hiketeia', 100. Women are in his view significant for the ritual because inviolate.
[48] 'For I too have a righteous mind, and my heart is not made of iron, but is pitiful [*eleēmōn*]'; *Od.* 5. 190–1.
[49] *Od.* 7. 75–7. See Heubeck, edn. cit. 316–19.
[50] *L'Odissea d'Homero tradotta in volgare Fiorentino* (Florence, 1582), 188.

Bacelli's version shows how tempting it is for later and quite literal translators of the *Odyssey* to attribute its hero's return and reintegration into society, not to supplication, but to pity. This shift in emphasis responds to tendencies in the *Odyssey*: in this poem to be *philoxeinos*, willing to accept strangers, is not just a matter of understanding a nexus of rituals and obligations to the gods: it is also overshaded with feeling the right sorts of sympathy, and even, perhaps, with taking a fancy to people. Once Odysseus has reached a land where he can appeal to such a mingling of pity, feelingfulness, and divinely required hospitality, he is practically home. His return to Ithaca, after he has successfully supplicated and won over the Phaeacian court, is magically easy: a Phaeacian ship whisks him home under a supernatural anaesthetic.

The ability to tell and respond to stories also helps Odysseus on his way. He is consistently associated with narratives on the boundaries of fiction: Telemachus first learns of his progress after leaving Troy from a tale within a tale, as Menelaus tells him how the fabular Old Man of the Sea, Proteus, told him of Odysseus's incarceration by Calypso.[51] A cloud of fiction continues to surround the hero: all his most magical adventures— the encounters with the Cyclopes, with the Sirens, with Scylla and Charybdis, and so on—are related by him to the Phaeacian court as the concluding part of his integration into their society (after all of which the king, Alcinous, drily remarks that he has told the stories like a professional story-teller[52]). This huge narration of the past comes after he has successfully supplicated Arete, proved himself to be more than a run-of-the-mill beggar in the Phaeacian games, and given intimations of a heroic past by responding strongly to the court bard Demodocus's tales of Troy. His narrative also immediately precedes his departure home. Odysseus's narration of his past also occurs in a context of pitiful responses to stories, which accumulates around it a powerful aura of affective force, sufficient to suggest that telling the past, and thereby establishing a bond of feeling between his past and his audience, helps him home. His tale is immediately preceded by an extraordinary instance of the power of story-telling to create affinities between subject and audience. Odysseus weeps when the bard Demodocus sings of the Trojan war:

The famous minstrel sang this song. But Odysseus's heart was melted. Tears flowed from his eyes and wet his cheeks. And as a woman howls and flings herself about her dear husband, who has fallen in front of his city and his people in attempting to ward off the pitiless day from his city and his children; and, when she sees him dying and gasping for breath, she clings to him and shrieks aloud, while the enemy behind her hit her back and shoulders with

[51] *Od.* 4. 491–569.   [52] *Od.* 11. 363–9.

their spears, and lead her away to captivity to endure labour and suffering, her cheeks wasted with pitiable mourning: so did pitiful tears fall from the eyes of Odysseus.[53]

The stories people tell in the *Odyssey* (unlike in the *Iliad*) are often lies, unscrupulously told in order to establish a fictional version of the tie with a listener that Glaucus generated by telling Diomedes about his genealogy on the battlefield. The power of a fictional past to create a bond between an audience and their narrator is often manipulated by Odysseus: he routinely conceals his identity behind fables which tie him to someone dear to his listener.[54] Characters as lowly as the swineherd Eumaeus show a weary familiarity with the dangers of listening to someone's story and accepting a tie with them on the strength of what may well be lies.[55] The safest (and the most frequently accurate) way to identify someone in the *Odyssey* is to watch their responses to tales of the past. Emotional responses to narratives are a key index of who someone is, because in the *Odyssey*, as in the *Iliad*, the enabling condition of feeling grief at a story is self-recognition in the tale, combined with memory or anticipation that its content is true also for the listener. Emotions are tied to memory in the poem, and memorial emotions are never feigned. Menelaus recognizes Telemachus as Odysseus's son not by his own protestations, but by his tears when he hears a story of Odysseus.[56] Similarly, Alcinous, the king of Phaeacia, begins to speculate about Odysseus's identity when he notices that his strange guest throws his cloak over his head to hide his private tears when Demodocus sings of the matter of Troy.[57]

This concern with the affective power of story-telling underlies the simile which describes Odysseus's response to Demodocus's song. His reaction is entirely private, and is tied in with his memory (it is perhaps to avert this form of emotional memory that Helen drugs her audience before she sings of the Trojan horse, and the more slippery aspects of the Trojan war, to one of its key participants, Menelaus, and Telemachus, the son of another[58]). The simile suggests a sudden mind-swap with a woman in a sacked city, after Odysseus has heard a story of his own

[53] *Od.* 8. 521–31.

[54] See e.g. *Od.* 13. 256–86; 14. 199–359. Murnaghan, *Disguise and Recognition*, 148 notes how reunited characters regularly tell each other stories.

[55] *Od.* 14. 122–47. In his response to Odysseus's fictional tale he explicitly denies that his guest's association with Odysseus affects him: 'Ah, wretched stranger, you have stirred my heart deeply in telling the tale of your sufferings and wanderings ... It is not for this [your alleged connection with Odysseus] that I will show you respect or kindness, but from fear of Zeus, the stranger's god, and from pity for yourself.' *Od.* 14. 361–89. Note that Eumaeus is himself an exile, and so has a particular interest in the story, *Od.* 15. 390–484.

[56] *Od.* 4. 113–19. Telemachus begins to look like Odysseus after this, *Od.* 4. 138–46.

[57] *Od.* 8. 83–96.

[58] *Od.* 4. 219–34.

sacking of a city. This is not quite, *pace* Colin MacLeod's brilliant account of the subject,[59] an indication of how Homer thinks poetry in general functions, since it is so closely tied in with particular circumstances. It shows a particular story striking a particular man with the force of memory, a memory that makes him recognize the kinship between his own grief and that of a woman in the city which he sacked. This sympathy is not founded on an understanding that suffering is universal; rather, it particularizes Odysseus. He is the only person to respond in this way to the story, because he is the only person who has the experience to enable him to respond in this way. The rest of the court regard his reaction as sufficiently particular to identify him. Alcinous asks if he had some relative at the sack of Troy, or perhaps was there himself. The emotion identifies Odysseus—indeed it locks him into the solitude of his own experience— more conclusively than a dozen of his own fables. And the location of the simile shows its full significance. It precedes Odysseus's naming of himself—which he has ostentatiously delayed up to this point—and the story of his past. Sympathy precipitates his identification and full acceptance into the Phaeacian court; it also precedes his tale of his past, which in turn precedes his return home. This sequence could be read as attributing enormous powers to the sympathy created by fiction: it is a major constituent in the forces which lead to Odysseus's return to Ithaca.

The *Odyssey* frequently associates the reintegration of Odysseus into society with an affective return to the past. It is part of the deep structure of the poem. Telemachus's first act of self-assertion is to insist that his mother continue to listen to tales of Troy, despite her tears: 'For not just Odysseus lost his day of return, but many others also perished.'[60] This self-assertion reads at first as though it grows from a tough pity: 'Accept that death occurs', Telemachus appears to say, 'and listen to these tales of death.' But it is replete with the combination of emotional truth and factual duplicity which surrounds the spoken word in the *Odyssey*: Athene has just indicated to Telemachus that his father might still be alive. His demand that his mother accept the deaths of the returning Trojan heroes consequently unites a sense of universal fragility with a privy attempt to ensure that Penelope continues to remember Odysseus, and so remains willing and able to receive him home. The journey which follows this first adult act continues to associate the homecoming of Odysseus with listening to the past: Telemachus collects stories from his father's fellow warriors about his past history and present whereabouts. There are moments when listening to the past could delay his progress, especially

[59] *Collected Essays*, 1–15. [60] *Od.* 1. 354–5.

in the court of Menelaus;[61] but Telemachus's willingness to hear and respond to tales of Odysseus is linked with his emergence as someone able to assist his father's return. There is a very deep association in the poem between hearing and responding to stories, and becoming a person of fixed identity and power. The poem insinuates that the ability to respond to stories is what it means to have an identity.

Scholars have established that Homer's verbal style associates certain oral formulas and narrative motifs in certain contexts;[62] but the poet also instinctively associates forms of narrative with particular modes of feeling. The most startling flashback in either of the Homeric poems occurs when the nurse Eurycleia recognizes Odysseus's scar, and the poet pauses to relate the story of Odysseus's naming, his parentage, and the occasion on which he came by the scar. The significance of the episode has been much debated; but it is worth reflecting that this huge flashback occurs at the end of the process of 'recognizing' Odysseus, both in the sense of according him status in the society of Ithaca and of determining his name and history. It occurs where it does because in the *Odyssey* the acceptance or recognition of strangers is instinctively associated with stories about the past. This sudden extended narrative recoil into Odysseus's earlier history is not attributed to a particular unreliable human narrator, or associated directly with the memory of either Eurycleia or Odysseus.[63] It is just related as the moment of recognition, when the past is present, and brings about both emotion and the acceptance of a stranger into a society. The instinctive association in the Homeric poems of the boundary between the inside and outside of a culture with narratives about the past, and of narratives about the past with emotional recognition, makes the flashback occur when it does. It may not be certainly or simply so, but by the end of the *Odyssey* it begins to look as though some version of compassion—sharing the experience of a sufferer—lies behind many of the most strikingly unseasonable of Homer's transitions.

The same web of associations might even be used to explain that strangest of unseasonable transitions, the moment when Circe tells Odysseus that he must go to the house of the dead before he returns home. When he arrives in Hades, Odysseus hears stories from the dead about their pasts, and encounters dead friends, who affirm that all men live under death. The sudden and inexplicable leap which occurs when Circe

---

[61] *Od.* 4. 594–608.

[62] See e.g. Fenik, *Battle Scenes, passim*; Nagler, *Spontaneity and Tradition*, 21.

[63] *Od.* 19. 386–475. See Terence Cave, *Recognitions* (Oxford, 1988), 10–24, and cf. Erich Auerbach, *Mimesis: The Representation of Reality in Western Literature*, trans. Willard R. Trask (Princeton, NJ, 1953), 3–23. Austin, 'Function of Digressions', 82, relates it more closely than the text warrants to the particular experiences of Eurycleia.

tells him to undergo this journey could indicate an interpolation, or some jolt in the mind of the poet, or it could betoken the kind of coyness which Pope's annotator finds in it. But the whole sequence, from supplicating Circe to the house of the dead, follows one of the main narrative contours of the Homeric poems. Circe's sudden command occurs immediately after Odysseus has supplicated her to be allowed to leave; and, since stories of the past and a trace of sympathy are so often associated with the acceptance of a suppliant in the poem, the tales of dead heroes could be seen as a displaced completion of a nexus of ideas: supplication, sympathy, a sudden shift in tense, person, or place are part of the narrative grammar of the Homeric poems. 'Homer', be he or she one or many, repeatedly and mysteriously links these ideas and structures. And the mysteriousness of the linkage allows, almost compels, subsequent poets to try to make sense of the association. Those strange moments where the thought behind a sequence of narrated events seems at once not to be fully explicable, and yet to tempt explication, are the points in the Homeric poems which urge later poets to provide a governing idea with which to assimilate them. Virgil was the first poet systematically to attempt such an assimilation.

2

Virgil

A writer who sets out to assimilate a past text will always alter emphases, and make elements which had been peripheral or only latent in the original text central and patent. This is often compulsive, since there will always be ideas and contours of emotion in the past which will have a beguiling apparent similarity to some present idea or mode of feeling. These inevitable misinterpretations are also often overlaid and augmented by the wish of imitators to make the past text look as though it has become their own, or that of the cultural ideals within which and for which they write.

But in the case of writers who are imitating a narrative, there are strong limits to these freedoms. If the subsidiary episodes in a main plot are revised, remotivated, misread, or updated, then the overall goal or ending of the original narrative can begin to look distant and unlikely. Unless a writer sets out deliberately to render the outcome of a story strange or improbable, the need to arrive at the set of concluding events related by his predecessor puts quite strict limits on how he can re-motivate or embellish the actions and emotions which lead up to that conclusion. The process of imitating a narrative is not a simple linear movement towards accuracy or fidelity: it is an oscillation between indulging a new interpretation and deliberately restraining that interpretation in the interest of returning to the overall shape of an earlier story. This process has an unsteady kind of fidelity built into it: a work can approach the shape of its original by at first remaking it in the image of the present—by changing how its hero feels, or what he does—and then restraining the tendencies of its remaking in order to return to the overall structure of its source. It is a process which will never quite arrive at identity between past and present text, however. To move towards the shape of an earlier narrative will almost invariably lead to the deliberate suppression of little details or large-scale modifications which one knows to be one's own. It is not easy to suppress part of oneself: traces of the effort to do so will always remain.

Virgil's response to Homer is of this self-suppressive kind. He repeatedly intensifies the affective force of episodes in the Homeric poems which do not advance the purpose of the main plot. In this he is following a dynamic established by the Homeric poems themselves: digressions into the past, or away from the overall goal of the narrative, carry a much greater emotional weight in the *Odyssey* than they do in the *Iliad*. But in the *Odyssey*, as we have seen, this intensification of the emotional effect of digressions is accompanied by a shadowy impression that these digressive episodes are actually assisting the forward movement of the plot: when Odysseus weeps at Demodocus's story of the Trojan past, this precipitates his recognition and return. The closest parallel to this episode in the *Aeneid* is the moment when Aeneas sees a narrative picture of the Trojan War in the Temple of Venus. The tableau elicits a powerful, but powerfully solitary, response from Aeneas:

> constitit et lacrimans 'quis iam locus,' inquit, 'Achate,
> quae regio in terris nostri non plena laboris?
> en Priamus. sunt hic etiam sua praemia laudi,
> sunt lacrimae rerum et mentem mortalia tangunt.'[1]

He stopped and, weeping, said 'What place, Achates, what area of the world is not full of our labour? Here is Priam. Even here too there are the rewards of praise; even here tears fall for human affairs, and mortality touches the heart.'

There is a vestige here, an experimental approximation of, Homeric sympathy: mortal things, the mortality of things, touch the mind. Aeneas's rapt pause before the image of Troy might well recall Odysseus when he weeps for the tale of Troy as told by Demodocus. But Aeneas's momentary, paralysing isolation of feeling is amplified beyond all personal content and beyond all functional role in the narrative: Aeneas's response does not help to identify him, since the content of his emotion is entirely general; and there is no one with him who does not know his identity, from whom his grief might win acceptance. The object of his emotion is probably of more instrumental importance to his goal of arriving in Italy than the emotion itself, since the existence of the picture of Troy in such a remote spot shows that Aeneas's *fama* is sufficiently widespread to win him acceptance and recognition anywhere.[2] Although the affective force of this vision of the past is learnt from Homer, the faint suggestion in the *Odyssey* that an emotional response to the past could be dynamic and purposive, and could actually help one home, is stripped away from the episode. This leaves a powerful but purposeless emotion, an emotion amplified from its source, but checked, repressed in its relation to the main narrative line.

This model of imitation, whereby Virgil amplifies the latent emotion

---

[1] *Aen.* 1. 459–62. Text and translation adapted from *Aeneidos liber primus*, ed. R. G. Austin (Oxford, 1971).

[2] Dido's reception of the Trojans alludes to her knowledge of their ordeal, 1. 565–6. On the ecphrasis, see further Page DuBois, *History, Rhetorical Description and the Epic from Homer to Spenser* (Cambridge, 1982), 32–5.

in Homer and then denies it even an implicitly collaborative role in the development of the main plot, also applies, and applies cruelly, to the episode which surrounds Aeneas's vision of Troy's past in the Temple. Aeneas encounters Dido, queen of Carthage, and delays his imperial mission while he helps to found a surrogate and spectral version of Rome. The early stages of the episode in Carthage are scattered with allusions to Odysseus's time with the Phaeacians. Aeneas is met by his mother Venus, and their language recalls the exchanges of Odysseus and Nausicaa; Dido and her companions are compared to the Chorus of Diana's Nymphs, in an explicit allusion to a simile used to describe the gaggle of Phaeacian girls whom Odysseus encounters.[3] There are repeated hints and wistful allusions to a marriage between Odysseus and Nausicaa in Books 6–9 of the *Odyssey*, and these sketchy details are fleshed out in the *Aeneid* to the point of carnality. After the two have retired to a cave together during a storm, Dido thinks she has married Aeneas, although Aeneas later claims he is not so sure. The latent marriage with, and the assisting fancies of, Nausicaa have become ambiguous but none the less substantial realities. This development of a suggested fancy into a love-affair is precipitated by another amplification of Homer: Virgil attributes massive affective power to narration. With the collaboration of Venus, Aeneas's story of the Trojan War and of his subsequent Odyssey in Books 2 and 3 turns Dido's initial flicker of excitement into passion. Odysseus's tale of his past is transformed into a story which creates love; and love retards rather than assists Aeneas's return.

Virgil needs to exaggerate the power of fiction, and the attendant rather less reliable power of fancying, in order to make up for a major conceptual gap. Roman literature attaches far less importance to supplication and the attendant obligation to establish guest-friendship with a wandering stranger than its Greek prototypes. Given this dwindling of one major possible explanation for Dido's acceptance of Aeneas, Virgil has to create a cocktail of motives, expanded from the peripheries of Homer's text, in order to motivate his own: a sense of imperial affinity, a vestige of shared suffering, and plain passion combine to motivate the acceptance of his Odysseus in his version of Phaeacia.[4] This substitution of feelings for the fulfilment of ritual obligations may be a deliberate or an unconscious rereading, or a mixture of the two; but it does have drastic consequences. The Phaeacian

---

[3] 1. 498–502; cf. *Od.* 6. 102 ff. Austin, ad loc.

[4] *Aen.* 1. 628–30: 'me quoque per multos similis fortuna labores | iactatam hac demum voluit consistere terra; | non ignara mali miseris succurrere disco.' Cf. Dryden: 'For I my self, like you, have been distress'd; | Til Heav'n afforded me this place of rest. | Like you an Alien in a Land unknown; | I learn to pity Woes, so like my own.' *The Poems*, ed. James Kinsley, 4 vols. (Oxford, 1958), 888–91.

episode is turned from an exploration of the collaborative power of charm and supplication to gain access to civility, into an out and out love affair, which is catastrophically irrelevant to the main plot of a hero's return home. It becomes an episode which could possibly lead Virgil to a scandalous revision of the *Odyssey*: his new Odysseus could marry his Nausicaa, and live on.

Virgil has two options, given his necessary remotivation of the episode: he could drop the whole structure of the *Odyssey* and turn his hero into an amorous vagrant from his imperial future; or he could invent some force sufficient to stun the power of the motives which he has invented to take the place of guest-friendship. The price of turning latent suggestion into patent eroticism is subsequent repression. The poem is the ultimate, originating instance of the self-suppressive processes of imitation: it rewrites Homer, developing hints and suggestions into sub-plots and powerful emotions. Then it reasserts the need for a main plot which follows the shape of the Homeric homecoming.

The moment which most fully dramatizes this process of self-suppression is Aeneas's departure from Dido. Mercury is sent from Jove to tell Aeneas to leave his delusory alternative empire at Carthage and move on to Rome. Aeneas relays this command to Dido, who rages:

> nec tibi diva parens generis nec Dardanus auctor,
> perfide, sed duris genuit te cautibus horrens
> Caucasus Hyrcanaeque admorunt ubera tigres.[5]

No, you had no goddess for a mother, no Dardanus began your line, but the Caucasus, jutting with hard cliffs, bore you, and a Hyrcanian tigress suckled you.

These lines derive ultimately from Patroclus's words to Achilles after the Achaeans have supplicated him to return to battle. Patroclus rages at Achilles in similar terms: 'Pitiless man, your father was not the horseman Peleus, nor was Thetis your mother; but the grey sea bore you, and the craggy cliffs, your heart is so unbending.'[6] In the *Iliad* this cry precedes one of those bifurcations in the narrative line by which the poet frequently avoids attributing divided emotions to a single character: the kindly Patroclus disguises himself as Achilles and goes to battle, while the wrathful Achilles remains in his tent. The two possible responses to the supplication become, as it were, two alternative versions of Achilles. Virgil does not split people in two like this: through Euripides and Apollonius Rhodius the hero with a passionately divided mind, but a tragically indivisible body, had become a central element in heroic narrative. Instead Virgil creates the impression that Aeneas wishes he could split in two.

---

[5] *Aen.* 4. 365–7. Text and parallel in *Aeneidos liber quartus*, ed. R. G. Austin (Oxford, 1955).
[6] *Il.* 16. 33–5.

There are two potential stories in play at the moment of departure: Aeneas could pitifully respond to his near-wife's passion, or he could leave her:

> At pius Aeneas, quamquam lenire dolentem
> solando cupit et dictis avertere curas,
> multa gemens magnoque animum labefactus amore
> iussa tamen divum exsequitur classemque revisit.[7]

But dutiful [*pius*] Aeneas, although he longed to calm her grief with consolation and to lessen her sorrow with words, groaning many things, and overcome in spirit with great love, none the less carried out the commands of the gods and went back to his fleet.

Two verbs, 'cupit' and 'exsequitur', pull violently against each other here. The desire to stay and console has a weighty pile of clauses on its side, all of which nearly overtopple duty, and nearly turn into action: 'labefactus amore' (usually translated by some routine and forceless phrase like 'shaken with love') employs a participle from 'labefacio', which can mean 'incite to mutiny'.[8] The verb can be used of people whose resolve crumples and topples as they abandon what they should do. But it does not have the energy here to become a main verb: the string of mildly insubordinate subordinate infinitives and participles which accompany 'cupit' only intimate a suppressed, potential, alternative narrative in which Aeneas stays with and consoles Dido. What he actually does is leave a woman who is unconscious with grief.

It is hard to like Aeneas (or Virgil) here. But—at the risk of letting them both off a hook on which they deserve to squirm—the problems they both face are not simply the result of personal caddishness. Virgil is forced by his desire to imitate the large-scale structure of the *Odyssey* to make Aeneas leave. And he is forced to invent a reason for the departure sufficiently compelling to oust the passion which he had imputed to the Phaeacian episode. Aeneas's dilemma is more than just a personal conflict: it is a crisis point for the structure and motivating forces of the narrative, a moment when Virgil has to curtail the eroticism of his reading of Homer.

The main force which he uses to pull his poem back into shape is the *pietas* of his hero: it is *pius* Aeneas who leaves, in response to a command from Mercury. This epithet is widely reckoned to be central to the argument and uncertainties of the poem. It has a wide range of meanings. Cicero treats *pietas* as primarily concerned with the just performance of offices towards the gods and the state. He does acknowledge, however,

---

[7] *Aen.* 4. 393–6.   [8] Lewis and Short IIa; cf. Austin, ad loc.

that *pietas* also embraces the more intimate reciprocal ties of clientship and family.[9] The familial element of the virtue connects it with the softer sentiments of love and affection between parents and children. Aeneas's characterizing virtue consequently extends from areas which we would now regard as relatively abstract, to personal bonds which generate emotion. The extent and richness of the term is indicated by the way it gives us two words which are now completely distinguished in morphology and meaning: 'pity' and 'piety' both derive from Aeneas's virtue. Some commentators have indeed suggested that compassion is at the forefront of Aeneas's characterizing virtue,[10] but most modern critics have tended to see the range of meanings and the set of associations which cling to the term as a means of articulating the ambivalences of imperial experience: the *Aeneid* explores the progressive bleaching from *pietas*, and from Aeneas, its chief exemplar, of the warmer aspects of the virtue. Aeneas loses his wife and country in the sack of Troy; his father dies; and he is left in the second half of the poem to seek a land to which he is tied only by the commands of the gods, and by the obligation to find a country for his descendants.[11] *Pietas* gradually loses its familial warmth and acquires more and more of what might be called a 'deontic' force: it becomes cold obligation. The episode with Dido is on this view a transitional moment, the last point at which *pietas* might encompass a modicum of sympathetic affection for a near-wife and near-family member such as Dido.

But Virgil does not investigate the term simply in order to explore what it means to be an imperial hero. It is also a means of getting back on course with both the narrative structure and the ethos of his Homeric

---

[9] 'est enim pietas iustitia adversum deos' (*pietas* is justice towards the gods), *De natura deorum* 1. 116; 'Quid est pietas nisi voluntas grata in parentes?' (What is *pietas* if not a willing thankfulness towards one's parents?), *Pro Plancio* 33. 80; 'iustitiam cole et pietatem, quae cum magna in parentibus et propinquis, tum in patria maxima est' (Cultivate justice and *pietas*, which is great towards parents and relations, but greatest in relation to one's country), *De re publica* 6. 16. See the useful note to line 393 in *Aeneidos liber quartus*, ed. Arthur Stanley Pease (Cambridge, Mass., 1935).

[10] Paul Fécherolle, 'La Pietas dans L'Énéide', *Études classiques*, 2 (1933), 167–81 finds 'douceur d'âme, mansuétude, miséricorde' at 1. 545, 6. 403, 769, and 11. 292; but on all these occasions *pietas* is linked with *armis*, and there is nothing in the context to warrant the belief that the virtue mitigates martial powers. Viktor Pöschl, *The Art of Virgil: Image and Symbol in the Aeneid*, trans. G. Seligson (Ann Arbor, Mich., 1962), 53, finds Aeneas 'prefigures the Christian hero, whose heart remains gentle through struggle and sorrow and beats in secret sympathy with all suffering creatures'. A similar view is expressed in James Henry, *Aeneidea, or Critical, Exegetical, and Aesthetical Remarks on the Aeneis*, 4 vols. (London, 1873–89), i. 175–87. For the vanity of compassion, see W. R. Johnson, 'Virgil and the Ironies of Pietas', *Classical Journal*, 60 (1965), 360–4. For a more Roman view of *pietas*, see M. Owen Lee, *Fathers and Sons in Virgil's 'Aeneid'* (Albany, NY, 1979), 17–23, 180–1; W. B. Anderson, 'Sum pius Aeneas', *Classical Review*, 44 (1930), 3–4.

[11] Cf. Adam Parry, 'The Two Voices of Virgil's *Aeneid*', *Arion*, 2: 4 (1963), 76–7. J.-P. Brisson, 'Le "pieux Énée"!', *Latomus*, 31 (1972), 380, notes that it is only when Aeneas has begun his epic quest that he is called *pius*; in Books 2 and 3, which relate events which occurred before his mission proper, the epithet is not used. For the bleaching of the hero, see D. C. Feeney, 'The Taciturnity of Aeneas', *Classical Quarterly*, NS 33 (1983), 204–19.

prototypes. *Pietas* pulls the narrative back into shape after an amorous episode; but it is also through the ambiguities of *pietas* that Virgil attempts to reconstitute the combined ruthlessness and compassion of the Homeric hero. The ambivalences of the term roughly correspond—or to a Roman would appear to correspond—to the contours of Homeric tough pity. *Pietas* is founded on justice, the due offering of services to gods and to the state, but it also requires emotions, such as gratitude and affection. This means that the virtue could unite rigorous dutifulness with warm remorse, and so provide the conceptual foundation for a simultaneously dutiful and regretful departure from a woman who is almost a wife. The most vital factor determining the ethos and form of the *Aeneid* is that Virgil cannot quite replicate the form of Homeric compassion, the solitary sense of an analogy between one's own condition and that of another. This emotion can make one feel sympathy for but not assist a sufferer; it can also lead one simultaneously to pity and to leave a woman without being torn in two: Hector leaves Andromache while pitying her, in the consciousness of a shared response to a shared catastrophe. Virgil cannot replicate this knowing grief in departure: pity is for him an emotion which keeps emerging from *pietas*, but which he struggles continually to restrain. Pity is what unsuccessfully rebels against the nagging commands of Mercury; it does not collaborate with the motives for departure. The result of this effort to replicate Homeric compassion, which slides just slightly off-centre, is a desperate Aeneas, who wants to be two people at once, who is ordered to go but who wants to stay, whose *pietas* is splitting into two incompatible senses, a dutiful sense and a pitiful sense. His conflict grows from Virgil's inability to find a motive which will both override and absorb into itself the vagrant amorousness which he imputed to the Phaeacian episode.

The *Aeneid* does retain many of the episodic digressions and some of the marvellous and mythical elements in Homer. Its hero shares the name of the character who is most frequently associated with magical resurrections in the *Iliad*, and Virgil's Aeneas remains true to the mingling of divine good fortune and magic which surrounds his Homeric prototype. The Trojan fleet is turned by Jove into nymphs in order to avoid being burnt by Turnus; and more of this magical good fortune surfaces when Aeneas is miraculously cured by Venus after being wounded by an arrow in battle.[12] The *Aeneid* is not so single-mindedly concerned with the establishment of the Roman people as to eradicate all of Homer's moments of magic. But it has few of those resonantly sudden shifts of scene and time which add such a power of suggestion to the *Iliad* and the *Odyssey*.

---

[12] *Aen.* 9. 117–22, 12. 318–424.

Many of the most strikingly irrelevant or detachable episodes in the Homeric poems do find a place in it, but they are thought in, encoded into its fabric of ideas, and encompassed by its structures of motive, rather than being allowed simply to intrude like alien relics from past texts. And this effort of assimilation puts enormous pressure on the structures of thought used to contain Homer. Odysseus's trip to the underworld is startlingly ill-prepared for: Circe gives no reason for her sudden command that he should visit Teiresias before his return. But in the *Aeneid* the episode is squeezed forcibly into a motive shape. Aeneas's descent to Hades might appear at first to be another episode which has been assimilated by *pietas*, since it originates in a command from the ghost of Anchises in Book 5,[13] and concludes with a vision of the imperial history which is to spur the hero on through the 'horrida bella'[14] which lie immediately before him. It consequently enacts a movement between two aspects of *pietas*, from family loyalty to a concern for the well-being of the state. But this flexibility in the meaning of the term points to a problem: the controlling motive of *pietas* slips and slides, as though placed under enormous strain by the effort to make Homer's episode seem smoothly integrated into a new fabric of ideas. Different aspects of Aeneas's virtue seem at different times to be the underlying reason for the descent. When the hero asks the Sybil to be permitted to make the journey, he does not appeal to an idea of empire, or produce a sonorous invocation of the gods. He asks for the compassion which is owed to filial affection:

> quin, ut te supplex peterem et tua limina adirem,
> idem orans mandata dabat. gnatique patrisque,
> alma, precor, miserere.[15]

For this reason Anchises gave pleading orders that I should seek you as a suppliant and approach your doors. Mother, pity a son and a father, I beg you.

This appeal for a compassionate response to the dutiful affection of father and son is a distant descendant of the moment when Odysseus supplicates Circe to be allowed home. But here familial emotions dominate the supplication, and swamp both the Homeric background of ritual gesture and the Virgilian concern for imperial obligations. The soft emotions which so often emerge in the poem through family feeling also blur over into the Sybil's view of Aeneas's motives for descending: she attributes

---

[13] *Aen.* 5. 724–39.
[14] *Aen.* 6. 86.
[15] *Aen.* 6. 115–17.

his wish to undertake such a task to *amor* and *cupido*,[16] rather than to a pious desire to learn of Roman history. The motive by which Virgil attempts to explain and integrate Homer's sudden shift of subject will not remain fixed. It is mutable and slippery, occluding but not neutralizing personal passions under the profession of higher purposes. And when Aeneas encounters Dido in the underworld its range of meanings becomes suspiciously convenient. At this moment of desperate self-justification, Aeneas lays claim to the most austere motives for his descent:

> sed me iussa deum, quae nunc has ire per umbras,
> per loca senta situ cogunt noctemque profundam,
> imperiis egere suis.[17]

But the commands of the gods compel me to carry out their instructions, to go through these shadows, through places laden with dankness and deepest night.

This is very close to being a lie. It is true enough that Mercury ordered him to leave Dido; but commentators have accepted too readily Aeneas's less ingenuous protestation that he also descended to Hades merely in response to a divine command: Anchises does issue divine orders, but these concern the pursuit of Rome. His actual request for a visit does not mention the gods. For all Aeneas knows this trip to Hades is simply a family outing.[18] The hero's wavering account of why he is there may well be an authentic confusion deriving from the strong associations established by *pietas* between family, gods, and state: Aeneas sees them all as one. But he is always suspiciously keen artificially to bolster the forces behind his actions when excusing his conduct to Dido: he claims in Book 4 that he seeks Italy unwillingly, and at the command of both his father and the gods, although at that point only Mercury had definitely appeared to him.[19] This slippage, which may either be disingenuous or encoded in the Roman shape of feeling (or both), is fundamental to the poem: the meaning of *pietas* tends to modulate towards the higher, more abstract elements of the virtue at moments when it is inconvenient for Aeneas to acknowledge that he is motivated by family emotion. The ambiguity of the term, which allows the mind to slither from a feeling, into divinely sanctioned dutifulness, and back again, may have seemed quite natural to

[16] *Aen.* 6. 133. On the recurrent association of the father/son relationship with tenderness and supplication, see M. C. J. Putnam, '*Pius* Aeneas and the Metamorphosis of Lausus', *Arethusa*, 14 (1981), 145.

[17] *Aen.* 6. 461–3.

[18] The gods are mentioned at *Aen.* 5. 726; but the request for a visit is scrupulously unrevealing: 'Ditis tamen ante | infernas accede domos et Averna per alta | congressus pete, nate, meos' (However, first go to the infernal house of Dis, and seek a meeting with me, my son, through the deep house of Avernus), *Aen.* 5. 731–3.

[19] *Aen.* 4. 351–9. On ancestor worship at Rome, see Michael Grant, *History of Rome* (London, 1978), 128.

its first audience. But these modulations—and the way the 'higher' forces of empire and the gods are often apparently used to mask over emotion—can look now like dishonesty. Homer's compassion has many aspects, and can—as when Achilles kills Lycaon—appear ruthless; but it is a complex set of attitudes to the shared fragility which circumscribes all human beings, rather than a punning combination of several differing attitudes under a single word. Virgil replaces the multi-aspected cognitive compassion of Homer with a term which is conveniently ambiguous rather than many-dimensioned. He does 'integrate' and provide a motive for the descent to the underworld: but the pressure of assimilation makes the motive he constructs look suspiciously plural, even as though it is on the verge of fragmentation.

This violent use of the ambiguities of *pietas* to assimilate Homeric digressive episodes also creates the most pathetic tale in the *Aeneid*: the story of Nisus and Euryalus in Book 9. This episode derives from the one part of the *Iliad* which is almost universally agreed to be a late interpolation, the 'Doloneia', which takes up the whole of Book 10.[20] The contents of *Iliad* 10 are unusually separable from the main narrative: the Achaeans, at their most desperate, hold an emergency nocturnal council of war, which resolves to send out Ulysses and Diomedes on a scouting mission, either to extract some information or to kill a few Trojan stragglers.[21] Their mission succeeds on both counts, but has no impact at all on the fighting which follows or precedes it. The ghoulish scenery—horses squelch over dead flesh, corpses rot around the council—is unlike the rest of the *Iliad*, and the adventures of the two Achaeans—capturing a scout, killing Trojans as they sleep, and hijacking horses—have no effect on the course of the battle. The entire episode seems excisable, and alien to the rest of the poem.

Virgil takes this unnecessary episode and makes its unnecessariness pointed. His story originates with Nisus's confused deadly desire, 'dira cupido', either to fight or to perform some great deed.[22] He and Euryalus enter a nocturnal council of war, and ask to direct this desire towards the

[20] See F. Klingner, Über die Dolonie', *Hermes*, 75 (1940), 337–68; Kirk, *The Songs of Homer* (Cambridge, 1962), 310–12. On the comparison with Virgil, see K. W. Gransden, 'Virgil's *Iliad*', in Tom Winnifrith *et al.* (eds.), *Aspects of the Epic* (London, 1983), 49–57. See also Barbara Palock, *Eros, Imitation, and the Epic Tradition* (Ithaca, NY, and London, 1990), 87–112. This study reached me too late to play any part in the development of my argument. On the role of the scholia in determining how Virgil read the 'Doloneia', see Robin R. Schunk, *The Homeric Scholia and the 'Aeneid': A Study of the Influence of Ancient Homeric Literary Criticism on Vergil* (Ann Arbor, Mich., 1974), 59–81.

[21] The ambiguous aim of the mission nearly proves fatal, when Diomedes wonders whether to kill more men or take more booty; but Pallas directs him to flee, *Il.* 10. 503–14. Odysseus does not hesitate. This is the origin of Virgil's distinction between the behaviour of his two scouts.

[22] *Aen.* 9. 184–7.

serious imperial purpose of informing the absent Aeneas of the Rutulian
attack. But the end of the episode betrays its origins in confused desire,
as their mission rapidly degenerates into the heated quest for glory and
gain of their Homeric prototypes. The two scouts butcher their sleeping
enemies and seize trophies of their conquest; and, as they lose their
imperial impulse, the story becomes marginal and pathetic. Euryalus is
killed by Volcens, the commander of the Rutulian band, and a concluding
simile culled from the amorous field of Catullus compares him with a
marginal beauty destroyed by cultivation:

> purpureus veluti cum flos succisus aratro
> languescit moriens, lassove papavera collo
> demisere caput pluvia cum forte gravantur.[23]

As when a purple flower sliced by a plough wilts in death, or as poppies hang
down their weary heads when they are weighed down by a chance shower.

The episode, like its prototype, is excisable: it could be sliced like a
delightfully unnecessary ornament from the structure of the poem. But
its very unnecessariness ties it back in with the concerns of the *Aeneid*.
The story reflects and exaggerates the shifts in motive which surround
Aeneas's descent in Book 6. Both episodes begin with the motivating
'cupido'[24] of their instigators; but the story of Nisus and Euryalus, unlike
Aeneas's visionary digression, splinters off from the main design of the
poem when this original desire supplants imperial purpose. It is made to
become irrelevant from within, by the unregenerately Homeric desire of
its main characters just to do a spot of killing, rather than to perform an
imperial mission.

But resting just beneath this cupidinous irrelevance lies the warmth,
not just of wild desire, but of family feeling. At the Trojan Council
Euryalus asks Iulus to look after his mother, but does not himself risk
seeing her before his heroic departure, because 'nequeam lacrimas perferre
parentis' (I would not be able to bear my parent's tears).[25] Parental tears
have such motivating power that to witness them opposing an imperial
mission would prevent it altogether. Aeneas's son, Iulus, is struck with
the familial emotion which he shares with Euryalus, 'atque animum
patriae strinxit pietatis imago' (And the image of paternal piety seized his
mind).[26] This line has resonances of Homer's sympathetic self-recognition
in the other, and suggests a moment when self and sufferer seem to share

---

[23] *Aen.* 9. 435–7; cf. Catullus 11. 21–4.

[24] The Sibyl attributes Aeneas's descent to 'tantus amor menti... tanta cupido' at 6. 133.

[25] *Aen.* 9. 289. On this element in the episode, see Rory B. Egan, 'Euryalus' Mother and *Aeneid*
9–12', in Carl Deroux (ed.), *Studies in Latin Literature and Roman History II, Collection Latomus*,
168 (1980), 157–76.

[26] *Aen.* 9. 294; cf. 10. 824.

common vulnerability. But it has subtly shifted emphasis away from its prototype: Iulus's shiver of shared *pietas* is founded not on an analogy between the circumstances or experience of the sufferer and himself, but on a perceived similarity between their moral priorities. Kinship of values, rather than a sense of shared experience, or of shared fragility, creates Iulus's form of feeling: the image of *pietas*, of a shared set of priorities, creates the affinity between the two sons. This suggests a terrifyingly minimized view of the way in which it is possible to experience an affinity with another person: it requires more than just an analogy of experience; it requires an identity of attitudes. Virgil responds to Homer by tying episodes from his original into the ethical concerns of his own poem, and this habit in his way of integrating his predecessor is a manifestation of his imperial version of sympathy: those you feel with are those with whom you share values. Past texts similarly only take on a meaning for him in the present when they can be made to manifest a familiar structure of ethical thought, rather than when they present an experience which all mortals share.

Yet to write one's own values over those of another leaves faint traces, like a poor palimpsest, of what was there before. *Pietas* will not simply absorb into itself the varieties of experience which derive from Homeric compassion. It struggles to contain that alien compassion within an imperial form. Iulus's momentary *frisson* of ethical identity with a victim of Rome's history does not result in any action: he does not, for instance, try to prevent the departure of Euryalus because of their shared *pietas*. Rather, the episode moves immediately away from the emotions aroused by family, towards duties and commands: Iulus 'multa patri *mandata dabat*' (gave many instructions to his father), which the two scouts are to deliver. The same phrase — 'mandata dabat' — was used by Aeneas when asking to be allowed to descend to Hades.[27] The energy required to rewrite Homer again makes Virgil's chief motive seem on the brink of fragmentation: the need to send and receive commands again emerges through and drowns out whatever motive power there might be in sympathetic feeling. Such feelings have to be suppressed if Virgil is to follow the shape of his original: a Iulus who told Euryalus to stay, sensing kinship with him, would be a hero from a kind of poem which could not accommodate the brutally episodic form of the 'Doloneia'. The story would have to continue; Euryalus would live on, saved by sympathy. Such a poem Virgil consistently suggests might be possible; but he refuses to write it, swerving between a sense of the power of familial emotion, and a wish to impose the lineaments of imperial *pietas* on his Homeric original.

[27] *Aen.* 9. 312; cf. 6. 116.

The emotions released by family kinship do, though, emerge from the episode, and seem almost for a moment to deflect the poem from its purpose. The two warriors, unlike their Homeric prototypes, both die. The episode then is (apparently) closed off with an encomiastic apostrophe, describing the *fama* which the deaths of Nisus and Euryalus acquire in Virgil's poem. But at once it reopens like a fresh wound, as the news of the heroic death reaches the live nerve of feeling. Euryalus's mother hears of her son's end and vainly complains:

> figite me, si qua est pietas, in me omnia tela
> conicite, o Rutuli, me primam absumite ferro.[28]

Transfix me, Rutulians, if you have any pity, hurl all your arms at me, kill me first with your swords.

This is the only moment in the *Aeneid* when *pietas* is definitely forced towards its later sense of 'pity' by the pressure of vain family feeling in hostile circumstances. Virgil is only willing to release such feeling when it is completely locked off from motive force, when it is enclosed in an irrelevant Homeric digression. This twisted form of *pietas* only provides a little unexpected coda to a closed episode: it will not revive Euryalus. Even his mother's desperate plea for compassionate execution is unheard by the Rutuli. Squeezed dry of emotion, Euryalus's mother is dropped from the narrative and never appears again. The episode advances Rome's history not at all.

The unnecessary episode of Nisus and Euryalus is one of the most characteristic in the *Aeneid*. The poem releases stray emotions—rebellious desires, non-imperial loves, unmartial compassions—which will not be absorbed into its main story. These desires are acknowledged, but given no motive force to direct the narrative. Writers have consistently responded most actively to Aeneas's actions—the episode with Dido in Book 4, or the descent to Hades in 6—when they delay rather than directly advance the main narrative. The history of Virgil's influence suggests that the imaginative drive of the *Aeneid* lies in its digressions, in the way vagrant desires are stunned and discarded. This makes it a powerfully perverse poem: its energy lies in what it asserts to be irrelevances. This perversity haunts the imagination of later writers, as they in their turn seek to grasp hold of and contain the divergent energies of the *Aeneid*. But the peculiarly constructive incoherence of the poem is explicable. The *Aeneid* creates a massive structural paradox: the means to realize the overall goal of the

---

[28] *Aen.* 9. 493–4. See Fécherolle, 'Pietas', 172. He also cites *Aen.* 2. 536, 'Di, si qua est caelo pietas quae talia curet' (Gods, if there is in the heavens a *pietas* which cares for such things), in which the reciprocal ties between man and gods nudges the sense towards 'compassion'. See *Aeneidos liber secundus*, ed. R. G. Austin (Oxford, 1964), ad loc.

main plot, to establish the Trojan race in Rome, is not just to proceed directly towards Italy. Rather, this overall purpose entails the *creation* of digressions: it is only by turning alternative or subsidiary stories into dead ends—literally dead ends—that the main plot can assert its dominance.[29] In order to pursue his Roman goal Aeneas has to make major incidents seem like mere digressions, by killing off whatever does not lead to Rome. Alternative possible plots, such as the story of Dido, or the heroic sortie of Nisus and Euryalus, have to be abruptly terminated in order to achieve the overall goal of the poem. It is for this reason that the episodic structure of the Homeric poems becomes painfully pointed: each episode *must* stop or the poem will never reach its intended goal. This also suggests why the chief Homeric episodes in the poem are encompassed by a fragmenting form of *pietas*: the duplicity of this term, spreading from an urgent pang of ethical identification to an austerely impersonal concern for the emergence of an empire, catches the range of emotions required both to create and to respond to a digressive structure. As the plot advances, *pietas* has to assume the power to destroy whatever does not suit its goal. This intensification of violence, however, puts enormous pressure on the meaning of the term: whatever traces of pity lie latent in its austerely Roman form grow into full strength as the imperial plot moves forward. The very savagery to which a purposeful linear plot gives rise creates the vain pathos which clings so consistently in the *Aeneid* to its opponents. The more the poem suppresses and marginalizes the alternative stories which Virgil intimates could occur, the more plangently necessary they appear to be.

As the *Aeneid* turns to war in its second half, Aeneas, the agent of the linear unifying plot of settling in Rome, becomes himself increasingly the creator of pathetic digressive episodes. When Magus supplicates him on the battlefield with an appeal 'per patrios manis et spes surgentis Iuli' (by the paternal spirit of the dead Anchises, and the growing hope of Iulus), Aeneas replies that since Turnus broke the 'commercia belli' (agreements of war) by killing Pallas, such appeals can no longer guarantee salvation, 'hoc patris Anchisae manes, hoc sentit Iulus' (The spirit of Anchises knows this; Iulus knows this).[30] A supplication leads only to a martial episode, which terminates in a sudden, ruthless slaughter. It is only *after* the killing that Aeneas realizes with compassionate shock that his victim, who dies saving his father, shares his virtue:[31]

---

[29] See David Quint, 'Epic and Empire', *Comparative Literature*, 41 (1989), 1–32; esp. 15: 'Epic views all such romance alternatives as dead ends...stories which, unlike its own narratives of missions accomplished, have no place to go.'

[30] *Aen.* 10. 524, 534.

[31] On belated emotion in the *Aeneid*, see R. O. A. M. Lyne, *Further Voices in Vergil's 'Aeneid'* (Oxford, 1987), 170.

> ingemuit miserans graviter dextramque tetendit,
> et mentem patriae subiit pietatis imago.[32]

He groaned deeply and pitied, and stretched out his right hand. There came into his mind the image of his paternal piety.

As with Iulus's feeling for Euryalus, compassion for Lausus springs not so much from a sense of shared suffering as from a sense of moral identity with his victim, whose death makes Aeneas think of his own *pietas*. This is not simply sorrow for another's harm, since it is dependent upon recognizing that his victim shares his virtue. And again the emotion released by this sense of ethical identity is insulated from any narrative consequence: it comes too late to provide the motive for an action. It rises unnecessarily like the hero's groans over Dido, like the cries of Euryalus's mother. Homer's Achilles acknowledges a kind of kinship with Lycaon as he kills him which is a distorted derivative of the compassion that underlies so much of the rest of the poem. Aeneas is driven more inwardly both to become and even to create that which he is struggling to conquer: he generates the reasons for the pity which he must struggle to exclude, as he becomes the kind of ruthless Homeric creator of terminal martial episodes which he is attempting to transcend.

 This paradox comes to a head in the poem's final moment, when Aeneas defeats his Homeric adversary Turnus in single combat:

> ille humilis supplex oculos dextramque precantem
> protendens 'equidem merui nec deprecor' inquit;
> 'utere sorte tua. miseri te si qua parentis
> tangere cura potest, oro (fuit et tibi talis
> Anchises genitor) Dauni miserere senectae
> et me, seu corpus spoliatum lumine mavis,
> redde meis . . .'
>
>   .   .   .   .
>
>   stetit acer in armis
> Aeneas volvens oculos dextramque repressit;
> et iam iamque magis cunctantem flectere sermo
> coeperat.[33]

He, humbly suppliant, stretching out his right hand and gazing on him, said: 'I have deserved this, and so beg for nothing. Use your good fortune. If the grief of an unhappy father can touch you, I beg (and you had a similar father in

---

[32] *Aen.* 10. 823–4.   [33] *Aen.* 12. 930–41.

Anchises) pity the old age of Daunus, and return me, or my body despoiled of life if you prefer, to my family.' . . . Aeneas stood eager in arms, rolling his eyes, and held back his sword arm. And more and more this speech began to affect him as he delayed.

That wordless hesitation is a stutter brought about by revisionary instincts. Aeneas is recreating and modifying Achilles's ruthless execution of Hector. In the *Iliad* Hector is already mortally wounded before he addresses Achilles, and there is no possibility that his killer could do more than agree to return his corpse. Here, though, there is a faint possibility that Turnus could be allowed to live on. And the reason for his continued life would presumably be that form of ethical compassion which Virgil imposed on Homer. Turnus supplicates for the return of his own body to his father, not by appealing to a common store of grief but by exploiting shared moral and emotional values: 'You too have a father who is dear to you; apply your *pietas* also to my father, and so return my body or spare me for his sake.' The difference from the form of compassion which Achilles shows to the suppliant Priam is subtle but crucial: Aeneas is not asked to contemplate the grief he shares with his suppliant, nor is he asked to pity Turnus, but to be moved by his own filial piety to pity Turnus's father.[34] This complex emotion, permeated by the ethical, is represented only by a silent pause. And this final silence indicates both a huge effort to understand Homeric compassion, and a sense that something new, something less deadly than its prototype, might be on the brink of emerging—and something which might lead Virgil to depart from the main lineaments of Homer's plot.

But in a final subjection of his new motives to the narrative structure of his original, Virgil terminates this vestige of a pitiful delay. It is checked by a blast of *furor* as Aeneas sees over Turnus's arm the baldric stripped from the body of the boy Pallas, whom Turnus had killed, and whom Aeneas had agreed to protect:

> ille, oculis postquam saevi monimenta doloris
> exuviasque hausit, furiis accensus et ira
> terribilis: 'tune hinc spoliis indute meorum
> eripiare mihi? Pallas te hoc vulnere, Pallas
> immolat et poenam scelerato ex sanguine sumit.'

[34] This is controversial. Putnam, '*Pius* Aeneas and the Metamorphosis of Lausus', 152, suggests the parallel with *Iliad* 24, but thinks that *ira* overcomes *pietas* (which he construes as tending to pity) in the death of Turnus. Similar views are found in Johnson, 'Ironies of Pietas'; K. W. Gransden, *Virgil's Iliad: An Essay on Epic Narrative* (Cambridge, 1984), 144, 211–15. But Lee, *Fathers and Sons*, 103, Pöschl, *Art of Virgil*, 136, and Lyne, *Further Voices*, 187, infer that Aeneas hesitates because he piously remembers Anchises's advice 'parcere subiectis' (to spare the subject). Since Aeneas is actually asked to pity Turnus's father and remember his own, it is more natural to assume that is what he does.

hoc dicens ferrum adverso sub pectore condit
fervidus; ast illi solvuntur frigore membra
vitaque cum gemitu fugit indignata sub umbras.[35]

He, once he had drunk in with his eyes those relics and monuments of grief, burning with rage and awesome in his frenzy: 'Are you, clad with the spoils of my friends, to escape from me? Pallas gives you this wound, Pallas sacrifices you, and drinks punishment from your defiled blood.' Saying this in passion, he buried his sword in the breast turned towards him; the limbs of Turnus collapsed into coldness, and his life fled with indignation to the shadows beneath.

Something of a past text can be evoked just by giving a sense that there is something out of the ordinary happening, which does not readily fit established forms of language. Stories—particularly old stories—do enable such strange modes of feeling to be evoked: a sequence of events can be built up which intimates an unknowable and alien emotion, which does not need to be spoken, or expressed, or even directly imputed to a character, provided the surrounding narrative constructs the events which would give rise to such an unspeakable emotion. But there is another much simpler method of evoking the past, which is to attach some familiar and simple label to its mode of experience. This is perhaps more like appropriation, and almost always involves a distorting simplification. The death of Turnus shows both these ways of responding to the past. It is Virgil's last and most desperate attempt to evoke and transfigure Homeric compassion: that strange emotion emerges transformed into a wordless sense of affinity for the priorities of an enemy. This alien, almost inexpressible motive, which might have the power to change the outcome of Homer's story entirely, is glanced at wordlessly by Aeneas's silent delay over his antagonist. But this hesitant stutter, this momentary suggestion of ethical compassion, is then blown away by a simple passion, which has the power to goad Aeneas into reliving the action of Achilles in killing Hector or Lycaon, but which lacks any complexity or wonder at the modes of experience related by Homer. There are strange vestiges of Achilles still in Aeneas: his suggestion that Pallas will take the blood of Turnus in sacrificial atonement for his death has a faint, religiously transformed, residue of Achilles's wild threat to eat Hector's flesh once he has killed him.[36] But what enables Aeneas to replicate the action of Achilles is a combination of *furor* and *ira*. Virgil needs those simple passions in order to follow and motivate the outlines of Achilles's action— and his simplified motives lived on into the increasingly operatic idiom of later epic, in which heroes oscillate between passions of rage and pity at the touch of a buckler. But it is the hesitant, enigmatic silence of

---

[35] *Aen.* 12. 945–52.   [36] *Il.* 22. 347.

Aeneas, in which Virgil strives to penetrate the character of compassion, which was to give later writers space in which to construct more complex versions of heroic emotions, and with those feelings, their own narrative forms.

3

Ariosto

Italian romances have a splendidly free and uninhibited attitude to earlier books. In Boiardo's *Orlando innamorato*, the hero—who is a thick, mildly lecherous, thoroughly ineffectual version of the hero of the *Chanson de Roland*—at one point comes across a monstrous creature that asks a familiar literary riddle: 'What goes on four legs in the morning, two in the afternoon, and three in the evening?' Orlando scratches his head for a moment or two, before he decides the problem is too tricky for him. So he draws his sword and pushes the creature off a cliff.[1]

Bookish readers would hear behind this episode the voice of the Sphinx, and might see Boiardo's hero as a jokey version of Oedipus, the first person to solve its riddle. The joke is both at the wimpish circumspection of the cerebral Oedipus, who thinks where he cannot kill, and at the dim, abrupt warriors of old French epic, who swipe around rather than thinking. A reader is given a few familiar learned reference points, which seem all to point in different directions, and finally to vanish in a haze of comical uncertainty. The feeling that the joke rests finally on the bookish reader is confirmed by the way the story continues. Orlando gallops on for a mile or so, then remembers that he has been given a magic book that answers all questions. He pauses for a moment to look up the answer to the riddle of the Sphinx, then, presumably, decides it was not a good riddle, and stupidly gallops on. There is no room in Boiardo for any struggle for mastery between the writing of the present and that of the past; earlier texts seem to vanish with a teasing sparkle into the air.

This playful, dislocating attitude to ancient literature is part of the delight of reading Italian epic romances. They swirl around, playing tricks, frustrating, enchanting, and getting nowhere with perfect charm. Readers have often felt this rootless detachment in the early sixteenth-century continuation of Boiardo, the *Orlando furioso* by Ludovico Ariosto. The heroes of *Orlando furioso* desperately seek the unbearably attractive Saracen princess Angelica, in many directions and with enormous rapidity. Whenever they reach her she vanishes, or they are unable to get their armour off to enjoy her, or with delicious wilfulness Ariosto abandons them before they achieve the consummation for which they so devoutly

---

[1] *Orlando innamorato*, ed. Giuseppe Anceschi, 2 vols. (Milan, 1978), v. 68–78.

wish, and picks up another of the various threads of his manifold, exfoliating weave of narratives, leaving them, and us, panting. Even his own stories are not followed through to their anticipated conclusions, and are thrown away with wilful delight.

If Ariosto's earlier critics were to be believed, it would seem unlikely that the poet who explodes the chivalric ideal with the dispassionate irony of a sixteenth-century Oscar Wilde,[2] or who explores the ceaselessly complex energy of aberrant human desire,[3] should have any need of a poem so drivingly concerned with the motive power of self-conscious morality as the *Aeneid*. The majority of the male characters in the *Orlando furioso* are driven frantically to pursue beauty under the guise of Angelica, Olimpia, or Alcina, until they succumb to amorous insanity, or perform outrageously uncivic deeds. Appetitive desire, rather than the staid and ostentatious correctness of Aeneas, causes most of the events in Ariosto's romance: Orlando pursues Angelica to distraction; Rinaldo chases her under the pretence of performing state missions; and Ruggiero deserts his dynastic mate Bradamante in order to dally with the seductive charms of Alcina.[4] The centralized devotion to an imperial cause which is manifested in Aeneas's *pietas* appears to be completely lacking from the poem. *Orlando furioso* seems indeed almost to be an explosively decentred revision of the epic plot, in which the multiplicity of episodes so violently prevented by Aeneas become the chief object of writing.[5]

Yet there are odd moments at which Virgil's dutiful efforts to contain desire do surface, and with these moments comes something of Virgil's strained, self-corrective probity in imitation. Ruggiero, for example, leaves the sorceress Alcina with something of Aeneas's purposeful heroism.[6] But this hero is rescued from his Dido not by an admonitory visit from Mercury, but by the Mage Melissa, who disguises herself as his guardian Atlante, and rebukes the feminized hero for deserting his historical mission to found the Estense dynasty. Her language is that of Virgil's Mercury:

> Se non ti muovon le tue proprie laudi,
> e l'opre escelse a chi t'ha il cielo eletto,

---

[2] See e.g. Francesco De Sanctis, *Storia della letteratura italiana*, ed. B. Croce, 2 vols. (Milan, 1912), ii. 1–41; Benedetto Croce, *Ariosto, Shakespeare e Corneille*, 4th edn. (Bari, 1950), 1–69.

[3] See Giorgio De Blasi, 'L'Ariosto e le passioni; Studio sul motivo poetico fondamentale dell'*Orlando furioso*', *Giornale storico della letteratura italiana*, 129 (1952), 318–62; 130 (1953), 178–203.

[4] *OF* xxiv; xlii. 42; vii.

[5] See David Quint, 'Epic and Empire', *Comparative Literature*, 41 (1989), 1–32.

[6] Peter De Sa Wiggins, *Figures in Ariosto's Tapestry: Character and Design in the 'Orlando furioso'* (Baltimore and London, 1986), 67, sees him as 'a kind of Aeneas in reverse, [who] repeatedly postpones his destiny in order to fulfil more immediate commitments.' See also Andrew Fichter, *Poets Historical: Dynastic Epic in the Renaissance* (New Haven, Conn., and London, 1982), 71.

> la tua succession perché defraudi
> del ben che mille volte io t'ho predetto?[7]

If your own glory does not move you, and the high labours for which you are chosen by heaven, why do you cheat your offspring of the benefits which I have prophesied to you a thousand times?

The scene is set for a revisitation of Aeneas's reluctant departure from Dido. But this does not occur. Melissa's initial Virgilian rebuke to Ruggiero only succeeds in moving him to wordless shame, rather than motivating his flight.[8] Ariosto feels the need to add a second phase to Melissa's imperial exhortation, in which the Mage places the Ring of Reason on Ruggiero's finger and returns to her proper shape in order to tell the hero that she has been sent from his love, Bradamante, to restore him to her.[9] The Ring reveals that Alcina is a withered hag whose charms are feigned; and once Ruggiero sees how truly disgusting his mistress is, it is scarcely surprising that he bolts:

> Miracol non è dunque se si parte
> de l'animo a Ruggiero ogni pensiero
> ch'avea d'amare Armida, or che la truova
> in guisa, che sua fraude non le giova.[10]

It was no wonder then if all thought of loving Alcina vanished from Ruggiero's mind, now that he found her a sham, so that her trickery no longer worked.

There is no single ethical ideal like Aeneas's *pietas* which accounts simultaneously for Ruggiero's reversion to his historical task and his ability to conquer his retarding desire. Ariosto splits the motivation of the departure in two, and makes the first, Virgilian phase a shady, ineffective fake, in which a false image of a surrogate father reminds Ruggiero of his destiny and produces only a slight bashfulness. The second phase, in which the object of his desire is defaced, successfully drives the hero on his way. This second phase of Ariosto's revision of Virgil is formed by the prevailing medieval allegorization of Aeneas's departure from Dido, according to which the admonitory voice of Mercury is variously identified as adult rationality, or the power of virtue, which

---

[7] *OF* vii. 60; *Aen*. 4. 272–6: 'si te nulla movet tantarum gloria rerum | . . . | Ascanium surgentem et spes heredis Iuli | respice, cui regnum Italiae Romanaque tellus | debetur' (If the glory of these affairs does not move you at all, consider the growing Ascanius, and the hope which rests in your heir, to whom the kingdom of Italy, and the country of Rome, are owed).

[8] *OF* vii. 65.

[9] Ibid. 68.

[10] Ibid. 74.

routs adolescent desires from the hero.[11] But Ruggiero does not, like Aeneas, leave the desired presence of a beautiful woman for a higher, rationally apprehended purpose: he ditches an old hag who has duped him, and whom he has ceased entirely to desire. Ariosto responds with incredulity to Virgil's episode: he cannot credit the perversity with which the hero leaves his love despite his desire to stay. He needs to root out passion in its object before he can make his hero depart: Ruggiero goes without necessarily overcoming his susceptibility to beauty.[12] And the underlying motives of the whole episode paradoxically demonstrate the strength of love: both stages of Melissa's intervention derive ultimately not from draining obligations to gods, family, and state, but from Bradamante's love for Ruggiero. Ariosto's revision of the departure lacks the core motivating principle of *pietas*, but fills the gap with a motive love which finds the means to extirpate rival passions.[13]

The priority of love as motive is the most obvious and important fact about *Orlando furioso*. And it accounts for one of the main things missing from Ariosto's departure scene. He cannot afford to allow his Dido to be present imposing her charms on the hero as he leaves, nor can he permit her a torrid diatribe to the departing hero, which appeals to his love, faith, and compassion,[14] since in the *Furioso* these sentiments provide the main grounds for action. It is almost impossible for Ariosto's heroes to

[11] 'Mercurius enim deus ponitur ingenii; ergo ingenio instigante aetas deserit amoris confinia' (The god Mercury represents the intellect; therefore youth leaves the confines of love at the urging of the intellect), Fabius Plancias Fulgentius, *Opera*, ed. R. Helm, Teubner Texts (Stuttgart, 1970), 94–5. Cf. Bernardus Silvestris, *The Commentary on the First Six Books of the 'Aeneid' of Virgil*, ed. J. W. and E. F. Jones (Lincoln, Nebr., and London, 1977), 25. Giovanni Boccaccio, *Genealogie Deorum gentilium libri*, ed. Vincenzo Romano, 2 vols. (Bari, 1951), ii. 723: 'Virgilius sentit [by Mercury] seu conscientie proprie morsum, seu amici et eloquentis hominis redargutionem a quibus, dormientes in luto turpitudinum, excitamur, et in rectum pulchrumque revocamur iter, id est ad gloriam' (Virgil means by Mercury either the qualms of conscience, or the urging of a friend and man of eloquence, by which we arouse those slumbering in a mire of vices, and call them back to the true and beautiful way, that is, to glory). Cf. 'Enea ci rappresenta uno prudentissimo heroe, Giove la parte superiore dell'anima humana, Mercurio la discorsiva & ragionevole, & Didone la parte inferiore & sensuale' (Aeneas represents a most prudent hero, Jove the superior part of the mind, Mercury the discursive and rational part, and Dido the inferior and sensual element), Gianbattista Giraldi Cinthio, *Didone Tragedia* (Venice, 1583), 4–5.

[12] Landino similarly notes that Aeneas's reluctant departure indicates that he has not eradicated, but only suppressed, his desires. He is a continent rather than a temperate man, 'quod si veram temperantiam adeptus fuisset non lachrimans sed laetus [voluptatem] reliquisset: poeta nam non ipsum a principio sapientem fingit: & vera virtute ornatum: sed eum qui a perturbationibus animum vendicare cupiens se paulatim a vitiis redimat: & post varios errores in italiam idest ad veram sapientiam perveniat' (because if he had acquired true temperance he would have abandoned pleasure not with tears, but with delight. For the poet does not depict him as wise, and bedecked with virtue, right from the start; but as a man who, desiring to drag his mind from passions, little by little draws himself from vice, and, after various wanderings, comes to Italy, that is, to true wisdom), *Quaestiones Camaldulenses Christophori Landini* (Venice, ?1505), sigs. g3^b–4^a.

[13] Fichter, *Poets Historical*, 91–5, argues that Ariosto is attempting to Christianize Virgil in this episode.

[14] Cf. *Aen.* 4. 305–30.

see a lady suffering or to hear a lady appeal for pity without responding. And that means not just feeling, but acting. Ruggiero shows later in the poem that his native amorousness was only temporarily inhibited by the rational defacing of his object of desire,[15] when he sees Angelica naked and chained to a rock:

> E come ne' begli occhi gli occhi affisse,
> de la sua Bradamante gli sovenne.
> Pietade e amore a un tempo lo trafisse,
> e di piangere a pena si ritenne.[16]

And when he fixed his eyes on her beautiful eyes, he recalled his Bradamante. Pity and love simultaneously pierced him through, and he barely restrained himself from weeping.

By an amorous quirk of perception, Ruggiero's love for his fiancée amplifies rather than restrains his desire for Angelica, whom he pauses to assist. The analogy he perceives between his love and the woman in front of him does not lead him to melt sympathetically into her concerns: he tries vainly to rape her before the embattled lady manages to put the ubiquitous Ring of Reason into her mouth, and vanishes from sight.[17] Compassionate amorousness is only checked by the disappearance of its object. Given a lovely lady of pitiful beauty, however, all obligations to other women or to the tasks of state prove frail and ineffective.

This primary emotional contour of the *Furioso* re-forms another version of Aeneas's departure, in which the Emperor Carlo sends Rinaldo off to England, and away from the quest for Angelica which has previously been his determining desire:

> Rinaldo mai di ciò non fece meno
> volentier cosa; poi che fu distolto
> di gir cercando il bel viso sereno
> che gli avea il cor di mezzo il petto tolto:
> ma, per ubidir Carlo, nondimeno
> a quella via si fa subito volto
> et a Calesse in poche ore trovossi.[18]

Rinaldo never did anything less willingly, since he was torn from going searching the serenely beautiful face which had torn the heart out of the middle of his breast. But, to obey Carlo, none the less he at once turned in that direction, and in a few hours found himself in Calais.

There is something of Aeneas's reluctance in the wrench which pulls

---

[15] Wiggins, *Ariosto's Tapestry*, 86, argues that Ruggiero learns circumspection in leaving Alcina.
[16] *OF* x. 97.   [17] *OF* xi. 1–6.   [18] *OF* ii. 27.

('distolto') Rinaldo from what pulls out ('tolto') his heart. Yet, unlike Aeneas, Rinaldo does not leave the presence of a desirable lady; he deserts merely the idea of Angelica, who is only a yearning absence rather than a palpably charming presence when he goes off to Calais. The subsequent history of his mission shows how strongly the cupidinous prevails over the deontic in this romance. Once Rinaldo has reluctantly deferred his pursuit of Angelica to please his emperor, he almost immediately deserts this new objective in order to assist Ginevra in her attempt to avoid the rigorous penalties imposed by Scottish law for premarital amorousness.[19] He pauses to impose on the strict letter of the law compassionate indulgence for the irresistible sentiment of love. And whilst he is engaged on this truancy from the task of Empire in the service of pity, he is further delayed by Dalinda, who is being assaulted by villains and prays for *pietà*. Since he is *pietoso*, he stops and helps this woman before he helps Ginevra, and before he performs Carlo's mission.[20] This sequence of events shows how little power political devotion has over the form of the poem. The pitifulness of its heroes does not involve much in the way of identification with those they see suffering: it is more like a compulsive reflex to assist, to desire, and to desert their previous purpose. This unreflective pity generates the sprawling, ceaselessly self-renewing structure of the poem. Stories superfoetate, as pitiable ladies spring up and make overpowering demands on amorous heroes, who defer all longer-term goals in order to assist them.[21] Compassion is not linked with vain regret for the damage done to the victims of imperial advancement: it is liberated from the restraints placed on it by Virgil, and is made to drive the involved movement of the poem. Rinaldo's mission is a linear extrapolation of the emotions which Virgil's Aeneas feels when leaving Dido: an action which expresses imperial dutifulness is followed by a string of episodes in which amorous and pitiful emotions are exuberantly indulged.

In liberating Virgil's repressed remorse Ariosto was not acting entirely on his own, nor was he just mischievously decentring the narrative of the *Aeneid*. The involutions of his narrative form often derive from a revision of Virgil's heroic priorities, in which pitifulness becomes the key chivalric

---

[19] Wiggins, *Ariosto's Tapestry*, 22–30, argues Rinaldo is cynical in this episode—a rather severe judgement, since he is merely articulating the ethos of the poem.

[20] *OF* iv. 51–72.

[21] Cf. Eugenio Donato, '"Per Selve e Boscherecci Labirinti": Desire and Narrative Structure in Ariosto's *Orlando furioso*', in Patricia Parker and David Quint (eds.), *Literary Theory/Renaissance Texts* (Baltimore and London, 1986), 33–62, in which the narrative structure of the poem is taken to embody the 'problematics of desire'. See also Patricia Parker, *Inescapable Romance: Studies in the Poetics of a Mode* (Princeton, NJ, 1979), where this process of deferral is (predictably enough) related to the infinite pursuit of the signified.

virtue. There is a large tradition of exegetical writings on the *Aeneid*
which sees in the hero's *pietas* the early stages of the semantic shift which
was to pull the word towards its Italian derivative *pietà*, and the English
'pity'. This tradition was sufficiently entrenched by the early sixteenth
century to make Virgil's hero appear deeply perverse. Servius takes *pius*
to mean that Aeneas is a just upholder of the old religion, but frequently
suggests that the hero also possesses the virtue of compassion. He identifies
pietas with justice in his note to 'insignem pietate virum' (a man famous
for *pietas*);[22] yet later in the same Book, at 'nec pietate fuit' (not for
pietas), he establishes a distinction between the two qualities. *Pietas* is to
severitas as mercy is to rigour: 'multum interest inter iustitiam et pietatem;
nam pietas pars iustitiae est, sicut severitas' (There is a big difference
between justice and *pietas*; for *pietas* is a part of justice, like severity).[23]
And, when Aeneas leaves Dido, Servius argues that the hero shows his
ruthfulness in groaning for her, and his *religio* in leaving her at Jove's
orders:

bene autem excusat Aeneam 'pium' dicendo, cum ei et gemitus dat, et ostendit
solacia dolenti velle praestare, et probat religiosum, cum deorum praeceptis
paret.[24]

He excuses Aeneas well by calling him *pius*, since he both gives a groan and
shows that he wants to afford consolations to one who is grieving. He also shows
himself to be religious, since he obeys the commands of the gods.

Servius introduces the predominant response to the Aeneid and its hero
in the Middle Ages. Augustine describes his own tearful response to the
pitiable Dido in the *Confessions*,[25] and attributes a similar larmoyance to
the hero when he interprets the line 'mens immota manet, lacrimae
volvuntur inanes' ('His purpose remains unshaken; tears roll in vain') to
mean that Aeneas weeps in vain, rather than recognizing the veil of
bashful ambiguity which Virgil places over this reading: the syntax and

---

[22] *Aen.* 1. 10: 'Nam si iustus est Aeneas, cur odio deorum laborat?' (If Aeneas is so just, why does
he labour under the hatred of the gods?), *Servii Grammatici qui feruntur in Vergilii Carmina
Commentarii*, ed. G. Thilo and H. Hagen, 2 vols. (Leipzig, 1878–83), i. 15.

[23] *Aen.* 1. 545; edn. cit. i. 167.

[24] Edn. cit. i. 535.

[25] 'Quid enim miserius misero non miserante se ipsum et flente Didonis mortem, quae fiebat
amando Aenean, non flente autem mortem suam, quae fiebat non amando te, deus' (For what can be
more miserable that an unhappy man not pitying himself, and weeping the death of Dido, which
resulted from her love of Aeneas, but not weeping his own death, that resulted from not loving you,
God?), *Confessions*, trans. W. Watts, 2 vols., Loeb Classical Library (Cambridge, Mass., and London,
1912), i. 38 (1. 13).

context allow that the tears could be Anna's.[26] He also remarks on the hero's compassion for Lausus.[27] A long section of Macrobius's *Saturnalia* discusses the *Aeneid* as a rich source for the rhetoric of compassion.[28] And although Orosius is unusual in emphasizing Aeneas's ruthless martial exploits,[29] Lactantius is so convinced that the primary sense of *pietas* is 'compassion' that he rages incredulously against the execution of Turnus, on the grounds that no truly pitiful man could have performed such a deed.[30]

This line of interpretation affects vernacular translations of the poem. Compassion slides to the centre of the hero's nature under cover of the beguiling phonetic and etymological kinships between *pietas*, *pietà*, and *pité*. The anonymous *Roman d'Eneas* is often regarded as initiating the amorous and inward idiom of twelfth-century romance.[31] Some caution is necessary in accepting this view, however, since the author does not show any signs of understanding the way familial *pietas* draws the Roman hero into compassion for Lausus: this episode is clipped to a killing without a trace of pious compassion.[32] The pity which Aeneas does feel for Dido's ghost in the underworld ('miseratur euntem'—he pities her as she goes)

---

[26] *Aen.* 4. 449; *City of God against the Pagans*, trans. G. E. McCraken, W. M. Green, D. S. Wiesen, P. Levine, E. M. Sanford, and W. C. Green, 7 vols., Loeb Classical Library (Cambridge, Mass., and London, 1957–72), iii. 166 (9. 4). 'Virgil is purposely ambiguous', *Aeneidos liber quartus*, ed. R. G. Austin (Oxford, 1955), ad loc.; cf. 'Those tears are his', R. O. A. M. Lyne, *Further Voices in Vergil's Aeneid* (Oxford, 1987), 163–4.

[27] 'Unde enim apud Vergilium pius Aeneas laudabiliter dolet hostem etiam sua peremptum manu?' (*Pius* Aeneas is praised for his grief over an enemy, who was killed by his own hand), *City of God*, i. 312 (3. 14); referring to *Aen.* 10. 823–4.

[28] *The Saturnalia*, trans. P. V. Davies (New York and London, 1969), 256–81 (4. 2–6). The original terms used are *oiktos*, *pathos*, and *misericordia*. See *I Saturnali*, ed. Nino Marinone (Turin, 1967).

[29] 'quantos populos inplicuerit odio excidioque adflixerit [Aeneas], ludi litterarii disciplina nostra quoque memoriae inustum est' (the number of peoples he enveloped in his hatred, and afflicted with destruction, remains in our training in secular literature, and in our memory), *Historiarum adversum Paganos libri VII*, ed. C. Zangemeister, in *Corpus Scriptorum Ecclesiasticorum Latinorum*, 5 (Prague, 1882), 70 (1. 18).

[30] He quotes *Aen.* 11. 81–2 and complains 'ubi est igitur, o poeta, pietas illa quam saepissime laudas?' (Where is that pity, o poet, which you praise so often?), and continues 'quisquamne igitur hunc putet aliquid in se virtutis habuisse, qui et furore tamquam stipula exarserit et manium patris per quem rogabatur oblitus iram frenare non quiverit? nullo igitur modo pius qui non tantum non repugnantes, sed etiam precantes interemit' (For who would imagine someone to have a shred of virtue, who burns with rage like a rush, and who, forgetful of his father's memory, by which he is besought, is not able to restrain his rage? He cannot at all be called *pius* who kills not only those who fight back, but also those who beg for mercy'), L. Caelius Firmianus Lactantius, *Opera Omnia*, ed. S. Brandt and G. Laubmann, in *Corpus Scriptorum Ecclesiasticorum Latinorum*, 19 (Prague, 1890), 430–1.

[31] See e.g. W. P. Ker, *Epic and Romance* (London, 1922), 346–52; Jerome E. Singerman, *Under Clouds of Poesy: Poetry and Truth in French and English Reworkings of the 'Aeneid', 1160–1513* (New York and London, 1986), 50–2. A more accurate view is offered by Erich Auerbach, *Literary Language and its Public in Late Latin Antiquity and in the Middle Ages*, trans. Ralph Manheim (London, 1965), 181–233.

[32] *Eneas: Roman du XIIe Siècle*, ed. J.-J. Salverda de Grave, 2 vols., Classiques français du moyen âge (Paris, 1983–5), ll. 5909–26.

is also excised.[33] Yet Aeneas's wordless pause over Turnus is filled, as it is in the anonymous *Excidium Troiae*, with a speech in which the hero confesses he was moved to *pité* until he saw Pallas's ring (a detail which may also indicate the author knew the *Excidium*) on his victim's hand.[34] And Dido's tirade to the departing hero does include the accusation that, despite his *pieté* he lacks *pité*.[35] The hero is not purely a ruthful man, partly, perhaps, because French maintains the distinction between pity and piety in these variant spellings. Yet there is a suggestion in the departure scene that Aeneas is offstage for the better part of Dido's pathetic complaint[36]—a sign that the author, like Ariosto, could not quite believe in a pitiful hero who withstood the force of feminine pathos, and could not fully conceive the pattern of responses which derives from *pietas*.

This detail also indicates a debt to Ovid's *Heroides* 7, in which the deserted Dido complains of her maltreatment in a verse epistle to a perfidious Aeneas.[37] In this version of the story the framework of imperial destiny which justifies and motivates Aeneas's departure is dropped, and the hero is a stonily absent addressee of a letter, who fails to join author and reader in their orgy of compassion. Under the influence of this work, Aeneas loses his imperial epithet *pius* in Chaucer's *House of Fame* and becomes a villainous lover:

> But let us speke of Eneas,
> How he betrayed hir, allas.
> And lefte hir ful unkyndely.[38]

---

[33] *Eneas*, 2651–62; cf. *Aen.* 6. 472–6. See Raymond J. Cormier, *One Heart One Mind: The Rebirth of Virgil's Hero in Medieval French Romance*, Romance Monographs, 3 (Oxford, Miss., 1973), 140.

[34] 'Etiam Eneas proximus fuit ei misereri . . . "Poteram te patri tuo vivum dimittere; sed quia adhuc tiranide letaris de spoliis mortuorum, merito dolor Pallantis cuius brachi<a>lem cingeris te occidit"' (Aeneas came close to pitying him. 'I would have been able to send you home alive to your father; but because tyrannically you despoil the dead, it is deservedly that grief for Pallas, whose bracelet you wear, kills you'), *Excidium Troiae*, ed. E. B. Atwood and V. K. Whitaker, The Mediaeval Academy of America Publications, 44 (Cambridge, Mass., 1944), 54. Cf. 'Ge aüsse pitié de toi, | ne perdisses vie ne menbre, | mais par cest anel m'en remenbre, | de Pallas que tu oceïs; | el cuer m'en as molt grant duel mis: | ne t'ocirra mie Eneas, | mais de toi se venche Pallas' (I would have pitied you, and you would not have lost life nor limb, but I am reminded by this ring of Pallas whom you killed. My heart has given me great pain for this. It is not Aeneas who kills you; but Pallas avenges himself upon you), *Eneas*, ll. 9804–10. Cf. *Aen.* 12. 947–9.

[35] ll. 1803–6.

[36] See the analysis in Cormier, *One Heart*, 129.

[37] *Eneas*, edn. cit. ii. 132. For the Dido-centred works influenced by Ovid's heroine, see Peter Dronke, 'Dido's Lament', in *Festschrift Franco Munari* (Hildesheim, 1986), 364–90.

[38] *House of Fame*, 293–5. Text from *The Riverside Chaucer*, ed. L. D. Benson *et al.*, 3rd edn. (Boston, 1987). On Chaucer's *Aeneid*, see Louis Brewer Hall, 'Chaucer and the Dido-and-Aeneas Story', *Medieval Studies*, 25 (1963), 148–59; Albert C. Friend, 'Chaucer's Version of the *Aeneid*', *Speculum*, 28 (1953), 317–23; and John M. Fyler, *Chaucer and Ovid* (New Haven, Conn., and London, 1979), 112–13. See further Meyer Reinhold, 'The Unhero Aeneas', *Classica et Mediaevalia*, 27 (1966), 195–207; Götz Schmitz, *The Fall of Women in Early English Narrative Verse* (Cambridge,

This is Chaucer's equivalent of Virgil's delicately poised departure sentence. Aeneas has failed to show the chivalric virtues of *trouth* and *pitee*—despite Dido's plea 'Have pitee on my sorwes smerte'.[39] And, as in the *Roman*, Aeneas is effectively absent while Dido complains. There is no indication of what he feels, or even that he is present listening to Dido's complaint. This is partly because Chaucer draws on Ovid's verse epistle, in which, obviously enough, the recipient is absent. But it is also because he lacks the language to describe Aeneas's actions or emotions. Caxton's redaction of the *Aeneid*'s departure sentence shows why this is:

Wherof Eneas, how be it that he had grete pyte and compassyon of her, and desired sore to comforte her wyth swete & amyable woordes, for to assuage her sorowe in grete sobbynges | for grete displaysure & sorowe that he had, to see his swete love suffre suche a peyne | Always he determyned hymself, & went his wayes for to see his shippes |[40]

Caxton has misunderstood *pius*: 'how be it that he had grete pyte and compassyon of her' translates the adjective with its derivate, 'pity'. So a ruthful Aeneas leaves Dido; and the departure becomes inexplicable, since the characterizing adjective, and everything Aeneas feels, pulls violently against what he does. And Caxton, like Chaucer, has removed the gods' admonishment. These departures couched in the language of romance founder because in their idiom action frequently derives from sentiment, rather than from commands or imperatives. To feel pity for someone is to attempt to comfort their wretchedness—as when Theseus starts down from his horse to assist the woebegone women at the start of the 'Knight's Tale', 'For pitee renneth soone in gentil herte'.[41] The behaviour of the 'pitiful' Aeneas, who feels compassion without acting on it, is so inexplicable on these terms that he can only be edited out, or regarded as an inscrutable cad.

The same problem of interpretation besets the full, and quite literal, translation of the whole *Aeneid* into Middle Scots by Ariosto's near contemporary Gavin Douglas. Douglas prides himself on his ability to

1990), 17–43; and Barbara J. Bono, *Literary Transvaluation: From Vergilian Epic to Shakespearean Comedy* (Berkeley and Los Angeles, 1984), esp. 41–82.

[39] *House of Fame*, 316.

[40] *Eneydos*, ed. W. T. Culley and F. J. Furnivall, EETS Extra Series, 57 (Oxford, 1890), 74. See further Louis Brewer Hall, 'Caxton's *Eneydos* and the Redactions of Virgil', *Medieval Studies*, 22 (1960), 136–47.

[41] 'Knight's Tale', fr. I, ll. 1761, 948–53; cf. 'Squire's Tale', fr. V, l. 479; 'Merchant's Tale', fr. IV, l. 1986. See the lucid study of the 'feminine' pitiful Chaucerian hero in Jill Mann, *Geoffrey Chaucer* (Hemel Hempstead, 1991), 165–85.

render the real *Aeneid*;[42] but he still cannot capture the imperial conflict. *Pietas* again becomes pity, since in Middle Scots, as in Middle English, the conceptual distinction is not lexically marked:[43]

> Bot ȝyt, althocht the reuthful Eneas
> The dolorus queyn to meyss full bissy was,
> To do hir comfort, and hir dyseyss asswage,
> And with hys wordis return hir sad curage,
> Bewalyng mekill hyr sorow and distress,
> Proplexte in mynd by gret luf; netheless,
> The command of the goddis, by and by,
> He execut, and vysseys hys navy.[44]

If Aeneas is so ruthful (and Douglas claims in a note 'I interpret that term quylys for "rewth", quhils for "devotion" and quihilis for "pyete" and "compassion" '[45]), why does he leave? This entrenched tradition of interpretation twists the perversity of the *Aeneid* into an explosive tension, in which the apparent motives of the hero violently conflict with his actions. Ariosto's two versions of the departure from Dido attempt to unwind this tension by making one hero leave a disgusting hag who makes no claims on either sympathy or desire, and another leave an *absent* lady on a wildly indirect imperial mission from which he is continually deflected by pitiful ladies. The involuted plots of Ariosto's imperial heroes express the author's desire to create a narrative which follows the motive instincts of writers like Augustine and Douglas, and thereby to eliminate the perverse antagonism of action and motive which made an intelligible and sympathetic reconstruction of Virgil's Aeneas practically impossible in the later Middle Ages. The only way to imitate the *Aeneid* for anyone under the influence of this tradition would be to rewrite its plot, to follow the instincts of the pitiful Aeneas away from the central forces of Empire, and towards the peripheries of Virgil's text, towards digressive interludes which explore the pitiful actions of heroes towards suffering women. The form of romance, the wild, enfolding, unstoppable flow of stories, substantially derives from a revision of the *Aeneid*'s central motive.

Ariosto untangles the impossible perversity of the medieval Virgil most

---

[42] Douglas expresses his intention 'Virgillis versys to follow and no thing feyn', *Eneydos*, ed. D. C. Coldwell, STS, 4 vols. (Edinburgh and London, 1957–64), 1. Proem 266. On this translation, see further Priscilla Bawcutt, *Gavin Douglas* (Edinburgh, 1976); Bruce Dearing, 'Gavin Douglas' *Eneados*: A Reinterpretation', *PMLA* 67 (1952), 845–62; Louis Brewer Hall, 'An Aspect of the Renaissance in Gavin Douglas' *Eneados*', Studies in the Renaissance, 7 (1960), 184–92.

[43] *A Dictionary of the Older Scottish Tongue*, ed. W. A. Craigie *et al.* (Chicago, London, and Aberdeen, 1937–   ), lists 'dutifulness' as sense 4b of 'Piete', after 'clemency'.

[44] Edn. cit. IV. vii. 63–70.

[45] Edn. cit. 45. Turnus's words: 'Begouth inclyne hym to reuth and mercy', XII. xiv. 128. At XIII. xi. 75 'reuthful Aeneas' is added to Mapheus Vegius.

fully in his version of the most pathetic and pathetically redundant episode in the *Aeneid*, the story of Nisus and Euryalus.[46] Ariosto's revision of this pathetic interlude begins with the simile which marked Euryalus's end, which immediately intimates that there is a deliberate topsy-turviness to the imitation. The simile is adapted to describe the death of Dardinello, who is the 'signor' of Ariosto's equivalent of Virgil's pair, Cloridano and Medoro:

> purpureus veluti cum flos succisus aratro
> languescit moriens, lassove papavera collo
> demisere caput pluvia cum forte gravantur.[47]

As when a purple flower sliced by a plough wilts in death, or as poppies hang down their weary heads when they are weighed down by a chance shower.

> Come purpureo fior languendo muore,
> che'l vomere al passar tagliato lassa;
> o come carco di superchio umore
> il papaver ne l'orto il capo abbassa.[48]

As a purple flower dies languishing, which the plough in passing has cut, or as the poppy in a meadow, fraught with heavy dew, lays down its head . . .

This image of death in its new setting, though, does not motivate (as it does in Virgil) desperately vain grief, or provide a narrative with a mortal conclusion. Medoro, the younger of Ariosto's two friends, is moved by love of his 'signor' to persuade the older Cloridano to rescue Dardinello's body. This is an important modification of previous night missions, since it devolves the power to instigate episodes away from the centres of authority, and binds this power in with affection and friendship. Homer's 'Doloneia' begins right at the top, with agitation in the Greek leaders, which diffuses down the ranks and issues in an ill-defined attempt to pick off stragglers or to acquire a smidgeon of information, which succeeds on both counts. In Virgil the episode starts with the confused 'dira cupido' of Nisus, the older partner, who proposes the mission to his superiors, and concludes with the fatal booty-hunting of the younger. Ariosto follows Statius, and continues the devolution of the heroes' motives from the centre of authority: Cloridano and Medoro, like Hopleus and Dymas in the *Thebaid*, seek their commander's body at their own instigation, without

---

[46] On Virgil's episode, see K. W. Gransden, *Virgil's Iliad* (Cambridge, 1984), 102–19. Walter Moretti's penetrating article, 'La storia di Cloridano e Medoro: Un esempio della umanizzazione ariotesca delle idealità eroiche e cavalleresche', *Convivium*, 37 (1969), 543–51, argues the modifications of Virgil amount to 'the exaltation of the invincible goodness of the human heart' (549). See also Barbara Palock, *Eros, Imitation, and the Epic Tradition* (Ithaca, NY, and London, 1990), 170–86.

[47] *Aen.* 9. 435–7; cf. Catullus 11. 21–4.

[48] *OF* xviii. 153.

consulting their superiors.[49] Yet Ariosto eases the episode further away from the political by making the action start with the love of the *youthful* member of the pair for his king. He treats the story as an 'esempio raro | di vero amore' (a rare example of true love).[50] The force of love pulls Virgil apart. The vain emotion released by the episode in the *Aeneid*, as it were, ingeminates the story, pulling it into two strands. Dardinello dies with the pathos of Euryalus; but love draws Medoro to become a second, resurrected Euryalus, who sets out at night to find his prince, and, like his Virgilian prototype, slaughters his enemies as they drunkenly doze. He and Cloridano then flee with the body, which his companion drops on the approach of a hostile troop led by Zerbino. At the equivalent point in Virgil, the Rutulian commander rushes on Euryalus ('saevit atrox Volcens'—fierce Volcens raged[51]) and, after protestations from Nisus, stabs the boy. Yet Ariosto is again moved to fracture his original by his conviction that the pathos of doomed youth must have motive power over his executioner:

> Or Zerbin, ch'era il capitano loro,
> non poté a questo aver più pazienza.
> Con ira e con furor venne a Medoro,
> dicendo:—Ne farai tu penitenza.—
> Stese la mano in quella chioma d'oro,
> e strascinollo a sé con violenza:
> ma come gli occhi a quel bel volto mise,
> gli ne venne pietade, e non l'ucisse.[52]

Now Zerbino, who was their captain, ran out of patience with him. With rage and fury he came at Medoro, saying 'You'll regret this.' He reached out his hand and grabbed his golden locks, and pulled him sharply towards himself. But when his eyes fell on that beautiful face, he was overcome with pity, and did not kill him.

Pietà, compassion, again pulls the Virgilian model off course, and prevents a killing. Douglas had squeezed vain ruth out of Aeneas's hesitation over Turnus:[53] Ariosto follows his emotional instincts in narrative form by sparing the suppliant Medoro—momentarily, at least,

---

[49] *Thebaid* 10. 347–449. References to *Statius*, ed. J. H. Mozley, Loeb Classical Library, 2 vols. (Cambridge, Mass., and London, 1928). On this episode in relation to Virgil, see David Vesey, *Statius and the Thebaid* (Cambridge, 1973), 116–17. For Ariosto's debt to Statius, see Pio Rajna, *Le fonti dell'Orlando furioso: Richerche e studi* (Florence, 1876), 216–18.

[50] *OF* xviii. 165. But modern readers have often read the story as an example of *fede*. See Eduardo Saccone, *Il 'soggetto' del 'Furioso' e altri saggi tra quatri e cinquecento* (Naples, 1974), 161–201.

[51] *Aen.* 9. 420.

[52] *OF* xix. 10.

[53] 'Et iam iamque magis cunctantem flectere sermo | coeperat' becomes 'And mor and mor thir wordis, by and by, | Begouth inclyne hym to reuth and mercy.' *Aen.* 12. 940–1/Douglas XII. xiv. 127–8.

before the violence of the Virgilian warrior resurfaces, displaced on to a disobedient subordinate:

> In questo mezzo un cavallier villano,
> avendo al suo signor poco rispetto,
> ferì con la lancia sopra mano
> al supplicante il delicato petto.[54]

In the middle of all this a low-ranking soldier, who had little respect for his master, swung his lance down and struck the delicate breast of the suppliant.

Ariosto's displacement of brutality down the chain of command signifies his reluctance to believe that any noble character could lack *pietà*. But this alteration to Virgil's story is also strangely suggestive of those moments in the *Iliad* when two possible alternative responses to some moment of crisis are accommodated by different versions of the same character—when one of the Atreides spares a suppliant, while the other kills, or when a ghostly Aeneas dies while the real one lives. Ariosto splits multiple motives into their constituent elements and embodies each emotion in a different character in a way that is suggestive of a near-allegorical anatomy of passion. Bigi suggests (ad loc.) that the nameless subordinate who wounds Medoro recalls Volcens, the leader of Virgil's squadron. But again Ariosto is fragmenting Virgil by following a hint from Statius. In the *Thebaid* 'Amphion equites', the leader of his troop, orders Dymas and Hopleus to stop, and hurls a warning javelin across their bows; but Aepytus is less gentle:

> at non magnanimus curavit perdere iactus
> Aepytus, et fixo transverberat Hoplea tergo.[55]

But great-hearted Aepytus did not want to waste a throw, and struck Hopleus through the back.

Ariosto wants this division of roles to be ethically significant, and probably developed Amphion into a softly chivalric figure on the strength of his being called 'equites' (knight), and of his prohibition on violence ('quamvis saevire vetaret | Amphion'[56]). In the conceptual scheme through which Ariosto read the classical epic, according to which *pietà* and *amore* were the principal indices of nobility, this decision had as its inevitable concomitant that Statius's 'magnanimus' slayer would become 'villano',

---

[54] *OF* xix. 13.   [55] *Thebaid* 10. 399–400.   [56] Ibid. 420–1.

both low-class and unfeeling.[57] But whatever the precise literary genesis of the division of roles, Ariosto is drawn to revise and fragment the Virgilian story by his conviction that pity motivates.

Medoro, though, is left for dead, and appears to become a second vainly slaughtered Euryalus. At this point there occurs the most staggering and important ethical *peripeteia* in the poem, the moment above all others when Ariosto rebels against—and consciously rewrites—the stagnant, ineffective compassion of the *Aeneid*. Angelica arrives on the battlefield 'a caso'.[58] Now, all the main protagonists of the *Furioso*, even the irascible Rodomonte, feel the pull of *pietà* sooner or later.[59] Savages, birds, beasts, and the very stones feel pity.[60] But Angelica, though she is often the object of these amorous sympathies, is as flinty-hearted and pitiless as a Petrarchan mistress.[61] When she hears Sacripante's desperate plaint for her love she is ghoulishly attentive, but entirely ruthless:

> ma dura e fredda più d'una colonna,
> ad averne pietà non però scende,
> come colei c'ha tutto il mondo a sdegno,
> e non le par alcun sia di lei degno.[62]

But she was more hard and cold than a column, and so did not deign to pity him, like someone who despised the whole world—and no one to her seemed to deserve her.

She makes temporary use of his services, and then flits away. So when this chilly attractiveness makes an appearance on the battlefield in which Medoro is lying, she is likely only to stir the semi-animate warrior with unrequited passion. Yet she sees the wounded youth and, for the first time, experiences the governing sentiment of the poem:

> Quando Angelica vide il giovinetto
> languir ferito, assai vicino a morte,
> che del suo re che giacea senza tetto,
> più che del proprio mal si dolea forte;

---

[57] Lactantius offered Ariosto no guidance on this reading, although he takes Hopleus's supplication as aimed 'ad iniiciendam misericordiam hostibus' (at inspiring pity in his enemies), *Statius Thebais cum Lactantii Commentariis* (Venice, 1494), fol. 155ᵃ. Erasmo di Valvasone's translation of 'quamvis saevire vetaret Amphion' may show the influence of Ariosto, however: 'benche l'usar atto *villano* | Prohibisse Anfion quanto poteva' (Although Amphion had prohibited any act appropriate to a villein, as best he could), *La Thebaide di Statio ridotta in ottava rima* (Venice, 1570), fol. 125ᵇ.

[58] *OF* xix. 17.

[59] *OF* xxxi. 73–4, in which Fiordiligi successfully pleads with him in the name of the dead Isabella to help Brandimarte. See Wiggins, *Ariosto's Tapestry*, 41.

[60] For pitiful savages, see *OF* viii. 65; for compassionate birds and beasts, see xlv. 95; for pitiful echoes, see x. 22 and xxvii. 117.

[61] On Ariosto and Petrarch, see C. P. Brand, *Ludovico Ariosto: A Preface to the 'Orlando furioso'*, Writers of Italy, 1 (Edinburgh, 1974), 58.

[62] *OF* i. 49.

> insolita pietade in mezzo al petto
> si sentì entrar per disusata porte,
> che le fe' il duro cor tenero e molle,
> e più, quando il suo caso egli narrolle.[63]

When Angelica saw the youth—who mourned the misfortune of his king, who lay headless, more than his own misfortune—lie wounded, near enough dead, she felt unaccustomed pity enter the middle of her breast through unused doors, which made her hard heart soft and mild—even more so when he told her his story.

Dido loves Aeneas's story too. Angelica pities, cures, loves and retires with Medoro to a cave which has familiar literary associations: 'ch'ebber, fuggendo l'acqua, Enea e Dido' (like that which Dido and Aeneas went into as they fled the storm).[64] Her start of unaccustomed compassion causes a continuing narrative to grow from Virgil's terminal digression. Ariosto's second Euryalus lives to dally with a Dido because of the pathos released by his wounding. The chief moments when Ariosto rewrites Virgil all concern the power of love to overcome the terminal pressures of the *Aeneid*'s imperial plot. His chief hero, Ruggiero, does eventually marry—and will eventually produce dynastic offspring with—his Bradamante, whereas the *Aeneid* ends before its hero is finally united with Lavinia. His transformation of the dead and irrelevant Euryalus into the one character who succeeds in winning the compassion and so the love of Angelica is another massive revision: it suggests that it is in the nature of a Christian epic to avoid the terminal, to turn the dead and infertile into the continuingly vital.[65] And the new Euryalus has a greater power over the continuing narrative of the poem even than this: Orlando's discovery of the green testimony of Angelica's love for this unknown soldier carved on trees is what finally drives him 'furioso'.[66] Ariosto makes Virgil's dead episode thrill with continuing life, and cause the main action of his poem. And when Astolfo finally captures Orlando in order to make him sniff his wits back from their lunar storage bottle, he too is transfixed by a pity which introduces the raving hero's return to sanity.[67] Pathos lies at the motive centre of the poem, and marks the beginning and end of its major action; it is moved from the margins to the centre of a dynastic romance.

The argument so far has run counter to the general view that Ariosto mischievously and idiosyncratically parodied Virgil in order to overgo

---

[63] *OF* xix. 20.
[64] *OF* xix. 35.
[65] Neo-Latin epic often associates Euryalus with Christ. See pp. 275–6 below.
[66] *OF* xxiii. 96–136.
[67] *OF* xxxix. 46.

him.[68] Rather, the action of the *Aeneid* is repeatedly altered in order to harmonize with the established medieval understanding of its ethos. But things change in the poem. Ariosto increasingly loses any trace of that throwaway attitude to earlier books that had been so important in Boiardo; and as he does so the character of compassion alters. The later stages of *Orlando furioso* gravitate towards Virgil, and strive to make an equivalent for the actions and motives of his epic predecessor in the language of chivalry.[69] This process involves a particularly Virgilian pattern of thought: Ariosto increasingly discards his own revisions of Virgil's ethos as he attempts to approach the motive structures of his predecessor's poem. At the end of canto xxxvii Ruggiero and Bradamante separate with a sense that it is the nobleness of life to do thus, and in the proem to the next canto the poet justifies this stern action to his audience of 'cortesi donne':

> Pur, per salvar l'onor, non solamente
> d'escusa, ma di laude è degno ancora.[70]

For rescuing his honour he deserves not just to be excused, but to be praised.

Melissa had only elicited a vain blush from Ruggiero by mentioning his 'proprie laude'; but now consciousness of honour and praise has been promoted up the scale of motives to a place above amorous appetency. And, with its careful justification, this heroic departure introduces a new phase of Virgilian imitation which dominates the remainder of the poem. *Orlando furioso* ends with the ruthless execution of Rodomonte by Ruggiero in imitation of the death of Turnus,[71] and much of its action from canto xxxviii onwards prepares the motive grounds for this denial of the romance hero's pitiful instincts. It has often been noticed that, in the later phases of the poem, *fede* (faith) becomes a central issue.[72] This shift in moral concern, however, is also paired with a new preoccupation with the closing phase of the *Aeneid*. Many of the major actions in this phase of the *Furioso* derive from the Iliadic second half of the *Aeneid*. The interrupted single combat between Aeneas and Turnus which takes up the bulk of *Aeneid* 12, for example, generates the confrontation between Ruggiero

---

[68] Daniel Javitch, 'The *Orlando furioso* and Ovid's Revision of the *Aeneid*', *Modern Language Notes*, 99 (1984), 1023–36, argues that Ariosto showed unprecedented literary-historical acumen in perceiving and emulating the parodic relation of the *Metamorphoses* to the *Aeneid*. Cf. Parker, *Inescapable Romance*, 39–44. Thomas M. Greene, *The Descent from Heaven: a Study in Epic Continuity* (New Haven, Conn., and London, 1963), 125–9, analyses the Medoro episode as an example of the poet's 'freedom from any tradition' (129).

[69] C. P. Brand, 'Ludovico Ariosto—Poet and Poem in the Italian Renaissance', *Forum for Modern Language Studies*, 4 (1968), 101: 'from a relatively light-hearted romance atmosphere in the early cantos [it] progresses to a relatively serious, religious and epic note in the latter half.'

[70] *OF* xxviii. 3.

[71] *OF* xlvi. 140; *Aen.* 12. 950–2.

[72] See Wiggins, *Ariosto's Tapestry*, 48.

and Rinaldo in Ariosto's canto xxxviii. But this increasing debt to the narrative content of the later *Aeneid* is accompanied by a twisting up of the instincts which motivate Ariosto's heroes. The single combat in the *Furioso*, as in its model, is interrupted by a general outburst of fighting which breaks a truce.[73] Ruggiero and Rinaldo swear that each will desert their respective king if they discover that he was responsible for this breach of faith. This sets up a triple division of loyalties in Ruggiero when he discovers that Agramante, his prince, was the guilty party: his vow to Rinaldo and his promise of marriage to Bradamante are set against his oath of allegiance to his king.[74] He opts to remain faithful to Agramante and desert Bradamante and her brother. The rival claims of *fede* establish a structure of imperatives which override desire; and these dutiful obligations, structurally akin to *pietas* in their opposition to personal feeling, are established during a hiatus in a Virgilian combat.

As the poem continues, Ariosto continues to gravitate towards the grimmer fare of Virgil's closing movement. War predominates, and creates further conflicts of obligation and emotion. Brandimarte joins in a final battle against Agramante with the restored Orlando, and is mortally wounded by Gradasso. His death scene is imbued with the pious compassion which marks the hero's end in the *Chanson de Roland*,[75] and with the imperial remorse which animates the death of Virgil's Pallas.[76] Yet despite the enormous pathos of Brandimarte's protracted death scene, here, unlike in the Medoro episode, compassion has no power to avert his end. Indeed, his wounding releases a new form of motive feeling which is close to the remorseless violence which the death of Pallas unleashes in Aeneas.[77] Orlando finally completes his reversion from insane amours to martial frenzy because of Brandimarte's death. But martial frenzy is not a motive sufficiently strong to compel the story forward without a justificatory pause:

> Non so se in lui poté più il duolo o l'ira;
> ma da piangere il tempo avea sì corto,
> che restò il duolo, e l'ira uscì più in fretta.

---

[73] *OF* xxxviii. 77–xxxix. 9; *Aen.* 12. 113–310.

[74] *OF* xl. 62–6.

[75] It is significant that Ariosto's only apparent allusion to his hero's martial ancestor is to the one moment in the *chanson de geste* which causes a general outbreak of *pité*. Angels descend for Brandimarte at *OF* xlii. 14 as for Roland in *La Chanson de Roland*, ed. F. Whitehead, Blackwell's French Texts, 2nd edn. (Oxford, 1946), ll. 2389–96. See Bigi ad loc. General pity strikes at 2418–19: 'Il nen i ad chevaler ne barun | Que de pitét mult durement ne plurt' (There was no knight or baron who did not pity him bitterly and weep), and at 3120: 'Plurent Franceis pur pitét de Rollant' (The Franks wept for pity of Roland).

[76] Cf. *OF* xliii. 169–74 and *Aen.* 11. 42–71.

[77] *Aen.* 10. 510–605.

Ma tempo è ormai che fine al canto io metta.[78]

I do not know if anger or grief had more power over him; but he had such a short time to weep that his grief remained checked, and anger rushed rapidly out. But now it is time that I put an end to this canto.

Orlando moves out of the narrator's ken, as motive anger stifles a moment of tearfulness. Pity in *Orlando furioso* is a familiarizing emotion: it is founded on an instinctive ability to recognize the suffering of someone who is weak, and who is attractive to the pitier. It is also for Ariosto the most familiar motive imaginable, as it motivates the chief actions in scores of romance narratives. These two facts make it an extremely easy sentiment through which to assimilate a past text: it is intrinsically assimilative, and it is familiar. But anger is different. In order to enter into the mind of someone who is angry one has either to share the anger or, perhaps, to see its justice. But one does not exactly enter into the spirit of anger by recognizing its causes: it is more like decoding or explaining the emotion. Anger inherently resists attempts to identify with it which do not undo its character as a passion. It would also not have been an emotion of which Ariosto was primed to approve. Most commentators praised Aeneas for his pity, but deplored the vestiges of the wrath of Achilles that led him to kill Turnus at the end of the poem. All these distancing factors lead Ariosto to break the dynamism of Orlando's strange and alien rage by starting a new canto with a burst of justificatory explanation, which acknowledges that rage, well, it is not exactly *his* field:

> E s'a crudel, s'ad inumano effetto
> quell'impeto talor l'animo svia,
> merita escusa, perché allor del petto
> non ha ragione imperio né balia.
> Achille, poi che sotto il falso elmetto
> vide Patroclo insanguinar la via,
> d'uccider chi l'uccise non fu sazio,
> se nol traea, se non ne facea strazio.[79]

And if this impetus of feeling divert the mind sometimes towards cruel and inhumane actions, it deserves excuse, because at such moments reason has neither power nor control over the heart. Achilles, when he saw Patroclus under his borrowed helmet bloody the ground, was not sated by killing the man who killed him, unless he dragged him around and lacerated him.

The argument runs: even if one does not like this irrational cruelty, classical epic shows us that it is natural for a warrior to lose his *umanità*

---

[78] *OF* xli. 102.   [79] *OF* xlii. 2.

when his friend is wounded. The *Iliad* is introduced to explain an emotion which Ariosto regards as enigmatic. He needs help from the alien past in order to justify Orlando's response to the death of his friend. There is a trace here of Boiardo's deliberately destabilizing invocation of past texts: if you can swallow Achilles, then you can stomach Orlando, he says, in the knowledge that most readers would regard Achilles as a monster of irascibility. But this instability is directed at more than the creation of a haze of detached uncertainty. The ironical unsettling of a reader is used to create shocking contact with the strangeness of a strange form of passion. The poet is pursuing the morally alien outlook of the classical epic back to its ultimate origin, without himself feeling deep sympathy for it, and without fully expecting his readers to do so either. Orlando's rage is alien, and while a respect for classical precedent might lead one to respect such rage, this will not lead to its full assimilation, since it is not quite clear that classical epic is fully likeable. But Ariosto is inclining towards the strange, desperately playing with notions in order to arrive at what he perceives to be the alien forms of feeling which motivate classical epic. And this process continues to produce dislocating results with the simile that describes Orlando's rage with Agramante:

> Qual nomade pastor che vedut'abbia
> fuggir strisciando l'orrido serpente
> che il figliuol che giocava ne la sabbia
> ucciso gli ha col venenoso dente,
> stringe il baston con colera e con rabbia . . .[80]

As a vagrant shepherd, who has seen the horrid snake flee hissing which, with poisonous fangs, has killed his son as he was playing in the sand, brandishes his stick with rage and fury . . .

There are several classical similes in which a timid warrior is compared to a shepherd who stumbles on a snake in a mountain grove, and leaps back in fear.[81] In Homer the warrior simply sees the snake; Virgil has the man tread on it. Ariosto takes these straightforward similes and turns them into the contorted syntax and violently retributive content of his own description of death and vengeance. The alteration to the classical model indicates that the poet is entering a strange new world of feeling; but the simile retains a trace of his earlier concern with the motive power of love: it becomes a description of how paternal love motivates vengeful

---

[80] *OF* xlii. 7.

[81] *Il.* 3. 33–7; *Aen.* 2. 379–81: 'improvisum aspris veluti qui sentibus anguem | pressit humi nitens trepidusque repente refugit | attollentem iras et caerula colla tumentem' (As someone who, stepping securely on the ground, has trodden on a snake hidden in sharp brambles suddenly starts back in terror as it rises in anger and puffs out its purple neck). Cf. *OF* i. 11; xxxix. 32. This connection is not noted in Kristen Olson Murtaugh, *Ariosto and the Classical Simile*, Harvard Studies in Romance Languages, 36 (Cambridge, Mass., 1980).

rage. Ariosto understands even the angry side of classical epic as a
consequence of affection, and affection is connected with the family. And
the way fury originates in family feeling is vital to the impact of the
simile in its narrative context, since Orlando's paternal fury is not
unmitigatedly terminal. It is followed by another ingemination of the
narrative line. Orlando first kills Agramante in rage, but then familial
warmth resurfaces from his anger and he spares Sobrino:

> e confortollo con parlar benigno,
> come se stato gli fosse parente;
> che dopo il fatto nulla di maligno
> in sé tenea, ma tutto era clemente.[82]

And comforted him with friendly speech, as though he were a parent, who after
the deed was done bore no grudge against him, but was totally clement.

This is a split imitation, which gives some residual motive force to the
compassion which emerges from Aeneas's ruthless executions of Lausus
and Turnus. Aeneas's victim is, as it were, divided in two, and each of
his impulses is given a narrative consequence: one is killed, the other is
compassionately spared. But Orlando, in deciding to spare his adversary,
differs significantly from Ariosto's earlier compassionate heroes. Unlike
Zerbino when confronted by the winning gaze of Medoro, Orlando does
not feel simple *pietà* for his victim: he feels as though he had been the
parent of Sobrino. Both Orlando's rage and his clemency are linked to
family ties. Sentiment is no longer entirely unmediated by collective social
obligations, but involves a perceived link between the pitied and the
pitier. Ariosto is attempting to refigure something of the ethical feeling
generated by family ties in the *Aeneid*. He never quite grasps the shocking
sense of moral kinship which leads Aeneas belatedly to pity Lausus: he
thinks people have to imagine *actual* rather than *ethical* kinship with those
who suffer in order to be moved to revenge or pity them. He never quite
makes sympathy become a cognitive identification with the sufferer; if he
were to do so he would have achieved the parallel interpretive goal of
entering into the ethical structure of the *Aeneid*. But he is gravitating towards
Virgil, puzzling over the pattern of emotion developed in the *Aeneid*, and
attempting to reduplicate it. He is impeded from full sympathetic union
with his original by a touchingly recurrent literalism about the nature of
compassion: it involves some literal tie, some family bond.

His inclination towards Virgil, though, continues in the longest episode
which Ariosto added to *Orlando furioso* in 1532. Ruggiero fights Leone,
is captured and released by him, and agrees to win Bradamante for his

---

[82] *OF* xlii. 19.

courteous captor. The episode draws its movement from Leone's gently perverse love for the *valore* of the warrior who defeats his forces:[83]

> Come bambin, se ben la cara madre
> iraconda lo batte e da sé caccia,
> non ha ricorso alla sorella o al padre,
> ma a lei ritorna, e con dolcezza abbraccia...[84]

As a child, if his dear mother has become angry and beats him, or chases him from her, does not flee for safety to his sister or father, but returns to her and embraces her with love...

The simile is subtly wrong: Ruggiero's ability to defeat Leone is an intrinsic part of the *valore* which makes him admirable; but the ability to chastise is not essentially what makes mothers nice. The tenor contaminates the vehicle, and gives a faintly masochistic tincture to family love, which connects the Leone episode with the new complexities of family sympathy and rage which run through almost every episode of the later *Furioso*. But the simile also acknowledges the dutiful scruples which distort family relations in the immediately surrounding narrative. Bradamante's parents take a rigorously Aristotelian view on the need for a man to have money and noble birth in order to be noble,[85] and refuse to allow the poor but virtuous Ruggiero their daughter's hand. This sets Bradamante's filial love against her passion for Ruggiero, and wrings from *pietà* a newly dutiful sense:

> Avrà, misera me! dunque possanza
> la materna pietà, ch'io t'abandoni,
> o mio Ruggiero, e ch'a nuova speranza,
> a desir nuovo, a nuovo amor mi doni?[86]

Oh, misery! Will maternal piety win out, so that I abandon you, o my Ruggiero, and I give myself to new hope, new desire, and new love?

'Materna pietà' introduces the idea, new to the poem, that love is a voluntary emotion, which can be renounced and taken up in response to

[83] For 'cortesia' in the Leone episode, see David Marsh, 'Ruggiero and Leone: Revision and Resolution in Ariosto's *Orlando furioso*', Modern Language Notes, 96 (1981), 144–51; and Giuseppe dalla Palma, 'Dal secondo al terzo *Furioso*: mutamenti di struttura e movimenti ideologici', in Cesare Segre (ed.), *Ludovico Ariosto: Lingua, stile e tradizione. Atti del congresso organizzato dai communi di Reggio Emilia e Ferrara 12–16 ottobre 1974* (Milan, 1976), 95–105. For 'fede', see Eduardo Saccone, 'Prospettive sull'ultimo Ariosto', *Modern Language Notes*, 98 (1983), 55–69. Walter Moretti, *L'ultimo Ariosto* (Bologna, 1977), 61–94, regards the episode as showing the rise of a new, hostile, bourgeois world.

[84] *OF* xliv. 92.

[85] Aristotle, *Politics* 1283ᵃ. This notion would be recognizably archaic to Ariosto's readers. See Quentin Skinner, *The Foundations of Modern Political Thought*, 2 vols. (Cambridge, 1978), i. 45–6.

[86] *OF* xliv. 42.

the moral demands of family. The power of familial duty is, as in the
Aeneid, driving out desire and simple pity. And love undergoes a similar
process of gravitation towards the deontic when Leone rescues Ruggiero:

> Leone Ruggier con gran pietade abbraccia,
> e dice:—Cavallier, la tua virtute
> indissolubilmente a te m'allacia
> di voluntaria eterna servitude.[87]

Leone embraced Ruggiero with great *pietà*, and said 'Sir, your virtue has bound
me to you indissolubly in eternal voluntary servitude.'

'Pietade' could conceivably mean 'pity' here, since Ruggiero has been
languishing in prison, and so merits a dose of compassion. But its
association with 'voluntaria eterna servitude' makes it encompass a feeling
of loyalty which is voluntarily directed towards an object of admiration.
And this must be the nature of the grateful emotion which Ruggiero feels
towards Leone, since nothing at all makes his liberator deserve compassion:

> Il primo tutto era odio, ira e veneno;
> di pietade è il secondo e d'amor pieno.[88]

At first all was hatred, anger, and poison; the next was full of piety and love.

Ruggiero decides to abandon his love for Bradamante not simply through
fede towards Leone, or gratitude for his *cortesia*, but for this composite
dutiful *pietà*. His decision to fight Bradamante in order to win her for his
rival is an almost unbearably magnified version of Aeneas's sacrifice in
Aeneid 4, which involves renouncing not only the person he loves, but
also transforming the romance ethos which has previously motivated his
actions. The poem and its heroes are turning against their own earlier
values in order to accommodate the alien structures of feeling found in
the *Aeneid*. This emergence of dutiful *pietà* in Ariosto's largest addition
to his romance is the last phase of his attempt to understand Virgil. The
Orlando furioso moves from early pitiful misprisions of the *Aeneid* towards
this final vision of a piety which drains the motive power from the hero's
spontaneous feelings. This transformation of values is analogous to that
described in the *Aeneid*: a man of amours becomes a taciturn warrior,
who kills his opponent without saying a word. But it is also more deeply
analogous to the processes of imitating a narrative poem enacted by
Virgil: reinterpretations of the motives which underlie peripheral episodes
produce a poem which is on the brink of springing free from its original,
of creating something so new and independent that it could never reabsorb
itself into the overall narrative shape of its predecessor. But, like Virgil,

---

[87] *OF* xlv. 46.   [88] Ibid. 51.

Ariosto curbs and curtails the freedom of his own digressive revisions in order to return to something like the structure and ethos of his chief original. This involves a degree of self-mutilation: few readers have preferred the later phases of *Orlando furioso* to the freewheeling ease of its earlier sections. But the later parts of the poem show Ariosto gravitating towards Virgil as Virgil gravitated towards Homer. For both Ariosto and Virgil this process of approaching the idiom of their predecessors involves renouncing a bit of themselves. Ariosto needed to add the Leone episode to his earlier drafts in order to fashion an ethos which would explain the last action of his poem, and make it coincide with the last action of the *Aeneid*; he needed an episode which would pull his hero from pity to pious ruthlessness, and into a new phase in the imitation of classical epic, in which the Aeneas who killed Turnus could convincingly be recreated— as when Ruggiero finally destroys Rodomonte:

> il ferro del pugnale a Rodomonte
> tutto nascose, e si levò d'impaccio.
> Alle squalide ripe d'Acheronte,
> sciolta dal corpo più freddo che giaccio,
> bestemmiando fuggì l'alma sdegnosa,
> che fu sì altiera al mondo e sì orgogliosa.[89]

He buries his sword to the hilt in Rodomonte's forehead, and ensured thereby his own safety. The disdainful soul, which had been so haughty and full of pride in life, fled cursing to the muddy banks of Acheron, torn from a body more cold than ice.

[89] *OF* xlvi. 140; cf. *Aen.* 12. 945–52.

4

Tasso

Ariosto's heroes, in their mad gallops around the world, often find themselves in labyrinthine forests, where they lose their way, and very often their loves. The forest is the perfect place to contain the directionless process of their multiple quests for Angelica: in a thicket of trees it is hard to tell where, or even who, anyone is, let alone who is a good guide to its intricate shape, and who a bad. Tasso's *Gerusalemme liberata*, however, has a very different setting. Most of its action takes place on the clear, open spaces of a plain around the city of Jerusalem. Two opposed camps are set against one another in this open space: Jerusalem is occupied by Saracen forces, while a Christian alliance under Tasso's hero, 'pio Goffredo', besieges them and seeks to regain the town for his religion. There are a few moments when characters wander from the battlefield into a landscape of trees and greenery, and find a pastoral seclusion which is valued above the polarities of the battle; but these are rare.[1] Sometimes a prospect across the plain—through the crepuscular gloom which Tasso excels at evoking—reveals the flash of an unidentified helmet. But more usually the poem matches its open setting with correspondingly clear indications of which side people are on. This limits the possibilities for the moral and narrative entanglements in which Ariosto so delights: the very geography of Tasso's poem suggests a polarized confrontation between Christian virtue and pagan sacrilege.

The clear landscape of the poem is also reflected in its structure. *Gerusalemme liberata* contains few episodic chance encounters with the pitiable ladies of dubious parentage and virtue, of the kind who repeatedly pull Ariosto's narrative thread into intricate tangles. When some episodic accident happens, it is likely to originate either with God or with the Devil, and Tasso usually tells which of these two great opposed forces lies behind a given episode before it begins. When 'pio Goffredo' relives the episode from the *Aeneid*, in which 'pius Aeneas' is wounded, it is

---

[1] See e.g. Erminia's flight, *GL* vii. 1–22. This episode was excised from the *Gerusalemme conquistata*, from which Tasso banished several of the episodes which are closest kin to Ariosto. See C. P. Brand, *Torquato Tasso: A Study of the Poet and of his Contribution to English Literature* (Cambridge, 1965), 119–32.

not a partisan pagan deity that comes to his rescue and cures him, but an angel sent from God.[2] On the other hand, women who play on the passions of Christian knights, and lead them from the assault on Jerusalem, are often inspired to do so by the Devil. This stark demonizing of the erotic means that the divisions between the two armies fighting on the plain are rarely broken down by a love which cuts across religious boundaries. The one pagan woman not to have a dire effect on her Christian paramour is Clorinda. She, though, is not allowed to live. Her lover, Tancred, mortally wounds her as she fights him under the anonymity of a helmet. With her last gasp she renounces her old faith, and, through his remorseful tears, he baptizes her.[3]

Tasso urgently seeks to curtail, and if not curtail, then sanctify, any momentary deflections of his heroes from their main purpose of 'liberating'—that is, reconquering—Jerusalem. But there is one magnificently unsettling episode, deep in the heart of *Gerusalemme liberata*, where the simple clarity of opposed armies fighting on a plain breaks down. In canto xiii the Christians need wood to replace their siege engines. The pagan enchanter-in-chief, Ismeno, summons up spirits to haunt the only available grove, and so thwart their purpose. These spirits make terrifying sounds, and create the appearance of fire, with sufficient vigour to deter the Christians from entering the wood; but Tasso does not allow these spectres to become quite real. The place remains no more than a shady grove of nightmarish fantasy:

> Qual semplice bambin mirar non osa
> dove insolite larve abbia presenti,
> o come pave ne la notte ombrosa,
> imaginando pur mostri e portenti,
> così temean, senza saper qual cosa
> siasi quella però che gli sgomenti,
> se non che 'l timor forse a i sensi finge
> maggior prodigi di Chimera o Sfinge.[4]

As a simple child does not dare to look where strange new forms might appear, or as he trembles in the shadows of the night, imagining monsters and portents, so the Christian forces were afraid, without knowing what it might be that terrified them, unless perhaps fear created worse horrors than the Chimera or the Sphinx.

The effects of the grove are associated with the products of the imagination, the faculty which, in Renaissance psychology, can recombine sense

---

[2] *GL* xi. 54–7, 68–75; *Aen.* 12. 318–23, 383–440.
[3] *GL* xii. 52–71.
[4] *GL* xiii. 18.

impressions when freed from the guiding hand of reason, and so create
strange hybrids like the Chimera and the Sphinx.[5] The effort to destroy
the grove is an assault on these self-created fears, and on the delusive
faculty which creates them. This urge to assault the imaginary sources of
fiction runs deep in Tasso, and creates a strange and giddying alliance
between his poem and its ideological enemies. His mocking comparison
of the Christian forces with deluded children derives from an extraordinary
source for a Christian poet attempting to advance the cause of the
Christian forces: it is from Lucretius's *De rerum natura*, which attempts
to put forward a materialist Epicurean account of the world with sufficient
force to overcome the childlike (and imaginative) fears of death.[6] A pagan
sceptic—who was widely regarded as an atheist—is enlisted to assault the
feeble, imaginary delusions of Christian heroes. Ariosto's forest is turned
into a source of delusive superstition; and the whole success of the
Christians' siege depends on its destruction and transformation into
weapons of war. The allusion to Lucretius suggests that destroying this
most cherished and typical romance environment, full of the delusions
which draw Ariosto's heroes so deliciously astray, will lead his heroes to
renounce a part of themselves: they must abandon the imaginary for the
sceptical scorn of an ancient pagan, in order to overcome the delusive
murkiness of the forest.

After one Christian knight has failed in his attempt to enter the haunted
grove, Goffredo summons Tancred from his bed, where he is mourning
the death of Clorinda. He sails through the wall of imaginary flame with
ease; but at the centre of the grove he confronts a tougher adversary. He
smites the trunk of a huge, lone cypress, which begs him to cease in the
voice of Clorinda:

> Qual l'infermo talor ch'in sogno scorge
> drago o cinta di fiamme alta Chimera,
> se ben sospetta o parte anco s'accorge
> che 'l simulacro sia non forma vera,
> pur desia di fuggir, tanto gli porge
> spavento la sembianza orrida e fera,

---

[5] See further W. Rossky, 'Imagination in the English Renaissance: Psychology and Poetic', *Studies in the Renaissance*, 5 (1958), 49–73.

[6] *De rerum natura*, ed. C. Bailey, 2nd edn. (Oxford, 1922), 2. 55–61: 'nam veluti pueri trepidant atque omnia caecis | in tenebris metuunt, sic nos in luce timemus | interdum, nilo quae sunt metuenda magis quam | quae pueri in tenebris pavitant finguntque futura. | hunc igitur terrorem animi tenebrasque necessest | non radii solis neque lucida tela diei | discutiant, sed naturae species ratioque.' (And as children tremble, and fear everything in the blinding darkness, so we sometimes fear in daylight, things which are no more to be feared than what children tremblingly imagine to be about to happen in the darkness. It is not the rays of the sun, nor the light threads of day which are needed to expel this fear from the mind, but an understanding of the orderly system of nature.)

tal il timido amante a pien non crede
a i falsi inganni, e pur ne teme e cede.[7]

As a sick man, who sees in his sleep a dragon, or a huge Chimera girded with flame, even if he fully suspects, or half-believes, that the simulacrum is not a real thing, yet still he wants to flee, so much does the horrid and strange apparition terrify him; so the fearful lover did not exactly believe the false delusions, but none the less feared and retreated from them.

Talking trees frequently occur in earlier epic. Virgil's Polydorus, although turned into a tree, speaks to Aeneas; Dante hears the pitiful voice of Pier delle Vigne emanating from a tree in the *Inferno*; and Ariosto's Astolfo makes a noise like the pained crackles of sappy logs on a fire when Ruggiero tears off one of his branches.[8] Only Ariosto's hero is released from his wooden prison, partly as a result of the pity he elicits in Ruggiero: the others stay metamorphosed in a fixed shape within closed episodes. Several sixteenth-century critics debated whether an epic poem should contain such miraculous events, or whether they should be driven from the genre.[9] For Tasso this debate becomes a battle within his hero. Tancred confronts and half-credits his own delusive, digressive fictions and the desires from which they stem; and these fabulous imaginings are associated with fictional sources of dubious propriety. The poem requires him to kill Clorinda his love twice, once in reality, and then again in an imaginary surrogate, redolent with the energies of Ariosto, in order to further the Christian campaign. He cannot kill Clorinda a second time, and with her the memory of past romance episodes, since they are tied in with his own very recent experiences. She has only just, with pitiful perversity, died at his hand. The proximity of this loving and pitiful death, which has not driven out, but merely frustrated amorous desires, means that Tancred leaves the tree intact. The forest stands inviolate, and the Christian battle incomplete.

Tancred's effort to unpick a delusive confusion between what is valued as part of the self and of the imagination, and what is alien and to be destroyed, is a recurrent, unwinnable battle for the heroes of *Gerusalemme liberata*. It is also a huge, tensely dynamic, and irresolvable problem for Tasso. He attempts to pierce through the idiom of Ariosto towards a more unified, classically centred form of plot; but to do so involves destroying a large part of the received modes of feeling—and of interpreting classical epic—which were alive to him. Even the poem's most

---

[7] *GL* xiii. 44.

[8] *Aen.* 3. 22–68; *Inferno* xiii; *OF* i. 27–8.

[9] For Tasso's contribution to this debate, see Bernard Weinberg, *A History of Literary Criticism in the Italian Renaissance*, 2 vols. (Chicago, 1961), 628–34, and Tasso's *Discourses on the Heroic Poem*, ed. and trans. Mariella Cavalchini and Irene Samuel (Oxford, 1973), 34–6.

complete (and at times its most completely flat) hero, 'pio Goffredo',
struggles at times to contain the digressively amorous energies that lurk
within his characterizing adjective. The first and most crucial of these
moments of heroic restraint occurs, significantly enough, in Tasso's canto
iv, when Goffredo avoids the temptations of Armida as Aeneas overcame
his love for Dido in Virgil's Book 4.[10] But Goffredo's re-creation of the
narrative form which flows from the structure of Virgilian heroism is by
no means easy. Armida arrives at the Christian camp at the instigation of
Satan, and uses the magnetic beauty of a romance heroine to sow disunity
in the Christian camp. The 'cupide turbe' (impassioned crowd) of
Christians are dazzled like so many Orlandos by a latter-day Angelica.
Eustazio is drawn to her:

> Come al lume farfalla, ei si rivolse
> a lo splendor de la beltà divina.[11]

As a butterfly round a light, so he fluttered round the magnificence of her
heavenly beauty.

She tells a piteous tale of usurpation by her own family, and, like Ariosto's
Olimpia, seems about to cause piteous truancy in her male audience.
Finally she appeals to Goffredo for pity and assistance in her cause. It is
a dangerous moment for Goffredo's intention to pursue no goal but the
recapture of Jerusalem; but it is also a crucial moment for the structure
of the poem, since if he were to run after Armida the continuity of the
narrative line would be lost, together with its fidelity to the contours of
Virgil. Her appeal is brilliantly tricksy, insinuating itself within two
conceptual systems at once:

> Ma se la nostra fé varia ti move
> a disprezzar forse i miei preghi onesti,
> la fé, c'ho certo in tua pietà, mi giove,
> né dritto par ch'ella delusa resti.[12]

But if our different Faith moves you perhaps to scorn my honest prayers, the
certain faith which I have in your *pietà* encourages me; and it does not appear
that this faith will be disappointed.

She transposes the terms of loftily religious heroism into those of secular
romance. 'Fé' initially marks a firm religious division between Armida
and the Christian general, but her secular 'preghi' prepare the way for a
'fé' of a very different kind: that of personal confidence in 'pietà'. And it
is faith in *pietà* of the pitiful rather than the pious sort, of the sort which

---

[10] Paolo Beni praises Goffredo for his resistance to Armida, and contrasts him with the amorously
servile Aeneas, *Comparatione di Homero, Virgilio, e Torquato* (Padua, 1607), 20.
[11] *GL* iv. 34. 1–2.
[12] Ibid. 42. 1–4.

can cut across religious boundaries, and lead a Christian hero to pursue a pagan princess. Armida slithers from religious to romance language within three lines, and, as a result, the secular *pietà* for which she appeals seems sanctified and ennobled. She could be saying 'the religious devotion which I have to your piety', whereas in fact she means 'the confidence I have in your ruthfulness'. Goffredo, however, unlike any hero in Ariosto, sees this semantic wiliness and—with epoch-making precision—separates pity from piety and opts for the former: 'Or mi farebbe la pietà men pio' (Now pity would make me less pious).[13] This refusal of a romance digression does not come without a moment of doubt, when his 'pietoso affetto | . . . che non dorme in nobil petto' (pitiful affection that does not sleep in a noble breast)[14] takes Armida's part; but Goffredo successfully suppresses this eager swelling of his romance subtext, that undercurrent of compassion in his *pietà*. By this critical temperance he prevents himself from wandering off into the mazes intricate of the Ariostan landscape.

The severity and narrative restraint of *Gerusalemme liberata* in comparison with the free-wheeling abundance of *Orlando furioso* is commonly attributed to the two main cultural forces operating in the years between 1532 and 1575: the Counter-Reformation and the rise of Aristotelian literary theory.[15] But these forces for religious orthodoxy and formal unity were linked with changes in interpretative attitudes towards the content and character of classical epic, which have received rather less critical attention.[16] 'Pio Goffredo' was not the only person to distinguish pity from piety in the sixteenth century. Julius Caesar Scaliger in his *Poetics* shows a newly circumspect understanding of Aeneas's characterizing virtue:

Est autem pietas vox ambigua . . . Existit autem pietas aut in affectu, aut in officio: ac distribuitur humanis animis aut erga deos, aut erga patriam, aut erga parentes, uxorem, liberos, affines, amicos . . . Pietas interdum misericordiam quandam significat.[17]

---

[13] Ibid. 69. 7.

[14] Ibid. 65. 7–8. For Goffredo's fusion of chivalric clemency and Virgilian *pietas*, see Walter Moretti, *Torquato Tasso* (Rome and Bari, 1973), 41; Giorgio Petrocchi, 'Virgilio e la poetica del Tasso', *Giornale italiano di filologia*, NS 2: 23 (1971), 1–12, esp. 4.

[15] See e.g. Thomas M. Greene, *The Descent from Heaven* (New Haven, Conn., and London, 1963), 176–80; Francesco De Sanctis, *Storia della letteratura italiana*, ed. B. Croce, 2 vols. (Milan, 1912), ii. 135–76; Giuseppe Toffanin, *La fine dell'umanesimo* (Turin, 1920), 2. Gaetano Firetto, *Torquato Tasso e la controriforma* (Palermo and Milan, 1939), *passim*; Brand, *Tasso*, 94; and R. M. Durling, *The Figure of the Poet in Renaissance Epic* (Cambridge, Mass., 1965), 182–210, argue that these forces were internalized by the poet.

[16] Guido Baldassari, *Il sonno di Zeus: Sperimentazione narrativa del poema rinascimentale e tradizione omerica* (Rome, 1982), discusses how the declining interest in love as a heroic motive changes the structure of 16th-cent. epic, but he does not relate this to reinterpretations of the outlook embodied in classical epic.

[17] *Poetices libri septem* ([Lyons], 1561), 92. Scaliger goes on none the less to accord *misericordia* prime place in Aeneas's character.

Pietas, however, is an ambiguous term...*Pietas* comes into play either with
regard to affections, or in relation to obligations, and it flows from human minds
either towards the gods, or towards one's country, or towards parents,
wife, children, neighbours, friends...*Pietas* also from time to time means
'pity'.

This critical understanding is very important for shape, content, and
indeed the influence of *Gerusalemme liberata*. Malatesta Porta, a champion
of Tasso against the Accademia della Crusca,[18] juxtaposed in dialogue two
rival views of the *Aeneid*. The stooge, Paci, argues that 'si possa fermamente
conchiudere, la Pietà d'Enea esser favola dell'*Eneide*' (one can firmly
conclude that *pietà* is the narrative subject of the *Aeneid*).[19] When his
opponent and instructor, Beffa, enquires what *pietà* is, Paci tentatively
identifies it as 'una passione dell'anima nostra, che ci fà sentir dispiacere
dell'altrui miserie' (a passion of our mind, which makes us feel displeasure
at the pain of others).[20] Beffa pounces on this outmoded notion, with all
the acumen of 'pio Goffredo':

voi ingannate voi stesso col nome 'pietà' che secondo un tal uso commune, e
popolare si toglie sovente in iscambio di 'compassione' di cui è la diffinitione, da
voi data alla pietà.

You are tricking yourself with the word *pietà*, which, according to a popular and
vulgar usage is taken as a synonym for 'compassion', to which the definition
belongs that you give to *pietà*.

When asked to come up with something better, Paci produces a definition
which is close to Scaliger's:

la Pietà, della quale ragionamo è una passione dell'Anima nostra, che ci fà amatori
di Dio, osservatori delle piè cerimonie del culto divino, ubbidienti a' maggiori,
solleciti nella cura della patria, e de' padri nostri, e pronti all'amico, ed al
prossimo.[21]

Pietà, about which we are arguing, is a passion of our spirit, which makes us
lovers of God, observers of pious ceremonies in religious worship, obedient to
our superiors, active in our concern for our country, and our fathers, and swift
to help our friends and neighbours.

This dialogue by a follower of Tasso shows how the theoretical debates
on the nature of epic created an environment alive to the tricks which

---

[18] *Il Rossi: o vero del parere sopra alcune obiettioni, fatte dall'Infarinato Academico della Crusca.
Intorno alla Gierusalemme liberata* (Rimini, 1589). 'Infarinato' was the pseudonym of Lionardo
Salviati.

[19] *Il Beffa, o vero della favola dell'Eneide, dialogo* (Rimini, 1604), 12.

[20] Ibid. 15.

[21] Ibid. 15–16.

could be played on interpreters of Virgil by the engaging apparent
similarities between his ethical language and that of the present. There
was an extensive debate about the form of *Orlando furioso* in the mid-
sixteenth century, and a side-shoot of this debate also reached into the
ethical, rather than simply the formal, aspects of the poem. A major
strand of this argument concentrated on the later stages of *Orlando furioso*.
The episode which carried the burden of Ariosto's effort to move closer
to Virgil, the story of Ruggiero and Leone from the 1532 *Orlando furioso*,
was, surprisingly enough, not admired by Tasso and his followers. Paolo
Beni, for instance, thought Ruggiero acted dishonourably in fighting for
Leone:

essendo già Bradamante vera sposa e consorte di Ruggiero, non par che questi
potesse senza bruttissima macchia d'honore farsi Campion di Leone contra di
Bradamante.[22]

since Bradamante was already the true wife and consort of Ruggiero, it does not
seem that he could make himself Leone's champion against Bradamante, without
some vile blot on his honour.

Tasso himself outlines the reasons against Ruggiero's decision to fight his
fiancée in order to gain her for another, and goes on to criticize him as a
misguided cad:

Ma fù nondimeno anteposto Leone a Bradamante, e in questa maniera tutti i
debiti dimenticati, & tutti gli uffici furono perturbati nella persona di Ruggiero:
percioche prima siamo obligati a Dio, poi al Re, nel terzo luogo alla moglie, o
all'amante, che ama di casto amore; nel quarto all'amico, che ha per fine l'utilità,
e l'ambitione.[23]

But none the less Leone was placed before Bradamante, and in this way all
duties were forgotten, and the hierarchy of obligations was confounded in the
person of Ruggiero; because we are firstly tied to God, then to our King, then,
in the third place, to our wife, or to a lover who loves with a chaste love; in the
fourth place we are tied to a friend, whom one has for the sake of utility or
ambition.

This hostility to Ruggiero's tortured preference for *fede* and *cortesia*
towards a man who has saved his life over love is surprising, since the
episode has often been seen as anticipating Tasso's wary treatment of

[22] Beni, *Comparatione*, 247. On Beni and Tasso, see P. B. Diffley, *Paolo Beni: A Biographical and Critical Study*, Oxford Modern Languages and Literature Monographs (Oxford, 1988), 121–35. For a full account of the controversy, see Weinberg, *Literary Criticism*, ii. 954–1073; and Daniel Javitch, *Proclaiming a Classic: The Canonization of Orlando furioso* (Princeton, NJ, 1991).
[23] *Apologia in difesa della Gierusalemme liberata, a gli Accademici della Crusca* (Ferrara, 1586), 136–7.

romance sentiments.[24] But the version of love which Tasso finds lacking
in this episode is not the primitive appetency of the early *Furioso*; it is an
emotion founded on an orderly sequence of duties, to God, to the King,
then to a wife, and last of all to opportune friends. This hierarchy of
'uffici', obligations arising from one's formal social relations with others,
is disrupted by Ruggiero's decision to help his friend rather than continue
in the higher loyalty to his love. At the start of his 'Discorso dell'amor
vincendevole tra 'l padre e 'l figliuolo', Tasso discusses filial piety, or
dutiful affection, in the *Aeneid*:[25] a new intimacy with Roman values
underlies his attack on Ariosto. The differences between the two poems
are often attributed by modern formalist critics to Tasso's theoretical
writings, and their advocacy of a single main action for the heroic poem.[26]
But they also derive from the ideas which underlie and create form, the
two poets' differing views of the ethos embodied in the hero of the *Aeneid*.

Although Tasso reaches out for pious unity in the epic, he never quite
realizes his goal, since to do so would involve his performing the kind of
imaginative exorcism of his own experience of which Tancred proves
incapable. He would have to destroy his own modes of feeling, and equip
his heroes with the pagan motives which were almost universally regarded
as dangerously equivocal in this period. In the intricate debates of
sixteenth-century Italian literary theory, several defenders of romance
argued that the classical unity required of epic poets by Aristotelian critics
was not appropriate to the modern period, since literary forms change as
customs change.[27] Tasso takes up this crucial element in the debate which
associates changing outlooks with changing literary forms. In one vital
passage of his *Discourses on the Heroic Poem*[28]—which explains so much
of the pained antagonistic attraction which Tasso feels for the narrative
mode of Ariosto—he accepts the main foundation of the digressive plot
structure of *Orlando furioso*: the modern heroic poem must embody love
rather than pagan rage:

---

[24] C. P. Brand, *Ludovico Ariosto*, 175–82. Margaret W. Ferguson, *Trials of Desire: Renaissance Defenses of Poetry* (New Haven, Conn., and London, 1983), 57, argues that Tasso's defence of the genre is bound up with his desire to defend his father's romance.

[25] *Le prose diverse*, ed. Cesare Guasti, 2 vols. (Florence, 1875), 215–26.

[26] So Giulio Cattaneo, 'Varietà e unità nella *Gerusalemme liberata*', in Carlo Ballerini (ed.), *Atti del convegno di Nimega sul Tasso* (Bologna, 1978), 15–34.

[27] The principal proponent of this view is Giovambatista Giraldi Cinthio: 'I maintain that it is better to follow the usage of the time made reputable by worthy writers than to follow in the steps of those who wrote when such usage had not been introduced', *On Romances: Being a Translation of the 'Discorsi intorno al comporre dei romanzi*, ed. and trans. Henry L. Snuggs (Lexington, Ky., 1968), 44. See Weinberg, *Literary Criticism*, ii. 960–8.

[28] Pirated 1587; first published with Tasso's consent in 1594. On the chronology of Tasso's prose, see Emanuela Minesi, 'Indagine critico-testuale e bibliografica sulle *Prose diverse* di T. Tasso', *Studi Tassiani*, 32 (1984), 123–46; 33 (1985), 125–42.

Ma qual delle due passioni fosse più conveniente, l'ira o l'amore. Omero stimò senza dubbio più conveniente l'ira, perché altrimente avrebbe formato il poema dell'amor d'Achille e di Polissena. E oltre ciò, la ragione e l'autorità di Platone par che più ci confermi quella d'Omero, perché tra le tre potenze dell'animo nostro, io dico la ragione e l'appetito irascibile e 'l concupiscibile, senza fallo nobilissima <è> la ragione, e quasi regina dell'altre; ma il concupiscibile appetito somiglia più tosto al rubbello popolare, il qual, sollevandosi e facendo tumulto nell'animo, nega di prestare obedienza alla ragione, là dove l'irascibile è quasi guerriero e ministro della ragione in raffrenare l'altro che le fa contrasto. Dunque dell'ira più tosto che dell'amore dee prendere soggetto il poeta eroico. E ciò peraventura sarebbe vero se gli eroi fossino tutti e sempre soggetti alle passioni; ma se l'amore è non solo una passione e un movimento dell'appetito sensitivo, ma uno abito nobilissimo della voluntà, come volle san Tomaso, l'amore sarà più lodevole ne gli eroi, e per conseguente nel poema eroico. Ma gli antichi o non conobbero questo amore, o non volsero descriverlo ne gli eroi; ma se non onorarono l'amore come virtù umana, l'adorarono quasi divina; però niuna altra dovevano stimar più conveniente a gli eroi.[29]

But which of the two passions would be more appropriate, anger or love? Homer without doubt thought that anger was more appropriate, otherwise he would have made his poem about the love of Achilles and Polyxena. And apart from this, the reason and authority of Plato appears further to affirm that of Homer, since among his three faculties of the human mind (I mean reason, the irascible faculty, and the concupiscible faculty), without doubt the most noble is the reason, and as it were the queen of the others; but the concupiscible appetite is most like a fractious populace, which, splintering itself away from and making chaos in the mind, refuses to obey reason. Whereas the irascible is, as it were, the warrior and counsellor of reason in controlling the others which rise up against it. And so the heroic poet should take as his subject anger rather than love. And this indeed would be true if heroes were all, and always, subject to passions; but if love is not only a passion and a movement of the sensitive appetite, but a most noble habitual movement of the will—as Aquinas has it— love will in that case be more praiseworthy in heroes, and consequently in the heroic poem. But the ancients either did not know this kind of love, or did not want to describe it in their heroes; but if they did not honour love as a human virtue, they adored it, as it were, as divine. But they ought to have thought no other virtue more appropriate to heroes.

Although this passage was written some time after *Gerusalemme liberata*, it resonates with the problems of structure and motive which run through the poem.[30] It proposes a model of heroism which would create two quite different plot structures: the one, linear and transcendent, would direct love towards a goal which is ultimately divine. Traces of this almost

---

[29] *Discorsi dell'arte poetica e del poema eroico*, ed. Luigi Poma (Bari, 1964), 106.
[30] For a full account of the composition of the *Discorsi*, see edn. cit. 263–70.

unwritable kind of linear plot might be felt in Goffredo's pious substitution
of divine for human desire in the Armida episode. But the passage also
suggests a far more fractious and disunified plot: irrational passions arise
and are arrested by reason. This narrative structure repeatedly surfaces
through the relations between Goffredo and his subordinates, as Tasso
suggested in his much-abused allegory of the poem:[31] 'love, which maketh
Tancredie and the other woorthies to dote, and disjoine them from *Godfrey*,
and the disdaine which entiseth *Rinaldo* from the enterprise, doe signifie
the conflict and rebellion which the *Concupiscent* and *Irefull* powers doe
make with the reasonable'.[32] The commonplace anatomy of mental faculties
into the irascible, concupiscible, and rational elements—which derives
ultimately from Plato—does run deep in the narrative foundations of
Gerusalemme liberata.[33] When Rinaldo's *ira* is in danger of becoming
excessive in the first main battle, his prince sends a messenger to restrain
him:

> —Tornatene,—dicea—ch'a le vostr'ire
> non è il loco opportuno o la stagione;
> Goffredo il vi commanda.—A questo dire
> Rinaldo si frenò...[34]

'Turn round,' he said, 'this is not the right place or time for your anger; Goffredo
commands it.' At this speech, Rinaldo reined himself in.

His rage is duly checked, and the possible excesses of this martial episode
are curtailed in order to restrain it within decorous bounds.[35] Form is an
ethical issue in *Gerusalemme liberata*.

But Tasso's remarks on the contrasting foundations of pagan and

---

[31] 'Si direbbe che il Tasso ha scritto l'allegoria di malavoglia, non convinto' (One could say that
Tasso wrote the allegory in bad faith), Adolfo Jenni, 'Appunti sul Tasso', *Studi Tassiani*, 17 (1967),
27. Cf. Roberto Weiss, who mistakenly attributes it to Fairfax: 'Fairfax explained the hidden meaning
of the *Gerusalemme*, a meaning which Tasso had naturally never dreamt of.' *Jerusalem Delivered: The
Edward Fairfax Translation* (London, 1962), p. xii. But see the fine defence of the Allegory by Luigi
Derla, 'Sull'allegoria della *Gerusalemme liberata*', *Italianistica*, 7 (1978), 473–88. The allegory was
printed with editions of the poem from 1581. For the Italian text, see *Prose*, ed. Guasti, i. 297–313.
[32] *Godfrey of Bulloigne: A Critical Edition of Edward Fairfax's Translation of Tasso's 'Gerusalemme
liberata'*, ed. K. M. Lea and T. M. Gang (Oxford, 1981), 90.
[33] Plato, *Republic* 439–41. Cf. Robert Durling: 'The *Gerusalemme liberata* grows from the Renaissance ethical and religious tradition in which it is rooted and fed, and the allegories Tasso constructed
accurately reflect it.' *Poet*, 195. Cf. Moretti, *Tasso*, 40.
[34] *GL* iii. 53. 3–6.
[35] See Francesca Savoia, 'Notes on the Metaphor of the Body in the *Gerusalemme liberata*', in
Luisa Del Giudice (ed.), *Western Jerusalem: University of California Studies on Tasso* (New York,
1984), 57–70. See also Tasso's letter of 15 Apr. 1575 to Scipione Gonzaga 'i molti cavalieri sono
considerati nel mio poema come membra d'un corpo, del quale è capo Goffredo, Rinaldo destra; sì
che in un certo modo sì può dire anco unità d'agente, non che d'azione' (the many heroes are treated
in my poem as limbs of one body, of which the head is Goffredo, and Rinaldo the right hand; so
that in a way one can talk at least of unity of the agent, if not of action). *Le lettere*, ed. Cesare Guasti,
5 vols. (Naples, 1852–5), i. 63.

Christian heroism also create a remarkable and bewildering overlap between the two. His argument begins with a scrupulous acknowledgement of the alien motive priorities of past texts. He also recognizes that to change the ethos of the past would involve changing the subject-matter of its poems: if Homer had regarded love, rather than anger, as the chief heroic passion, he would have written the *Iliad* about the love of Achilles and Polyxena. But this radical revision of classical epic is almost exactly what Tasso appears to propose at the end of the extract, when—with audacious anachronism—he claims that pagan poets should have made love the prime heroic motive. This uneasy oscillation between recognizing the separateness of past values and assimilating them to a superior modernity is also apparent in the part of his argument concerning the motive power of anger. Ariosto had invoked Homer in his bewildered attempt to justify the rage of Orlando; Tasso invokes both Plato and reason to provide a far more stable justification of rage: it fights on the side of reason. The pagan motive of anger is consequently given massive force in the mind. Its alien force could be deployed in support of the supremacy of reason, and of the structural unity of the poem. It might perhaps even provide a positive force of sufficient power to drive out from his poem the residuum of Ariosto's pitiful fluency in slipping from one episode to another. This ancient motive could be deployed in the modern battle to recreate the past, as a violent means of terminating the rebellious and digressive impulses of the romance plot.

Throughout *Gerusalemme liberata* Tasso sets predominantly wrathful pagan heroes, filled with *ira* and *sdegno*, against amorous and predominantly pitiful Christians.[36] Since the pagans' feelings gravitate more readily towards the irascible passions,[37] they are in a curious and unsettling way closer to Tasso's chief project than their Christian counterparts: they are naturally prone to a rage which drives out potentially digressive erotic feeling, and so can aid Tasso in his effort to exorcize from his imagination the loose and loving structure of Ariosto. Where Tancred stands paralysed by an imaginary love in the enchanted forest, one of Tasso's pagans would probably strike out against these delusions in rage. And this ability of the pagan forces to overcome pity by anger can make them participate in the re-creation of the Virgilian terminal pathos which had been so alien to Ariosto. In canto ix Lesbino, Solimano's page, enters fresh-faced, with

---

[36] 'Tasso's pagans, heirs of the classical heroic tradition, suffer defeat at the hands of Christian warriors whose literary ancestors can be traced primarily to Romance.' Judith A. Kates, *Tasso and Milton: The Problem of a Christian Epic* (London and Lewisburg, Pa., 1983), 89.

[37] The opposition continues until the last episode in the poem, when Rinaldo feels 'pudica pietà' for the pagan Armida, who weeps tears of blended 'amor e sdegno'. On wrath in *GL*, see Walter Moretti, *Cortesia e furore nel rinascimento italiano* (Bologna, 1970), 37–74.

such grace as to make his 'sdegnoso rigor', his pagan harshness, seem 'dolce'.[38] He is killed by Argillano, and lies dead, like Virgil's Euryalus 'quasi bel fior succiso' (like a beautiful flower plucked), breathing 'pietà'.[39] But he is relentlessly allowed to die; the sentiment released by his death is converted into the pagan Solimano's vengeful fury:

> Ma come vede il ferro ostil che molle
> fuma del sangue ancor del giovenetto,
> la pietà cede, e l'ira avampa e bolle,
> e le lagrime sue stagna nel petto.
> Corre sovra Argillano e'l ferro estolle,
> parte lo scudo opposto, indi l'elmetto,
> indi il capo e la gola; e de lo sdegno
> di Soliman ben quel gran colpo è degno.[40]

But when he saw the hostile blade still fuming with the blood of the young man, pity abandoned the field, and rage grew up and boiled, and tears stayed choked in his breast. He rushed over Argillano and pulled out his sword, split his enemy's shield in two, then the helmet, then the head and the throat. And that great stroke was worthy of the disdain of Solimano.

This is a ruthless exorcism of romance sentiment. It issues in a terminal rage which stagnates tears and curtails the motive force of compassion. Solimano's mind is briefly split between the two passions, but the sight of Lesbino's blood makes his own blood boil so violently that he forgets his split motives in the interests of splitting the body of a Christian in two.

Tasso is drawn to moments when the mind hovers between two feelings, but rarely indulges Ariosto's urge to bifurcate the narrative line when such divided emotions occur. Emotions often overlap, and then lead nowhere. And such moments of consequenceless, psychological division are not exclusively limited to pagan characters. Christian *pietà* is often mingled with a faint, blurry suggestion of irascibility, as when Odoardo is given a choice between rushing to the aid of his wounded wife Gildippe or stopping to avenge her death:

> Che far dee nel gran caso? Ira e pietade
> a varie parti in un tempo l'affretta:
> questa a l'appoggio del suo ben che cade,
> quella a pigliar del percussor vendetta.
> Amore indifferente il persuade
> che non sia l'ira o la pietà negletta.

---

[38] *GL* ix. 81.

[39] Ibid. 85–6. Caretti, ad loc., notes parallels with *Aen.* 9. 433–6.

[40] *GL* ix. 87.

Con la sinistra man corre al sostegno,
l'altra ministra ei fa del suo disdegno.[41]

What should be done at such a terrible moment? Anger and pity at the same time pulled in different directions; the latter moves him to support his stricken wife, the former to take revenge on the man who had struck her. Love—equally disposed to both—persuaded him that neither anger nor pity should be neglected. With his left hand he rushed to support her; the other he made the executor of his vengeance.

Odoardo's efforts to be the wrathful Homeric warrior at the same time as remaining the amorous Christian knight has a tragic outcome: he dies trying to fight Tasso's ruthless and indomitable Solimano with only one hand. Odoardo's death does display that dutiful compassion for his love which Tasso found lacking in Ariosto's Ruggiero: *pietà* is used here precisely on the boundary between simple compassion and ethical devotion to a wife. But his death springs from a tragic indecision about motive which is deeply akin to Tasso's own theoretical uncertainties.[42] The episode follows the outline of Tasso's statement of modern heroic priorities: love ultimately controls both *pietà* and *ira*. But this predominant emotion does not make his story continue towards resurrection. It ends it fatally.

Yet the story of Gildippe and Odoardo is not simply a pathetic digression. It begins with an apostrophe to the *fama* of the couple which consciously recalls Virgil's address to the pathetic duo Nisus and Euryalus.[43] It also ends with *Fama* bearing news of their deaths to Rinaldo, as *Fama* told Euryalus's mother of her son's death.[44] These allusions have a deep resonance: Ariosto used the compassion released by the death of Euryalus to revive Medoro in the central action of *Orlando furioso*. And Tasso too is not quite willing to let his stories end brutally with a pitiful death. Rinaldo hears of the couple's death, whereupon

Sdegno, dover, benivolenza e duolo
fan ch'a l'alta vendetta ei si converta.[45]

Disdain, duty, kindness and grief made him turn to high vengeance.

This is a bewildering parallel to the way that the pathetic death of Lesbino motivates the pagan Solimano to kill. The list of motives reads like a feeble attempt to mask the similarity between this Christian warrior and

[41] *GL* xx. 97. Cf. the wrath of Homer's Odysseus at the death of Tlepolemus, *Il.* 5. 668–73. In Homer the choice is not between wrath and pity, but between two forms of vengeance: whether to kill Sarpedon or his less elusive men.

[42] Lanfranco Caretti, *Ariosto e Tasso* (Turin, 1961), 81, argues that the characters' emotional conflicts parallel the governing impulses of the poem.

[43] *GL* xx. 94; *Aen.* 9. 446–9. Caretti, ad loc.

[44] *GL* xx. 101; *Aen.* 9. 473–5. Caretti, ad loc.

[45] *GL* xx. 101.

his pagan counterpart: it is hard to see what part 'benivolenza' plays in motivating Rinaldo's subsequent slaughter. The word is thrown into a miscellaneous list in order to indicate that he is not just overwhelmed by blood-lust. But the uncertain wavering between passions here is not just Rinaldo's or Tasso's: it is deeply encoded in the structure of post-Homeric epic. The strange simultaneity of compassion and the ability to kill in Homer's warriors derives from the nature of Homeric pity: it can be a pity which kills. This attitude cannot be readily reproduced in an idiom which reifies passion: the complex attitude of the Homeric hero becomes two quite separate emotions, rage and pity, with two quite distinct probable narrative consequences. Tasso attempts at first to provide an equivalent for this killing pity by piling up alternative categories of experience. But he then inclines towards the Homeric nexus of feeling in a powerfully perverse way: he gives anger a structural role in the development of the story which is analogous to Ariosto's *pietà*. Although it is anger, rather than pity, which gives the story of Odoardo a sequel, a sequel it does have: the episode lives on through rage. The irascible Rinaldo is goaded to his final execution of Solimano by the deaths of Gildippe and Odoardo: Euryalus is not revived, but an allusion to his death provides the spur for the rage which motivates the final, ruthless action of the poem, in which a Christian hero violently slays a pagan antagonist. Tasso creates the prospect of a poem in which continuing episodes grow one from another, not through pity, but through anger.[46]

The price of writing an epic that lives with Christian instincts is radical revision of classical prototypes: compassion must flow on, revising the narrative, pushing it towards endlessness. But to incline towards the pagan past, Tasso is drawn towards a deep and self-thwarting paradox. His Christian heroes must blur over into the pagan, and seek to overwrite their pitiful natures with a violence capable of destroying an antagonist. It is a paradox similar to that which runs through the *Aeneid*, and its partial effort to turn the warriors of Homer into the violent enemies of the Roman hero: if the values of a literary predecessor are made so alien that modern heroes come to fight the embodiments of those values, then there will inevitably come a moment when the new type of hero will have to use the methods of their antagonists in order to defeat them. Fighting against an irascible past eventually leads to a strange community with it, since anger is needed to defeat it. When Aeneas kills the Homeric Turnus, in a burst of fury at the sight of Pallas's baldric, he comes closest to reproducing the wrath of Achilles at the very moment when he defeats a Homeric antagonist. Tasso was unusually sympathetic to this harsher,

---

[46] I must thank A. D. Nuttall for making this point.

almost self-implosive side of Aeneas's heroism, and appreciated Virgil's efforts to differentiate his hero from the antiquated figure whom he destroyed. He defended Aeneas's dispatch of Turnus as of its age:

Giusta fu dunque la vendetta e lecita al cavaliero gentile (il quale non può esser riputato crudele da' gentili, o in comperazione degli altri [cavalieri gentili]), e molto più convenevole che la vendetta fatta d'Achille: peroché l'uno, come abbiam detto, uccise il difensor de la patria, che non aveva alcuna colpa nel periurio o nel violar de'patti; ma l'altro tolse la vita al rompitor de' patti e al perturbator de la pace.[47]

For vengeance was just and permitted to a pagan knight (who could not be counted cruel by the pagans, or different from the others), and it was much more warranted by circumstances than the vengeance exercised by Achilles. He, as we have said, killed a man who was defending his country, who had never broken his oath or violated a truce. But Aeneas took the life of one who broke pacts and disturbed the peace.

Cinthio, the chief advocate of suiting epic action to cultural conditions, also defended Aeneas against the charge of ruthlessness. 'Justice', he wrote, 'prevailed over clemency.' And 'Aeneas was less piteous than just.'[48] But sixteenth-century Italian translators of the *Aeneid* were as eager as the *Eneas* poet to extract all the ruth they could from Aeneas's wordless hesitation over the suppliant Turnus, and so redeem him from the alienness of rage. Lodovico Dolce, who edited *Orlando furioso* and translated Homer and Virgil into *ottava rima*, produced the most sentimental redaction of Aeneas's pause:

> Et Enea, che di Pio seco portava
> Il cognome gentil meritamente,
> Fermossi a le parole; e cominciava
> A intenerir la generosa mente.[49]

And Aeneas, who carried with him the gentle surname of pitiful deservedly, stopped at his words, and allowed his generous mind to begin to soften.

Tasso caught just a touch of this pity in his main attempt to re-create the end of Turnus, when Tancred conquers Argante.[50] But he attempts to grow closer to the ethos of the past text in the only way he can: by all

---

[47] *Discorsi*, 160.
[48] *Romances*, 168.
[49] *L'Enea di M. Lodovico Dolce* (Venice, 1558), fol. 129ᵃ. Freely rendering *Aen.* 12. 940–1: 'et iam iamque magis cunctantem flectere sermo | coeperat' (and now more and more the speech began to move him as he delayed). Cf. *L'opere di Vergilio tradotte in versi sciolti*, trans. Alessandro Sansedoni *et al.* (Venice, 1573), fol. 279ᵇ: 'Et già gl'incominciavan le parole | A piegar l'alma a giusto sdegno volta | Al cammin di pietà, con dolce forza' (And already his words began to turn his spirit from just disdain to the path of pity, with sweet force).
[50] *GL* xix. 20–6; cf. *Aen.* 12. 919–52.

but eradicating the modern view of heroism from his imitation. Tancred overwhelms his opponent, and asks the kneeling pagan to yield. Argante echoes Turnus's 'utere sorte tua' (use your fortune), but Tancred does not press home his advantage at once. His opponent rises enraged to continue the battle.[51] Whereupon Tancred realizes that his hesitant *pietà* was misplaced, and yields once more to anger:

> Infuriossi allor Tancredi, e disse:
> —Cosí abusi, fellon, la pietà mia?[52]

Tancred then flew into a rage, and said, 'Is this how you abuse my pity?'

The Christian's ruth nearly makes him botch his attempt to emulate Aeneas: he needs two attempts to kill his victim. The imitation is flustered by the motive of its modern hero, and nearly grows into a digression motivated by compassion; but Tasso and Tancred do manage eventually to reproduce the undigressive rigour of their original. Yet it needs a blast of *furor* to disperse the narrative energy released by the prevailing view of Aeneas's nature. Anger is used as a means of thwarting the form and ethos of romance-based readings of the *Aeneid*. The price of this is high: the Christian hero does not manifest his loving nature at the moment when he achieves the supremacy of his ethos.

Tasso's acceptance of anger as part of a Christian warrior's make-up did, however, also enable him to re-create the most alien episode in the *Aeneid* to writers in the romance tradition, the moment when Aeneas leaves Dido. Ariosto had found this episode impossibly perverse; but much of Tasso's poem can be seen as an elaborate preparation of the emotional ground for an imitation of Aeneas's *pius* departure, which discards Ariosto's pitiful reading of the hero. Tasso concentrates his transforming powers on the story of Rinaldo, who at first irascibly abandons the Christian force when he is not allowed to head the squadron sent out to assist the pitiable Armida, and kills its appointed leader in jealous rage. A shadowy double of his corpse is discovered; but it subsequently emerges that he has been ensnared by Armida and lives on in love, dallying with a cupidinous Dido-figure. He spends the bulk of the poem in erotic seclusion, leaving his amorous double Tancred to do the bulk of the fighting. He does, however, eventually depart from Armida in a manner which is clearly reminiscent of Aeneas's desertion of the

---

[51] *Aen.* 12. 932; *GL* xix. 22: 'Usa la sorte tua.'
[52] *GL* xix. 26. 1–2.

Carthaginian queen: Armida, like Dido, faints, he leaves, and she curses him.[53]

Characters in the early *Furioso* tend only to leave absent or uglified ladies; Tasso's effort to make his hero succeed where earlier warriors had failed involved the complex deployment of a number of sources. The genesis of Rinaldo's departure scene is intricate, but worth examining in detail, since it marks an epoch in the history of Renaissance epic: it is the most sustained attempt to construct a motive which would intelligibly re-create, from the inside, as it were, Aeneas's departure. The sequence begins when a band of Christian warriors comes to rescue Rinaldo through the labyrinths of Armida's palace, and shows him a mirror in which he sees his uxorious servility. This shameful vision recalls Statius's *Achilleid*,[54] in which Ulysses holds a gleaming shield up to Achilles, who is languishing in woman's clothing in the court of Deidamia. The hero sees his reflection, and is thrilled with horror and shame:

> ut vero accessit propius luxque aemula vultum
> reddidit et simili talem se vidit in auro,
> horruit erubuitque simul.[55]

As he came closer the mimicking light returned his reflection, and he saw himself as he was in the gold. He shrank back and blushed at once.

Tasso approached past texts by editing out what seemed anachronistic from modern versions of them; but he saw them first through a layer of modernity. This is true of his use of Statius here. He was prompted to link the *Achilleid* with *Aeneid* 4 by reading Giraldi Cinthio's epic *Dell'Hercole*.[56] Cinthio's hero is rebuked by Aretia—a figure, like Ariosto's Melissa, who represents virtue (*aretē*)—for his enslavement to Omphale. She holds up 'duo bei christalli' to Hercules, which show his former glories in contrast with his current amorous servitude. He, like Achilles, is goaded by shame to leave:

[53] Cf. Armida's complaint at *GL* xvi. 57–60 and Dido's at *Aen.* 4. 365–87. See Annagiulia Angelone dello Vicario, *Il richiamo di Virgilio nella poesia italiana (momenti significativi)* (Naples, 1981), 77. Rinaldo's initial departure is modelled on the withdrawal of Homer's Achilles. See John M. Steadman, 'Achilles and Renaissance Epic: Moral Criticism and Literary Tradition', in Horst Meller and Hans-Joachim Zimmermann (eds.), *Lebende Antike: Symposion für Rudolf Sühnel* (Berlin, 1967), 139–54.

[54] See Steadman, 'Achilles', 142–4.

[55] *Achilleid* 1. 864–6. Text from *Statius*, ed. J. H. Mozley, Loeb Classical Library, 2 vols. (Cambridge, Mass., and London, 1928).

[56] Salvatore Multineddu, *Le fonti della 'Gerusalemme liberata'* (Turin, 1895), 180–1, regards the *Hercole* as the main source of the episode (in apparent ignorance of the *Achilleid*), but scholars have forgotten this modest discovery. For Tasso's relation to earlier Italian epic poetry, see Roberto Agnes, 'La *Gerusalemme liberata* e il poema del secondo cinquecento', *Lettere italiane*, 16 (1964), 117–43. Tasso refers to Giraldi's poem in the *Discorsi*, edn. cit. 73, 97.

> Tutto pentito de l'error commesso,
> più che fuoco, vermiglio in viso venne,
> e gli occhi vergognoso à terra tenne.[57]

All repentant of the fault he had committed, a red brighter than flame suffused his face, and he turned his eyes to the ground, overwhelmed with shame.

Cinthio assimilated the departures in the *Achilleid* and *Aeneid* 4 to the predominant medieval allegorical interpretation of the Dido episode, according to which Aeneas overcomes childlike desires by the rational virtue embodied in Mercury. He is also drawn to the main medieval and early Renaissance view of the emotions expressed on the literal level of the story: Omphale appeals in vain for *pietà*, and then curses Hercules with all the vigour of Dido. The hero then leaves, a pitiful rather than a pious man, 'Et potea ogni sua forza restar vinta: | Da la pietà, che n'hebbe' (And all his strength could have remained overcome by the pity which he had for her).[58]

Tasso's Rinaldo responds to the admonitory image of himself in the mirror rather differently. The starts of pity which colour Cinthio's hero are painted over with harder feelings. At first Rinaldo feels shame; then, with the self-mutilating instincts of Tasso himself, he rends away his effeminate clothing, and feels *anger*:

> Ma poi che diè vergogna a sdegno loco,
> sdegno guerrier de la ragion feroce,
> e ch'al rossor del volto un novo foco
> successe.[59]

But then shame gave place to disdain, disdain the fierce warrior of reason, so that a new fire replaced the red of his face.

Ariosto wrote 'poté la pietà più che'l timore' (pity can do more than fear),[60] and Tasso rewrote the line to show his different psychological priorities: 'più che 'l timor poté lo sdegno' (disdain can do more than fear).[61] At this crucial testing point for Tasso's martial, religious, and rational heroic ethos, the new priority of *sdegno* enables Rinaldo to be a new Aeneas, rather than another Ariostan acratic. As Tasso said in the passage from the *Discorsi* quoted above:

il concupiscibile appetito somiglia più tosto al rubbello popolare, il quale, sollevandosi e facendo tumulto nell'animo, nega di prestare obedienza alla ragione,

---

[57] *Dell'Hercole* (Modena, 1558), 225–6; cf. *OF* vii. 56–65.
[58] *Dell'Hercole*, 230–1. Allusions to *Aen.* 4. 296–396 abound.
[59] *GL* xvi. 34. 3–6.
[60] *OF* xvii. 48. 5.
[61] *GL* ii. 55. 6.

là dove *l'irascibile è quasi guerriero e ministro della ragione* in raffrenare l'altro che le fa contrasto.[62]

The concupiscible appetite is very often like a rebellious populace, which, rising up and making a riot in the mind, refuses to give obedience to reason; whereas the irascible appetite is, as it were, the warrior and servant of reason in restraining the other appetite which opposes it.

In this passage, Tasso is recalling the moment when Rinaldo refigures Aeneas's departure from Dido. It is 'sdegno *guerrier de la ragion* feroce' which draws the warrior back from his cupidinous rebellion to the assault on Jerusalem. The passage in the *Discorsi* on the relative powers of love and anger in pagan and Christian epics draws on Tasso's own practical experience of translating a moment of crisis in a classical epic into modern terms. And this breakthrough in motivating the epic hero haunted Tasso throughout his subsequent career as a literary and ethical theorist. The discussion of Rinaldo in the Allegory quotes the line on *sdegno*, and accords it a specially significant role in the psychological meaning of the poem.[63] In his discussion 'Della virtù eroica e della carità' Tasso emphasizes the need for more than passive prudence in the epic hero by further reference to this Platonic notion.[64] He had Plato in mind—almost certainly in Ficino's translation—when he constructed a new motive for his hero's departure:

Itaque sermo testatur, iram saepe pugnare adversus concupiscentiam . . . iram asserimus animae partibus inter se dissidentibus pro ratione arma capessere.[65]

And so this anecdote shows that anger often fights against desire . . . we say that, when the parts of the mind are warring with each other, anger takes up arms for reason.

It is likely that this was among the 'alcune postille' (few bits) of Plato which the poet reread when he composed his Allegory.[66] The parallel

---

[62] Edn. cit. 106.

[63] 'Questa virtù impetuosa, veemente ed invitta, come che non possa interamente essere da un sol cavaliero figurata, è nondimeno principalmente significata da Rinaldo; come ben s'accenna in quel verso ove di lui si parla: "Sdegno guerrier della ragion feroce."' (This forceful, vehement, and invincible virtue, although it could not be entirely represented by a single knight, is none the less chiefly signified by Rinaldo, as is clear in that verse where it is said of him 'Disdain, fierce warrior of reason'); *Prose*, ed. Guasti, i. 306.

[64] 'da l'una parte par che sia suo ufficio il por freno a le passioni; da l'altra Platon vuole, che *l'ira sia guerriero della ragione*; e buon guerriero non può essere chi con molta veemenza e ferocità non combatte' (on the one hand it appears that its duty is to restrain the passions; on the other hand Plato has it that *anger is the warrior of reason*; and a good warrior cannot be someone who does not fight with great vehemence and ferocity). Ibid. ii. 193. Published 1582.

[65] *Omnia Divini Platonis Opera tralatione Marsilii Ficini* (Basle, 1532), 584, translating *Republic* 440a–b. Ficino captures, as modern translators do not, the martial metaphors of the Greek which caught Tasso's imagination.

[66] *Lettere*, ed. Guasti, i. 187.

with Rinaldo's rational *sdegno* when leaving Armida shows that Tasso also had Plato's treatment of anger as a rational emotion in the *Republic* at the front of his mind when composing the *Liberata*.[67]

But it was not just Plato who helped Tasso's revision of the *Aeneid*. The allegorical conquest of love by *sdegno* is also prefigured by Ariosto's qualifications of the romance ethos in the later *Furioso*. Tasso's pointed hostility to the later part of the poem cannot disguise the role it played in making his own. In canto xlii, Ariosto tells how Rinaldo sets out for the last time on his pursuit of Angelica under the pretext of capturing Baiardo for his emperor. As he mopes over Angelica's marriage, the amorous hero is assaulted by an allegorical figure of Jealousy, from whom he is rescued by an anonymous Knight, whose name, it transpires, is Sdegno. He and Rinaldo join forces, and together stumble on the fountain which removes love. Rinaldo drinks, is cured of his passion, and returns in earnest to his imperial task.[68] *Sdegno* covers the semantic ground of disdain for a lover as well as martial vehemence.[69] In Ariosto's episode the Knight operates on the boundary between the amorous and the martial senses of the term: his martial activity conquers Jealousy, and it is in the company of Sdegno that Rinaldo finally loses his love. Yet this tale of love's death remains an allegorical, rather than a naturalistic account of the role played by *sdegno* in conquering passion. In Tasso's Armida episode the structure of emotion is the same; but the allegorical foundation for the action leaks through into the literal level of motive. Tasso's anatomy of passion makes Rinaldo's departure grow from his martial nature, rather than resulting from the intervention of allegorical figures like Ariosto's Sdegno, or his Melissa, or Cinthio's Aretia, who make the hero act against his pitiful emotions. Rinaldo is a soldier even when Armida clings to him:

> Prendergli cerca allor la destra o 'l manto,
> supplichevole in atto, ei *s'arretra*,

---

[67] See further Michael Murrin, *The Allegorical Epic: Essays in its Rise and Decline* (Chicago and London, 1980), 87–127. Tasso remarked apropos of the Allegory (to Scipione Gonzaga, 15 June 1576) 'Lessi già tutte l'opere di Platone, e mi rimasero molti semi ne la mente de la sua dottrina' (I read all the works of Plato a while ago, and many seeds of his teaching remained planted in my mind); *Lettere*, ed. Guasti, i. 187. His use of the past historic tense shows that his debt to Plato was long-standing, rather than, as Murrin suggests, p. 98, developed by his recent reading. He did not simply apply an allegorical gloss of Platonic psychology to his poem in the late 1570s and early 1580s.

[68] *OF* xlii. 40–67.

[69] It is often opposed to *pietà* in Petrarch: 'Ogni angelica vista, ogni atto umile | che giamai in donna ov'amor fosse apparve, | fora uno sdegno a lato quel ch'io dico' (Every angelic look, every humble act, which ever had appeared in woman or in love, is like disdain beside that of which I speak); *Petrarch's Lyric Poems: The 'Rime Sparse' and Other Lyrics*, ed. and trans. Robert M. Durling (Cambridge, Mass., 1976), 123. 9–11; cf. *OF* i. 49.

resiste e vince; e in lui trova impedita
Amor entrata, il lagrimar l'uscita.[70]

She tried to take his right hand or his cloak in a gesture of supplication; but he drew himself up, resisted, and conquered; Love found the way to him blocked, and tears found the way out blocked.

'Arretrare le truppe' means to draw back or rally troops. Rinaldo's ability to leave Armida may be a psychological allegory of how the irascible passions make the cupidinous subject to Reason, but it is also a story about a soldier who rallies his mental resources, resists and fights off a woman—a story which is told in language that fits its hero like a gauntlet.

Once *sdegno* has driven out love, Tasso allows his hero a belated concession to the emotional make-up of his Italian forefathers. He experiences compassion which, like its Virgilian ancestor, has no motive power:

Non entra l'Amor a rinovar nel seno,
che ragion congelò, la fiamma antica;
v'entra pietate in quella vece almeno,
pur compagna d'Amor, benché pudica.[71]

Love did not come back to renew its presence in his breast, since reason had frozen over the old passion; in its stead came pity, the pure companion of love, though chaste.

Tasso's hero does not have to feel his way through the jungle of conceptual entanglements which hinders the early attempts of Ariosto's heroes to proceed in a straight line towards their duty. In the early *Furioso* love and *pietà* and desire and action are all aspects of the muddlesome appetency of the human mind; for Tasso they are carefully, perhaps too carefully, distinct. Pity without love, and love without active assistance, are almost inconceivable until the last phase of *Orlando furioso*; but here the almost allegorical anatomy of passion allows that pity—or is it dutiful affection for a woman who loves him?—be felt without love, and without any necessary connection to amorous errancy.

Rinaldo's first major action on his return to the Christian camp is to attempt the task in which his cupidinous double, Tancred, had failed: to destroy the enchanted grove. It has grown in voluptuousness and imaginary richness during his absence. He has to wander through bird-song, cross over a stream on a magic golden bridge which collapses behind him, and witness a bevy of slinkily clad maidens emerge from the womb of an oak

---

[70] *GL* xvi. 51. 5–8. Tasso boasted to Luca Scalabrino: 'Ma certo, o l'affezione m'inganna, tutte le parti de l'allegoria son in guisa legate fra loro, ed in maniera corispondono al senso litterale del poema' (But surely, unless my affection blinds me, all the parts of the allegory are in a way interconnected, and in a way correspond to the literal sense of the poem). *Lettere*, ed. Guasti, i. 179.

[71] *GL* xvi. 52. 1–4.

tree and dance round him. Armida then emerges from an amorous myrtle
tree, and begs him to take off his helmet for a kiss:

> Seguia parlando, e in bei pietosi giri
> volgeva i lumi e scoloria i sembianti,
> falseggiando i dolcissimi sospiri
> e i soavi singulti e i vaghi pianti,
> tal che incauta pietade a quei martíri
> intenerir potea gli aspri diamanti;
> ma il cavalier, accorto sí, non crudo,
> piú non v'attende, e stringe il ferro ignudo.[72]

She carried on talking, and in lovely piteous rounds rolled her eyes, and changed
her colour, feigning the sweetest sighs, such that an unwary pity of such sufferings
could soften the hardest diamond. But the knight, curt but not cruel, listened
no more, and drew his naked sword.

Rinaldo shows no incautious pity as he smites at the trunk of the tree
until it falls to the ground. The phantoms of the forest vanish as its trunk
splinters. His violent action is given no motivating passion at all: it is a
bare, blank fact, a destruction of his amorous past, which requires him
simply not to hear Armida's theatrical gestures of pity, and to evacuate
all feeling from the heart. Those things which pity renders possible—the
magical crossing of religious boundaries, the creation of fantastical edifices
in which one sees one's own desires projected in the world—are all
killed.

And this is deeply uncomfortable, the more so when one recognizes
that Rinaldo's ruthless destruction of the grove is a re-enactment of a
strangely violent source. The chief classical figure to destroy a haunted
grove is Julius Caesar in Lucan's *Pharsalia*. He is the most burningly
equivocal character in classical epic, who releases a suicidal energy on
Rome, in which political ideals collapse into their opposites, as the
Republican leader fights to become the absolute ruler of Rome. The civil
wars he sets loose on his city lead to a general rushing of self against self,
an implosion of ideals in violent insanity, in which even the sober Roman
virtue of *pietas* is turned into no more than a motive for killing one's
wounded relations with swiftness and precision.[73] Caesar's destruction of
the sacred grove, which is haunted by the memory and fear of earlier
deities, is his first violation of a Roman sanctum, and it marks a terrifying
willingness to take sacrilege upon himself:

---

[72] *GL* xviii. 33.
[73] *Phars.* 4. 565–6. See further pp. 181–3 below.

inplicitas magno Caesar torpore cohortes
ut vidit, primus raptam librare bipennem
ausus et aeriam ferro proscindere quercum
effatur merso violata in robora ferro:
'iam ne quis vestrum dubitet subvertere silvam,
credite me fecisse nefas.'[74]

When Caesar saw that his cohorts were paralysed with inertia, he dared to be first in seizing up and swinging an axe, and chopped a high oak. Driving the blade into the desecrated tree, he said: 'Now whoever fears to overturn the wood, think that I performed the sacrilege.'

Lucan's wood is fraught with numinal fears, filled with rotting images of unknown and antiquated gods. If Caesar's destruction of this wood is a liberation from past terrors, it is still, none the less a 'nefas', a sacrilegious crime. Tasso's use of this episode to provide the core, pivotal moment of his poem, when Rinaldo returns to active service after his dalliance with Armida, is powerfully charged with self-destructive perversity. In order to loosen the hold of contemporary versions of pitiful heroism on his hero, Tasso identifies him with the most unbalanced, and urgently destructive, hero from past epic. Pagan sacrilege translates into Christian virtue. The episode is locked into the ruthless logic of reviving the past: if modern categories of experience—simple passions like pity and rage—seem not to re-create the contours of past feeling, then one option remains: the alien energy of the past can at least be approached through the ruthless destruction of these present anachronisms. If a modern passion impedes the progress of a text towards its prototype, then it must be killed. But such a destruction of the modern remains a violation of one's own mode of seeing, a kind of sacrilege against the experiences of the present. The sword of Rinaldo, sinking into the image of Armida in the myrtle, is desperately suggestive of the self-violating imagination which led Tasso to hack large sections of romance episodic intrusions from his poem in the interests of a return to formal, classical unity, when he came to recast the poem into the *Gerusalemme conquistata* after his ordeal with the Inquisition. But the poem is more deeply, anguishingly heretical than even Tasso or his inquisitors would recognize: it had taken the violence of pagan sacrilege into the heart of its hero, into the innermost crannies of its structure. This is what it means for Tasso to re-create the past: it is to mutilate the constructions of the present, by means of an alien energy.

[74] *Phars.* 3. 432–6.

5
Spenser

Some form of sympathy is an essential part of a response to the past. Without a sense of genealogical affiliation, or a more chancy, friendly sense that the concerns of past and present overlap, past modes of feeling seem the products of a strange country, separated by alien rites and strange practices from present modes of thought. To enter this strange domain without some sense of kinship with its modes of feeling requires either the extreme violence of conquest, in which present values are imposed upon past structures of thought, or else a similarly violent effort to eradicate present attitudes from the mind. There is no author so prey to this double violence against self and past as Tasso; and there is no author who feels so keenly the tortured energy released by an antiquarianism which seeks vainly to strip away layers of anachronistic misreadings from past texts.

The Faerie Queene might seem at first to be written in a quite different spirit. It is a bewildering amalgam of topicality and timelessness, which seems to celebrate the power of the author to blend different periods, different writers, and different idioms into one vast composite, with little sign that such a process is difficult or dangerous. Spenser's language mingles archaism with contemporary usage, and his imaginary location, Faerie-land, is at once a distant, idealized space, and a parallel version of things going on next door. The poem's allegory ranges from the very recent history of England to an atemporal world of myth, from which people, and even time itself, are, for brief instants, banished. These visionary moments, such as the dance of the Graces in Book VI, or the endless self-regeneration of Adonis in Book III, are fragile and private myths of seclusion. Such episodes fearfully remind the prying eyes of their interpreters that they, like Time with his 'flaggy wings' rampaging through the Garden of Adonis, could destroy the beauties they admire. A love of such fleeting moments, which remain in the mind as glimpses of glory, is what it means to love Spenser. And part of the love the poem evokes is a fearful recognition that these visions can be violated, that a backward glance to gloss or to anatomize could destroy them. *The Faerie Queene* has remained a classic partly through its ability to persuade interpreters that their activity is a kind of sacrilege—that to attach unified interpretations to the poem is less what it means to experience Spenser than to mull over his writing, absorb its rhythms, and misremember it. Readers, like the intrusive Faunus, who spies on Diana in the *Mutabilitie Cantos*, or the over-eager Calidore, who frightens the Graces from the poet Colin Clout in Book VI, and makes the poet substitute a pedantic gloss for his dancing vision, could unmake the world which they seek to relish.[1]

The chapter which follows does not attempt to nail meanings to such elusive moments, but to work into them through their literary and historical genealogy. It argues that *The Faerie Queene* tries to transcend the epic romance tradition, for reasons which have to do both with difficulties ingrained in the genre, and with the more immediate pressures which faced an Elizabethan epic poet. The poem attempts both to deploy and to overgo the ferocious negativity wrought into the mode by Tasso. For Tasso, the way to return to the narrative shape and motive structures of classical epic was to fight off pity; and he was self-sacrificially aware that this process can terminate only in a wasteland, the ruins of an enchanted forest, destroyed by a ruthless warrior. Spenser responded powerfully to this dynamic force in the tradition: his knights often hover between pity and rage, before they act in anger. When Guyon undergoes a mini-Odyssey to the Bowre of Blisse, the Palmer, with a voice that blurs into that of Tasso, warns him to keep a straight course, and to resist the alluring cries for pity which beseeching damsels utter from the shore. When Guyon duly arrives at the Bowre, the sneaking influence of the erotic remains in his sideways glances at the damsels who bathe naked there; but the linear plot of his epic task continues purposefully forward, and terminates in a blast of rage. His 'rigour pittilesse' destroys the whole delightsome edifice, and nothing withstands 'the tempest of his wrathfulnesse'.[2]

Such moments, in which pity is violently resisted, take on a new and highly topical dimension in Elizabethan England. Queen Elizabeth I, to whom the poem is dedicated, and whose image is refracted and multiplied through the many female characters in the poem, nurtured and strategically deployed a reputation for pity in a more systematic way than any ruler since Virgil's Augustus. Part of the purpose of *The Faerie Queene*, I shall argue, is to use epic romance—a mode which creates, then abruptly cuts off pitiful digressions—to urge Spenser's Queen to a less wilfully random mode of supremacy. But *The Faerie Queene* also, at the same time, seeks to create some alternative to the increasingly attenuated, bleachingly irascible, episodes of *Gerusalemme liberata*, to provide some vision of life,

---

[1] *FQ* VII. vi. 36–55; VI. x. 4–29.
[2] *FQ* II. xii.

as it were, after the savage renunciation of pity which leads to the destruction of the Bowre of Bliss.

It is these two pressures that create the visionary moments in *The Faerie Queene*. The poem generates a narrative mode which enfolds within itself and overgoes both the aimless, processful wanderings of Ariosto, and the devoted linearity of Tasso. Spenser's desire to create such a narrative mode—an alternative version of epic romance—leads him towards timeless, placeless myths, which dwell on reproduction and change. These mythical, personless moments, which include the evocation of endless mutability which animates the Garden of Adonis, and the living digressions of the *Mutabilitie Cantos*, are the centres of the Spenserian experience: they seem to grow beyond human concerns, into a realm magically removed from topicality. But their magic is intertwined with what is, perhaps, the chief aim of *The Faerie Queene*. These visionary episodes are part of an attempt, which runs though the whole poem, to create a language which might obliquely persuade a queen who prided herself on her pity, and on her rigid virginity, that there are times to kill and conquer; that there are times to follow the law, and not the clement instincts of the monarch; that there are better ways to make life continue than through the whimsical pardonings of a queen; and, above all, that there are times to breed. As this chapter will argue, these pressures from inside and outside the genre of epic romance combine to make the most intimate, oblique, and mythically charged moments in *The Faerie Queene*.

SPENSER AND ARIOSTO: *THE FAERIE QUEENE*, BOOK III

The Faerie Queene may well have begun life as an effort to emulate the sparkling disparateness of Ariosto.[3] *Orlando furioso* was *the* epic model in Spenser's circle during the formative period of its composition. Gabriel

---

[3] Josephine Waters Bennett, *The Evolution of 'The Faerie Queene'* (Chicago, 1942), esp. 138–53. On relations between the two poets, see Robert M. Durling, *The Figure of the Poet in Renaissance Epic* (Cambridge, Mass., 1965), 223, who writes that Spenser is 'informed with the passionate idealism that is very different from Ariosto's Horatian equanimity'. Cf. Mario Praz, *The Flaming Heart: Essays on Crashaw, Machiavelli and Other Studies in the Relations between Italian and English Literature* (New York, 1958), 298; R. E. N. Dodge, 'Spenser's Imitations from Ariosto', *PMLA* 12 (1897), 151–204; A. H. Gilbert, 'Spenser's Imitations from Ariosto: Supplementary', *PMLA* 34 (1919), 225–32. A more sensitive account is in Graham Hough, *A Preface to 'The Faerie Queene'* (London, 1962), 25–47. On Ariosto in England, see further Jacob Schoembs, *Ariosts Orlando furioso in der Englischen Literatur des Zeitalters der Elizabeth*, Strasburg Doctoral Thesis (Soden, a.T., 1898); Anna Benedetti, *L''Orlando furioso' nella vita intellettuale del popolo inglese* (Florence, 1914); Joseph Gibaldi, 'The Fortunes of Ariosto in England and America', in Aldo Scaglione (ed.), *Ariosto 1974 in America* (Ravenna, 1974), 135–77; Peter De Sa Wiggins, 'Spenser's Anxiety', *Modern Language Notes*, 103 (1988), 75–86.

Harvey's lost epic poem *Anticosmopolita*, which may have been begun in the 1580s, comprised 'sundrie royale Cantos, (nigh as much in quantitie, as Ariosto) in celebration of her majesties most prosperous, & in truth glorious government'.[4] Even the verbose Harvey may have sought to emulate *Orlando furioso* in more than simple bulk; but Spenser stated his intention, very early on in his thought about *The Faerie Queene*, to 'overgo', rather than simply to imitate, Ariosto.[5]

This intention issues chiefly in an effort to contain the digressive force of love by allegorically redirecting it towards images of virtuous nobility, and ultimately to a goal of active sexual fertility. This would make two apparently disparate motives collapse together: concern for honour would melt into love. Arthur's quest for Gloriana—by whom, Spenser wrote to Ralegh, 'I meane glory in my generall intention'[6]—is the largest and most obvious example of this redirection of desire: the Prince seeks her both as an allegorical image of Glory and, presumably, as a dynastic partner. Such a fusion of love and honour into the composite motive 'love of honour' seems to be the serenely idealistic unifying purpose of *The Faerie Queene*. It runs through Book III, which may well contain many of the earliest fragments which Spenser composed:

> that sweet fit, that doth true beautie loue,
> And choseth vertue for his dearest Dame,
> Whence spring all noble deeds and neuer dying fame.[7]

This sounds simple enough: love directed to a noble object ennobles itself, and gives rise to noble actions. But motives as disparate as love and honour cannot be made to melt together simply by an authorial assertion. And these lines, when placed in their context in Book III, seem conscious of the difficulties of the project they propose. They occur in the middle of a flashback which tells how Britomart came to love Artegall. Her initially timid love for a man in a mirror comes eventually to motivate her entry into the world of chivalric action; and this description of heroic love comes precisely at the transitional moment between girlish narcissism and active martial pursuit.[8] This translation of desire, from something purposelessly random, into something directedly purposeful, would be one way of overgoing Ariosto: dutified emotion could tame the erotic energy of *Orlando furioso*. But the goal evoked by these lines is shown by

---

[4] Quoted in Virginia F. Stern, *Gabriel Harvey: His Life, Marginalia, and Library* (Oxford, 1979), 51.

[5] *The Works of Edmund Spenser: A Variorum Edition*, ed. E. Greenlaw *et al.*, 10 vols. (Baltimore, 1932–49), x. 471. Cited as *Var*.

[6] *Var*. i. 168.

[7] *FQ* III. iii. 1.

[8] Kathleen Williams, *Spenser's World of Glass* (Berkeley and Los Angeles, 1966), 93–4.

the surrounding action to be implicated in the complex processes of correctively imitating past texts, and of redirecting their modes of feeling, and this process is shown to be fraught with difficulty. The early section of Britomart's story is modelled on a passionately erotic, and ultimately fatal, love story of dubious provenance. Her love for Artegall derives very closely from a pseudo-Virgilian poem called *Ciris*, which is an erotic epyllion of a decidedly uncivic character, rather than an epic poem. In *Ciris*, the mythical girl Scylla falls in love with her country's enemy, Midas, and destroys her city by cutting off her father's purple lock of hair, which magically protects the town against invasion.[9] Scylla's love is consummated only in her metamorphosis into a bird, as Midas drags her through the sea to punish her amorously motivated treachery. Spenser drew most of Britomart's childish love—her frantic pining, her desperate complaints—from the section of *Ciris* which describes the height of Scylla's uncivic passion, as she proceeds tremblingly at night to murder her father.[10] Treason is in the air. And the destructive metamorphosis of Spenser's heroine seems imminent, as her nurse, Glauce, compares Britomart to Myrrha, Biblis, and Pasiphaë. The heroine herself caps these lustful metamorphoses with that of Narcissus:

> I fonder, then *Cephisus* foolish child,
> Who hauing vewed in a fountaine shere
> His face, was with the loue thereof beguild;
> I fonder loue a shade, the bodie farre exild.[11]

It is shortly after this super-Ovidian perversity that Spenser talks of the ennobling power of 'that sweet fit' of passion. The story suddenly swerves away from its original: it relates not its heroine's metamorphosis, but the metamorphosis of love, from frenzied girlish passion into a love of nobility.

The new form of desire introduced in the proem to canto iii is far from the kind of emptily sententious idealizing which readers so often find, and then find objectionable, in Spenser. It sits uneasily against the uncivic and narcissistic love of an epyllion, struggling to transform it into the motive force of an active and fertile life. It is a shocking assertion of the novelty, and a suggestion of the improbability, of such a love. If this

---

[9] *Ciris: A Poem Attributed to Virgil*, ed. R. O. A. M. Lyne (Cambridge, 1978), ll. 220–377; see Merritt Y. Hughes, *Virgil and Spenser* (Cambridge, Mass., 1929), 348–54.

[10] See James Nohrnberg, *The Analogy of 'The Faerie Queene'* (Princeton, NJ, 1976), 446–7. William Nelson, *The Poetry of Spenser* (New York, 1963), 142–3, regards this imitation as 'perverse', and Jan Karel Kouwenhoven, *Apparent Narrative as Thematic Metaphor: The Organization of 'The Faerie Queene'* (Oxford, 1983), 136, makes the extraordinary assertion that 'Britomart resembles Scylla in helplessly causing the state's doom in her love.'

[11] *FQ* III. ii. 44.

radical revision of the ethos of the original could be sustained, a closed metamorphic tale would have to be turned into an open-ended dynastic tale of chivalric pursuit. But this process of transformation is by no means easy. Glauce takes Britomart to Merlin's cave, where the heroine witnesses a prophecy of the heroic offspring that her love will create. This encounter is a close parallel to a breezily random episode at the start of *Orlando furioso*, when Bradamante—who is already desperately seeking Ruggiero— is lured into a pit, where, by chance, she encounters Merlin and Melissa, who tell her, quite unnecessarily, that her love has a grand future. Since his advice is gratuitous, Merlin can only tell Bradamante to keep on with the good work ('segue animosamente il tuo sentiero'[12]). The Italian episode is fortuitous, is without motive effect on its heroine, and fits in only with the chaotic randomness of the early *Furioso*. In Spenser's version, however, it breathes directed purpose: it is a sought encounter which starts Britomart on her quest. At the end of the prophecy, Britomart is showered with *exempla* of female prowess which spur her to act. The prophecy, and the dynastic awareness which it brings, is vital to the progress of the narrative, and to the transformation of its heroine's motivation: without it the events of Book III would never have occurred.[13] Glauce precipitates the girl's departure by describing the Saxon warrior Angela and the heroines that Britomart's family has produced:

> And sooth, it ought your courage much inflame,
> To heare so often, in that royall hous,
> From whence to none inferiour ye came,
> Bards tell of many women valorous
> Which haue full many feats aduenturous
> Performd, in paragone of proudest men.[14]

Ariosto's throwaway prophetic interlude is modelled on the vision of Rome's future glories which Aeneas receives from his father in *Aeneid* 6. Although Spenser draws far less descriptive detail from Virgil's descent to Hades than Ariosto,[15] his version of the episodes is none the less much closer to the structural effect of the prophecy in the *Aeneid*. After the revelations of Book 6, Aeneas becomes less nostalgic and more taciturn, and the poem as a whole becomes more forward-looking and martial.[16] Glauce's exhortation, and the knowledge of her future, similarly inspire

---

[12] *OF* iii. 19. 4; see *Var.* iii. 227, and appendix V, ibid. 367–76.

[13] See further Andrew Fichter, *Poets Historical: Dynastic Epic in the Renaissance* (New Haven, Conn., and London, 1982), 156–206.

[14] *FQ* iii. iii. 54.

[15] *Aen.* 6. 756–853; Hughes, *Virgil and Spenser*, 354–7.

[16] See e.g. Viktor Pöschl, *The Art of Virgil*, trans. G. Seligson (Ann Arbor, Mich., 1962), 38: 'Memory becomes hope; retrospective longing for Troy gives way to a visionary longing for Rome'; K. W. Gransden, *Virgil's Iliad* (Cambridge, 1984), 32; Fichter, *Poets Historical*, 6–8.

Britomart with a newly martial mode of feeling:

> Her harty words so deepe into the mynd
> Of the young Damzell sunke, that great desire
> Of warlike armes in her forthwith they tynd,
> And generous stout courage did inspire.[17]

Introverted love is transformed into 'great *desire* | Of warlike armes', and the heroine is moved by her new ethos into the public realm. Britomart emerges from her seamy epyllion world by emulating her ancestors' deeds as related by poets. Spenser shows a consciousness of the purposive shape of Virgil which lies behind the random encounter in Ariosto; but he does not aspire to take on that shape. His revision of *Orlando furioso* is not a direct effort to return to the original which lies behind it; his transformation is deeply topical and contemporary. In order to turn Britomart from a schoolgirl with a crush into a heroine with a purpose, he relies on a commonplace of humanist thought in the sixteenth century, that a hereditary aristocracy should continually renovate its ancestral virtue in order to merit its supremacy: 'it fortuned by the providence of god that of those good men were ingendred good children, who beinge brought up in vertue, and perceivinge the cause of the advauncement of their progenitours, endevoured them selfes by imitation of vertue, to be equall to them in honour and autoritie.'[18] This mode of thinking forces his heroine's passion into martial ambition, and helps to transform an epyllion and a prophetic interlude in a romance into a unified tale of love's growth, a tale that feels strongly directed to a purpose, and which has a Virgilian purposiveness to it.

The *Ciris*/Merlin episode is the start of Britomart's story in literal time; but it is not the first episode which Spenser relates in the tangled sequence of narration which makes up Book III.[19] We do not learn of the purpose which underlies Britomart's actions at the opening of her adventure. The first thing she does in the narrative sequence of Book III seems, indeed, to be strikingly random and unnecessary: she unhorses

---

[17] *FQ* III. iii. 57. 'Spenser, unlike his Italian contemporaries, but like Vergil, makes knowledge of the nation's history and destiny the final preparation for the hero', W. Stanford Webb, 'Vergil in Spenser's Epic Theory', *ELH* 4 (1937), 76. Cf. Thomas P. Roche, jun., *The Kindly Flame: A Study of the Third and Fourth Books of Spenser's Faerie Queene* (Princeton, NJ, 1964), 61–2, who ignores the motive power of Angela. See also Fichter, *Poets Historical*, 158–61.

[18] Sir Thomas Elyot, *The Boke Named the Governour*, ed. H. H. S. Croft, 2 vols. (London, 1880), ii. 28. See further Ruth Kelso, *The Doctrine of the English Gentleman in the Sixteenth Century*, University of Illinois Studies in Language and Literature, 14 (Urbana, Ill., 1929), esp. 24–5.

[19] Cf. the Letter to Ralegh: 'a Poet thrusteth into the middest, even where it most concerneth him, and there recoursing to the thinges forepaste, and divining of things to come, maketh a pleasing Analysis of all', *Var.* i. 169. Catherine Rodgers, *Time in the Narrative of the 'Faerie Queene'*, Salzburg Studies in English Literature, 5 (Salzburg, 1973), 51–61, notes some of the disruptions in fictive time in Book III.

Guyon in a joust. After the two knights are reconciled, Florimell flees past the posse of warriors, whereupon the male members of the party disperse in pursuit of this vagrant version of Ariosto's Angelica, who flees past them with a Foster in hot pursuit. The sequence provides no reference points for a reader: even the heroine's identity is concealed, and the knights show no centred purpose, but flee off in all directions. And when the episode is compared with its chief source, this randomness seems all the stronger: all motive seems to have been evacuated from it. Britomart's fight with Guyon derives from Bradamante's first action in *Orlando furioso*, when she attacks Sacripante in order to prevent his raping Angelica.[20] This lustful purpose is tidied away in Spenser, and the encounter becomes a chivalric romp with honour rather than pursuit of a woman as its object. Having been dishonoured by his defeat, Guyon is angry as men of honour tend to be when humiliated. Coëffeteau wrote that the main cause of choler is 'that men desire passionately to see themselves honoured':[21]

> Full of disdainefull wrath, he fierce vprose,
> For to reuenge that foule reprochfull shame...[22]

The Palmer suppresses this wrathful outburst; then follows another piece of apparently serene idealizing, in a stanza which has caused more flak to fly at Spenser than any of his other imitations from Ariosto:

> O goodly vsage of those antique times,
>   In which the sword was seruant vnto right;
>   When not for malice and contentious crimes,
>   But all for praise, and proofe of manly might,
>   The martiall brood accustomed to fight:
>   Then honour was the meed of victorie,
>   And yet the vanquished had no despight:
>   Let later age that noble vse enuie,
> Vile rancour to auoid, and cruell surquedrie.[23]

This imitation of Ariosto's slippered irony is generally reckoned to reel on stilted rhetoric.[24] Its original occurs when Ariosto asserts for the first

[20] Bennett, *Evolution*, 145; W. J. B. Owen, 'Narrative Logic and Imitation in *The Faerie Queene*', *Comparative Literature*, 7 (1955), 332–3.

[21] *A Table of Humaine Passions, with their causes and effects*, trans. E. Grimestone (London, 1621), 568. Cf. Pierre de la Primaudaye, *The French Academie*, trans. T[homas] B[owes] (London, 1589), 296.

[22] *FQ* III. i. 9.

[23] Ibid. 13; see *Var.* iii. 368–9.

[24] Dodge, 'Spenser's Imitations', 171–2; Ernest de Selincourt, *The Poetical Works of Spenser* (Oxford, 1912), p. xlii; cf. Alfonso Sammut, *La fortuna dell'Ariosto nell'Inghilterra elisabettiana* (Milan, 1971), 52–5.

time that pursuit of ladies is the overriding force in his poem. Ferraù and
Rinaldo, rivals hammering on each other's helms only a moment before,
join forces to pursue Angelica after she has suddenly disappeared and
thereby rendered their battle pointless:

> Oh gran bontà de' cavallieri antiqui!
> Eran rivali, eran di fé diversi,
> e si sentian degli aspri colpi iniqui
> per tutta la persona anco dolersi;
> e pur per selve oscure e calli obliqui
> insieme van senza sospetto aversi.[25]

Oh, the amazing goodness of the ancient knights! They were rivals, they were
of different faiths, and they still felt the pain of hard, unfair blows all over their
bodies; then, through dark woods and twisted ways they went forward together
without suspicion.

The reconciliation of the two knights, with this stanza of commentary,
defines the motive force of the *Furioso*'s early stages, with a delicate jab
at the *bontà* of those ancient knights, whose goodness consists solely in
taking the easiest means to further their desires. Spenser's stanza is
apparently less ironic in defining the main motive of his poem; but in its
setting, this direct statement of motive priorities loses much of its
certainty. It does not mark a return to a stable 'antiquity' which simply
eradicates the lustfulness of Ariosto. His praise of the 'goodly usage'
comes directly after Guyon's violent rage at his defeat, which is the direct
consequence of a concern for personal honour. This potentially dissident
fragment of the synthetic motive 'love of fame' is checked by the Palmer
for prudential reasons rather than abstract principles of right. He 'gan to
feare | His toward perill and vntoward blame'. And, no sooner have the
knights been praised for pursuing honour in battle than they rush off in
pursuit of Florimell, as she flies from the Foster. They strive to out-
Foster the Foster:

> Which outrage when those gentle knights did see,
> 　　Full of great enuie and fell gealosy,
> They stayd not to auise, who first should bee,
> 　　But all spurd after fast, as they mote flie.[26]

Editors may try all they like to tease antiquated and noble senses out of
'enuie' and 'fell gealosy'; but to most sixteenth-century readers they
would sound suspiciously randy motives for noble knights to pursue.[27]

[25] *OF* i. 22.
[26] *FQ* iii. i. 18.
[27] See *The Faerie Queene*, ed. A. C. Hamilton (London, 1977), ad loc.

The whole sequence does have an irony, but an irony which is structural rather than tonal: the knights are praised for an antique excellence which the narrative shows they do not possess.

The entire opening sequence of Book III illustrates the most important fact about Spenser's ethos: it is synthetic. He attempts to yoke together the motive of love with the motive of honour, and these two elements are always on the brink of springing apart. A captious desire for personal glory is one degenerate form of his ideal; and uncontrolled lustful pursuit is the other. He places examples of both these forms of defect on either side of his most open statement of the ideal, and as a result the ideal seems elusive, to be no more than a wish, wryly conscious of its own failure to revive antique perfection.

Yet in between Guyon's angry outburst and the amorous errancy that follows it, Britomart stands unmoved and enigmatic. She is an unknown force when she encounters Guyon, and (apparently) feels nothing about the encounter. When the others rush off, her 'constant mind, | Would not so lightly follow beauties chace'.[28] Spenser protectively displaces all the deviant emotions she might feel on to other figures, leaving her almost a blank. This blankness of the heroine has something to do with the way his chief professed narrative motive is all but impossible to represent: it is not easy to show someone actually in the process of amorously pursuing honour, without representing them as either honour-conscious to the point of irascibility, or as simply loving. Spenser's ideal, since it is a synthesis of intrinsically irreconcilable forms of feeling, can only be represented in opposition to deviant forms of behaviour—be they desiring appetency or wrathful consciousness of honour. The ideal of an honour-loving chaste heroine as developed in cantos i and ii is illusory: so long as Britomart is represented externally, she appears to be resolutely pursuing Artegall; but as the plot moves forwards, so the story moves backwards, and we learn that this impassive heroine was once a wildly passionate little girl like the pseudo-Virgilian Scylla.[29]

And as the remarkably retrograde plot moves further forwards, so the story continues to move backwards. By canto iv it finally gets around to explaining the origins of the event with which the Book began: Florimell's provocative flight. And, most remarkably, it was Britomart who caused it. For critics who believe that Spenser tried in vain to imitate Ariosto in Book III, the fact that Britomart initiates Florimell's flight by wounding Marinell after the terrified lady has already rushed past her and her

---

[28] *FQ* III. i. 19.

[29] 'The *story* is the raw materials of the narrative, that is, the events in their chronological sequence. The *plot* is the narrative as actually shaped.' Robert Scholes, *Structuralism in Literature* (New Haven, Conn., and London, 1974), 80.

companions is the most glaring example of Spenser's inability to tell a story.[30] But Spenser's most characteristic technique is to unfold his meaning by *plot*, the order in which events are related, rather than by *story*, the actual order in which events occur. Britomart's belated initiation of Florimell's flight shows again the deep instability of Spenser's ethos. He acknowledges that to translate the texts of the immediate past into antique perfection is an impossibility: his praise of the 'goodly usage' is undercut by the mass desertion of the knights of maidenhead in pursuit of the first woman who moves; his representation of Britomart's 'constant mind' is followed by the story of her near-suicidal, near-treasonable youthful love. This in turn is followed by an account of how Florimell came to flee because of Britomart's amorous pique when Marinell gets in her way. These 'completing analepses'[31] fill in Britomart's past in such a way as to make her apparent constancy at the opening of Book III seem no more than apparent. She wounds Marinell with just the arbitrary passionateness with which her fellow knights pursue his fleeing love:

> Her former sorrow into suddein wrath,
> Both coosen passions of distroubled spright,
> Conuerting, forth she beates the dustie path;
> Loue and despight attonce her courage kindled hath.[32]

Spenser's synthesis of love and honour is just as likely to split into desperate love and frustrated rage in his heroine as in the hotheaded knights who seem at first to be so unlike her. And it is his heroine's susceptibility to those passions which initiates the circular, undynamic flow of the early stages of Book III.

The largest and most significant borrowing from *Orlando furioso* in Book III of *The Faerie Queene* displays the same desire to correct Ariosto, and shows the same resigned sense of the impossibilty of doing so perfectly. In canto v, Belphoebe rescues Timias from the Fosters, and nurses him back to physical health, whilst unwittingly inspiring him with a desperate unrequited love. This episode is closely and unmistakably modelled on the Angelica and Medoro episode in *Orlando furioso*, when Angelica pities, rescues, revives, loves, and marries Medoro. This moment is the imaginative core of *Orlando furioso*, where Ariosto's pitiful ethos liberates the melancholy sentiment of Virgil's story of Nisus and Euryalus, and turns pity into a motive which leads to sex, and thence to marriage. In *Orlando furioso*, Angelica feels unaccustomed pity for her version of the wounded Euryalus:

[30] Bennett, *Evolution*, 147–8.
[31] Gérard Genette, *Narrative Discourse*, trans. J. E. Lewin (Oxford, 1980), 51.
[32] *FQ* III. iv. 12.

insolita pietade in mezzo al petto
si sentì entrar per disusate porte,
che le fe' il duro cor tenero e molle.[33]

She felt unaccustomed pity enter the middle of her breast through unused doors, which made her hard heart soft and mild.

Spenser's heroine is less overwhelmed by her emotion:

Saw neuer liuing eye more heauy sight,
That could haue made a rocke of stone to rew,
Or riue in twaine: which when that Lady bright
Besides all hope with melting eyes did vew,
All suddeinly abasht she chaunged hew,
And with sterne horrour backward gan to start:
But when she better him beheld, she grew
Full of soft passion and vnwonted smart:
The point of pitty perced through her tender hart.[34]

The episode draws massive erotic dynamism from its original, which Spenser struggles to contain. In the episode as a whole he displaces Angelica's pitiful love from Belphoebe to the Squire, making him the main sufferer in the erotic drama; and this urgent need to protect Belphoebe (as a type of his chaste queen) from unchaste thoughts puts great pressure on the syntax of this stanza. A residuum of erotic pity remains. Line 4 fluidly leaves it in doubt whose eyes are melting. Hamilton opts for Belphoebe,[35] but the phrase may well continue the description in the previous stanza of the 'Christall humour' around Timias's eyes—and it is surely Timias who is 'besides all hope'. Yet the construction leaves Belphoebe the faintest glimmer of a sympathetic tear, which precedes, and perhaps precipitates, her violent recoil. Pity is represented as a more painfully intrusive passion ('point...perced') than in the source stanza: the heroine puts up an initial chaste reaction to its penetrative force, and ultimately does not allow compassion to cause her sexual surrender. Like Tasso, Spenser is fighting pity; like him too, he only succeeds by emptying his hero of emotion: Belphoebe's feelings, after this early burst of compassion, are left largely undescribed.

The Squire has the burden of repressing the libidinous subtext:

Long while he stroue in his courageous brest,
With reason dew the passion to subdew,
And loue for to dislodge out of his nest...

---

[33] *OF* xix. 20.
[34] *FQ* III. v. 30.
[35] Hamilton, edn. cit. ad loc.

> Vnthankfull wretch (said he) is this the meed,
> With which her soueraigne mercy thou doest quight?
> Thy life she saued by her gracious deed,
> But thou doest weene with villeinous despight,
> To blot her honour, and her heauenly light.[36]

Consciousness of honour, this time in the sense of 'sexual purity' stalls the Squire, and again prevents Spenser's episode from blossoming into a repeat of Ariosto's; and it is combined with an attempt to establish the due supremacy of reason over the rebel passions—a commonplace of humanist thought which was elegantly expressed by Spenser's schoolmaster: 'To keepe thinges in order, there is in the soule of man but one, though a verie honorable meane, which is the direction of reason: to bring things out of order there be two, the one strongheaded, which is the commaundement of courage, the other many headed, which is the entice ment of desires.'[37]

Overlaying both these familiar forces, set against the insurgent erotic subtext of Ariosto, is Spenser's elevation of pity from Ariosto's simple sentiment for a wounded soldier to a regal virtue, and ultimately to divine grace. Belphoebe's intervention is explicitly providential, unlike that of Angelica, which is attributed to 'caso';[38] and, on meeting his virgin rescuer, Timias initially echoes Aeneas's providential meeting with Venus.[39] The Squire recognizes his salvation as an act of grace, or 'soueraigne mercy', which he should requite by some fitter means than an attempted rape. John Stubbes, who was condemned to lose a hand for publishing *The Discovery of a Gaping Gulf whereinto England is like to be Swallowed by an other French Marriage* in 1579, offered devotion akin to that afforded God for his grace as recompense for the saving mercy which he sought from the Queen. Stubbes makes a chilling joke about the obligation he would have felt had the Queen pardoned him: 'There is nothing in me alredie to move youe, neither can I promisse any newe and worthy recompense of service dewe for so great a grace; for alasse! what can my poor hand performe?'[40] Mercy expresses power, and ensures devoted obedience, since its enabling condition is the capacity to save a subject. Its beneficiaries can never requite such saving grace. The sexual dynamics of Ariosto's episode are interrupted by the overlapping concepts of political obedience,

---

[36] *FQ* III. v. 44–5.
[37] Richard Mulcaster, *Positions, wherein those primitive circumstances be examined, which are necessarie for the training up of Children* (London, 1581), 73.
[38] *FQ* III. v. 27; *OF* xix. 17.
[39] 'Mercy deare Lord (said he) what grace is this, | ... Angell, or Goddesse do I call thee right?' III. v. 35; cf. *Aen.* 1. 328. See further Merritt Y. Hughes, 'Virgilian Allegory and *The Faerie Queene*', *PMLA* 44 (1929), 696–705.
[40] Printed in *Nugae Antiquae*, ed. Thomas Park, 2 vols. (London, 1804), i. 153.

religious devotion, and love for a gracious monarch.[41] The pressure of the contemporary once again transfigures Ariosto: courtly devotion to the Queen is used to put a stop to his unstoppable eroticism.

But the erotic force of Ariosto is suppressed rather than completely obliterated. Immediately after his monologue on his debt to Belphoebe, Timias yields himself completely to love, and as a result nearly dies. The canto ends with an elaborate description of Belphoebe's rose tree, which represents the 'soveraigne salve' of her virginity which she denies him. Roses are consistently associated in the romance tradition with vulnerable sexual purity. In *Orlando furioso* Ariosto coyly describes Medoro's conquest of Angelica as 'plucking the rose';[42] and the *Romaunt of the Rose* provides another urgent subtext in which a description of a rose tree is a prelude to prolonged attempts by the infatuated dreamer to pluck its buds.[43] The literary associations of the passage scream out that the Squire is about to make an assault on Belphoebe—and even his monologue on self-restraint insistently exploits the sexual potential of 'die'.[44] Yet Spenser subjects the forward-looking and erotic narrative instincts of a reader versed in the romance tradition to massive disappointment.

For his story does not go forward towards sex. It goes backwards. This interrupted seduction is followed immediately by the canto dealing with the Garden of Adonis. Spenser jolts suddenly back into a timeless past, in order to escape the erotic power which Ariosto's story brought with itself. In the funniest lines in *The Faerie Queene* (this, perhaps, indicates that its humour is not exactly side-splitting), Spenser tells his readers that all along they have been wondering, not about what the Squire will do next, but about the origins of Belphoebe:

> Well may I weene, faire Ladies, all this while
> Ye wonder, how this noble Damozell
> So great perfections did in her compile,
> Sith that in saluage forests she did dwell.[45]

No readers in their right mind—let alone someone who had read Ariosto—would have been wondering about where Belphoebe came from. The transition is the most violent example of Spenser's use of the narrative

---

[41] See further Michael O'Connell, *Mirror and Veil: The Historical Dimension of Spenser's 'Faerie Queene'* (Chapel Hill, NC, 1977), 107–24.

[42] *OF* xix. 33; cf. i. 42; Catullus 62. 39–47.

[43] Chaucer's translation of *The Romaunt of the Rose* follows the *Canterbury Tales* in both Thynne's *Workes of Geoffray Chaucer* (London, 1532) and Speght's *Workes of our Antient and Learned Chaucer* (London, 1598): Spenser would have seen it as one of Chaucer's major works.

[44] *FQ* III. v. 45–7.

[45] *FQ* III. vi. 1. Clarke Hulse, *Metamorphic Verse: The Elizabethan Minor Epic* (Princeton, NJ, 1981), 277, calls it 'the most "ingenious" of Ovidian transitions to so exalted a vision'.

technique which has (brilliantly) been called 'cantus interruptus'.[46] Ariosto loves to stop stories short, just tantalizingly short, of an expected climax. This technique was described by the ponderous Giovanni Battista Pigna as having two possible effects: it can occur at an opportune moment, in which case the mind rests content; or at an unexpected moment, when 'l'animo resta sospeso, & ne nasce perciò un desiderio che fa diletto' (the mind remains in suspense, and there grows from this a desire which makes delight).[47] Spenser's interruption of the narrative at the point of the Squire's languishing desire is, however, aimed at producing more than just delightful desire. It uses Ariosto against himself. One of the chief narrative devices of the *Furioso* is used to break off the one moment when Ariosto actually does show Angelica succumbing to a lover. Spenser then displaces and redirects the reader's prurient desire to see the story's consummation into dynastic curiosity. The intrusive narrator who begins canto vi knows exactly what he has created: a half-finished love story, and a love story which could never be finished for political reasons. Elizabeth, wrinkling, and increasingly hostile to any unsolicited advice about marriage in the 1580s, would not welcome a story about one of her types falling for a squire of low degree. John Stubbes, whose name was to become unfortunately appropriate, needed to beg for Elizabeth's saving mercy because he had published a pamphlet attacking her rumoured match with Alençon; he lost his hand despite his appeal. The axe falls across Spenser's version of the Angelica and Medoro story, too: better to cut off a story than represent a queenly type mingling with a squire, and risk losing that warm scribe his hand.

Spenser's greatest strength as a poet is his ability to turn the pressures of contemporaneity into myths, myths which transform the dynamics of earlier writers into something that seems at once to be timeless and rooted in the Elizabethan present. Two of the most substantial temporal digressions in the poem are the *Ciris*/Merlin episode and the canto dealing with the Garden of Adonis. Both occur at moments where queenly characters are unduly entangled in amorous affairs, and both use a flashback to contain and cap dangerous narrative material. But such digressions also have a powerful imaginative purpose in *The Faerie Queene*, with the strange identity of imaginative power and political fear that is so typical of this period:[48] in them Spenser takes episodes from his

---

[46] Daniel Javitch, '*Cantus Interruptus* in the *Orlando furioso*', Modern Language Notes, 95 (1980), 66–81.

[47] *I Romanzi* (Venice, 1554), 45.

[48] See Annabel Patterson, *Censorship and Interpretation: The Conditions of Writing and Reading in Early Modern England* (Madison, Wis., 1984), esp. intro. and ch. 1.

predecessors and transforms them into his new ethical vision.[49] The rapid
and embarrassed shift of tack to the birth of Belphoebe, and thence to
the Garden of Adonis, cuts off the erotic dynamism of the Belphoebe and
Timias story. The result is a curtailed version of Ariosto's story of
Cloridano and Medoro, which lacks its amorous sequel of Angelica's
deflowering. This termination of Ariosto's story is again strangely redolent
of Virgil: like the story of Euryalus, the tale of Timias is rudely
inconclusive, releasing passions which have no direct narrative consequences. Spenser's flashbacks point towards an epic past which predates
the sensuous delights of Ariosto.

But he does not simply amputate Ariosto's romance coda in order to
reduplicate the deadly, stagnant compassion of Virgil's tale; he uses the
residual erotic power of his romance predecessor to make an alternative
vision of sexuality. Timias's bungled and suppressed desires have no
direct historical sequel, but the narrative sequence grants them a chastened
consummation in the burgeoning sexuality with which canto vi begins.
Spenser turns to the origins of Belphoebe and Amoret. And he begins
their story with conception. The sexual union towards which he cannot
push his characters in the main narrative is acknowledged in a distant,
personless form:

> But wondrously they were begot, and bred
>> Through influence of th'heauens fruitfull ray,
>> As it in antique bookes is mentioned.
>> It was vpon a Sommers shynie day,
>> When *Titan* faire his beames did display,
>> In a fresh fountaine, farre from all mens vew,
>> She bath'd her brest, the boyling heat t'allay;
>> She bath'd with roses red, and violets blew,
> And all the sweetest flowres, that in the forrest grew.

> Till faint through irkesome wearinesse, adowne
>> Vpon the grassie ground her selfe she layd
>> To sleepe, the whiles a gentle slombring swowne
>> Vpon her fell all naked bare displayd;
>> The sunne-beames bright vpon her body playd,
>> Being through former bathing mollifide,
>> And pierst into her wombe, where they embayd
>> With so sweet sence and secret power vnspide,
> That in her pregnant flesh they shortly fructifide.[50]

---

[49] See further my essay 'Original Fictions: Metamorphoses in *The Faerie Queene*', in Charles
Martindale (ed.), *Ovid Renewed: Ovidian Influences on Literature and Art from the Middle Ages to the
Twentieth Century* (Cambridge, 1988), 99–119.
[50] *FQ* III. vi. 6–7.

The scene in which Chrysogone conceives is fraught with reminiscences of another erotic poet, whose treatment of love is far more perverse than that of Ariosto. Ovid's *Metamorphoses* have as their most distinctive narrative content sterile pursuit terminating in metamorphic fixity, and these frustrated pursuits through a deserted landscape often start in pastoral seclusion similar to that in which Chrysogone is discovered at the start of canto vi.[51] Noontime by a pool is a dangerous moment for Ovidian nymphs.[52] Had Ovid told the story of Chrysogone's conception, though, it would have indubitably ended with a preventive metamorphosis, or the rape of the heroine, say, by Apollo. Spenser cuts this anticipated violent climax, and substitutes for it sweet silent conception. As with the premature termination of the Squire's lust, the amorous urges of a predecessor are abruptly curtailed.

The story of Chrysogone is not a dead end, however; her spontaneous generation becomes the archetype of all generative processes. And to represent this ideal fecundity, Spenser once more uses one aspect of his predecessor's idiom to drive out another. He turns to another side of Ovid:

> Miraculous may seeme to him, that reades
>   So straunge ensample of conception;
>   But reason teacheth that the fruitfull seades
>   Of all things liuing, through impression
>   Of the sunbeames in moyst complexion,
>   Doe life conceiue and quickned are by kynd:
>   So after *Nilus* invndation,
>   Infinite shapes of creatures men do fynd,
> Informed in the mud, on which the Sunne hath shynd.
>
>   Great father he of generation
>   Is rightly cald, th'author of life and light;
>   And his faire sister for creation
>   Ministreth matter fit, which tempred right
>   With heate and humour, breedes the liuing wight.
> So sprong these twinnes in wombe of *Chrysogone* . . .[53]

This is almost a paraphrase of the *Metamorphoses*. Spenser adapts the account of the rebirth of animal life after the flood from Book 1 of Ovid's poem, but transforms it from a unique past event into a continuing process:

[51] Hugh Parry, 'Ovid's *Metamorphoses:* Violence in a Pastoral Landscape', *Transactions and Proceedings of the American Philological Association*, 95 (1964), 268–82. Cf. *Met.* 2. 417–24, 3. 407–12, 4. 297–304, 5. 577–603. For Spenser's use of these sinister *loci amoeni*, see Richard J. DuRocher, *Milton and Ovid* (Ithaca, NY, and London, 1985), 210–16.

[52] C. P. Segal, *Landscape in Ovid's 'Metamorphoses'*, Hermes, 23 (Wiesbaden, 1969), 4.

[53] *FQ* III. VI. 8–9.

Cetera diversis tellus animalia formis
sponte sua peperit, postquam vetus umor ab igne
percaluit solis, caenumque udaeque paludes
intumuere aestu, fecundaque semina rerum
vivaci nutrita solo ceu matris in alvo
creverunt faciemque aliquam cepere morando.
sic ubi deseruit madidos septemfluus agros
Nilus et antiquo sua flumina reddidit alveo
aetherioque recens exarsit sidere limus,
plurima cultores versis animalia glaebis
inveniunt et in his quaedam modo coepta per ipsum
nascendi spatium, quaedam inperfecta suisque
trunca vident numeris, et eodem in corpore saepe
altera pars vivit, rudis est pars altera tellus.[54]

The earth bore of its own accord the other animals in their sundry shapes. After the primeval damp had been warmed by the fire of the sun, and the slime and wet marshes had swollen with heat, the vital seeds of things, fed with the living soil as though in a mother's womb, grew, and gradually took on some form. So, when the seven-streamed Nile has left the soaking fields, and has returned its streams to its former bed, and the fresh mud has been scorched by the sun's rays, farmers find masses of living things in the sods which they turn over. Among these they see some now just begun to cohere, and on the verge of being born, and some bodies which have not reached their full form. Often in the selfsame body one part lives, and the other part is still rude earth.

The allusion is clearly intended to be noticed: 'fecunda semina' becomes 'the fruitfull seades', for example. Ovid is, and yet is not, the fictional 'antique booke' which mentions the birth of Belphoebe. Spenser does not simply revive this antiquity, however: in the timeless space of a narrative retrospect he reverses the priorities of his original, and makes it live and grow. In Ovid, the life in a mother's womb is an incidental comparison with the genesis of animal life ('ceu matris in alvo'); and this burgeoning rebirth of animal life is in ostentatious contrast to the event it follows: the barren regeneration of the human race from the stone-throwing of Pyrrha and Deucalion.[55] Spenser appropriates the story of animal creation to illustrate the human miracle of conception. And this shows a remarkable power to fuse. In the 1570s and 1580s there were two widely held but deeply conflicting views of the *Metamorphoses*. Change of shape was frequently interpreted as a fitting punishment for those who were

---

[54] *Met.* 1. 416–28. Noted by Upton, *Var.* iii. 251.

[55] This contrast is explicit in *Met.* 1. 414–15: 'inde [i.e. from the stony origins of mankind] genus durum sumus experiensque laborum | et documenta damus qua simus origine nati' (Hence we are a tough breed, and suffer labour, and give evidence of the origin from which we grow).

inhumanly lustful in life.[56] The second view (often held by the same writers) was that the poem put forward a unified historical vision of the world as flux. Sabinus regards the creation as 'prima & maxime admiranda metamorphosis' (the first and most amazing metamorphosis), the start of a continuing history of change.[57] Elizabethan commentators attached great importance to the philosophy of flux expressed in Ovid's opening cosmogony and in the discourse of Pythagoras.[58] For Golding, a traditional moralizer of the poem, the *Metamorphoses* also showed

> That nothing under heaven dooth ay in stedfast state remayne.
> And next that nothing perisheth: but that eche substance takes
> Another shape than that it had.[59]

These two sides of received opinion about Ovid in the 1570s do not quite add up. The universe changes with burgeoning and perpetual abundance, but man becomes fixed in punishment for his bestiality. But then Ovid does not quite add up. He is the most serious opponent for a poet attracted to procreative dynastic love, since his heroes and heroines never willingly convert lustful pursuit into generative embraces. Almost no human couples in the *Metamorphoses* have children by entirely natural means who survive to connect man with the perpetual creativity of the universe. Ceyx and Alcyone are married and of child-bearing age, but without offspring until they are changed to birds. Medea kills her children. Tereus eats his son. Baucis and Philemon are apparently childless; and when Pyrrha and Deucalion are told to repopulate the world after the flood, they start not by amorous embracements, but by throwing stones over their shoulders.[60] The poem is an extraordinarily tense mixture of

---

[56] See e.g. Georgius Sabinus, *Fabularum Ovidii Interpretatio* (Cambridge, 1584), sig. ¶8[b]: 'Finguntur enim hic converti ex hominibus in belluas, qui in hominis figura belluae immanitatem gerunt: quales sunt ebriosi, libidinosi, violenti & similes, quorum appetitus rectae rationi minime obtemperat' (Those who, in the shape of men, emulated the brutality of beasts are feigned here to be converted from men to beasts: among such are the drunkards, lechers, violent, and the like, who scarcely tempered their appetite to the demands of right reason). Cf. John Lyly's *Euphues*: 'Why art thou not enamoured of thy father knowing that *Mirha* was so incensed? these are set down that we viewing their incontinencie, should flye the like impudencie, not follow the like excesse.' *Complete Works*, ed. R. W. Bond, 3 vols. (Oxford, 1902), i. 240.

[57] Sabinus, *Interpretatio*, 2.

[58] *Met.* 1. 1–88; 15. 60–478; Charles Segal, 'Myth and Philosophy in the *Metamorphoses*: Ovid's Augustanism and the Augustan Conclusion of Book XV', *American Journal of Philology*, 90 (1969), 278–90; cf. L. P. Wilkinson, *Ovid Recalled* (Cambridge, 1955), 213–19; Brooks Otis, *Ovid as an Epic Poet*, 2nd edn. (Cambridge, 1970), 82, 295.

[59] *Metamorphoses: The Arthur Golding Translation, 1567*, ed. J. F. Nims (New York and London, 1965), The Epistle, ll. 10–12. Golding goes on to note the historical scheme of the poem, and to deplore the bestiality of those metamorphosed.

[60] *Met.* 11. 410–748, 7. 394–404, 6. 647–66, 8. 631–724, 1. 350–415.

the generative and the perverse. And Ovid is not interested in reconciling them.

But Spenser is. Through the story of Chrysogone he unites the two sides of the *Metamorphoses* which are so extraordinarily divergent. The changeful, blooming, unstoppable material world of the philosophical sections of the poem is put in the space where one would expect a rape or a sterile metamorphosis. Chrysogone conceives with the natural, changeful vitality of Ovid's earth. This union of Ovid's two divergent aspects does more than redeem the Roman poet's view of humanity, however.[61] It concludes and consummates Timias's love for Belphoebe in a suitably displaced, temporally distant, and tactful form. The narrative sequence, which places the story of Belphoebe's birth after her refrigerated encounter with the Squire, intimates that people fall in love *and then they breed*.

But any dangerously direct suggestion that virgin queens are incapable of permitting stories livingly to continue is carefully masked behind a sanitizing myth, which is calculated to smooth the angry creases which might have formed on the brow of Spenser's queenly patroness. Elizabeth was the daughter of Henry VIII and Anne Boleyn. After Anne's fall from favour, Henry declared Elizabeth illegitimate and debarred from succession.[62] To transfigure this messy historical sequence into the immaculate conception of a nymph by a sunbeam is safely flattering. But to use that flattery to suggest, as the narrative sequence implies, that breeding is properly how futureless love stories like that of Timias and Belphoebe should end is little short of a poetic miracle. Tact and historical euphemism combine with a powerful implied criticism. Ovid and Ariosto are transformed into fertility, as a result of Spenser's need to create a mythical language which would fuse praise with criticism.

In the course of the digression into the past of Belphoebe, Spenser slips, via the birth of Belphoebe, through an encounter between Venus and Diana, to the upbringing of her twin, Amoret, in the endlessly fertile Garden of Adonis, in which the continuation of life is a pleasurable process:

> There wont faire *Venus* often to enioy
> Her deare *Adonis* ioyous company,
> And reape sweet pleasure of the wanton boy.[63]

The transition to this delighted love so gently diffuses lust into procreation that it is easy to forget where it began. The longing of Timias is forgotten,

---

[61] The story also suggests the incarnation. See Roche, *Kindly Flame*, 103–10.
[62] See J. E. Neale, *Elizabeth I and her Parliaments* (London, 1953), i. 34.
[63] *FQ* III. vi. 46.

and the whole sequence lifts romance on to a new plane: fertility overrides sterile pursuit and pitiful appetency. Spenser replaces the frustrated metamorphosis of the Virgilian Scylla by a dynastic vision; and he replaces the erotic climax of *Orlando furioso* by a generative metamorphosis transformed. The main exemplars of European erotic narrative are re-written as dynastic romance in the timeless spaces of *The Faerie Queene*. Frustrated love, and vain pity, are metamorphosed into living process.

BEYOND ROMANCE: SPENSER AND TASSO

A large quantity of Elizabethan propaganda represented the monarch as merciful, sometimes divinely so. Often the Queen's willingness to pity a particular person who had injured her led propagandists to suggest that she was in absolute control of all her subjects through her gracious power to spare them. In 1578 Thomas Appeltree accidentally discharged a gun across the bows of a barge in which the Queen was relaxing. Her boatman was injured, and the ball passed within 6 feet of Her Majesty. Her courtiers (a familiar type) insisted 'That hangyng was to good a death',[64] but the Queen spared Appeltree. Sir Christopher Hatton praised her for superhuman restraint, and passed from this encomium to an elaborate expression of servile obeisance:

A notable action of compassion proceding from a heavenly minde, and so farre different from the common nature of man, forced into a fearefull jealousie of losse of life, as hath never bin read or heard of ... God for his mercie directe us, ever to be so [loyal subjects], and with our due gratefulnesse to sacrifise at hir kinglie feete our bloud and lyves for hir service sake.[65]

The Faerie Queene is dedicated to Elizabeth, and is designed to appeal to her interests. But at every level of its structure and argument it privily resists this pitiful image of her. It is rootedly hostile to the manipulation of authority through the pretence of loving concern, which so delights Hatton. And this hostility to pity is encoded in its structure. The poem is punctuated by the swift dispatch of pagan or papist antagonists by heroes who seldom even pause with the ruth that retards Aeneas's dispatch

---

[64] 'A newe Ballade, declaryng the daungerous Shootyng of the Gunne at the Courte', *The Harleian Miscellany*, 10 vols., ed. Thomas Park (London, 1813), x. 273.

[65] *A True Report of the most gratious and mercifull message of hir most excellent Majestie ...* (London, 1579), sigs. B1b–B2a.

of Turnus.[66] Its heroes and heroines separate with remarkable ease.[67] And human love is repeatedly associated with painful servility, with that burning sense of exclusion from reciprocal love which Timias feels before Belphoebe, or which the subject feels for a gracious but unattainably distant monarch.

This leads Spenser both to draw on and to transform many of the techniques used by Tasso to explore the waverings of his heroes when confronted by an object of desire. In Book I—which in all likelihood was composed after Book III, and after Spenser had drunk Tasso into his system—Redcrosse confronts the first obstacle to his quest. He is made to dream that Una, his lady, is coupling with a Squire; then he awakes to find his dream flesh. A phantasmal image of Una is hanging wantonly over his bed:

> All cleane dismayd to see so vncouth sight,
>   And halfe enraged at her shamelesse guise,
>   He thought haue slaine her in his fierce despight:
>   But hasty heat tempring with sufferance wise,
>   He stayde his hand, and gan himselfe aduise
>   To proue his sense, and tempt her faigned truth.
>   Wringing her hands in wemens pitteous wise,
>   Tho can she weepe, to stirre vp gentle ruth,
> Both for her noble bloud, and for her tender youth.

> . . . .

>   My weaker yeares
>   Captiu'd to fortune and frayle worldly feares,
>   Fly to your faith for succour and sure ayde:
>   Let me not dye in languor and long teares.

> . . . .

>   Her doubtfull words made that redoubted knight
>   Suspect her truth: yet since no'vntruth he knew,
>   Her fawning loue with foule disdainefull spight
>   He would not shend, but said, Deare dame I rew,
> That for my sake vnknowne such griefe vnto you grew.[68]

The ambiguous waverings of the knight, between a curious pitiful lust and sudden surges of violence, are direct offshoots of the responses of

[66] Spenser alludes to *Aen.* 12. 896–8 during Arthur's battle with Maleger, whom he ruthlessly kills, *FQ* II. xi. 35. Arthur also kills Corflambo without hesitation as 'auengement' for his assault on Timias (who has a role similar to that of Pallas) at IV. viii. 45. Sansfoy and Sansjoy are assaulted unmercifully, I. ii. 19, I. v. 13; Pollente at v. ii. 18; Grantorto at v. xii. 23.

[67] *FQ* I. xii. 41, IV. vi. 42–7, V. vii. 43–5. On all these occasions only the woman shows any apparent sorrow.

[68] *FQ* I. i. 50–3.

Tasso's Christian knights to the insinuating charms of Armida. The erotic suggestions hidden in the most innocent language delude the hero into confusion: Redcrosse almost kills the phantasm at first, but pauses with a desire to 'tempt' her truth—a phrase that fuses erotic desire to try how true she is with an exemplary caution to test whether she is criminally false.[69] 'Since no'vntruth he knew' similarly hovers in uncertainty: it could refer to the knight's doubts about Una's intentions in coming to him, and mean 'since he did not know certainly that she was untrue'; but it could also express a narrator's violent response to lustful suggestion, and mean 'the only reason that he did not kill her as she deserved was because he was so ignorant of evil'. This righteous, almost disembodied, anger rises disruptively through Redcrosse's incipient amorousness; but when he decides not to give it rein, ruth supervenes. Passions fragment, overlap, and oscillate. They blend only through dangerous erotic puns. The phantasm claims to rely on Redcrosse's 'faith', punning on 'religious devotion' and 'chivalric constancy'. Like Tasso's Armida, she attempts to winkle the feelingful knight from the pious warrior: 'la fé, c'ho certa in tua pietà...' (the certain faith that I have in your *pietà*...).[70] The whole seduction attempt, which aims to redirect Redcrosse's sober religious mission towards a pitiful desire, is confounded by the marvelling bemusement of innocence. Redcrosse, unlike Tasso's Rinaldo, does not run off after this pitifully desirable woman. Pity is an ornament to bemused inaction. He apologizes, and sends her to bed. The episode closes there: pity has no narrative consequence, nor does savage ruthlessness. Redcrosse's plot, for a moment at least, continues along its simple course.

The episode with the phantasm does illustrate one major change which Spenser makes to the dreamlike suspension between motive forces which is Tasso's chief contribution to the epic tradition. Power intrudes into the relation between Redcrosse and the phantasm as in no equivalent moment in earlier epic romance. This is not entirely surprising: appeals for pity usually happen when one party is either not suffering from the pain of the other or is capable of alleviating some discomfort that the sufferer is powerless to escape. Pity is consequently a relation founded on a disparity of power between the sufferer and the pitier. The phantasm plays on this connection very strongly. In the course of her sobbing appeal to Redcrosse (in lines omitted from the extract above), she conflates her lustful appeal with the language of justice:

---

[69] Cf. Rosamund Tuve, *Allegorical Imagery: Some Medieval Books and their Posterity* (Princeton, NJ, 1966), 121: 'fidelity not rightness is being spoken of'.

[70] *GL* iv. 42. 3.

> Die is my dew: yet rew my wretched state
> You, whom my hard auenging destinie
> Hath made iudge of my life or death indifferently.

According to her 'dew' she should die; but she appeals to his clemency, fused with the amorousness of romance ('rew'), to ensure her safety and his sexual entrapment. She is not just teasing lust from pity; she is also tempting Redcrosse to use the power that 'having someone at one's mercy' implies.

This connection between pity and power recurs throughout *The Faerie Queene*, and repeatedly contaminates the relations between men and women. The episode of Chrysogone and the sunbeam evokes an ideal, power-free fusion between the sexes. But such equable relations between men and women are never attained by any of the major human characters in the poem. *The Faerie Queene* is a poem in which rivers, and the odd minor character, marry; but its major characters repeatedly encounter barriers of power, which prevent the emergence of a perfect mutuality between them. This is partly because Spenser moralizes faithful loves as 'fierce warres'. To explore the relations between men and women in terms of fights inevitably causes power to permeate the relations of the sexes, since in most fights someone wins and someone else loses. A love which begins in, leads to, or expresses itself in fighting, or which grows in an environment of conquest, will never be a sweet, temperate mingling of two bodies like the union of Chrysogone with a sunbeam.[71] At the end of Spenserian battles defeated knights often throw themselves at their conqueror's mercy, and beg for a pity which is elicited at the price of subjection. This is one side of the politics of mercy which taints loving relations in the poem. But the distracting associations of pity with power extend much more widely than this: in several of the poem's erotic battles, a conqueror pities and spares his victim, whereupon the victim gains control over the victor. This process of self-subjection evokes the voluntary yielding of a lover to a mistress; but, since it grows from a relation of physical dominance, it is unlikely ever to become a form of love which is entirely devolved from power. When Artegall shears off Britomart's ventail, he is overcome by her beauty. His response to her recalls one of Tasso's most agonized attempts to make violence and pity collide, when Tancred unhelms the wounded Clorinda, and is overwhelmed at once by her beauty, and by amorous pity for the wounds which he has inflicted.[72] Artegall, though, falls before Britomart in obeisance rather than desire:

---

[71] On a similar pressure in Chaucer, which underlies much of Spenser's anguish about amorous servility, see the excellent discussion by Jill Mann, *Geoffrey Chaucer* (Hemel Hempstead, 1991), esp. ch. 3, 'The Surrender of *Maistrye*'.

[72] *GL* iii. 21–30.

> And as his hand he vp againe did reare,
>   Thinking to worke on her his vtmost wracke,
>   His powrelesse arme benumbd with secret feare
>   From his reuengefull purpose shronke abacke,
>   And cruell sword out of his fingers slacke
>   Fell downe to ground, as if the steele had sence,
>   And felt some ruth, or sence his hand did lacke,
>   Or both of them did thinke, obedience
> To doe to so diuine a beauties excellence.
>
> And he himselfe long gazing thereupon,
>   At last fell humbly downe vpon his knee,
>   And of his wonder made religion,
>   Weening some heauenly goddesse he did see.[73]

This passage is drenched in Tasso's deliquescent mingling of passions. The pitiful sword is drawn from Argillano's merciless execution of Solimano's page in *Gerusalemme liberata*, when the sword, but not the warrior, flinches from its task.[74] This source enables Spenser protectively to displace pity from the mind of his hero. Artegall himself does not slacken his anger: his sword and arm feel his pity for him. Artegall's religiously devoted obedience is, though, a distinctively English emotion, a political version of pity, which, like the Squire's impotent devotion to Belphoebe, is on the brink of decaying into lust. Artegall tries to restrain his amorous urges:

> Whereby the passion grew more fierce and faine,
> Like to a stubborne steede whom strong hand would restraine.[75]

Religiously motivated devotion is not a stable form of allegiance in *The Faerie Queene*. It can lead to a subjection so absolute as to stimulate faint suggestions of rebellion, because it is founded on a massive disparity of power between the worshipped and the worshipper. Such disparity cannot unite the sexes, or enable human characters to participate in the myths of generation represented in the Garden of Adonis. It can only produce a political parody of love, which is on the brink of decaying into a form of resentful servitude.

The instabilities which are latent in Artegall's devotion to Britomart

---

[73] *FQ* IV. vi. 21–2.

[74] *GL* ix. 84; H. H. Blanchard, 'Imitations from Tasso in *The Faerie Queene*', *Studies in Philology*, 22 (1925), 217. Cf. T. K. Dunseath, *Spenser's Allegory of Justice in Book Five of 'The Faerie Queene'* (Princeton, NJ, 1968), 43: 'Although he is not to be blamed when the sword falls from his hand—that is providential—Artegall is guilty of prostrating himself before beauty's shrine.' Fichter, *Poets Historical*, 204, says that Artegall feels 'true "ruth"' here. Neither interpretation has much hold on the text.

[75] *FQ* IV. vi. 33.

emerge fully and forcefully a little later on, when he fights and defeats the Amazon Radigund. She is gorgeously unhelmed in a second imitation of Clorinda, whereupon Artegall once more yields his advantage; but this time it is unequivocally through pity that he does so:

> At sight thereof his cruell minded hart
> Empierced was with pittifull regard,
> That his sharpe sword he threw from him apart,
> Cursing his hand that had that visage mard:
> No hand so cruell, nor no hart so hard,
> But ruth of beautie will it mollifie.[76]

She continues to fight, until Artegall 'to her mercie him submitted in plaine field'. Radigund then takes his shield, and strikes the subject knight with the flat of her sword 'And as her vassal him to thraldome tooke.' This parodies the ceremony of vassalage, in which a retainer is struck with a sword and given arms with which he is to fight for his overlord:[77] Radigund takes Artegall's sword and shield *away* in order to symbolize his complete subjection.[78] The relationship of lord and vassal came to be used in the seventeenth century as an argument for absolute monarchy: men have unconditionally yielded to their sovereign, and therefore his authority over them is absolute.[79] And this absolute domination is in *The Faerie Queene* far from being either the ideal political state or the ideal foundation of a relation between the sexes: Artegall is unmanned and imprisoned by his oath of allegiance to a manly woman whose supremacy derives from his pity.[80]

Spenser realized, more clearly than any other writer in the romance tradition, that pity forms a particularly dangerous part of the conceptual apparatus of absolute rule. For him, as for no other writer of epic romance, pity contaminates love with political servility. This shapes his responses both to the types of feminine supremacy which are represented in the poem and to the entire epic tradition; and the reasons for it lie very deep in the history of the sentiment. 'Pity', as an independent sense, probably began to emerge from its ancestor *pietas* during the death-throes

---

[76] *FQ* v. v. 13.

[77] *FQ* v. v. 16–18. *Pace* Hamilton: 'She dubs him her knight', edn. cit. ad loc.; cf. *Var.* v. 203.

[78] On the ceremony and its relation to dubbing for knighthood, see Maurice Keen, *Chivalry* (New Haven, Conn., and London, 1984), 64–71.

[79] J. G. A. Pocock, *The Ancient Constitution and the Feudal Law: A Study in English Historical Thought in the Seventeenth Century*, 2nd edn. (Cambridge, 1957, 1987), 168.

[80] Cf. the parody of feudal subjection when the false knight Bragadocchio defeats Trompart, *FQ* II. iii. 8. The only other character in Spenser's œuvre to offer obedience in such grovellingly feudal terms is the obsequious upstart briar in the *Februarie Eclogue*, ll. 150–3, when he beseeches the farmer to cut down the oak: 'O my liege Lord, the God of my life, | Pleaseth you ponder your Suppliants plaint, | Caused of wrong, and cruell constraint, | Which I your poore Vassall dayly endure.'

of the Roman Republic. Cicero associates *pietas* closely with justice; but in the early Empire the term came to be linked with *clementia* on coins which list the virtues of the emperors—a combination which begins with the triumphal shield of Virgil's Emperor Augustus,[81] and which suggests a gradual coincidence of the two virtues. This shift in the associations of *pietas* is connected with major constitutional changes. As republican forms of government declined, the rights of the citizenry ceased to be protected by the guarantee of equality before the law, and came increasingly to depend upon the personal discrimination and moral qualities of the emperor.[82] Such absolute power, if it is not to be tyrannical, creates the need for emperors to use their authority pitifully, with clemency, rather than with assertive violence. From this phase of Roman history comes Seneca's *De clementia*, a treatise intended to define and recommend to Nero a moral virtue which would restrain absolute rule from downright tyranny.[83] The idea that it is important to spare the subject—advice which Anchises gives to his son in Book 6, and which Augustus boasted to have followed[84]—developed in a period when the subjection of a people to the arbitrary will of an emperor was in danger of becoming absolute. It is not surprising that Calvin, the believer in a deity whose choice of the saved depended upon arbitrary decree rather than on a just assessment of meritorious deeds, wrote a commentary on the *De clementia* early in his career.[85] Nor is it surprising that Lucan, the poet who related the collapse of Republic into Empire, uses *pietas* repeatedly to mean something very close to 'pity'.[86] Pity, clemency, grace, compassion—this nexus of

[81] M. P. Charlesworth, 'The Virtues of a Roman Emperor: Propaganda and the Creation of Belief', *Proceedings of the British Academy*, 23 (1937), 114, notes that by the 3rd cent. 'we find a combination of *Pietas* and *Clementia*; but alas! it is nothing more than the indulgence of a conqueror towards the conquered whom he holds in his power'. *Res gestae Divi Augusti*, ed. P. A. Brunt and J. A. Moore (Oxford, 1967), 34. 2, p. 34: 'clupeus aureus in curia Iulia positus, quem mihi senatum populumque Romanum dare virtutis clementiaeque et iustitiae et pietatis caussa testatum est per eius clupei inscriptionem' (A golden shield was placed in the *curia Julia*, which was given to me by the senate and people of Rome by reason of my virtues of clemency, and justice, and *pietas*, as is witnessed by an inscription on the shield).

[82] C. Wirszubski, *Libertas as a Political Idea at Rome during the Late Republic and Early Principate* (Cambridge, 1950), 154. I am much indebted to this excellent book.

[83] Ibid. 150–3. *Moral Essays*, ed. J. W. Basore, Loeb Classical Library (Cambridge, Mass., and London, 1928), *De clementia* 1. 12. 3: 'clementia efficit, ut magnum inter regem tyrranumque discrimen sit' (Clemency brings it about that there is a great difference between a king and a tyrant).

[84] *Aen.* 6. 851–3; *Res gestae*, 3. 1, p. 18: 'Victorque omnibus veniam petentibus civibus peperci' (As a victor, I granted pardon to all states that sought it).

[85] Jean Calvin, *Commentary on Seneca's De Clementia (1532)*, ed. and trans. F. L. Battles and A. M. Hugo (Leiden, 1962). The commentary does not raise theological issues, but Calvin's reading of Seneca may influence *The Institutes of Christian Religion*, e.g. in the description of the holy man's reliance on God's clement power: 'he reclines upon him with sure confidence, and doubts not that, in the divine clemency, a remedy will be provided for his every time of need,—acknowledging him as his Father and his Lord, he considers himself bound to accept his authority in all things', trans. H. Beveridge, 2 vols. (London, 1957), i. 41–2.

[86] *Phars.* 4. 565–6; cf. 7. 320–2.

virtues grows from a time when rule by law was fading into absolute rule. Spenser associates pity with both divine grace and absolute domination, since there is an analytic as well as a historical link between these concepts: in a political or religious system governed by strict justice there is no need for the concepts of clemency, grace, or active pity, since all turns on due assessment of merit. These virtues only become necessary when rule according to the discretion of an absolute authority supplants strict procedural justice.

Spenser's anxious investigation of this web of imperial notions makes him the first epic poet after Virgil to grasp and explore the intricate conceptual foundations of political domination. But he does not return to the structures of the *Aeneid*; he attempts to transcend the political dimension of pity, and resolve its power into a form of union which does not generate servitude. The poem strains every sinew to create from earlier epic poems fictions which dramatize the emergence of an empowered equality between ruler and subject. In order to create such fictions, Spenser has to transform romance readings of classical epic, and move beyond them: his Aeneas should not merely pity, then kill his Turnus; he should ideally transform this relation into a form of empowered equality.

The clearest instance of this project occurs in Spenser's longest imitation of the archetypical imperial moment from Virgil's epic: the death of Turnus. Spenser's version of this episode, like so many Renaissance imitations of classical texts, is diffracted by a thick medium of contemporary versions of the original text; but it lies at the heart of his effort to transcend the sterile oscillation of passions with which Tasso had endowed Aeneas. Guyon faints after his ordeal without food and water in the Cave of Mammon, whereupon his two impassioned pagan antagonists, the irascible Pyrochles and the lustful Cymochles, begin to despoil his unconscious body. Arthur then comes to his rescue. He defeats one brother, then, like Aeneas, pauses before giving Pyrochles the *coup de grâce*:

> So he now subiect to the victours law,
>> Did not once moue, nor vpward cast his eye,
>> For vile disdaine and rancour, which did gnaw
>> His hart in twaine with sad melancholy,
> As one that loathed life, and yet despisd to dye.
>
> But full of Princely bounty and great mind,
>> The Conquerour nought cared him to slay,
>> But casting wrongs and all reuenge behind,
>> More glory thought to giue life, then decay,
>> And said, Paynim, this is thy dismall day;

> Yet if thou wilt renounce thy miscreaunce,
> And my trew liegeman yield thy selfe for ay,
> Life will I graunt thee for thy valiaunce,
> And all thy wrongs will wipe out of my souenaunce.
>
> Foole (said the Pagan) I thy gift defye,
> But vse thy fortune, as it doth befall,
> And say, that I not ouercome do dye,
> But in despight of life, for death do call.
> Wroth was the Prince, and sory yet withall,
> That he so wilfully refused grace;
> Yet sith his fate so cruelly did fall,
> His shining Helmet he gan soone vnlace,
> And left his headlesse body bleeding all the place.[87]

A sudden savagery is suppressed in the space between the penultimate line and the alexandrine, which suggests the mute violence which closes the *Aeneid*, and which eradicates all trace of the retarding pity which had delayed so many generations of romance Aeneases. But there are two significant details in Spenser's version of the death of Turnus which have no counterpart in Virgil. Arthur offers mercy at the price of subjection, as Aeneas does not; and Pyrochles disdainfully rejects life, whereas Turnus is 'humilis' when he accepts defeat. The second of these shows a debt to Italian ways of decoding the emotions which fill the silent spaces of the death of Turnus: many translators had read simple *pietà* into the hero's delay,[88] while the final pathetic epithet which Virgil uses to describe the soul of Turnus as it goes to Hades, 'indignata' ('indignant', with perhaps a trace of 'undeserving'), uniformly prompts Italian redactors of the poem to deploy some derivative of 'sdegnoso' (disdainful).[89] It also led Ariosto to make Ruggiero's final pagan adversary, Rodomonte, blaspheme as he bites the dust.[90] The Italian opposition between a pitiful hero and a

---

[87] *FQ* II. viii. 50–2.

[88] 'Et Enea, che di Pio seco portava | Il cognome gentil meritamente, | Fermossi a le parole; e cominciava | A intenerir la generosa mente' (And Aeneas, who carried with him the mild-mannered nickname of pitiful deservedly, stopped at his words, and his gentle mind began to grow compassionate). *L'Enea di M. Lodovico Dolce* (Venice, 1558), fol. 129ᵃ. Cf. *L'opere di Vergilio . . . trodotte in versi sciolti*, trans. Alessandro Sansedoni *et al.* (Venice, 1573), fol. 279ᵇ: 'Et già gl'incominciavan le parole | A piegar l'alma a giusto sdegno volta | Al cammin di pietà, con dolce forza' (And already his words began, with sweet force, to pull the spirit set on just disdain towards the way of pity).

[89] Dolce, loc. cit.: 'L'alma alhor si fuggì fiera e sdegnosa' (The fierce and disdainful spirit now fled). Cf. Sansedoni, edn. cit. fol. 280ᵃ: 'Et l'alma si fuggio colma di sdegno' (And the spirit, full of disdain, fled); *L'Eneida in Toscano del signor cavalier Cerretani* (Florence, 1560), 251: 'Disdegnosa fuggì l'alma al Inferno' (The disdainful soul fled to hell); *L'Eneide di Virgilio, del Commendatore Annibal Caro* (Venice, 1581), 556: 'Et l'anima di vita | Sdegnosamente sospirando uscio' (And the soul left the body, sighing disdainfully).

[90] *OF* xlvi. 140: 'bestemmiando fuggì l'alma sdegnosa, | che fu sì altiera al mondo e sì orgogliosa' (Blaspheming, the disdainful soul fled, which was so haughty and proud in life). Subsequent translators were influenced by Ariosto's version of the episode.

disdainful villain—which persists right up until Dryden[91]—provides part of the foundation for the early part of Spenser's death of Pyrochles.

But this simple opposition is entangled with the politics of mercy: Arthur attaches firm conditions to his gracious offer of life. There is a trace of an Italian intermediary in this detail too, since Tasso had also connected the death of Turnus with subjection, when Tancred sees Argante stagger:

> —Cedimi, uom forte, o riconoscer voglia
> me per tuo vincitore o la fortuna;
> né ricerco da te trionfo o spoglia,
> né mi riserbo in te ragione alcuna.—
> Terribile il pagan piú che mai soglia,
> tutte le furie sue desta e raguna;
> risponde:—Or dunque il meglio aver ti vante
> ed osi di viltà tentare Argante?
>
> Usa la sorte tua, ché nulla io temo
> né lascierò la tua follia impunita.[92]

'Yield to me, brave man, and recognize either me or Fortune as your conqueror. I seek no triumphal display nor spoils from you, nor do I seek to retain any hold on you.' The pagan frowned more terribly than ever, and drew together all his fury. He replied, 'So now you claim to have the better of me, and dare to accuse Argante of baseness? Use your fortune, since I fear nothing, nor will I leave your folly unpunished.'

Spenser borrows 'magnanimo' in 'great mind', and turns 'tua follia' into the brutally direct 'Foole' in order to make his debt clear. But his source is significantly clipped, pared back down to something like its shape in Virgil. Tasso is still prey to a vestigial romance version of the death of Turnus, which botches his imitation. His Tancred renounces his right to command or despoil his victim, and then fails to kill him. Whereupon Argante rises and starts the fight afresh:

> Infuriossi allor Tancredi, e disse:
> —Cosí abusi, fellon, la pietà mia?[93]

Then Tancred boiled with rage, and said: 'Do you dare abuse my pity, scoundrel?'

[91] Aeneas 'rowl'd his Eyes, and ev'ry Moment felt | His manly Soul with more Compassion melt.' And Turnus's death is disdainful, a term emphasized by a gory pun: 'The streaming Blood distain'd his Arms around: | And the disdainful Soul came rushing thro' the Wound.' xii. 1362–3, 1376–7. *The Poems*, ed. James Kinsley, 4 vols. (Oxford, 1958).

[92] *GL* xix. 21–2. Parallel noted by Upton, *Var.* ii. 277, but, like so many borrowings from Tasso, forgotten by modern critics. For Tasso's debt to Alamanni's *Avarchide* xxiii (where the new Turnus is outraged at the indignity of being offered mercy, although there is no mention of subjection), see Roberto Agnes, 'La *Gerusalemme liberata* e il poema del secondo cinquecento', *Lettere italiane*, 16 (1964), 126–7.

[93] *GL* xix. 26.

Belatedly, Tasso acknowledges that it *was* pity, rather than just a magnanimous desire to renounce all hold on his victim, that delayed the death of the Italian Turnus: the ruthful Christian has to try twice to kill his opponent, and only succeeds on the second attempt. Spenser has no such delay: he cuts the pitiful stammer from the Italian, pushing his episode back towards the leaner shape of its prototype in the *Aeneid*. And, unlike the overly magnanimous Tancred, Arthur insists on establishing lordship over the pagan as a condition of sparing him, then kills Pyrochles in anger when he refuses freely offered 'grace'.

On these slight alterations of detail hang vast differences in outlook. Spenser is correctively imitating Tasso: in his version, clement pardon is only appropriate when it renders the beneficiary subject to the victor's law; the gracious compassion which prolongs Argante's last stand in *Gerusalemme liberata* is dangerous, and has the potential, as in the case of Artegall's pity for Radigund, to be enslaving. This is no simple return to the austerity of Virgil: strong contemporary forces play a part in stamping out Tancred's pitiful stutter, and in transforming it into a ruthless assertion of authority. The central argument of Spenser's prose treatise *A View of the Present State of Ireland* is that, since English law is founded on English customs, the establishment of that law in Ireland would ideally require as its first step the imposition of English customs on the Irish. The only effective way to establish the common law in the province is, therefore, to eradicate all Irishness from the Irish. This savage policy has a hideous rationale: the razing of rebellion, and the social practices which give rise to it, are required in order 'to reduce thinges into order of Englishe lawe'.[94] But the Queen's disposition to mercy could fatally interrupt the initial violence:

But now when all thinges are brought to this passe and all filled with this rufull spectacles of soe manie wretched Carcasses starvinge, goodlie Countries wasted, so huge a desolacion and Confusion as even I that doe but heare it from youe and do picture in my minde do greatlie pittye and Comiserate, if it shall happen that the state of this miserye and lamentable image of thinges shalbe tolde and felingelye presented to her sacred majestye beinge by nature full of mercye and Clemencye whoe is moste inclynable to suche pittifull Complaintes and will not endure to heare such tragedies made of her people and pore subjectes as some aboute her maie insinuate, then shee perhaps for verye Compassion of suche Calamities will not onelye stopp the streame of suche violence and retorne to her wonted mildenes, but allso con them litle thankes which have bene the Aucthors and Counsellours of suche blodye platformes.[95]

---

[94] *Var.* x. 208. See further Nicholas Canny, 'Edmund Spenser and the Development of an Anglo-Irish Identity', *Yearbook of English Studies*, 13 (1983), 1–19.
[95] *Var.* x. 159.

The reply to this ballooning digression, in which the very syntax wanders with the romance instincts of the monarch, is that an offer of mercy may be used to bring Irish rebels under the Queen's sway; but only after they have been ground down by two years of violent campaigning.[96] Conquer, subject to English power, and then offer mercy and clement conditions of peace—this line of argument is strikingly similar to Arthur's response to his Turnus. It is the grim medium of ideas which diffracts Tasso into *The Faerie Queene*, and which helps Spenser transform Italian epic romance into something closer to the imperial rigour of the *Aeneid*.

But Spenser is not simply a poet of imperial domination, seeking to kill and rule Irish *furor*, as Aeneas killed Turnus. Arthur's pitiless conquest of Pyrochles is followed, as so often in earlier epic romance, by a twinned alternative version of the encounter, which belatedly acknowledges the graciousness of Tancred. Once the pagan brothers are defeated, Guyon awakes from his faint, and offers complete obedience as poor recompense for Arthur's gracious salvation:

> My Lord, my liege, by whose most gratious ayd
> I liue this day, and see my foes subdewd,
> What may suffise, to be for meede repayd
> Of so great graces, as ye haue me shewd,
> But to be euer bound[97]

The incommensurability of works and grace is, as so often in the poem, applied to political obedience, and once more feudal language ('liege') accompanies the offer of subjection. Yet Arthur forces a Virgilian half-line from Guyon, as he swiftly denies that he has performed an act of grace, and renounces his claim on the Elf's obedience. He denies himself his rights of conquest,[98] although he does so only when the knight at his mercy has confessed his subjection:

> To whom the Infant thus, Faire Sir, what need
> Good turnes be counted, as a seruile bond,
> To bind their doers, to receiue their meede?
> Are not all knights by oath bound, to withstond
> Oppressours powre by armes and puissant hond?
> Suffise, that I haue done my dew in place.[99]

---

[96] Ibid. x. 177–8.

[97] *FQ* II. viii. 55.

[98] It was a commonplace of Elizabethan thought that conquerors had an absolute right to impose their conditions on the subject people. See *Var.* x. 52. On conquest theory, see J. P. Sommerville, *Politics and Ideology in England, 1603–1640* (London, 1986), 66–9.

[99] *FQ* II. viii. 56.

The two brothers Pyrochles and Cymochles embody the two rebelliously passionate faculties of the mind. Once they are conquered, Spenser is left with a wide, free space, in which to construct a mode of feeling which goes beyond the entanglements of passion, and with them both the enslaving power of pity and the impassioned idiom of his immediate predecessors in the genre. Arthur willingly renounces the armlock of gracious salvation. With deliciously deliberate stupidity he claims that the only possible obligation resulting from being saved is the saviour's obligation to be thanked, which he forgoes. This is beautifully ignorant of the politics of mercy; it eradicates the servility of the saved by simply pretending it does not exist. The poem always is impelled by the irresolvable pressures of power to go beyond politics; it tries in this episode to see the expression of servitude as no more than a point on the way towards a gracious love which renounces all bonds. In this episode Spenser approaches the area of paradoxically overlapping ideas towards which so many earlier epic romances had tended: a mode of feeling beyond pity and wrath, which enfolds within itself traces of the power which both passions can produce. This mode of feeling is at the limits of the thinkable: Spenser had no readily available words, models or stories through which it could be articulated. But *The Faerie Queene* seeks restlessly for a space in which such a myth of perfect human relations could flourish. It is only by sleights of hand—like the way Arthur just ignores the feeling of servitude which he must inspire—that Spenser creates even momentary glimpses of some alternative to the constraints of power and passion.

And his sleight of hand becomes stronger and more desperately ingenious as the poem comes closer to contemporary politics. Book V canto ix represents the trial of Mary Queen of Scots by Elizabeth, under a transparent gloss of allegory, as the trial of Duessa by Mercilla. The episode is a masterpiece of strategic evasiveness, which shows another canny form of Spenser's repeated urge to enfold pity into a form of authority that is less impulsively arbitrary than the most domineering forms of that queenly virtue. At the end of canto ix, when Mercilla is supposed to pass sentence on Duessa, she appears to be at her most merciful; but she is in fact being ruthlessly just:

> But she, whose Princely breast was touched nere
>   With piteous ruth of her so wretched plight,
>   Though plaine she saw by all, that she did heare,
>   That she of death was guiltie found by right,
>   Yet would not let iust vengeance on her light;
>   But rather let in stead thereof to fall
>   Few perling drops from her faire lampes of light;

> The which she couering with her purple pall
> Would haue the passion hid, and vp arose withall.[100]

This is an impossibly brilliant reconciliation of demands put on the poet by context and subtext. There was general fear at the trial of Mary Queen of Scots that the Queen would give way to her pitiful nature and spare her kinswoman.[101] Sir John Puckering's speech for the Commons argued that 'Mercie now in this case towards her, would in the ende prove crueltie against us all, *Nam est quaedam crudelis misericordia*, and therefore to spare her is to spill us'.[102] Spenser—with all the slippery brilliance of the greatest court poet—makes Mercilla appear indeed to spare Duessa. This stanza, which describes a moment of judgement, looks as though it describes unrestrained mercy. It is the greatest re-creation of the moment when Aeneas (is he ruthful or dutiful?) leaves Dido:

> At pius Aeneas, quamquam lenire dolentem
> solando cupit et dictis avertere curas,
> multa gemens magnoque animum labefactus amore
> iussa tamen divum exsequitur classemque revisit.[103]

But dutiful Aeneas, although he longed to calm her grief with consolation and to lessen her sorrow with words, groaning many things, and overcome in spirit with great love, none the less carried out the commands of the gods and went back to his fleet.

Spenser performs a remarkable feat of *syntactic* imitation. The stanza moves with the same weighty contraflow of reluctance from 'But she...' ('At pius...'), except that the reluctance is not capped by 'iussa tamen...', but by a phrase which follows the adversative syntactic construction of Spenser's great original, whilst (apparently) pulling in diametrically the opposite direction: 'Yet would not let due vengeance on her light.' But 'let' is a saving pun: Spenser's use of it here to mean at once both 'hinder' and 'allow' encapsulates perfectly the psychological divisions of the heroic departure.[104] The pun makes the decision to sentence look like a pardon; but the tears which Mercilla 'lets' fall instead are an ornament to a judicial decision, which have no motive force. When Dido is left, Aeneas is in many Italian versions of the *Aeneid* 'pietoso', in the sense of 'pitiful':

---

[100] *FQ* v. ix. 50.

[101] See René Graziani, 'Elizabeth at Isis Church', *PMLA* 79: 1 (1964), 379.

[102] [Robert Cecil], *The Copie of a Letter to the Right Honourable the Earl of Leycester* (London, 1586), 9. For Spenser's debt to this and other works of anti-Marian propaganda, see J. E. Phillips, *Images of a Queen: Mary Stuart in Sixteenth-Century Literature* (Berkeley and Los Angeles, 1964), 117–42 and 201–3.

[103] *Aen.* 4. 393–6.

[104] O'Connell, *Mirror and Veil*, 152, writes: 'The canto ends with Mercilla unable to let "iust vengeance" fall upon Duessa.' The pun is noted and explored by Fichter, *Poets Historical*, 204.

'Enea, quantunque pio, quantunque afflitto . . .' (Aeneas, although pitiful, although afflicted . . .).[105] Spenser grants extraordinary apparent force to this romance reading of the heroic choice, but gives it no *motive* power at all. The next canto begins with Duessa dead. The vacant space between the two cantos contains the mute violence of an imperial duty performed.

Spenser's uneasy coincidence of pity and justice is akin to, and a descendant of, the dilemmas of Aeneas. Mercilla's action unites the appearance of pity with the reality of just condemnation. She embodies the wish to unite divergent concepts which makes epic romance: justice and mercy apparently blend. This fusion of antagonistic motives is not simply the product of generic pressures, however. It is made possible by, and articulates, contemporary unease about the relations between the emotions of monarchs and the law. Mercilla's judgement dramatizes the division between the role of prince and that of judge, as expressed by the political theorist Jean Bodin:

nothing is so proper unto a prince, as clemencie; nothing unto a king, as mercie; nothing unto majestie, as lenitie . . . Now nothing is more contrarie unto true justice, than pitie; neither anything more repugnant unto the office and dutie of an upright judge, than mercie . . . So that a prince sitting in judgement must take upon him two contrarie persons, that is to say, of a mercifull father, and of an upright magestrat; of a most gentle prince, and of an inflexible judge.[106]

It is necessary for a monarch to appear clement and gracious in order to be loved by his subjects, yet a judge must abide by the due process of the law. This division of roles is parallel to a distinction made by Max Weber, between 'bureaucratic' governments, which function by the due performance of offices, and 'charismatic' societies, in which the supremacy of a king or ruling class derives from transcendent excellence.[107] 'Charisma' is an appropriate term to describe Elizabeth's mode of supremacy, since it derives from *charis*, 'grace', or 'favour': the Queen's reputation for bounty and superhuman mercy did indeed associate her with the charismatic grace of a god.[108] Spenser's restless exploration of pity in *The*

[105] Caro, *L'Eneide di Virgilio*, 155. This tradition again persists to Dryden: 'But good *Aeneas*, tho' he much desir'd | To give that Pity, which her Grief requir'd . . .' iv. 568–9.

[106] Jean Bodin, *The Six Bookes of a Commonweale*, trans. R. Knolles (1606), ed. K. D. McRae, Harvard Political Classics (Cambridge, Mass., 1962), 509. For Bodin's influence in England, see George L. Mosse, 'The Influence of Jean Bodin's *Republique* on English Political Thought', *Medievalia et Humanistica*, 5 (1948), 73–83.

[107] For the distinction between charismatic and bureaucratic authority, see *From Max Weber: Essays in Sociology*, ed. and trans. H. H. Gerth and C. W. Mills (London, 1948), 196–252.

[108] In paradigm instances of charismatic authority ' "objective" law flows from the highly personal experience of divine grace and god-like heroic strength and rejects all external order.' Weber, *Economy and Society*, ed. G. Roth and C. Wittich, 2 vols. (Berkeley and Los Angeles, 1968), ii. 1115. For Elizabeth and 'charismatic authority', see Clifford Geertz, 'Centers, Kings, and Charisma: Reflections on the Symbolics of Power', in J. Ben-David and T. N. Clark ed., *Culture and its Creators: Essays in Honor of Edward Shils* (Chicago and London, 1977), 150–71; esp. 153–7.

Faerie Queene repeatedly returns to, and repeatedly attempts to limit, the practical effects of such charismatic authority. Underlying the poem's unease with pity is an uneasy and unanswerable question: what would happen if the Queen's pitiful charisma began to permeate the 'bureaucratic' function of the monarch as a distributor of justice: would the law survive such passionate, charismatic invasion?

This dangerous overlap between the passions of the monarch and the law was a great source of alarm in Elizabethan discussions about the relations between royal government and the supra-statutory form of justice known as Equity. Among Elizabethan lawyers, Equity was generally regarded as the means by which the Prince mitigated the severity of the law according to the dictates of his conscience, on occasions when strict application of the law would result in a decision which would be unjust.[109] Equity was also often, though, associated in less technical writings, such as sermons, with charismatic virtues such as mercy and divine grace.[110] It has been argued, notably by Frank Kermode, that the Mercilla episode in *The Faerie Queene* is part of a web of images which Spenser weaves in order to associate Elizabeth's supremacy with her power to use this supra-legal force,[111] and comprises part of an extensive project to praise his Queen as an imperial virgin ruler of absolute authority. This view is a tempting one, but highly partial. Throughout the late sixteenth century, discussions of Equity are underwritten by a fear that extending its power through the Queen's Prerogative courts, far from creating a truly imperial monarch, could endanger the traditional guarantee of English liberty: the supremacy of the common law.[112] William Lambarde expressed this

---

[109] William Lambarde, *Archion, or a Commentary on the High Courts of Justice in England* (London, 1635) [first Latin edn., 1568], 20: '*If Right be too heavy, then let him sue to the King*, &c. whereby it is meant, that hee should have the *Rigour* of the *Law* mitigated by the *conscience* of the *Prince*.' See the lucid discussion in J. H. Baker, *An Introduction to English Legal History*, 2nd edn. (London, 1979), 83–100.

[110] William Perkins in his *Epieikeia* extols Equity as 'moderation'—in both public and private life—of the strict requirements of justice, *Epieikeia, or a Treatise of Christian Moderation*, in *Workes*, 2 vols. (Cambridge, 1608–9), ii. 502–20. Cf. *Workes*, i. 515: 'God sheweth most admirable Equitie and moderation towards us, therefore ought we to shew it, one towards another.' Cf. Lodovick Bryskett, *A Discourse of Civil Life* (London, 1606), 71: 'equite is the tempering or mitigating the rigour of the law, which otherwise (like a tyrant) condemneth without mercy.' On early humanist attitudes to Equity, see Guido Kisch, *Erasmus und die Jurisprudenz seiner Zeit: Studien zum humanistischen Rechtsdenken*, Basler Studien zur Rechtswissenschaft, 56 (Basle, 1960), 55–68.

[111] Frank Kermode, *Shakespeare, Spenser, Donne* (London, 1971), 49–59. See also *The Classic* (London, 1975), 56–61. James E. Phillips, 'Renaissance Concepts of Justice and the Structure of *The Faerie Queene* Book V', *Huntington Library Quarterly*, 33 (1969–70), 103–20, claims that the end of the Book shows 'true clemency', which apparently involves not being clement at all. W. Nicholas Knight, 'The Narrative Unity of Book V of *The Faerie Queene*: "That part of Justice which is Equity"', *Review of English Studies*, NS 21 (1970), 283: 'England must be ruled by the wedding of Britomart (Equity) and Artegall (Justice).'

[112] See Stuart E. Prall, 'The Development of Equity in Tudor England', *American Journal of Legal*

concern in his analysis of Equity: '*Equity* should be appealed unto but onely in rare and extraordinary matters, lest... it should come to passe (as *Aristotle* saith) that a *Beast* should beare the rule.'[113] A legal system which allowed considerable power to the conscience of the monarch, or to his or her Chancellor, would be acutely vulnerable to abuse should the holders of these offices become impassionate or corrupt. Jurists such as Edward Hake expressed similar fears that Equity could destroy the English constitutional tradition that monarchs ruled by law, rather than at their own will. Hake endeavoured to detach Equity altogether from the will of the monarch, and tie it back into the common law. Equity, he argued, sprang from the common law's own provision to legislate in cases which are apparently beyond the purviews of its statutes.[114] Rule by law was for Hake the source of England's well-being, and the alternative was thraldom:

still happy, yea, twise happy, famous and renowned is the state of our government heere in England in that the rule of our Prince here is lymitted and directed by her lawes, and the obedience of her people rather yeelded by rule of love, and by the right levell of civility & knowledge then constrayned by servilitie and thraldome.[115]

This debate surfaced in constitutional form in 1616 when Sir Edward Coke attacked the Chancellor, Lord Ellesmere, for using his power to dispense Equity to diminish the authority of the common law.[116] Its ramifications could be seen in the violent hostility to extensions of the royal prerogative which marked the early phases of the Civil War. Even in the Elizabethan period, though, discussions of Equity tended to resolve into an argument between the merits of rule by law, as against rule by administrative fiat.[117]

There are deep-seated historical reasons for this association of Equity with mercy, grace, and absolutism. Like 'pity', Equity began to take on its modern appearance in the period when imperial power was being

---

History, 8 (1964), 1–19. Cardinal Wolsey tried to extend the powers of the Prerogative courts in order to diminish the influence of Parliament and the common lawyers, ibid. 7.

[113] *Archion*, 80.

[114] *Epieikeia: A Dialogue on Equity*, ed. D. E. C. Yale, Yale Law Library Publications, 13 (New Haven, Conn., 1953), 16: '*Equity* is not a parte or vertue attributory to the judge, but is a parte or vertue attributory to the lawe, and by the judge or expositor of the law to be applyed... according as the exigence of a particularity not expressed in the generality of the lawe shall geve the occasion.'

[115] Ibid., 80.

[116] See J. H. Baker, 'The Common Lawyers and the Chancery: 1616', *Irish Jurist*, 4 (1969), 368–92. The fear that Equity was by nature prone to be arbitrary led to John Selden's famous jibe that ''tis all one as if they should make the Standard for the measure wee call A foot, to be the Chancellors foot', *Table Talk of John Selden*, ed. F. Pollock (London, 1927), 43.

[117] Prall, 'Equity in Tudor England', 19. See further W. H. Dunham, jun., 'Regal Power and the Rule of Law', *Journal of British Studies*, 3: 2 (1964), 24–56.

extended at the expense of the traditional sanctions of legal redress, and when the Roman emperors began to acquire 'that element of influence or charisma which can have no legal basis or definition'.[118] The Roman concept of *aequitas*—originally appealed to as a general system of fairness underlying the law—came to be used synonymously with *benignitas* and *indulgentia*[119] only in the later Empire, and often came to be administered by the Emperor himself.[120] In the early Jacobean period several civil lawyers attempted to identify imperial *aequitas* with the royal prerogative to pardon offenders, and to overrule decisions reached by the common law, in the Prerogative courts.[121] The most famous of such absolutist civil lawyers, John Cowell, argued that the King is 'above the law by his supreme power', and attached a corresponding power to the Prerogative courts.[122] His *Interpreter* caused such an outcry in the Commons that James I was compelled to suppress it by proclamation in 1610. The supra-legal form of charismatic authority which Kermode detected in Mercilla's court was too absolutist to find acceptance even from James I, whose Scottish origins predisposed him in favour of the civil law, and whose own political works show a tendency to place the monarch above the law.[123]

Spenser makes no reference to the supremacy of the Queen's conscience in the Mercilla episode, and manages to imply by his syntax and his choice of subtext that Mercilla, like Aeneas, is subject to a higher power than her own will when she condemns Duessa.[124] In the English epic this is not the furtherance of Empire, but the constraint of justice. Mary

---

[118] H. F. Jolowicz and B. Nicholas, *Historical Introduction to the Study of Roman Law*, 3rd edn. (Cambridge, 1972), 324. Weber associates equity with charismatic authority, *Economy and Society: An Outline of Interpretive Sociology*, ed. Guenther Roth and Claus Wittich, 2 vols. (Berkeley and Los Angeles, 1968), ii. 1115–16; see also ibid. ii. 753–84: 'Emergence and Creation of Legal Norms'.

[119] W. W. Buckland and P. Stein, *A Textbook of Roman Law from Augustus to Justinian*, 3rd edn. (Cambridge, 1963), 55.

[120] W. W. Buckland, *Equity in Roman Law* (London, 1911), 8–14.

[121] See the rather outdated account in F. W. Maitland, *English Law and the Renaissance* (Cambridge, 1901); and Thomas Starkey, *A Dialogue between Reginald Pole and Thomas Lupset*, ed. K. M. Burton (London, 1948), 174. Cf. S. E. Thorne, 'English Law and the Renaissance', *Essays in English Legal History* (London and Ronceverte, 1985), 187–96. Roman law, with its provision for supra-legal and supra-personal *aequitas*, could be regarded as an ideal by which to reform the common law and so render its arcane statutes *less* in need of augmentation by the royal conscience. See Brian P. Levack, *The Civil Lawyers in England 1603–1641* (Oxford, 1973), 84.

[122] *The Interpreter* (Cambridge, 1607), sig. Qq1ᵃ; 'the Chanceler hath in this the kings absolute power, to moderate and temper the written lawe', sig. N2ᵇ. Cowell also defines the King's prerogative as 'preeminence, or priviledge that the King hath in any kinde, over and above the ordinarie course of the common lawe' and relates it to the civilians' *maiestas*, sig. Ddd3ᵇ. See Levack, *Civil Lawyers*, 103–5; and Jocelyn Simon, 'Dr Cowell', *Cambridge Law Journal*, 26 (1968), 260–72.

[123] Levack, *Civil Lawyers*, 82; *The True Law of Free Monarchies* (Edinburgh, 1598), sig. C7ᵃ.

[124] Spenser put forward a similar argument in the *View*: 'it is daungerous to leave the sence of a lawe vnto the reasone or will of the Judge whoe are men and maye be miscarried by affeccions and manye other meanes But the lawes oughte to be like stonye tables playne stedfaste and vnmoveable.' *Var.* x. 78.

Queen of Scots was finally executed at the insistence of the Commons,[125] and it has been convincingly argued that details of Mercilla's court recall the setting of the royal throne in Parliament.[126] These details create a strong *prima facie* case that the episode celebrates the waverings between human fears and superhuman justice that flow from the composite legislative power of the Queen in Parliament. Spenser offers the *appearance* of a benign imperial sovereign graciously dispensing justice according to the demands of her charismatically pitiful nature. But the narrative tells the true story: Parliamentary justice prevails.

Spenser was not an imperial poet. He insinuates unease with his Queen's modes of government in the silent spaces between episodes, and continually seeks to go beyond charismatic, imperial forms of authority—and the rigours of virginity—towards myths of sexual and juridical union between male and female, pity and justice. His critique in *The Faerie Queene* of Elizabeth's coercive use of pity is founded on the belief that reason and the law are respectively the psychological and political means of establishing a just commonwealth; a passion, such as pity, or a moral virtue, such as clemency, which are opposed to the strict operation of justice, are in principle antagonistic to this goal. And this view is ingrained in his whole project of 'fashioning a gentleman'. Many early humanists, writing educational manuals for potential rulers, proposed educational means to limit the potentially tyrannical passions of a monarch from within, by the sober bands of virtue and rationality. A commonplace of this genre is that monarchy approaches tyranny when the ruler governs by passion, rather than according to reason and the artificial rationality of the law.[127] Humanist conduct books also repeatedly urge that virtue is true nobility, and some also give tentative indications that an elective monarchy, in which the most virtuous and rational man is chosen to rule, would be the ideal state.[128] Impose on these pressures for the supremacy of rational virtue a Queen whose public image was of pitiful, charismatic supremacy, and a sublimely tense convergence of forces results. It is a combination of forces which cannot be reconciled without some startlingly evasive, staggeringly brilliant fictions. The battles fought by Tasso, between

---

[125] *The Copie of a Letter* (n. 102 above) 16.

[126] Douglas A. Northrop, 'Mercilla's Court as Parliament', *Huntington Library Quarterly*, 36 (1972), 153–8, and 'Spenser's Defence of Elizabeth', *University of Toronto Quarterly*, 38 (1968–9), 277–94.

[127] 'Those expressions of a tyrant, "Such is my will", "This is my bidding", "Let will replace reason", should be far removed from the mind of the Prince.' Desiderius Erasmus, *The Education of a Christian Prince*, ed. L. K. Born (New York, 1936), 189. 'Neither is it a state of servitude to live according to the letter of just laws. Nor is that a peaceful state in which the populace bows to every whim of the prince... Equity does not lie in giving everyone the same reward, the same rights, the same honour; as a matter of fact, that is sometimes the mark of the greatest unfairness.' ibid. 212.

[128] Erasmus, *The Education of a Christian Prince*, 139–40; 'Silenis Alcibiadis' in *Proverbiorum Chiliadas* (Basle, 1515), 470.

the pity of romance and the anger with which he sought to burn Ariosto from his mind, become vehemently alive in the 1590s. Romance is rooted in and given power by the political culture of the time; but the pitiful motives of the mode could give rise, in the personal sphere, to a vehemently humiliated sense of despairing subjection to an almighty, pitiful power; and, in the political sphere, an all-pitiful, all-powerful monarch would seem at once an inescapable fact and, potentially, a tyranically impassioned ruler. These uncertainties make epic romance, with its efforts both to fuse pity with wrath and to fight pity with wrath, *the* genre of the period.

ENDING EPIC ROMANCE

Philip Sidney's *Old Arcadia* ends with a wobbling unease which parallels Spenser's treatment of Mercilla in its desire to permit due force to rigid justice, whilst accommodating the endlessness towards which the romance mode is drawn. Euarchus unwittingly condemns his kinsmen, Pyrocles and Musidorus, to death for the murder of Basilius, according to the strict letter of the law. As a foreign ruler called in as a temporary judge, Euarchus has no power clemently to pardon them.[129] Pity is thereby excluded from playing a part in the human motives which determine the outcome of the plot. And yet the ending of *The Old Arcadia* does accommodate the impulses of romance, to make stories continue and heroes revive, in an impersonal form. Basilius, the supposedly murdered king, comes miraculously and comically back to life, and pardons the abject offenders. The revival of the clement king has been read as demonstrating the vital need for mercy, and for a power beyond the rigid letter of the law, such as Equity, in order to correct the potentially unjust justice of unmitigated legal processes.[130] This interpretation does not do justice (so to speak) to the full range of meanings and attitudes accommodated by Sidney's plot. The revival of Basilius faintly suggests that

[129] *The Countess of Pembroke's Arcadia (The Old Arcadia)*, ed. Jean Robertson (Oxford, 1973), 403–12: 'If rightly I have judged, then rightly have I judged mine own children, unless the name of a child should have force to change the never-changing justice', ibid. 411. Euarchus is defended in D. M. Anderson, 'The Trial of the Princes in the *Arcadia*, Book V', *Review of English Studies*, NS 8 (1957), 409–12; for W. D. Briggs, 'Political Ideas in Sidney's *Arcadia*', *Studies in Philology*, 28 (1931), 158, his behaviour implies 'that the crown is not above . . . constitutional laws, but subject to them'; Richard C. McCoy, *Sir Phillip Sidney: Rebellion in Arcadia* (Hassocks, Sussex, 1979), 129–31, notes the exclusion of motive pity; cf. the more hostile account by Elizabeth Dipple, '"Unjust Justice" in the *Old Arcadia*', *Studies in English Literature*, 10 (1970), 83–101.

[130] See esp. Arthur F. Kinney, 'Sir Philip Sidney and the Uses of History', in H. Dubrow and R. Strier (eds.), *Historical Renaissance: New Essays on Tudor and Stuart Literature and Culture* (Chicago and London, 1988), 293–314.

higher powers than human passions should override the operations of justice; but it also, simultaneously, leads to the triumph of arbitrary mortal powers over the law. The revival of the continuingly incompetent and perpetually impassioned Basilius magnificently accommodates a deep-seated Elizabethan unease about the values and dangers of having a royal power with a prerogative to mitigate the law: it is a distinctive product of the Elizabethan mode of epic romance. Life goes on; but at a price.

The New Arcadia also responds to this pressure—part generic, part political—to escape from and to submit to the structures of romance. It ends on the same strained chord as *The Old Arcadia*, combining destructive probity with endless compassion, but transposed into an epic key. Sidney had praised Aeneas in the *Apologie for Poetry* for leaving Dido 'though not only all passionate kindness, but even the human consideration of virtuous gratefulness, would have craved other of him'[131]—language which is almost *too* aware of the value of the emotions which Aeneas overcomes. And his re-creation of Turnus's end, very near the close of the section of his *Arcadia* which he lived to revise, is similarly torn:

Zelmane repressed a while her great heart—either disdaining to be cruel, or pitiful, and therefore not cruel. And now the image of human condition began to be an orator unto her of compassion, when she saw, as he lifted up his arms with a suppliant's grace, about one of them unhappily tied a garter with a jewel, which, given to Pyrocles by his aunt of Thessalia and greatly esteemed by him, he had presented to Philoclea, and with inward rage promising extreme hatred had seen Lycurgus (with a proud force and not without some hurt unto her) pull away from Philoclea, because at entreaty she would not give it him. But the sight of that was like a cipher signifying all the injuries which Philoclea had of him suffered; and that remembrance, feeding upon wrath, trod down all conceits of mercy. And therefore saying no more but, 'No villain, die! It is Philoclea that sends thee this token for thy love', with that, she made her sword drink the blood of his heart.[132]

Sidney is remarkable for recognizing the importance of memory and sympathy in Aeneas's last action. 'The image of human condition' is an almost Homeric acknowledgement of the humanity which the hero shares with his adversary. Pyrocles's victim, though, does not appeal to the shared value of *pietas*, but asks for mercy from his apparently female

    [131] *An Apology for Poetry*, ed. Geoffrey Shepherd, 2nd edn. (Manchester, 1973), 119.
    [132] *The Countess of Pembroke's Arcadia (The New Arcadia)*, ed. Victor Skretkowicz (Oxford, 1987), 462. Cf. *Aen.* 12. 945–9: 'Ille, oculis postquam saevi monimenta doloris | exuviasque hausit, furiis accensus et ira | terribilis: "tune hinc spoliis indute meorum | eripiare mihi? Pallas te hoc vulnere, Pallas | immolat et poenam scelerato ex sanguine sumit." ' (He, once he had drunk in with his eyes those monuments and relics of grief, ablaze with anger and awesome in his frenzy, said: 'Are you, clad in the spoils of my friends, to escape from me? Pallas gives you this wound, Pallas sacrifices you, and draws atonement from your impious blood.')

conqueror, and offers obedience as the price of salvation:

As you have taken from men the glory of manhood, return so now again to your own sex for mercy. I will redeem my life of you with no small services, for I will undertake to make my brother obey all your commandments. Grant life, I beseech you—for your own honour, and for the person's sake that you love best.[133]

Like Spenser, Sidney transposed the final episode of the *Aeneid* into a study in the politics of mercy—and, like Spenser, he rejected mercy. But his imitation cannot fully escape from the diffractive power of love. Pyrocles is asked to spare the suppliant, not through *pietas*, but 'for the person's sake that you love best'. Pallas's baldric is also transposed into a love token, and rage feeds on the memory of a violated lover, rather than of the boy whom Aeneas had an obligation to protect.[134]

This amorous element may well explain why the revised *Arcadia* ends as it does. There is a residuum of romance sentiment in the air, and such sentiment often creates radically divided emotions in authors who attempt to imitate the end of the *Aeneid*. Ariosto wished both to kill and to spare Turnus, and displays Aeneas's divided emotions in narrative form when Orlando kills Agramante in rage, but clemently spares Sobrino.[135] Sidney, too, deals with romance doubles: Pyrocles executes Lycurgus, and then continues the battle with his brother Anaxius—a battle which Sidney abandoned in mid-sentence. *The New Arcadia* reaches a point of ethical and generic crisis, similar to that so teasingly evoked at the end of *The Old Arcadia*, and which could only be resolved by a similar poetic miracle.[136] Sidney could choose between a second act of ruthlessness, or a pitiful pardon for Anaxius. The only alternative would be some fantastically brilliant fusion of the two. Neither simply sparing nor simply killing his second Turnus would capture the sparse depth of Aeneas's imperial delay, or transfigure into fiction the self-opposing political drives of his generation. It was probably with this confrontation of his impossible desire to write an epic in the language of romance, a work which praised vehement justice in a culture attuned to the power of pity, that Sidney's

[133] *New Arcadia*, 462.
[134] *Aen.* 8. 470–584; Servius, edn. cit. ii. 647 suggests that Aeneas remembers his obligation to Evander when he revenges Pallas: 'omnis intentio ad Aeneae pertinet gloriam: nam et ex eo quod hosti cogitat parcere, pius ostenditur, et ex eo quod eum interimit, pietatis gestat insigne: nam Evandri intuitu Pallantis ulciscitur mortem' (His whole intention pertains to the glory of Aeneas: for he shows him to be pitiful in that he contemplates sparing his enemy, and in that he kills him, he shows great signs of piety: for he avenges the death of Pallas out of consideration for Evander).
[135] *OF* xlii. 1–19.
[136] *Old Arcadia*, 415; see Stephen J. Greenblatt, 'Sidney's *Arcadia* and the Mixed Mode', *Studies in Philology*, 70 (1973), 269–78.

quill hit the desk for the last time.[137] His uncertainties are, like those of Spenser, more than generic: they grow from the sense of being in a state in which two conceptually distinct modes of government seem desirable. These forces both create and need poetic miracles in order to be expressed.

Similarly antagonistic forces also create Spenser's most majestically topical, timeless mythic structure, the *Mutabilitie Cantos*. These fragments, which were not published until 1609, may or may not have been intended as a conclusion for the poem; but, whatever their status, they are fraught with the divisions of motive which both Sidney and Spenser had tried to express through perilously temporary, unstable illusions, like the merciful justice of Mercilla, or the inconclusive rage of Pyrocles. The *Cantos* return once more to the anxieties of the Mercilla episode, and dwell on monarchs who judge cases which concern themselves. In the main plot, the pitifully irascible Jove seeks to condemn the Titaness, Mutabilitie, for her audacious challenge to his claim to possess the throne by right of conquest. He has all the passionate instability of Spenser's human heroes: at first he reaches in rage for his thunderbolt to destroy the usurper; then, confronted by his desirable rival, blinks between vengeful wrath and a kind of tenderly lustful pity:

> But, when he looked in her louely face,
>   In which, faire beames of beauty did appeare,
>   That could the greatest wrath soone turne to grace...[138]

Spenser's continual effort to go beyond this mortal unease in shifting between opposite passions, towards some higher, encompassing fiction, surfaces for the last time in the *Mutabilitie Cantos*: Jove's passions are absorbed into an independent judicial hearing of the case by Dame Nature, which Mutabilitie demands, and to which Jove agrees, prompted, presumably, by his smitten pity. And the trial is fixed for Arlo hill in Ireland.

At this point Spenser turns playful, and shifts to an unspecified, unpeopled, mythical past, with all the apparent randomness with which he leapt from the frustrated passion of Timias to the Garden of Adonis. He tells, in another timeless, retrospective narrative, which lives in the safely mythical space before the human complexities of the main narrative, how Arlo hill came to be at once fertile and desolate. In *The Faerie Queene* this movement of the narrative into a mythic past almost invariably brings

---

[137] Cf. McCoy, *Sidney*, 212–13, who summarizes rival views of the ending, and concludes 'the hero's potency is contained and neutralised without being crushed'; David Norbrook, *Poetry and Politics in the English Renaissance* (London, 1984), 106, argues that 'the work's serious religious and political concerns, and its increasing inwardness, were becoming incompatible with the courtly framework.'

[138] *FQ* VII. vi. 31.

with it a transforming vision, in which the energy of contemporary politics
is used to mutate past texts. The story of Arlo hill only gradually reveals
this power. It seems at first to evoke only a world on holiday, a past
landscape of Ireland which teems with life, in which even rivers immediately suggest associations with marriage. Molanna, the stream in which
Diana's entourage bathe, is so beautiful

> For, first, she springs out of two marble Rocks,
> On which, a groue of Oakes high mounted growes,
> That as a girlond seemes to deck the locks
> Of som faire Bride, brought forth with pompous showes
> Out of her bowre, that many flowers strowes...[139]

The rigid chastity of Diana is completely out of place in this landscape
which twinkles with desired weddings. And because this is a landscape
in love, the virgin goddess is exposed to the greedy eyes of Faunus, who
tempts the loving stream Molanna to give him a glimpse of her chaste
mistress by the offer of a lover:

> There-to hee promist, if shee would him pleasure
> With this small boone, to quit her with a better;
> To weet, that where-as shee had out of measure
> Long lov'd the *Fanchin*, who by nought did set her,
> That he would vndertake, for this to get her
> To be his Loue, and of him liked well...[140]

The whole stanza is full of love 'out of measure', as Faunus's eagerness
for Diana leads him to produce five feminine rhymes in a row—a number
of syllables beyond the measure of the line unsurpassed anywhere else in
the poem. Arlo hill is full of fast-talking hucksters and amorous possibilities. And when the goddess and her nymphs catch and sentence
Faunus, things do not change very much:

> At length, when they had flouted him their fill,
> They gan to cast what penaunce him to giue.
> Some would haue gelt him, but that same would spill
> The Wood-gods breed, which must for euer liue:
> Others would through the riuer him haue driue,
> And ducked deepe: but that seem'd penaunce light;
> But most agreed and did this sentence giue,
> Him in Deares skin to clad; and in that plight,
> To hunt him with their hounds, him selfe saue how hee might.[141]

---

[139] Ibid. 41.   [140] Ibid. 44.   [141] Ibid. 50.

There is one particular, brutal, judicial change which should occur here, but which gets lost in the rapid chatter of the nymphs. Ovid's Actaeon, who spies on Diana, is—with a savagery which is rare even in the *Metamorphoses*—transformed into a stag and torn apart by his own hounds. Faunus, a Spenserian descendant of Actaeon, suffers no such terminal change: he is just given a good run.[142] There is no final, fatal metamorphosis, no deadly triumph of destructive passion over the body. Ovid's savage ending is mollified by Spenser's primary imaginative drive: life must continue:

> Some would haue gelt him, but that same would spill
> The Wood-gods breed, *which must for euer liue.*

Spenser's central image of changeful perpetuity, Adonis, is subject to a similarly vital imperative: he 'may not | For euer die, and euer buried bee | In balefull night, where all things are forgot'.[143] Nor can Faunus die, since he supports the continuing generation of a whole breed of creatures 'which *must* for euer liue'. Generative perpetuity overrides metamorphic destruction. The need to live absorbs both the violence of punitive justice and the destructive power of passion. Impassioned government is superseded by a kind of mercy independent of the wishes of the judge, which is encoded in the fertility of the landscape. Molanna, the nymph who betrays her mistress, also survives the judgement of Diana, and lives on to marry:

> They, by commaund'ment of *Diana*, there
> Her whelm'd with stones. Yet *Faunus* (for her paine)
> Of her beloued *Fanchin* did obtaine,
> That her he would receiue vnto his bed.
> So now her waues passe through a pleasant Plaine,
> Till with the *Fanchin* she her selfe doe wed,
> And (both combin'd) themselues in one faire riuer spred.[144]

Those stones do not matter very much: this river's original desire is to marry, and she achieves this desire despite Diana. The landscape of the *Mutabilitie Cantos* retains at least the underlying pulse of vitality even after the goddess punishes it with transformation. She leaves:

---

[142] *Met.* 3. 192–252. Spenser's source for the version of the tale without the metamorphosis is probably Comes. Even in this version, however, Actaeon is mutilated: 'Alij dixerunt Actaeonem cervi pelle a Diana tectum laniatum fuisse a canibus ad eum lacerandum incitatis, ne Semelen uxorem duceret' (Others say that Actaeon was covered with a deerskin by Diana and torn apart by dogs goaded on to maul him, lest he should marry Semele), *Mythologiae, sive explicationum fabularum libri decem* (Paris, 1583), 666. See also Richard Ringler, 'The Faunus Episode', *Modern Philology*, 63 (1965), 14.

[143] *FQ* III. vi. 47.

[144] *FQ* VII. vi. 53.

All those faire forrests about *Arlo* hid,
  And all that Mountaine, which doth over-looke
  The richest champian that may else be rid,
And the faire *Shure*, in which are thousand Salmons bred.

Them all, and all that she so deare did way,
  Thence-forth she left; and parting from the place,
  There-on an heauy hapless curse did lay,
  To weet, that Wolues, where she was wont to space,
  Should harbour'd be, and all those Woods deface,
  And Thieues should rob and spoile that Coast around.[145]

Diana's effort at a judicial metamorphosis becomes a capricious and superficial vandalism, which is opposed to, yet cannot overwhelm, the forces which keep the salmon and wood-gods breeding. Such endless rebirth is beyond the virgin goddess's ken, and it remains beyond her authority. This world is not subject to the pitiful instincts of a monarch; it has mercy impregnated in it by the need for life to go on.

When Spenser returns from his digression to the main narrative, this mercy, which has no relation to passion, and pays no heed to virgin queens, retains its hold on the poem. It is the quality evoked in the final sentence of the hermaphroditic goddess Nature, once she has heard the evidence of Mutabilitie. She neither condemns nor pardons the aspiring Titaness; she just enfolds her into how things are:

I well consider all that ye haue sayd,
  And find that all things stedfastnes doe hate
  And changed be: yet being rightly wayd
  They are not changed from their first estate;
  But by their change their being do dilate:
  And turning to themselues at length againe,
  Doe work their owne perfection so by fate:
  Then ouer them Change doth not rule and raigne;
But they raigne ouer change, and doe their states maintaine.

Cease therefore daughter further to aspire,
  And thee content thus to be rul'd by me:
  For thy decay thou seekst by thy desire;
  But time shall come that all shall changed bee,
  And from thenceforth, none no more change shall see.
  So was the *Titaness* put downe and whist,
  And *Ioue* confirm'd in his imperiall see.
  Then was that whole assembly quite dismist,
And *Natur's* selfe did vanish, whither no man wist.[146]

---

[145] Ibid. 54–5.
[146] *FQ* VII. vii. 58–9.

Nature's judgement expresses a form of cosmic conservatism, which absorbs all rebellions, and all rebellious human passions, into a near-endless cycle of change and growth. There are some residual anomalies and evasions even in this apparently definitive conclusion, though; by a string of puns on 'change' (which she uses to mean both an irreversible shift of state and a continuing process of alteration), Nature makes history appear to be both a single process towards an apocalypse and an endless series of cycles. Her conservatism has a similar double edge. Jove, with his passionate affections, is not confirmed in his high see by this judgement at all, since it does not address his claim to rule by right of conquest. Nor are the claims of the rebel Mutabilitie rebutted. She is, like the antagonists in many romances, allowed to live on; but she lives on without acquiring or losing any power. Nature describes a processful force of change, which exists in a mythic space before and after human desires, and which is above any mortal authority. She perhaps evades, perhaps transcends, mortal questions about the nature of government. The whole enslaving fabric of human passions, powers, and aspirations is elegantly entangled in uncertainty by this merciful, generative, hermaphroditic justice, who lies beyond any specific location in time, and who has no need to assert her own authority. The enfolding of male with female, justice with mercy, in the complex figure of Nature is generated by Spenser's continuing battle to overcome the constraints of his inherited idiom, and from the closely related pressures of contemporary politics; if Nature lives in a space beyond time, and above mortal authority, it is because the poet has finally created a fiction which can avoid, or perhaps evade, the problems of power implicit in sexual and political relations.

6

Inglorious Spensers

Texts which offer the appearance of resolution, but which strike one as less unified the more one thinks about them, have an enormous power. Each generation can appropriate the apparent definitiveness of such works to sanction partial readings of them, while the residue of material which a dominant reading cannot explain enables the next generation to draw out some other aspect of the master-work to relish and exaggerate. *The Faerie Queene* presents an amalgam of antagonistic forces, which appear to be melting together in myths, but which are always restlessly shifting in relation to each other, interweaving or exfoliating into confusion and uncertainty. Such a combination of apparent unity and deep thematic instability gives the poem the potential to be reread and reinterpreted in order to suit a number of different occasions and attitudes. At some moments it appears that an active, martial rage is burning away the vestiges of Ariosto's pitiful eroticism from the minds of its heroes; at other times the chief force in the poem appears to be a kind of justice that transcends human passions altogether. Spenser also manages so scrupulously to look as though he is praising the gently manipulative forms of ascendancy practised by his queen that one could imagine a staunch Royalist reading his poem as a hymn to the clemency of imperial sovereigns.

The subsequent history of English epic can be seen as largely a string of differing responses to the pliable, unstable structures of *The Faerie Queene*. For its immediate successors, the aspects of the poem which seemed most urgent were its concerns with the pursuit of honour, and the rewarding of such honourable aspirations by a just monarch. A number of writers—particularly the authors of historical epics, and Chapman in his translations of Homer—began epic poems in the late 1590s which initially placed a romancish emphasis on pity and love, but which were subsequently revised in order to concentrate on heroes who burn with rage against monarchs who have denied them their dues. This strand in the English epic (which persists up to around the 1620s) is latent in the concerns of *The Faerie Queene* with the pursuit of glory, justice, and anger. But after this period many epic poems appear to abandon the civic concerns which had led Spenser to attempt to weld the opposing motives of love and honour into a single force, and turn to the internal regimen of the passions as the chief activity for the heroic mind. This tendency coincides with a period when few epics could boast the powerful patronage which had sustained, and given a political purpose to, the Elizabethan epic.

A further, and perhaps historically more important response to Spenser's poem emerges through the seventeenth century. Passions come to be seen as independent forces; heroes become agents who swing rapidly between these passions; and increasingly, through the works of Cowley and Dryden, Royal and Royalist characters are inclined to pitiful love, while dangerous rebels incline to anger. This is the line which ultimately leads to Dryden's *Aeneid*, in which a pitiful Aeneas confronts an irascible Turnus, and to his *Absalom and Achitophel*, in which a clement, all-powerful monarch confronts the mad rage of his rebellious antagonists. The precise stages of these developments are intricate, and often overlap and become entangled with each other. But the general movement, from the rich confusions of Spenser to the over-clarified idiom of Restoration epic, charted in the following two chapters, has enormous literary-historical importance. Most recent studies of English epic concentrate exclusively on Spenser and Milton. Several, under the heavy (or should that be heady?) influence of Harold Bloom, see the relations between those two poets simply (or complicatedly) in terms of a showdown between the anxieties of Milton and the text of his predecessor. The chief object of the following chapters is to correct this emphasis. The minor writers and translators discussed in this chapter and the next create a medium through which Milton read Spenser, and play a large part in creating the set of attitudes to the romance tradition which he inherited.

HARINGTON'S ARIOSTO

Sir John Harington made one mistake in life: he published a plan for a flushing lavatory in his treatise on courtly corruptions, punningly entitled *The Metamorphosis of A-Jax*. This has enabled critics ever since to sneer at him. Ben Jonson started the abuse when he said that Harington's *Orlando furioso* was 'under all translations . . . the worst'.[1] Jonson also may have been sending up the prophetic and heroic concerns of Harington's unpublished translation of *Aeneid* 6 in his gruesomely lavatorial poem *On the Famous Voyage*. This poem extracts the first murky shades of English mock heroic from the muck and slime of a failed voyage of discovery

---

[1] *Works*, ed. C. H. Herford and P. Simpson, 11 vols. (Oxford, 1925–52), i. 133.

through the sewers of London, and ends with a wish that 'My *Muse* had plough'd with his, that sung A-IAX'.[2]

Harington's translation of *Orlando furioso* does not deserve such a cloacal end, however. The fluent play of Ariosto is not quite Harington's thing; but his translation does have distinctive qualities of its own. It is at its best when rendering moments of rambunctious energy, as when an avaricious judge is tricked into sleeping with a Negro. This prompts Harington coyly to declare his control over the vernacular:

> But him with so large offers still he prest
> That in conclusion like a beastly sot,
> So as it might be done in hugger mugger
> The Judge agreed the Negro him should (   ).[3]

As this example indicates, Harington's translation does lack much of the amorous magic which keeps Ariosto's poem flowing delightedly from action to action. Things just lovingly happen in *Orlando furioso*; and the chief weakness of Harington's translation is that he often adds an intrusive violence to Ariosto's moments of amorous sympathy. When the Italian Orlando is sleeplessly lovelorn over Angelica, Ariosto plays his habitual trick of making love the source of all the energy in his poem. He takes Aeneas's martial unease in *Aeneid* 8 and crosses it with Dido's careful vigil in Book 4:[4] the tremors of love replace martial solicitude in an amorous renewal of a Virgilian simile:

> qual d'acqua chiara il tremolante lume,
> dal sol percossa o da' notturni rai,
> per gli ampli tetti va con lungo salto
> a destra et a sinistra, e basso et alto.[5]

---

[2] Ibid. viii. 89. See *The Sixth Book of Virgil's Aeneid, Translated and Commented on by Sir John Harington (1604)*, ed. Simon Cauchi (Oxford, 1991), p. xxi. A translation of *Aeneid* 4 in BL Add. MS 60283 has been wrongly attributed to Harington. See Simon Cauchi, 'Sir John Harington and Virgil's *Aeneid*', *English Manuscript Studies 1100–1700*, 1 (1989), 242–9. The fullest general study of Harington is D. H. Craig, *Sir John Harington* (Boston, 1985).

[3] Har. xliii. 133. All references to *Ludovico Ariosto's Orlando furioso translated into English Heroical Verse by Sir John Harington (1591)*, ed. Robert McNulty (Oxford, 1972).

[4] *Aen.* 8. 22–5: 'sicut aquae tremulum labris ubi lumen aënis | sole repercussum aut radiantis imagine lunae | omnia pervolitat late loca, iamque sub auras | erigitur summique ferit laquearia tecti' (As when in brass bowls a trembling ray of light, bouncing from the sun, or from the gleaming image of the moon, flits far and wide, and now leaps up and strikes the decorated ceiling of a building). Cf. Apollonius Rhodius, *Argonautica* 3. 744–65. For the contamination with *Aen.* 4. 522–32, see Fichter, *Poets Historical: Dynastic Epic in the Renaissance* (New Haven, Conn., and London, 1982), 74–7; Peter De Sa Wiggins, *Figures in Ariosto's Tapestry* (Baltimore and London, 1986), 112–14; D. S. Carne-Rosse, 'The One and the Many: A Reading of *Orlando furioso*, Cantos 1 and 8', *Arion* 5: 2 (1966), 222–5. Ariosto notices a connection hinted at by Virgil; see R. O. A. M. Lyne, *Further Voices in Vergil's Aeneid* (Oxford, 1987), 125–32.

[5] *OF* viii. 71. 5–8.

As the trembling light from clear water, struck by the sun or by the rays of the moon, goes in great leaps to left and right, high and low through a great building.

The impact of the light itself seems to cause the slight turbulence in the surface of the water that makes the reflection tremble. The water is 'percossa', physically struck by the light. This wondering delight is too fine for Harington, who misses the glimmer of Virgil:

> As circles in a water cleare are spred
> When sunne doth shine by day and moone by night
> Succeeding one another in a ranke
> Till all by one and one do touch the banke.[6]

Harington, as it were, throws a stone into the pool, and watches not the self-motive leap of the reflection, but the palpable rings that spread from the centre of the water which he has so violently disturbed. In general the translation moves with less amorous sympathy than its original. Moments of love never just emerge from a general environment of desire; they are forced to happen. Harington's version of Ruggiero's seduction of Alcina is typical for its new roughness:

> Come Ruggiero abbracciò lei, gli cesse
> il manto: e restò il vel suttile e rado,
> che non copria dinanzi né di dietro.[7]

When Ruggiero embraced her, her cloak slipped off, and there remained a subtle, luminous veil, which covered neither before nor behind.

The impersonal construction 'gli cesse' makes the amorous display occur almost without artifice, perhaps with the faintest assistance from Ruggiero, or with a yielding shrug from Alcina. Harington's knight, in full armour, is definitely the cause of this exposure:

> Yet so the champion hasted to the fight
> The mantell with his furie fell away,
> And now the smocke remaind alone in sight.[8]

Harington has to add little nudges, stones thrown into pools, or the enthusiasm of a mature warrior, in order to reproduce things which simply happen in Ariosto. The whole world of *Orlando furioso* is instinc-

---

[6] Har. viii. 63. John Stewart of Baldynneis is more delicately wrong: 'Lyk as the schadow befoir Phebus face | Of tuynkling vattir casting clairlie cleir, | Or as the nocturne beams quhilk dois appeir | But rest ay reilling throch the glansing sky'. *Poems*, ed. Thomas Crockett (vol. ii only), STS (Edinburgh, 1913), iv. 23–6.

[7] *OF* vii. 28. 5–7.

[8] Har. vii. 26. 4–6. Cf. C. S. Lewis, *English Literature in the Sixteenth Century Excluding Drama* (Oxford, 1954), 521: 'The great Italian, at his most wanton, is always elegant and civilized to his fingertips: Harington's waggishness is, by comparison, a little raw and provincial.'

tively sensitive to the lightest touch or the faintest trace of love; Harington's is not.

His toughness has an ethical correlative. With a consistency that amounts to programmatic modification of his original, Harington runs Ariosto's fresh appetency through moral categories. This has frequently been noted, variously deplored, and generally attributed to the thick medium of Italian allegorical commentaries through which Harington filtered *Orlando furioso* in order to make the spirited Italian acceptable to his sober English audience.[9] This is not entirely accurate: there are strong native forces at work in the translation. When Merlin reveals to Bradamante that she can look forward to noble progeny, Harington writes in the idiom of a subject in an elect nation:

> Acciò dunque il voler del ciel si metta
> in effetto per te, che di Ruggiero
> t'ha per moglier fin da principio eletta,
> segue animosamente il tuo sentiero.

Since then the will of heaven works through you, so that Ruggiero will have you for his wife, chosen from the beginning of time, pursue your course spiritedly.

> Wherefore sith God hath by predestination,
> Appointed thee to be Rogeros wife,
> And means to blesse thine heirs and generation
> With all the graces granted in this life,
> Persist thou firme in thy determination
> And stoutly overcome each storme of strife.[10]

'Eletta' probably jolted the English poet into the linguistic register of 'predestination' and 'grace': he regards his heroine as one of the elect, who needs none the less to exert herself against an opposing world in order to realize her calling.[11] This is far from the spirited pursuit of a

---

[9] For the influence of Simon Fornari, *La spositione sopra l'Orlando furioso*, 2 vols. (Florence, 1549), and Harington's text, *Orlando furioso di M. Lodovico Ariosto, nuovamente adornato di figure di Rame da Girolamo Porro . . . [con] una allegoria universale sopra tutta l'opera dell'Ariosto fatta da Giuseppe Bononome* (Venice, 1584), see Susannah Jane McMurphy, *Spenser's Use of Ariosto for Allegory*, University of Washington Publications in Language and Literature, 2 (Seattle, 1924), 16–21; T. G. A. Nelson, 'Sir John Harington and the Renaissance Debate over Allegory', *Studies in Philology*, 82 (1985), 359–79. Judith Lee, 'The English Ariosto: The Elizabethan Poet and the Marvellous', *Studies in Philology*, 80 (1983), 277–99, attributes the changes to the moral nature of English literary theory. Townsend Rich, *Harington and Ariosto: A Study on Elizabethan Verse Translation*, Yale Studies in English, 92 (New Haven, Conn., 1940), 142–54, doubts the seriousness of Harington's Allegories. For a more temperate account, see Hallett Smith, *Elizabethan Poetry: A Study in Convention, Meaning and Expression* (Cambridge, Mass., 1952), 312–22; and Daniel Javitch, *Proclaiming a Classic: The Canonization of Orlando Furioso* (Princeton, NJ, 1991), 134–57.

[10] *OF* iii. 19. 1–4; Har. 20. 1–6.

[11] On election, see Jean Calvin, *Institution of Christian Religion*, trans. Thomas Norton (London, 1561), fol. 252ᵇ, III. xxi–xxiv; esp. xxiii. 12 against the claim that the elect can live a vicious life of ease: 'If the marke of that election is directed unto be holinesse of life, it ought more to awake and sturre us up cherefully to practise that holinesse, than to serve for a ciokyng of slouthfulnesse.'

'sentiero' (delightfully suggestive of 'sentire') to which the Italian heroine is urged.[12] There are further suggestions of a distinctively English response to epic romance in Harington's treatment of this episode too. Spenser turned Merlin's revelation of Bradamante's noble progeny into an exhortation to Britomart that she emulate the ancestral virtue of her house, and used this exhortation to motivate her quest for Artegall.[13] This transformation was a response to the repeated insistence among humanistic writers that a hereditary aristocracy should reduplicate its ancestral virtue in order to merit its continuing supremacy. Harington's interpretation of Merlin's exhortation is very close to Spenser's:

In the great praise of *Rogero* and *Bradamant* his posteritie, noble men and gentlemen of good house may take comfort of their vertuous ancestors and thinke themselves beloved of God and blessed with great temporall blessings if themselves degenerate not from their worthy forefathers. Also we may note that commonly good parents bring good children.[14]

There is no evidence that Harington read Spenser while he was actually translating Ariosto (although he did know *The Faerie Queene* by the time he wrote the commentary, since it alludes to the poem in some detail[15]). But he does show a common way of interpreting romance. He shares the central animating ambition of *The Faerie Queene* to redirect desire towards Glory, and to see love quests as motivated by an aristocratic desire for a virtue which would bring a glorious past back to life—either literally, by breeding virtuous offspring, or more metaphorically, by reviving their glorious deeds. And this allegorical redirection of desire runs right through the translation, and explains some of the heaviness to which critics have repeatedly objected. Harington's wish to display an active love of virtue in his heroes often leads him to transform the rarefied beauty of Ariosto's women into much more sober charms. When, in the original, Orlando abandons his intention of rescuing Angelica from the Orc in order to help Olimpia, his action expresses the pitiful desire to help the beautiful which so often fertilizes the growth of one story from another in Ariosto's poem. Harington, with his very different model of human appetency in mind, changes the appeal to help an affable lady into a request from beleaguered virtue:

[12] Similar changes are also made to the delighted sightseeing of Ariosto's pilgrims in canto xv: their English equivalents undergo a hard journey to spritual remorse, and eventually attain a 'special grace': Har. xv. 71–6; *OF* 94–100.

[13] *OF* iii. 1–64; *FQ* III. iii. 15–62.

[14] Har. 47.

[15] Harington shows accurate knowledge of the 'excellent Poem of the Faery Queene' in the printed translation, Har. 513. The earlier manuscript, Bodleian MS Rawl. Poet. 125, contains no notes, and consequently offers no sure evidence that Harington knew *The Faerie Queene* before 1590.

E da parte il pregò d'una donzella,
ch'a lei venir non gli paresse grave,
la qual ritroverebbe, oltre che bella,
più ch'altra al mondo affabile e soave.

And he begged him on behalf of a damsel that he would not fail to go to her;
whom he would find—apart from being beautiful—more mild and sweet than
anyone else in the world.

How that a certaine dame of noble blood,
Of vertue verie great, of beautie rare,
Of sober cheare, and of behaviour good...[16]

Harington's Orlando pursues an image of virtuous nobility and sobriety,
where Ariosto's is tempted from his frenzied pursuit of Angelica by the
prospect of something sweeter. And this redirection of desire is a frequent
feature of the translation. Harington's women are often embodiments of
virtue and rank rather than just lovely:

Orlando domandò qual fosse tanto
scortese, ingiusto, barbaro et atroce,
che ne la grotta tenesse sepolto
un sì gentile et amoroso volto.

Orlando demanded who had been so discourteous, unjust, barbarous, and uncivil
as to hold buried in a cave a face so gentle and amorous.

Yet straight he enterd in examination
By whom in that same cave they had bene staid?
And who they were in so unseemly fashion
That kept a comely and a noble maid?
And said he saw it written in her face
Her nurture and her lynage were not base.[17]

The Italian Orlando—prompted by a sense that lovely faces should not
be kept in caves—regards the outrage on Isabella as a violation of the
primary chivalric rule that one should pity beleaguered damsels. Harington, however, is not appalled by the *scortesia* of those who mistreat a
maiden who is *amorosa*, but is intent on reading an ethical history into
Isabella's face. The violation is of rank: 'gentile' loses its suggestion of
softness to become 'noble', and Isabella's face becomes the embodiment
of an extended history of birth and nurture.[18] What, for Harington, makes
people attractive (in the literal sense of drawing others towards them) is
true worth, rather than pitiful beauty.

[16] *OF* ix. 19. 1–4; Har. 16. 1–3.
[17] *OF* xii. 93. 5–8; Har. 69. 3–8.
[18] Cf. *OF* xix. 17. 1–4; Har. 12. 1–4.

The network of ideas which underlies this change in human drive can be deduced from a significant addition which Harington makes to the genealogy of the treacherous Pinabello:

> che tra sua gente scelerata, solo
> leale esser non volse né cortese,
> ma ne li vizii abominandi e brutti
> non pur gli altri adeguò, ma passò tutti.

Who did not want to be alone among his family of scoundrels in being loyal and courteous, but in inhuman and brutal vices, not only equalled, but surpassed all.

> Borne in *Maganza* of that wicked race,
> Who like the rest so lewd a course did runne
> He holpe the more his lynage to deface:
> For onely vertue noblenes doth dignifie
> And vicious life a linage base doth signifie.[19]

The chivalric virtues of courtesy and loyalty are passed over in the English in order to show that Pinabello's unspecified wickedness lies in his pedigree. Harington's marginal note shows the doctrine that he reads into Ariosto, and which accounts for many of the attitudes that come through the English: *virtus vera nobilitas*, 'virtue is true nobility'. This doctrine is reiterated over and over again by the authors of humanist treatises on how to educate a gentleman: rather than simply relying on and relishing their high position, aristocrats should educate themselves in rational virtue in order to merit their position near the head of the body politic. The belief that virtue is true nobility could, theoretically, have a meritocratic edge, since it could be taken to imply that hereditary nobility is secondary to that won solely by virtue, and that, therefore, the ideal commonwealth would be one in which the most virtuous and rational ruled, irrespective of their rank. This interpretation of the doctrine could be, and occasionally was, used to advocate a meritocratic form of government which extended even to the monarchy: for Thomas Starkey, in a manuscript treatise composed in the early sixteenth century, the ideal that the most rationally virtuous should rule led to the startling suggestion that even monarchs should be elected to their offices.[20] The more conservative, and more usual, version of this outlook, however, was that implicit in Thomas Elyot's *Governour*: that the existing aristocracy should seek to educate itself so as to merit its elevated condition, and to exercise its role in

---

[19] *OF* ii. 58. 5–8; Har. 58. 4–8.

[20] *A Dialogue between Reginald Pole and Thomas Lupset*, ed. K. M. Burton (London, 1948), 153; for Lupset's views on the horrors of tyranny, see 100. For a detailed account of the sources and context of the dialogue, see Thomas F. Mayer, *Thomas Starkey and the Commonweal: Humanist Politics and Religion in the Reign of Henry VIII* (Cambridge, 1989).

government.[21] Writers on nobility in the 1590s often share the chivalric bias towards the high-born. William Jones, dedicating his translation of *Nennio, or a Treatise of Nobility* to Essex, praises his lordship for nobility both by descent and by virtue: 'both these conjoyned togither in your L. doe make you perfectly Noble'.[22] This encomiastic deployment of the theme takes the place of a preface to the Italian edition where Nennio speculates on the historical development of social rank in primitive society, which naturally has no place for inherited nobility.[23] Harington's reference to this nexus of ideas in the Marganorre episode is akin to this conservative position, since he implies an intrinsic relation between 'linage base' and a 'vicious life'. And this interpretation of true nobility lies deep in the chivalric tradition. Not only humanists voiced the *virtus vera nobilitas* doctrine:[24] it was also a commonplace of chivalric manuals, with a history which runs back to Juvenal's 'nobilitas sola est atque unica virtus'.[25] Guillame Fillastre, the second Chancellor of the Order of the Golden Fleece, voiced a commonplace when he said 'en vertu consiste noblesse',[26] and he certainly did not mean by this that plebs could become as good as lords.

The radical substratum of the doctrine does rest unsteadily beneath Harington's treatment of love in *Orlando furioso*, however, and explains a large number of his distortions to Ariosto and his commentators. Several of Harington's original notes explain why he so persistently identifies beauty with virtue: they repeatedly stress the importance of marrying virtue rather than blood and money, and so imply that desire and a concern for merit should ideally fuse into a single force.[27] This concern with loving merit also affects his reading of the *Furioso*'s core romance episode: when Angelica falls for Medoro, the episode does not show the

[21] *The Boke Named the Governour*, ed. H. S. S. Croft, 2 vols. (London, 1880), i. 5–6, ii. 28.

[22] Gianbattista Nenna da Bari, *Nennio, or a Treatise of Nobilitie: wherein is discoursed what true Nobilitie is, with such qualities as are required in a perfect Gentleman* (London, 1595), sig. A2ᵇ.

[23] *Il Nennio, nel qual si ragiona di nobiltà* (Venice, 1542), sigs. A1ᵃ–A2ᵇ.

[24] Quentin Skinner, *The Foundations of Modern Political Thought*, 2 vols. (Cambridge, 1978), i. 81, traces the development of this idea from the medieval *dictatores*; cf. Hans Baron, *The Crisis of the Early Italian Renaissance*, 2nd edn. (Princeton, NJ, 1966), 418–24, who also neglects its chivalric predecessors.

[25] *Satire* 8. 20. For a history of this saying in the Middle Ages, see George McGill Vogt, 'Gleanings for the History of a Sentiment: *Generositas Virtus, non Sanguis*', *Journal of English and Germanic Philology*, 24 (1925), 102–24. See also Maurice Keen, *Chivalry* (New Haven, Conn., and London, 1984), ch. 8, 143–61.

[26] *Le premier [et second] volume de la toison dor* (Paris, 1517), fol. 2ᵃ; see Michael Leslie, *Spenser's 'Fierce Warres and Faithful Loves': Martial and Chivalric Symbolism in 'The Faerie Queene'* (Cambridge, 1983), 136.

[27] 'Another good morall observation to be gathered in this canto is the choise of *Genevra* who being a great Ladie by birth yet chose rather a gallant faire conditioned gentleman then a great Duke', Har. 68. Cf. Harington's criticism of the way Bradamante's mother wants to see her daughter marry rank and money, Har. 527.

primacy of pity for Harington: it consummates the quest for honour:
'*Angelica* is taken for honor, which brave men hunt after by blood and
battells and many hardie feats and misse it, but a good servant with faith
and gratefulnesse to his Lord gets it.'[28] This note appears to have no
parallel in any Italian commentary. Ariosto's revived Euryalus becomes
the chief beneficiary of the *virtus vera nobilitas* theme, which overlays
pietà as the motivating principle of this central tale. Harington does not,
like Spenser, cut off the erotic conclusion of the story in order to stop
Angelica yielding to her lower-class lover; but he does tame it by closely
tying the desires it releases to a civic ideal of virtuous ascendancy.

   Harington's eagerness to impose the quest for virtue on the appetency
of *Orlando furioso* prevents him from producing a spirited version of the
amorous sympathies which motivate the energetic chaos of its early parts.
But his view of the poem does make perfect sense of—and substantially
derives from—Ariosto's drier, more duty-bound conclusion. He reads the
Furioso consistently through its ending. The story of Ruggiero and
Bradamante, as developed in Ariosto's additions of 1532, concludes with
a dramatization of the much-reiterated humanist debate on true nobility
and its relation to marriage. Good humanist ladies, like the heroine of
Henry Medwall's *Fulgens and Lucrece*, were meant, after due debate, to
choose the virtuous and low-born above the rich and ignorant. At the
end of *Orlando furioso* Bradamante's parents are opposed to her match
with the poor but virtuous Ruggiero, whom she, like the ideal woman in
early humanist debates on why one should marry, has chosen above rich
and royal suitors. Ariosto opposes her parents' old-fashioned Aristotelian
belief, that ancient riches make a man noble and eligible,[29] to the heroine's
conviction that the true nobility of virtue alone makes a man worthy to
wed. Her father says:

> né sa che nobiltà poco si prezza,
> e men virtù, se non v'è ancor ricchezza.
>
> Alas (quoth he) poore gentrie small availes
> And vertue lesse if lande and riches failes.[30]

Harington adds the contemptuous side-note 'Sentence. The common
opinion of the people' (although even someone as elevated as Lord

---

[28] Har. 218; cf. Har. 29, where Angelica is allegorized as 'pleasure or honor or whatsoever man
doth most inordinately affect'; ibid. 99: 'the passion of love or ambicion or whatsoever else may be
understood by *Angelica*'; ibid. 458: '*Angelica*, by which (as I have often noted) is meant pleasure or
honor.'

[29] *Politics* 4. 12 (1282^b–1283^a).

[30] *OF* xliv. 36. 7–8; Har. 33. 7–8.

Burghley put forward this position in his advice to his son[31]). Ariosto attempts at the end of the poem to reconcile the rival demands of love and service to the state by directing desire towards an embodiment of virtue. Aeneas can, as it were, be represented as staying with Dido provided that she is an embodiment of virtue and nobility. Harington is in complete, almost excessive, sympathy with this overall project. The concluding debate on true nobility perfectly consummates the ethos which Harington constructed for the poem:

> Degno d'eterna laude è Bradamante,
> che non amò tesor, non amò impero,
> ma la virtù, ma l'animo prestante,
> ma l'alta gentilezza di Ruggiero.

> Such was the noble *Bradamantas* mynd
> Who sought not after wealth and rich abilitie
> Nor state nor pompe that many women blynd,
> But after vertue pure, the true nobility.[32]

Ariosto intimates the substantive qualities in Ruggiero which make him lovable: 'l'animo prestante' is both nobly abstract high-mindedness *and* extraordinary high spirits; 'l'alta gentilezza' expresses both the peak of nobility *and* extraordinary tenderness. Harington, however, pulls the allegorical undercurrent to the surface: Bradamante's quest for Ruggiero also shows that she 'sought' true nobility for herself. The allegorical level sucks most of the juice out of the literal, leaving love a rather coldly abstract thing: Ariosto's poem, consistently read through its ending, does lose a lot of its energy. But Harington deserves praise for reading a quest for glory into the earlier, more wilful loves, of Ariosto's heroes: he is, as it were, just prematurely ageing the poem, pushing it towards its ending a little too soon.

There is another element, however, to Ariosto's resolution of Bradamante's conflict with her parents, which is rather more radical, and which imparts a real urgency to Harington's translation. Ariosto extends the *virtus vera nobilitas* doctrine to include the monarchy. Ruggiero is elected king of Bulgaria by virtue of his martial skill, and thereby obtains sufficient wealth and status to satisfy the most exacting parent. The Bulgarian heralds come to offer him a kingdom:

---

[31] He advises marrying money, 'for *Gentilitie is nothing but ancient Riches*: so that if the Foundation do sinke, the Building must needs consequently fall'; William Cecil, Lord Burghley, *Precepts, Directions for the well ordering and carriage of a mans life... left to his son* (London, 1637), 7. This treatise was composed *c.*1584; see *Advice to a Son: Precepts of Lord Burghley, Sir Walter Raleigh, and Francis Osborne*, ed. L. B. Wright (Ithaca, NY, 1962), pp. xvii–xix.

[32] *OF* xxvi. 2. 1–4; Har. 2. 1–4.

> Che quella nazion, la qual s'avea
> Ruggiero eletto re, quivi a chiamarlo
> mandava questi suoi, che si credea
> d'averlo in Francia appresso al magno Carlo:
> perché giurargli fedeltà volea,
> e dar di sé dominio, e coronarlo.

For this people, which had elected Ruggiero their king, had sent an embassy to fetch him, it being supposed that he was in France at Charlemagne's court. They wanted to swear obedience to him, to give him lordship over them, and to crown him.

> They said how that the people of their Nation
> To whom *Rogero* late such aide did bring
> Beyond all hope, beyond all expectation
> Had therefore chosen him to be their king,
> Rejecting all their owne kings generation
> And all his royall race (no usuall thing).[33]

The Estense were originally elected to a *signoria* in Ferrara, and Ariosto's narrative provides a reminder to his patrons that their power originated in their military abilities.[34] England's hereditary monarch could be expected to take less kindly to a dramatization of the doctrine that Princes are originally chosen for their virtue. This form of elective monarchy is readily assimilable to the premisses which underlie the idea that virtue is true nobility: if one accepts that the chief condition for social superiority is a superabundance of rational virtue, and that the defining quality of a monarch should be the extreme manifestation of such qualities, then to choose monarchs on the basis of their superiority in virtue would be entirely intelligible. Erasmus (in theory at least) advocated an elective rather than hereditary monarchy in order to ensure this due supremacy of virtue,[35] although he is characteristically evasive in his expressions of this idea. But it is an element in the social thought of early humanism which is continually on the brink of emerging from its underlying foundations. Unease with hereditary systems of monarchy and a tentative inclination towards elective monarchy repeatedly glimmer through the English epic tradition. In Sidney's *Arcadia*, Musidorus is elected monarch of Phrygia after liberating the country from a tyrant, but resigns the office, 'understanding that there was left of the blood royal, and next to the

---

[33] *OF* xlvi. 49. 1–4; Har. 32. 1–6.
[34] See L. Simeone, 'L'elezione di Obizzio d'Este a Signore di Ferrara', *Archivio storico italiano*, 93 (1935), 165–88; Werner L. Gundersheimer, *Ferrara: The Style of a Renaissance Despotism* (Princeton, NJ, 1973), 25–8.
[35] *The Education of a Christian Prince*, ed. L. K. Born (New York, 1936), 139–40.

succession, an aged gentleman of approved goodness'.[36] This legitimate, hereditary monarch appears with miraculous and comic ease, is dusted off, and given the crown with conditions imposed sufficient to prevent hereditary monarchy from declining once more into tyranny. Harington shares with Sidney a sympathy for meritocratic rule, which he too shrinks from explicitly affirming.[37] Elective monarchy is possible but, Harington cautiously adds, unusual. But like Sidney, he wrote an epic romance in which nobles pursue their own goals of virtue and high public office—even to the brink of monarchy—under the guise of amorous servitude.

Erasmus envisaged deposition of a monarch whose rule was not virtuous: 'If power is not joined to wisdom and goodness, it is tyranny not power; and that consent which the people once gave to that power can be withdrawn.'[38] Erasmus is also keen that the monarch should voluntarily limit his powers by acting within the law.[39] These notions are scatteringly presented rather than toughly argued through in Erasmus's works, but they flow from the chief premises of his arguments about monarchy: that kings should be rational, and that the supremacy of reason over the insurgent passions of a monarch should be established by educational means, supported by reasonable laws, and bolstered by the restraining presence of a strong, virtuous, conciliar nobility. This concern with the supremacy of reason leads Erasmus (as much as Spenser in *The Faerie Queene*) into a major area of difficulty when he attempts to describe how this rational and limited form of sovereignty should deploy charismatic virtues such as clemency and liberality. To exhibit such virtues might be necessary in order to elicit loving obedience from one's subjects; but it might also entail lovingly, clemently overthrowing the law. Erasmus also at one point confronts a more serious problem: that the *appearance* of these winning virtues could in theory be used by a Machiavellian tyrant

---

[36] *The Countess of Pembroke's Arcadia (The New Arcadia)*, ed. Victor Skretkowicz (Oxford 1987), 175. Harington was a friend of Sidney's brother Robert, and felt sufficient literary kinship with Sir Philip to insert several of his own jokes into a manuscript of the *Arcadia*, MS BL Add. 38892. See P.J. Croft, 'Sir John Harington's Manuscript of Sir Philip Sidney's *Arcadia*', in Stephen Parks and P.J. Croft (eds.), *Literary Autographs: Papers Read at the Clark Library Seminar 26 April 1980* (Los Angeles, 1983), 39–75. Harington shows knowledge of the printed editions, Har. 130. Michael G. Brennan, *Literary Patronage in the English Renaissance: The Pembroke Family* (London, 1988), 74, notes Robert Sidney's admiration of Harington's Ariosto; see also his 'Sir Robert Sidney and Sir John Harington of Kelston', *Notes and Queries*, 232 (1987), 232–7.

[37] Charles Merbury, *A Briefe Discourse of Royall Monarchie* (London, 1581), 22–37, attacks elective monarchies with a stridency which may indicate that advocates of this position were known to him.

[38] 'Siquidem potentia nisi sit cum sapientia, bonitateque coniuncta, tyrannis est non potentia, quam ipsam tamen populi consensus quemadmodum dedit, ita potest eripere', 'Silenis Alcibiadis' in *Proverbiorum Chiliadas* (Basle, 1515), 470, III. iii. 1.

[39] *The Education of a Christian Prince*, 212: 'Neither is it a state of servitude to live according to the letter of just laws. Nor is that a peaceful state in which the populace bows to every whim of the prince.' Cf. ibid. 221.

to bolster unjust rule.[40] Julius Caesar, as Erasmus notes, was famous for both tyranny and clemency: 'The clemency such as he feigned for preparing and bolstering up his tyrannical sway you should earnestly use to win for yourself the love of your subjects.'[41] Harington's refusal to make his heroes quite as completely amorous as those of Ariosto derives from a similarly equivocal attitude towards the relations between amorous supremacy, pity, and tyranny. Several of Harington's own notes to the translation emphasize the charming virtues of liberality, clemency, and faith (abiding by agreements), which often figure in Prince books as means to win obedience through grateful love;[42] and he shares something of Spenser's uneasy attachment to the view that subjects should obey monarchs primarily out of love for their superhuman virtues. But he feels the full stress of the amorous servitude implicit in such charismatic forms of rule. Harington's most vivid description of his Queen and Godmother is permeated with the power exerted by loving obedience, and is well aware of its practical effects:

Hir mynde was oftime like the gentle aire that comethe from the westerly pointe in a summer's morn; 'twas sweete and refreshinge to all arounde her. Her speech did winne all affections, and hir subjectes did try to shewe all love to hir commandes; for she woude saye, 'hir state did require her to commande, what she knew hir people woude willingely do from their owne love to hir.' Herein did she shewe hir wysdome fullie: for who did chuse to lose hir confidence; or who woude wytholde a shew of love and obedience, when their Sovereign said it was their own choice, and not hir compulsion? Surely she did plaie well hir tables to gain obedience thus wythout constraint: again, she coude pute forthe suche alteracions, when obedience was lackinge, as lefte no doubtynges whose daughter she was.[43]

---

[40] Niccolò Machiavelli, *The Prince*, trans. Edward Dacres (London, 1640), 122–41 (chs. 16–28), argues that a reputation for these virtues can be helpful, but that exercising them can be impolitic. Harington attacks 'that heathenish (nay divelish) saying of Machiavell that whom you have done a great injurie to, him you must never pardon', Har. 208.

[41] *The Education of a Christian Prince*, 202. Cf. the praise of Caesar's clemency in Francisco Patrizio, *Enneas de regno, & regis institutione* (Paris, 1519), 216.

[42] Har. 239, 457. See Erasmus, *The Education of a Christian Prince*, 206: 'The best formula is this: let him love, who would be loved, so that he may attach his subjects to him as God has won the peoples of the world to Himself by His goodness.' Erasmus goes on to praise clemency and affability (p. 209), preferment through merit (p. 219), and faith (p. 239). The matter is commonplace: 'Qui imperare cupiunt, Duo sibi proponere in primis debent. Unum ut liberales sint, Alterum ut clementes... Clementiam in quo esse senserimus, illum omnes admiramur, colimus, *pro* Deo habemus' (Those who want to rule ought first to make two resolutions: the first that they should be liberal; the second that they should be clement...We all admire a man in whom we sense clemency, we worship him, and hold him up as a god). Giangiovanni Pontano, *Opera Omnia* (Venice, 1518), fol. 87[b]; Innocent Gentillet, *A Discourse upon the Meanes of Wel Governing...against Machiavell*, trans. Simon Patericke (London, 1602), 255–308, defends all these virtues. See Skinner, *Foundations*, i. 127–8.

[43] *Nugae Antiquae*, i. 355–6.

He brilliantly evokes the ripple of Henrician muscle beneath the queenly crinolines, and elegantly plots the interrelations of love and servitude. Love naturally inspires willing obedience; but deliberate political deployment of amorous servitude turns voluntary subjection into a constraint both to obey, and to seem to obey willingly. While their arms are twisted up their backs, Elizabethan courtiers have to smile in contented obedience to a monarch they have to be seen to love. Harington knew well that charm can mask enslavement, as his allegorical commentary to the *Furioso* shows:

in that Bayardo striketh at *Sacrapant*, but yeeldeth to *Angelica*, it may be noted how the corage of our minds that can not be abated with any force are often subdued by flatterie and gentle usage till they be in the end even ridden as it were with slaverie.[44]

Harington's Gloriana has something of the domineering sweetness of his Godmother—and shares in what James Harrington was to call the Queen's 'perpetual love tricks' to win her subjects' obedience.[45] For Harington love, clemency, pity, and tyranny are all in very close contact. His unique allegory of Cimosco's tyranny advocates clemency and bounty as means of ensuring the informal obedience due to love, but there is again a residuum of dissatisfaction in his account of these soft virtues:

By *Cymoscos* tyrannie and death all Princes may take a warning that no engins nor strategems can keepe a tyrant safe in his estate but only clemency and bountie that to lawfull Princes breedes evermore love and loyaltie in the subject.[46]

His attempt to say that Princes win obedience by the charm of love has a slight ruffle in its syntax. 'No engins nor strategems can keepe a tyrant safe in his estate, but only clemency and bountie'—the suggestion that charisma keeps tyrants in their place is corrected by an attempt to limit such informal obedience to lawful Princes, but not before Harington has let slip a further suggestion that a tyrannical tempest might rumble behind the sweet breeze of his Godmother's nature. There is a faint trace of Spenser's fear that clement, winning ascendancy could initiate a slide into servitude.

There are also faint traces in Harington's works of an attraction to a period of overlap between Roman Republic and Empire in which government by law was supplanted by a less reliable form of rule. Such periods had a great fascination for writers in the 1590s: Shakespeare's *Lucrece* and *Titus Andronicus* (with its debate in Act I about the relative merits of heredity and meritocracy) both associate hereditary, or imperial, forms of

---

[44] Har. 29.
[45] *The Political Works of James Harrington*, ed. J. G. A. Pocock (Cambridge, 1977), 198.
[46] Har. 110.

supremacy with arbitrary acts of sexual violation. In the *Metamorphosis of A-Jax*, Harington translates Livy's description of how the whimsical charms of arbitrary monarchy lead Brutus's sons to reject Republican rule by law, and seek to reintroduce tyranny to Rome: they

concluded among them selves, that a king was better then a Consul, a Court better then a Senate; that to live onely by lawes, was too strict and rigorous a life, & better for pesantly then princely dispositions: that Kings could favour, aswell as frowne, reward, aswell as revenge, pardon aswell as punish, whereas the law was mercilesse, mute, and immutable; finally, they concluded it was ill living for them, where nothing but innocencie could protect a man.[47]

The cutting edge of the satire is reserved for the final clause: kingship attracts because it brings with it the power to pardon villains. The father of John Harington the Parliamentarian evidently admired the strict justice of the Roman Republic. He also praised Ariosto's Carlo for renouncing his power to dispense justice in person when the debate over Bradamante became unmanageably complex: 'he showd no manner of partiallity and in the end referred it to the determining of the free Court of Parliament'.[48] Like Spenser's Mercilla, Carlo justly defers to his counsellors in a doubtful case 'when the matter shall concerne great personages'. Although Harington did plan a treatise on clemency which would praise his Queen's bountiful government,[49] he habitually gravitates from clement sweetness to thoughts of tyranny. This habit of mind leads him to add a little biting aside when Angelica is tied (as Ariosto coyly puts it) to a naked rock:

> né l'orba tigre accesa in maggior rabbia,
> né ciò che da l'Atlante ai liti rubri
> venenoso erra per la calda sabbia,
> né veder né pensar senza cordoglio,
> Angelica legata al nudo scoglio.

---

[47] *A New Discourse of a Stale Subject, called the Metamorphosis of A-Jax*, ed. E. S. Donno (London, 1962), 116. Accurately translates Livy 2. 3. 1–5; see *The Romane Historie*, trans. Philemon Holland (London, 1600), 45. Cf. Har. 275: 'For that (indeed) is true clemencie in a Prince, to forgive that offence that is committed against . . . his owne person rather then that which is done against the law, for that is rather parciallitie and injustice then clemencie.'

[48] Har. 540.

[49] The notes to xvii translate Fornari, *Spositione*, i. 348, on the horrors of tyranny, to which Harington adds that he would write an encomium on 'the gracious and myld government of our Soveraigne save that so high and plentifull a matter requires an entire treatise . . . and therefore I reserve it wholly for an other worke of mine owne', Har. 195. There is no evidence that he ever wrote this work. Cf. 'In *Norandine* that finding he had done *Griffino* wrong is willing to make amends for it . . . we may see a notable example of princely clemencie which I could wish all Christian Princes to follow although indeed commonly they doe quite contrarie', Har. 208. He evidently followed Seneca in regarding compassion and clemency as virtues which would mitigate absolute rule: 'Clementia efficit, ut magnum inter regem tyrannumque discrimen sit' (Clemency brings it about that there is a great difference between a king and a tyrant), *De clementia*, edn. cit. 1. 12. 3.

Neither the pregnant tiger, worked up into a frenzied rage, nor the poisonous snake that on the red shores of the Atlantic wanders through the hot sand, could see, or think of without grief, Angelica tied to that naked rock.

> For sure no cruell beast were so unkind
> Nor Tyger in their greatest wrath and rage,
> Nor anie cruell tyrant can we find
> (Although there are good store in ev'ry age)
> That could behold or thinke without compassion
> A Ladie bounden in so vile a fashion.[50]

Harington does not catch Ariosto's difficult ellipsis for Libyan serpents;[51] but his venemous and ubiquitous brood of tyrants (perhaps spawned by the uncomprehending translator's desperate association of the East with despotism[52]) springs up in their place. *Every* age, Harington notes drily, has its store of tyranny. His Ariosto is not a placid work: it contains little pulses of unease with his Godmother's amorous and clement constraints on her subjects.

And it is far more concerned with tyranny and its remedies than any of its Italian sources.[53] Harington reads the tale of Marganorre's all-male kingdom in canto xxxvii as a lesson in life under tyranny.[54] This story, like much of the *Furioso*'s closing phase, traces the contorted forms into which pitiful desire is twisted when pursued to its limits. Marganorre's son Tanacro is led by his excessive amorousness to murder Drusilla's husband in order to possess her. She kills him in revenge. This violent consequence of unrestrained libidinousness prompts Marganorre to banish women from his country, through a twisted form of paternal love and *pietà*:

> Amor, pietà, sdegno, dolore et ira,
> disio di morte e di vendetta insieme
> quell'infelice et orbo padre aggira...[55]

Love, *pietà*, disdain, grief, and rage, desire of death and of revenge together goaded on this unfortunate, son-lorn father...

[50] *OF* viii. 67; Har. 59. 3–8.

[51] Bigi, ad loc., notes the allusion to *Inferno*, xxiv. 90.

[52] See C. A. Patrides, ' "The Bloody and Cruell Turke": The Background of a Renaissance Commonplace', *Studies in the Renaissance*, 10 (1963), 126–35.

[53] Harington ignores Fornari's note on Rodomonte's conduct in canto xxxv: 'si dinota che molte usanze ingiuste son da Tiranni imposte, & come quella pena, che ad altri attorto impongono, ultimamente sopra illor capo ricade' (It shows that many unjust practices are imposed by tyrants, and how the punishment which they wrongfully impose on others ultimately falls on their own heads), *Spositione*, i. 591; but in general he develops the theme.

[54] Harington's interpretation of this story may derive from *Orlando furioso...con alcune allegorie* (Venice, 1548), fol. 198ᵃ: 'In Marganorre [si vede] la crudeltà di Tiranno: ilquale al fine dopo molte offese trapposate senza castigo, è dal popolo ucciso' (In Marganorre one sees the cruelty of a Tyrant, who, after having performed many outrages without punishment, is finally killed by the people).

[55] *OF* xxxvii. 77. 1–3.

Ariosto's study in the perversity of passions takes on a political tone in Harington's version, however, when Drusilla contemplates her death and divine judgement:

> Se ti dirà che senza merto al vostro
> regno anima non vien, di' ch'io l'ho meco;
> che di questo empio e scelerato mostro
> le spoglie opime al santo tempio arreco.
> E che merti esser puon maggior di questi,
> spenger sì brutte e abominose pesti?

If you say that no one comes without merit into your kingdom, I say I have such merit, since I bring to His holy temple rich spoils. What merit could be greater than that of killing such a brutal and abominable monster?

> And if he say that none must there remaine
> But they that by good workes the same inherit,
> Tell him I have a cruell tyrant slaine,
> Of tyrants death I bring with me the merite;
> To kill a tyrant what can be more glorious
> Or in the sight of God more meritorious?[56]

As a murderess who is about to become a suicide, who believes that works might merit salvation, Drusilla is not the most likely spokesman for Harington's own opinions. But there is a precedent for her certainty of divine reward: several writers in the 1590s noted that the Greeks gave great honour to those who killed tyrants. Sir Walter Ralegh, for example, quotes at one point a passage from Cicero's *Pro Milone* 80, which accords praise to all types of tyrannicide.[57] Renaissance theorists generally agreed that usurping tyrants could justly be deposed by a subject;[58] but most followed Bodin in arguing that tyrannical but legitimate rulers like Marganorre and his son could only be deposed by a foreign prince.[59] Marganorre is deposed in orthodox manner by the errant Rinaldo and Marfisa, and so Harington's version seems contentedly orthodox. But that couplet on tyrannicide—'To kill a tyrant what can be more glorious | Or in the sight of God more meritorious?', which bounces along under the impetus of Harington's playgroundly jeering rhythm—shows no such

---

[56] *OF* xxxvii. 74. 3–8; Har. 63. 3–8.

[57] 'Also the *Grecians* did think it a service acceptable to murther the person of such an impious Prince. *Graeci homines deorum honores tribuebant iis qui Tyrannos necaverunt. Cic.*' Walter Ralegh, *The Cabinet Council* (London, 1658), 86. Cf. Louis Le Roy, *[Aristotle's] Politiques, or Discourses of Government*, trans. I.D. (London, 1598), 320: 'In old time great honors were set down in Greece for them that killed the Tyrans.'

[58] See W. A. Armstrong, 'The Elizabethan Conception of a Tyrant', *Review of English Studies*, 22 (1946), 161–81, and 'The Influence of Seneca and Machiavelli on the Elizabethan Tyrant', *Review of English Studies*, 24 (1948), 19–35.

[59] Jean Bodin, *Six Bookes of a Commonweale*, trans. R. Knolles (Cambridge, Mass., 1962), 221.

theoretical scruples: Drusilla's self-praise rings with confidence.

And she echoes one of the chief imaginative concerns of Harington's Ariosto. Harington sees the whole *Orlando furioso* in terms of a tyrannical strife between the passions and the reason. The *Apologie* prefixed to the translation makes tyrannicide an allegory of the establishment of reason's due regality, which, as in Drusilla's boast, is granted a heavenly reward. When Perseus killed Gorgon:

The Historicall sence is this: *Perseus*, the sonne of *Jupiter*, by the participation of *Jupiters* vertues that were in him, or rather comming of the stock of one of those kings of Creet or Athens so called, slew *Gorgon*, a tyrant in that country (*Gorgon* in greeke signifieth earth), and was for his vertuous parts exalted by men up into heaven.[60]

This myth and its allegory (Perseus's tyrannicide shows the elevation of man to divinity through eradicating tyrannous passions) probably caught Harington's eye in Leone Ebreo's *Dialoghi di Amore*[61] because it elevated one of his main imaginative concerns to a central place in moral psychology. His version of the story is crucially equivocal, though: Perseus's tyrannicide is justified *either* by his descent from royal blood *or* by his possession of Jupiter's virtue. Divine virtue as well as princely blood could sanction tyrannicide. Whoever does the deed, the execution of tyrant passion is a repeated theme in Harington's translation: for him the *Furioso* is about killing love.

When, towards the end of the poem, Bradamante's love for Ruggiero becomes painfully intertwined with filial devotion, Harington renders her conflict between love and loyalty not as an effort to wrest epic seriousness from youthful amours, but as an attempt to establish the regiment of the mind by destroying the tyrannous usurpation of love:

> So quanto, ahi lassa! debbo fare, so quanto
> di buona figlia al debito conviensi;
> io 'l so: ma che mi val, se non può tanto
> la ragion, che non possino più i sensi?
> s'Amor la caccia e la fa star da canto,
> né lassa ch'io disponga, né ch'io pensi
> di me dispor, se non quanto a lui piaccia,
> e sol, quanto egli detti, io dica e faccia?

I know, alas, what I must do. I know what is right for a good daughter to perform. I know all this; but what good is it to me, if reason cannot do as much

[60] Har. 5.

[61] (Venice, 1541), fols. 58^{a-b}. Harington's rendering is extremely close. See P. W. Long, 'A Detail of Renaissance Criticism', *Modern Language Notes*, 15 (1900), 84–9; noted independently by Robert Ellrodt, 'Sir John Harington and Leone Ebreo', *Modern Language Notes*, 65 (1950), 109–10.

as the senses? If love drives reason off, and makes her stand aside, and does not allow me to do as I like—no, doesn't even allow me to *think* of doing as I like—and when I only do and say what he wants and says?

> I know (alas I know) my duetie well,
> But powre I have not to performe the same.
> My fancie reasons rule doth quite expell
> And my well orderd thoughts put out of frame,
> And tyrant Love, gainst whom who dare rebell,
> Makes me cast off all feare of others blame:
> My speech, my deeds, my thoughts he doth dispose
> And ruleth them against my will, God knowes.[62]

Harington's conceited and tidied up revision of Bradamante's tangled complaint is not just a sign of (understandable) incomprehension. It derives from the doctrine implicit in his allegory of Perseus, that rationally ordered virtue should rule over the rebel passions. This doctrine shapes every aspect of Harington's *Furioso*. The final moment of the poem in Harington's allegory becomes the ultimate conquest of lust: '*Rodomont*, which is to be understood the unbridled heat and courage of youth ... is killed and quite vanquished by marriage.'[63] This interpretation derives, not from the Italian commentaries on *Orlando furioso*, but from allegorical interpretations of the end of the *Aeneid*. Fulgentius had interpreted Turnus as a representative of 'furor', which is conquered at the end of Virgil's poem by Aeneas. Harington transposes this reading into an amorous key.[64] For the English translator, Ariosto's romance relates the conquest, not of martial frenzy, but of rebellious *cupido*: the tyrannical passions are eradicated from the mind by marriage. The chief foundation of Harington's Ariosto is a kind of psychologized tyrannicide.

Harington's reading of *Orlando furioso* added a psychological and a political dimension to English epic romance, which may well explain why Milton read the translation twice.[65] A lesser light in the political turmoils of the succeeding generation was also very strongly influenced by Harington's political reading of Italian epic romance. Francis Rous (1579–1659) wrote

---

[62] *OF* xliv. 43; Har. 40.

[63] Har. 557. Cf. Fornari, *Spositione*, i. 758, who sees the combat as 'demonstrando in tanto come a vincere nei Duelli ha molto luogo l'haver la ragione dalla sua parte, l'ardimento del cuore, la destrezza, & l'arte, laquale fa divenir vana una immensa forza, & robustezza, & ogni furore, & rabbia' (demonstrating how useful it is to have reason on one's side, a zealous heart, dexterity, and skill, which can render ineffectual a great strength, total frenzy, and rage).

[64] 'Turnus enim Grece quasi turosnos dicitur, id est furibundus sensus; contra omnem enim furiam sapientiae atque ingenii arma reluptant' (Turnus is in Greek as it were *turosnos*, that is, the irascible appetite; for the arms of wisdom and virtue fight against all fury), *Opera*, ed. R. Helm (Stuttgart, 1970), 128.

[65] *The Works of John Milton*, ed. F. A. Patterson, 20 vols. (New York, 1931–40), xviii. 330–6.

Thule, or Vertues Historie (1598),[66] two books of a romantic epic in competent *ottava rima*, at the age of 16. Rous has all of Tasso's and Spenser's mistrust of amorous pity. One of his characters, Philedonus, reassures Viceina (a wandering Una-figure) with the concealed lustfulness of a late romance hero:

> Moved with pitie much, but more with lust,
> He dar'd not countermand her sad demaunds,
> But from his heart with pleasures flames combust,
> Vollied these words scarse shut in vertues bands:
> Come (fayre) and to my gentle mercie trust,
> And yeeld thy bodie to my embracing hands.[67]

Rous is not a subtle enough writer to match his understanding of Spenserian romance with a language that melts inconspicuously from pity to lust: Philedonus explosively reveals rather too much. Despite Rous's suspicion of pity, however, Ariosto presides over the structure of his first Book, which ends with a recollection of the final stanza of the *Furioso*: after the marriage of Doledra and Eumorpho, the wicked enchanter, who has opposed their match throughout, bites the dust with the blasphemous ferocity of Rodomonte.[68] Book I is a deliberate attempt at a compressed but complete romance narrative, which ends with a marriage and the death of a villain.

The first canto of Book II is occupied by political unrest, however, and shades over into more Haringtonian concerns. The subjects of Bdella (Greek, 'leech') have been bled white by, and are about to rebel against, their tyrannical but legitimate ruler Aimaran (whose name probably derives from the Greek *haima*, and so means, with Rous's youthful simplicity, that he is bloody). They enlist the help of the foreign knight Themistos (Greek *themis*, law or custom). Among Aimaran's crimes is the murder of Dicaea (Greek *dikē*, justice). All Rous's sympathies are with the popular rebellion against an unjust king. His writing is at its most energetic in violent apostrophes to evil counsellors[69] and to the tyrant himself:

> Heare how the trumpet of thy destinie,
> Looseth the bonds of blood ennurtur'd hate,
> That tingles in thine eares and bids thee die.[70]

---

[66] The poem is discussed in William Wells (ed.), 'Spenser Allusions in the Sixteenth and Seventeenth Centuries', *Studies in Philology*, Suppl. 68 (1971), 61–2.

[67] The Spenser Society, 23 (London, 1878), I. ii (p. 15).

[68] I. viii (p. 67). Rous imitates *OF* xlvi. 140, rather than *Aen.* 12. 951–2, since Turnus does not blaspheme during his death, and is killed before rather than after a marriage.

[69] II. i (p. 79).

[70] II. i (p. 77).

That last line is the best in the poem: tyrannicide was evidently as close to Rous's poetic heart as it was to Harington's. Since Themistos's name means 'law', Rous's allegorical intention is probably to suggest that a popular rebellion against a tyrant based on the law—whether he means common law, or simply a natural principle of fairness, is not made clear— is as legitimate as one which is supported by a foreign prince. One could not predict from *Thule* that Rous would become Provost of Eton and a mystic; but in this early work there are already signs of the attitudes which led him to publish an argument for political obedience to Parliament after the regicide of 1649,[71] and to become Speaker of the House of Commons during the Little Parliament. Like Harington, Sidney, and Spenser, he wrote an epic romance in the 1590s in which the limitation of royal power by general principles of justice was a major theme; unlike them he lived so long that he had to confront the practical consequences of his advocacy of political resistance in the Engagement controversy.

FAIRFAX'S TASSO

In Edward Fairfax's translation of Tasso (1600), all those erotic forces which Tasso attempted to push to the bottom of his text, and to drown in martial rage, come bouncing back to the surface. When Tancred fights (and eventually kills) Clorinda, Tasso produces one of his most intense displays of poetic restraint. The episode naturally shapes itself towards a deadly pathos, as an enamoured knight kills the woman he loves; but Tasso uses its climax to convert *pietà* into a religiose form: the final revelation of Clorinda produces only the eloquently restrained 'Ahi vista! Ahi conoscenza!'[72] whereupon Tancred baptizes his lady before she dies. During the battle Tasso mutedly suggests the parallels with a loving wrestle, but keeps this potential libidinousness on a very tight rein:

> Tre volte il cavalier la donna stringe
> con le robuste bracchia, ed altrettante
> da que' nodi tenaci ella si scinge,
> nodi di fer nemico e non d'amante.
> Tornano al ferro, e l'uno e l'altro il tinge
> con molte piaghe; e stanco ed anelante
> e questi e quegli al fin pur si ritira,
> e dopo lungo faticar respira.[73]

---

[71] *The Bounds and Bonds of Publique Obedience* (London, 1649).
[72] *GL* xii. 67. 8.
[73] *GL* xii. 57.

Three times the knight grasped the woman with his strong arms, and each time she escaped from those tight bands, bands of a fierce enemy, rather than a lover. They take up their swords, and each dyes the other red with many wounds; tired and breathless both at last withdrew, and took breath after long exertions.

Some of the deliberately lost opportunities here are taken up by Fairfax, who luxuriates in the suppressed erotic subtext:

> Thrice his strong armes he fouldes about her waste,
> And thrice was forst to let the virgine goe,
> For she disdained to be so embraste,
> No lover would have strain'd his mistresse soe:
> They tooke their swords againe, and each enchaste
> Deepe wounds in the soft flesh of his strong foe,
> Till weake and wearie, faint, alive uneath,
> They both retirde at once, at once tooke breath.

Fairfax revised the first stanza of his poem after it had been printed,[74] and these lines read as though they might once have had 'chaste' in a rhyming position. The adjective forces its way through the action (it very nearly surfaces in 'enchaste') because the translation describes what is almost an attempted rape: the 'virgine' does not simply escape, but chastely disdains Tancred's embraces. The swords do not simply tinge each of them with blood, they inflict wounds which unpleasantly suggest male penetration: 'Deep wounds in the *soft* flesh of *his* strong foe'. The final panting mutuality ('at once, at once'), in the place of Tasso's clearly separate retirement of the two warriors, brings the undercurrent of sexual embrace to its climax.

   This is not quite Tasso. When Tancred weeps at the plight of Clorinda he is first tempted ('invoglia') and then forced ('sforza') to put aside noble *sdegno* for softer feelings. The Ariostan core is there, but must force itself through martial restraint:

> In queste voci languide risuona
> un non so che di flebile e soave
> ch'al cor gli scende ed ogni sdegno ammorza,
> e gli occhi a lagrimar gli invoglia e sforza.[75]

In these fainting words was heard an unsayable something, tearful and sweet, which slipped to his heart and extinguished all disdain, and tempted, then forced his eyes to weep.

[74] See *Godfrey of Bulloigne: A Critical Edition of Edward Fairfax's Translation of Tasso's 'Gerusalemme liberata'*, ed. Kathleen M. Lea and T. M. Gang (Oxford, 1981), 69–70. All quotations from this edition. Stanza references are as for *GL*.
[75] *GL* xii. 66. 5–8.

Even now it is not his fault that he weeps; his *eyes* do it. In the English
the tears are expressive rather than just a reflex:

> His hart relenting nigh in sunder rave,
> With woefull speech of that sweete creature,
> So that his rage, his wrath and anger dide,
> And on his cheekes salt teares for ruthe downe slide.

Fairfax is too close to the fundamental elements of psychology fully to
see how Tasso masks the underlying amorousness of his hero: for him
this moment marks a shift from irascible to ruthful passions, so he elides
the delicate transitional processes in order to emphasize the shift. This
excess of conceptual clarity is his chief debt to Spenser. The political
elements of *The Faerie Queene* exert relatively little influence over him;
but he does owe a great deal to those moments in Spenser's epic when
heroes waver or jolt violently between clearly distinct passions. Tancred
succumbs to pity at the sound of Clorinda's voice as the ruthful Britomart
does when she reins in the wrathful Talus from his rigorously just
destruction of the Amazons:

> And now by this the noble Conqueresse
> Her selfe came in, her glory to partake;
> Where though reuengefull vow she did professe,
> Yet when she saw the heapes, which he did make,
> Of slaughtred carkasses, her heart did quake
> *For very ruth, which did it almost riue,*
> That she his fury willed him to slake.[76]

Violent pity nearly 'rives' the hearts of both Spenser's Britomart and
Fairfax's Tancred. 'Ruth' overcomes the externalized *furor* of Talus as it
overcomes the nearly personified wrath of Tancred. Fairfax's Tasso has
been fed through an interpretive grid which uncodes Tasso's complex
blends of anger and pity. But this grid is not just the product of the
allegory of passion which runs through *The Faerie Queene*; it derives from
a very gullible reading of that allegory. Fairfax is entirely seduced by the
appearance of pitiful feeling that is so often yoked with actual violence in
Spenser. He evidently felt that the episode in Mercilla's court, for
example—that *tour de force* of apparently motive, actually non-motive
pity—was a spectacular display of the power of pity. He thinks of the
Spenserian episode when Clorinda is moved by the plight of the pitiful
duo Sofronia and Olindo:

---

[76] *FQ* v. vii. 36; emphasis added.

> Clorinda intenerissi, e si condolse
> d'ambeduo loro e lagrimonne alquanto.

Clorinda became tender, and felt for and wept a little for the two of them.

> Clorinda chang'd to ruth her warlike mood,
> Few silver drops her vermile cheeks depaint.[77]

In Fairfax she switches emotional modes as though there were no intermediate stages between pity and wrath, as Arthur changes from martial to chivalric modes of feeling within one line during the Mercilla episode: 'That for great ruth his courage gan relent'.[78] With this Spenserian form of psychological representation comes a line which drips Spenser: 'Few silver drops her vermile cheeks depaint'. This heroic ruthfulness is filtered through Mercilla:

> But rather let in stead thereof to fall
> Few perling drops from her faire lampes of light.[79]

'Few silver drops', 'Few perling drops'—the verbal reminiscence is slight, yet points the similarity in idiom. Fairfax was drawn to this passage in which tears light instead of justice, and was taken in by its equivocations. In Spenser tears do not substitute for justice, they merely ornament it, while the poet maintains the illusion that Elizabeth pardoned her cousin. Fairfax recalled Mercilla, but forgot or failed to notice the narrative frame.

He also sprinkles ornamental tears over Tasso's 'Pio Goffredo', and shows a marked tendency to attribute to his hero the kind of clement ascendancy towards which both Harington and Spenser had shown such uneasy attraction. At one point this pitiful monarch weeps concealed tears over the death of Dudone:

> But he, withouten shew or change of cheare,
> His springing teares within their fountaines staid,
> His ruefull lookes upon the coarse he cast.[80]

Tasso's taciturn hero becomes less able to control his feelings: like Mercilla's, his tears do spring up (like ornamental fountains) although they are covered over. Goffredo simply restrains himself:

> ma con volto né torbido né chiaro
> frena il suo affetto il pio Buglione, e tace.[81]

[77] *GL* ii. 43. 1–2.
[78] *FQ* v. ix. 46.
[79] *FQ* v. ix. 50.
[80] *GL* iii. 67. 5–7.
[81] Guido Baldassari, *Il sonno di Zeus: Sperimentazione narrativa del poema rinascimentale e tradizione omerica* (Rome, 1982), 64–5, discusses Goffredo's Virgilian restraint here.

But, with a face neither clouded nor clear, the dutiful Duke reined in his emotion, and remained silent.

'Il *pio* Buglione' is probably the origin of the English Godfrey's 'ruefull lookes'. The semantic area of Ariosto's main ethical term which Tasso is so careful, so suspiciously careful, to hold in check has caught Fairfax's eye, because he writes with the feelingful side of Spenser in mind.

Even in Armida's appeal to Goffredo, when Tasso cautiously emphasizes that his hero is 'pio' in the religious rather than the feelingful sense, Fairfax picks out the suppressed sentiment. He is quite clear that Armida thinks of him as ruthful Godfrey (she speaks of his 'vertuous ruth');[82] and at the climax of the episode, Godfrey no longer contrasts his Tassan *pietà* with the Ariostan equivalent of the virtue. 'Or mi farebbe la pietà men pio' (Now pity would make me less pious)[83] becomes

> But if for pitie of a worldlie dame
> I left this worke, such pitie, were my shame.[84]

This emphasis on the pitiful nature of the Christian king shows the chief feature of Fairfax: he is an uncoder. His version of *Gerusalemme liberata* creates a much simpler opposition between pitiful Christians and disdainful pagans than its original. The lineaments of this opposition are there in *Gerusalemme liberata*, of course, but Tasso often deliberately blurs these outlines, reserving much irascible energy for his Christian knights, and allowing their pagan antagonists the odd sensation of unaccustomed pity. These blurred outlines take on much harder edges in their English form. One way in which Tasso managed to formulate the predominantly martial ethos of his pagans was through the Renaissance commonplace that secular glory follows from noble actions.[85] The chief spokesman for this point of view is Argante; and Fairfax realizes the pagan represents a distinct outlook when he says:

> ma il dico sol perché desio vedere
> in alcuni di noi spirto più invitto,
> ch'egualmente apprestato ad ogni sorte
> si prometta vittoria e sprezzi morte.

But I say this solely because I want to see in each of us a more invincible spirit, so that each of us is prepared for any kind of fate, whether promised victory or the death which we despise.

---

[82] *GL* iv. 36. 7–8.

[83] *GL* iv. 69. 7.

[84] When Godfrey prays, or is rescued by an angel, though, he becomes 'the godly Duke': both are moments where godliness counts: *GL* xviii. 62. 1–2; xi. 83. 2.

[85] See Maurice B. McNamee, *Honor and the Epic Hero: A Study of the Shifting Concept of Magnanimity in Philosophy and Epic Poetry* (New York, 1960), 140 *et passim*.

> I speake these words, for spurres I them esteeme
> To waken up each dull and fearfull spright,
> And make our harts resolv'd to all assaies,
> To winne with honour or to die with praise.[86]

Argante loses any trace of moderation in the English, and becomes a glory-seeking machine run wild. This clarity in defining the pagan ethos again owes much to Spenser, whose Cymochles is possessed by a similar honourable death wish, when he

> Resolu'd to put away that loathly blame,
> Or dye with honour and desert of fame.[87]

Fairfax repeatedly reads this kind of honour-conscious heroism into the pagan enemies of *pio Goffredo*. *Godfrey of Bulloigne* consequently makes a crucial development in the style of English epic: Fairfax splits an irascible pagan quest for honour from a tender Christian ruthfulness far more clearly than either Spenser or Tasso. It creates an idiom in which these two sets of motives are simply opposed, and in which the pagans are continually made to become just a bit more simply honour-conscious and martial than they are in his original. When Argante challenges the Christians to a duel, Fairfax makes an error which reveals this bias in his translation. The sentence is a difficult instruction to a herald in *oratio obliqua*; tell them, the warrior says, there is a knight frustrated by captivity

> e ch'a duello di venirne è presto
> nel pian ch'è fra le mura e l'alte tende
> per prova di valore, e che disfida
> qual piú de' Franchi in sua virtú si fida.

and who is ready to fight a duel on the plain which lies between the walls and the high tents, for a test of strength, and who lays down a challenge to show how much more than the Franks he trusts his force.

The English knight says something very different:

> That no devotion (as they falsly faine)
> Hath mov'd the French these countries to subdew;
> But vile ambition, and prides hatefull vice,
> Desire of rule and spoile, and covetice.[88]

Fairfax may well have misunderstood 'disfida' (rhyming with 'fida' it looks like a word for *dis*belief), and assumed that Argante was accusing

---

[86] *GL* x. 38. 5-8.   [87] *FQ* II. viii. 44.   [88] *GL* vi. 15. 5-8.

the Christians of irreligion rather than timidity. It is a good mistake,
though. The cruellest insult which a pagan could offer the Christians is
that their religious motive is bogus, and that they are as much motivated
by worldly ambition as their rivals. The misunderstanding shows that,
when foxed by detail, Fairfax could cover his incomprehension by patching
in a line or two which expressed the general contrast between the ethos
of each camp. This contrast in ethos, like much of the rest of the poem's
intellectual structure, he understood almost too well.

His willingness to split the poem up into two simple camps, however,
works an extremely influential change in the character of the English
epic. Spenser and Harington had both redirected Ariosto's desiring heroes
towards images of true worth. This had enabled them to use romance as
a political mode of writing, in which the prevalence of pity over reason
could suggest an amorous tyranny at the head of the body politic. But to
replace this unsteady synthesis by more or less ornamental oscillations
between passions, and to lock those oscillations between passions into an
increasingly rigid antithetical structure, leaves the epic mode sorely
depleted, private, withdrawn, and—above all—entirely predictable. A
reader versed in the conventions of such a clarified idiom could more or
less anticipate who will feel what in any given circumstances.

But Fairfax does have one foot strongly planted in the civic concerns
of his predecessors in the English romance idiom. He is very responsive
to moments when his original advocates the pursuit of virtuous ascendancy.
Tasso used the idea that virtue is the true nobility to sustain his revision
of the shield which Venus gives Aeneas in Book 8.[89] This is one of Virgil's
imperial symbols: a dense space contains impacted in it the whole destiny
of the nation, drawn in the time which is both the origin and the pattern
of Virgil's present.[90] Tasso's rewriting of it (the shield which Rinaldo is
given finally to wean him off the charms of Armida) is not a prophetic
image of future glory, but an exhortative vision of past virtues which have
been lost, and which should be reborn.[91] Tasso neatly looks back to and
renovates his literary ancestor in order to persuade Rinaldo to recall and
overgo his biological ancestors. The topos of reviving ancestral virtue is
once more used to assist the revival of an episode from classical epic:

[89]   *Aen.* 8. 626–728.
[90]   See Page DuBois, *History, Rhetorical Description and the Epic from Homer to Spenser* (Cambridge,
1982), 41–8.
[91]   Cf. Tasso on the moral function of epic in *Discorsi ... del Poema Eroico*, ed. L. Poma (Bari,
1964), 61: the readers of the poem 'riconoscendo le virtù del padre e de gli avi, se non più belle,
almeno più ornate con varii e diversi lumi della poesia, cercano di conformar l'animo loro a quello
essempio ...' (... recognizing the virtue of their father and ancestors, if not rendered more beautiful,
at least made more lavish by the various and different lights of poetry, seek to shape their own spirit
after that example).

—Alza la fronte, o figlio,
e in questo scudo affissa gli occhi omai,
ch'ivi de' tuoi maggior l'opre vedrai.

Vedrai de gli avi il divulgato onore,
lunge precorso in loco erto e solingo;
tu dietro anco riman', lento cursore,
per questo de la gloria illustre arringo.
Su, su, te stesso incita: al tuo valore
sia sferza e spron quel ch'io colà dipingo.[92]

Raise your brows, my son, and set your eyes now upon this shield, where you will see the labours of your ancestors. You will see the spreading fame of your predecessors, their long labours in steep and desolate places. You, though, hang behind, a slow runner in this race for glory. Up, up, urge yourself on: let that which I represent there be a goad and spur to your valour.

Fairfax provides an understanding paraphrase for this exhortation to take past glories as an *exemplum* to imitate:

'Looke up, my childe,
And painted in this precious shield behold
The glorious deeds of thy forefathers old:

'Thine elders glorie herin see and know,
In vertues path how they troade all their daies,
Whom thou art far behind, a runner slow
In this true course of honour, fame and praise.'

He heightens the language of honour, fame, praise, and virtue partly because he can never resist a good pile of synonyms, but partly also to emphasize the point that nobility must constantly renew its virtue in order to maintain its position. This is a theme which underlies Harington's version of Ariosto, and which adds an edge of radicalism even to the milder idiom of *Godfrey of Bulloigne*. At a few odd moments in the translation Fairfax adds or alters emphases in order to suggest that the ideal commonwealth is one in which high places are justly apportioned by a monarch who recognizes and rewards virtue. This idea causes a major and significant deflection from Tasso's course when Piero the hermit speaks in favour of monarchy on the very Tassan grounds that it is a rational principle that prevents *errando*:

Ove un sol non impera, onde i giudici
pendano poi de' premi e de le pene,
onde sian compartite opre ed uffici,
ivi errante il governo esser conviene.

---

[92] *GL* xvii. 64–5.

> Deh! fate un corpo sol de' membri amici,
> fate un capo che gli altri indrizzi e frene,
> date ad un sol lo scettro e la possanza,
> e sostenga di re vece e sembianza.[93]

Where one alone does not rule, on whom just rewards and punishments depend, by whom labours and offices are distributed, there the government must be erring. So, make yourselves one body of friendly members, make one head who rules and reins in the others, give to one man the sceptre and the right to rule, and keep up the appearance and substance of a king.

Fairfax is drawn aside from literal translation of the first section of this stanza by a very English form of satiric complaint:

> Where divers Lords divided empire holde,
> Where causes be by gifts not justice tride,
> Where offices be falsly bought and solde,
> Needes must the lordship there from vertue slide.
> Of friendly parts one bodie then upholde,
> Create one head the rest to rule and guide,
> To one the regall powre and scepter give,
> That henceforth may your king and soveraigne live.[94]

The latter end of this commonwealth forgets the beginning, since lines 2 to 4 do not present a single and cohesive argument against multiple rule, but string together several images of judicial corruption and false valuation of merit. These three lines do not show the consequences of divided rule as their Italian equivalents do; they represent a vision of a state in which distributive justice does not operate; where bribery prevents the just apportioning of punishment; where public offices do not go to those whose virtues deserve them. 'Premi' (rewards) is misconstrued as 'bribes', and 'compartite' (divided) is possibly confused with 'comprate' (bought). The conclusion ('Needes must the lordship there from vertue slide') may look like a *non sequitur*, but it does fit in with the preceding lines: in a state where principles of distributive justice do not operate, the governor will not be of a virtuous condition appropriate to his rank. Fairfax also implies by his choice of form that unless such principles do operate, turmoil will result, since his formal model is the pseudo-Chaucerian

---

[93] *GL* i. 31. Cf. *Il.* 2. 203–6.

[94] Lea and Gang cite a distant parallel in Milton, rather than noting Fairfax's changes. R[ichard] C[arew] provides a more accurate, but less expressive gloss: 'Where onely one doth not command, from whom | Judgement of paines and prices may depend: | From whom may offices and charges come, | There still the rule to eyther side wil bend: | Ah of these members friendly joyn'd, in some | One bodie make, and make a head to wend | And guide the rest, let one the Scepter beare, | And let him rule as King and Prince he weare.' *Godfrey of Bulloigne* (London, [1594]), 18–19.

prophecy quoted by Puttenham and borrowed by Lear's fool in his vision of the decay of England:[95]

> When faith fails in Priestes sawes,
> And Lords hestes are holden for lawes,
> And robberie is tane for purchase,
> And lechery for solace
> Then shall the Realme of Albion
> Be brought to great confusion.[96]

Fairfax's line 'Needes must the lordship there from vertue slide' fills the place of 'Then shall the Realme of Albion | Be brought to great confusion.' This prophetic shape lurking beneath the line hints that chaos will come if principles of just trial and just distribution of offices do not operate. And this form of prophecy is a great favourite among the Spenserian poets, whose relative lack of recognition by influential patrons helped to inspire a repeated concern with royal failures to reward merit. Drayton's *The Owle* uses a similarly paratactic complaint,[97] and one of the Harington family's poetic miscellanies contains a poem with a very similar theme and structure, but a more bloody force:

> Whear giltles men ar grevously opreste
> and faultie folks of favor boldly boste
> whear wrongs encrease eache day and none redreste
> whear wisdome wants and will dothe rule the roste
> whear crewelltie doth rain that bloody beast
> w^t innocents blood be sprinkling every poste
>
> .   .   .   .
>
> whear fleshe and blood doth rule and guid the gost
> And trouthe constraind, dothe offre costum place
> that piteous state doth stande in wofull cace.[98]

This poem is written on the verso of a leaf containing another poem about judicial corruption, and in the same hand as a draft of John Harington of Stepney's translation of *Orlando furioso*, xix. 1. Sir John Harington parodied this form in his Epigram 83:[99] it was evidently in his literary blood; and a watery version of the form found a way into Fairfax's

---

[95] *King Lear*, III. ii. 81–95.

[96] George Puttenham, *The Arte of English Poesie*, ed. Gladys Doidge Wilcock and Alice Walker (Cambridge, 1936), 224.

[97] ll. 1219–25. Text in *The Works of Michael Drayton*, ed. J. W. Hebel *et al.*, 5 vols. (Oxford, 1931–41).

[98] MS BL Add. 36529, fol. 44^b.

[99] He satirizes Jacobean court fashions: 'When Monopolies are giv'n of toyes and trashes: | When courtiers mar good clothes, with cuts & slashes | ... | When Lechers learn to stir up Lust with lashes, | When plainnesse vanishes, vainenesse surpasses, | Some shal grow Elephants, were knowne but Asses.' *The Letters and Epigrams*, ed. N. E. McLure (Philadelphia, 1930), 180.

poem. Edward Fairfax was a natural son of Thomas Fairfax the elder,[100] and so was an uncle of sorts to Lord Thomas Fairfax, the Parliamentarian general.[101] It is, of course, only too possible to swing from the branches of family trees to almost any destination;[102] members of the same family often fought on opposing sides in the Civil War, and as late as 1639 there was little sign that the Fairfaxes would take arms against the King—even Lord Thomas himself remained opposed to the regicide.[103] But Edward Fairfax's repeated emphasis on Godfrey's pitiful grace, on his virtues, and on the importance of distributive justice in maintaining the state provides a suitably undogmatic background for the wavering sympathies of the next generation of aristocrats: a concern with justice throughout the commonwealth supplants Tasso's statement of the abstract necessity of rule by a single man.[104] This is not an outlook inevitably prone towards Republicanism or regicide; but it shifts Tasso's constitutional balance away from monarchy, towards 'the lordship', the governing classes in general. The mixed constitutionalism of the Classical Republicans in the Civil War (in which a powerful aristocracy supreme in virtue was to play a leading role in government) is one extreme derivative of this outlook.[105]

[100] See Charles G. Bell, 'Edward Fairfax, a Natural Son', *Modern Language Notes*, 62 (1947), 24–7. Neither his illegitimacy nor his quarrel with his half-brother (Sir Thomas the younger) over his father's will cut the poet off from his family. See Lea and Gang, 5–8, and T. M. Gang, 'The Quarrel Between Edward Fairfax and his Brother', *Notes and Queries*, 214 (1969), 28–33. On the intricacies of the Fairfax family tree, see [Clements R. Markham], 'Genealogy of the Fairfaxes', *The Herald and Genealogist*, 6 (1871), 385–407; corrected, ibid. 7 (1873), 145–60.

[101] On the role of family history in forming the opinions of aristocratic Parliamentarians before the self-denying ordinance, see Vernon F. Snow, *Essex the Rebel: The Life of Robert Devereux, the Third Earl of Essex* (Lincoln, Nebr., 1970), and 'Essex and the Aristocratic Opposition to the Early Stuarts', *Journal of Modern History*, 32 (1960), 224: memories of the second Earl of Essex 'constituted the nucleus of the aristocratic opposition to the early Stuarts'. Cf. Jerrilyn Greene Marston, 'Gentry Honour and Royalism in Early Stuart England', *Journal of British Studies*, 13 (1973), 21–43. See also Blair Worden, 'Classical Republicanism and the Puritan Revolution', in Hugh Lloyd-Jones *et al.* (eds.), *History and Imagination: Essays in Honour of H. R. Trevor-Roper* (London, 1981), 182–200. J. T. Cliffe, *The Yorkshire Gentry from the Reformation to the Civil War*, University of London Historical Studies, 25 (London, 1969), offers precise accounts of some of the motives underlying opposition to Charles.

[102] A positively simian agility is displayed in 'Bacon's father married Gresham's wife's sister (though she was not Francis's mother).' Christopher Hill, *Intellectual Origins of the English Revolution* (Oxford, 1965), 85. Hill pays little attention to the origins of the aristocratic opposition.

[103] Thomas Fairfax the elder wrote to his grandson Thomas, 12 June 1639, when Charles raised troops to fight the Scots: 'I desire you to be mindful to serve God with all your soul, and the King with all your heart', *The Fairfax Correspondence*, ed. George W. Johnson, 2 vols. (London, 1848), i. 356. See John Wilson, *Fairfax: A Life of Thomas, Lord Fairfax* (London, 1985), 142–53.

[104] See further James E. Farnell, 'The Aristocracy and Leadership of Parliament in the English Civil Wars', *Journal of Modern History*, 44 (1972), 79–86, and 'The Social and Intellectual Basis of London's Role in the English Civil Wars', *Journal of Modern History*, 49 (1977), 641–60; Paul Christianson, 'The Causes of the English Revolution: A Reappraisal', *Journal of British Studies*, 15: 2 (1976), 40–75, and 'The Peers, the People, and Parliamentary Management in the First Six Months of the Long Parliament', *Journal of Modern History*, 49 (1977), 575–99.

[105] See Zera S. Fink, *The Classical Republicans: An Essay on the Recovery of a Pattern of Thought in Seventeenth-Century England*, Northwestern University Studies in the Humanities, 9 (Evanston,

Fairfax, in the more moderate environment of the late 1590s, is content with the ideal of a monarchical system topped by a clement and virtuous Prince.

While Fairfax's family were leaning towards one side of the Civil War, his literary heirs were playing a rather different role. Fairfax's greatest literary follower was Waller, who (according to Dryden) made his debt to Fairfax public knowledge.[106] Waller was a Member of Parliament who plotted to admit the King to London in 1643. He was banished and fined heavily for doing so. On returning from exile in 1651 he grovellingly praised Cromwell in *A Panegyrick to my Lord Protector*.[107] This poem shows a great debt to Fairfax's version of Spenser. Cromwell becomes what Spenser's Mercilla so nearly was, and yet clearly was not: an imperial peacemaker. In Waller's panegyrical deployment of the ideas which underlie earlier English epic poems, Cromwell's supremacy is justified both by his princely virtues and by his divinely inspired clemency:

> The onely cure which could from Heav'n come down,
> Was so much Power and Clemency in one.
>   One, whose extraction from an ancient Line,
> Gives hope again that well-born Men may shine...
> Born to Command, your Princely vertues slept
> Like humble *David's*, while the Flock he kept:
> But when your troubled Countrey call'd you forth,
> Your flaming Courage, and your Matchless worth
> Dazeling the eyes of all that did pretend
> To fierce Contention—gave a prosp'rous end.[108]

Waller is an equivocating, imperializing heir to the evasions of Harington and Fairfax: like them, he does not openly argue that some extremes of virtue merit a kingdom, but attempts to provide the Protectorate with sanctions of *both* noble blood and the virtues necessary to revive his country. He legitimates Cromwell's government by the unscrupulously vague '*Born* to command', and by not specifying which 'ancient Line' spawned his ruler. Fairfax's biological kin tended to Parliamentarianism;

Ill., 1945), 39, 96, *et passim*; Fritz Caspari, *Humanism and the Social Order in Tudor England* (Chicago, 1954), 207–8.

[106] W. L. Chernaik, *The Poetry of Limitation: A Study of Edmund Waller* (New Haven, Conn., and London, 1968), 219–21. See also *The Poems of John Dryden*, ed. James Kinsley, 4 vols. (Oxford, 1958), 1445. Later, in the Preface to *Fables Ancient and Modern*, he notes the importance of the whole school of Elizabethan epic writers: 'There was an *Ennius*, and in process of Time a *Lucilius*, and a *Lucretius*, before *Virgil* and *Horace*; even after *Chaucer* there was a *Spencer*, a *Harrington*, a *Fairfax*, before *Waller* and *Denham* were in being.' ibid. 1453. On Fairfax's role in the development of English verse, see Ruth C. Wallerstein, 'The Development of the Rhetoric and Metre of the Heroic Couplet, Especially in 1625–1645', *PMLA* 50 (1935), 169.

[107] Chernaik, *Poetry of Limitation*, 153; see further ibid. 154–71.

[108] *A Panegyrick to my Lord Protector* (London, 1655), 6–7.

but his literary heirs were more attracted to the Augustan ideal of clement rule. Waller's encomium of Cromwell—and his, and indeed Dryden's, portrayal of Aeneas[109]—is coloured by this wish for gentle supremacy. Pity is at root an imperial emotion: it gains its political meaning from a willingness to feel for the impotent victims of one's might. Throughout the later seventeenth century the willingness of a king to spare the subject, and to weep for the weak, is a key element in royal panegyrics. Fairfax's Spenserian reading of Tasso played a major part in the emergence of this idiom.

RAGING BARONS

The synthetic motive 'love of fame' does not just split with ornamental ease into two rival camps of pitiful heroes and disdainful villains in the late sixteenth century: it has the potential to explode, as the quest for glory is frustrated, and burns off the residual literal level of love. As Harington put it in his commentary on *Orlando furioso*:

For though indeed no subject (rightly considering his duety) ought to be moved by any ingratitude or injury of his soveraigne to forget his allegeance, yet seeing the nature of most men... is subject to the passion of revenge and can hardly bridle the same when they shall find themselves (as they thinke) disdayned or their services not well regarded, therefore the wisest and safest way and fittest for the Majesty of a Prince is to be liberall in rewarding or at least thankefull in accepting such mens services and to consider love and bountie are stronger bands of allegeance then feare and duetie.[110]

This is an unsettling view of informal amorous obedience. Those who lovingly pursue honour need to be rewarded, or their love will transform itself into rage. Such irascible frustration is a natural offshoot of the tendency among English writers of the epic to tie love and the quest for glory into one project: the pursuit of glory biases English epic romance towards justice, and a regard for the due distribution of honours. This strand in the Spenserian amalgam of epic impulses is the driving force behind the historical epics which sprang up, grew, and mutated through

---

[109] The crux, 'lacrimae volvuntur inanes', in which it is uncertain whether the vain tears pour from Aeneas or Anna (*Aen.* 4. 449), becomes 'And down his Cheeks though fruitless tears do roul, | Unmov'd remains the purpose of his soul', *Poems Written upon Several Occasions*, 3rd edn. (London, 1668), 185. See William Frost, 'Translating Virgil, Douglas to Dryden: Some General Considerations', in Maynard Mack and George deForest Lord (eds.), *Poetic Traditions of the English Renaissance* (New Haven, Conn., and London, 1982), 271–86, on the politics of translation. For Waller's Augustanism, see Howard Erskine-Hill, *The Augustan Idea in English Literature* (London, 1983), 198–212.

[110] Har. 398.

the later years of the sixteenth and the early part of the seventeenth centuries.

Underlying many of these works is a sense that writing a historical epic entails moving away from the subject-matter of romance, and towards the more austere fare of Lucan's *Pharsalia*. Lucan's poem is the most supremely adversarial in the corpus of classical epic. It pushes all genres towards ruination, in its effort to evoke the implosion of Roman values in civil war, and its relation to the epic tradition is self-consciously terminal.[111] After the battle of Pharsalia, Caesar hunts Pompey down through a landscape crammed with dead myths: he passes the Hellespont, scene of Hero and Leander's fatal love, and then pauses at Troy, to see the origins of the *Iliad* in the spot where Paris made his ill-fated judgement, and the ultimate source of the *Aeneid* in the grove where Anchises conceived Aeneas. He sees the site of Ajax's grave, and carelessly tramples on the bones of Hector.[112] Unlike Aeneas, who tours Pallanteum viewing the scenes of future Roman glories, Caesar witnesses the utter destruction of the past.[113] There is no literary resurrection from these monuments, which push even Lucan's own earlier imagery further towards death. The scene is overgrown by 'silvae steriles' (dead undergrowth) which clings to the ground by tired roots.[114] This wasted foliage reminds the reader that Lucan's own has-been of a hero has truly met his end: Pompey was compared in Book 1 to an oak 'nec iam validis radicibus' (with roots no longer sound);[115] now the roots cling even less tenaciously. We learn of Pompey in Book 1 'stat magni nominis umbra' (He stands the shadow of a great name),[116] but by Book 9 the past is still more terminally inanimate, for 'nullum est sine nomine saxum'.[117] This phrase

---

[111] See Charles Martindale, *John Milton and the Transformation of Ancient Epic* (London and Sydney, 1986), 224. The most vivid account of Lucan is John Henderson, 'Lucan/The Word at War', in A. J. Boyle (ed.), *The Imperial Muse: Ramus Essays on Roman Literature of the Empire to Juvenal through Ovid* (Victoria, 1988), 122–64. See also Jamie Masters, *Poetry and Civil War in Lucan's Bellum Civile* (Cambridge, 1992).

[112] *Phars.* 9. 950–79. All references to *The Civil War (Pharsalia)*, trans. J. D. Duff, Loeb Classical Library (Cambridge, Mass., and London, 1928). See W. R. Johnson, *Momentary Monsters: Lucan and his Heroes*, Cornell Studies in Classical Philology, 47 (Ithaca, NY, and London, 1987), 118–21.

[113] *Aen.* 8. 306 ff. See Lynette Thompson and R. T. Bruère, 'Lucan's Use of Virgilian Reminiscence', *Classical Philology*, 63 (1968), 16–19. Lucan's verbal allusions to his predecessors tend to have all the life crushed out of them by the weight of their setting. On 'reversals of normality' in Lucan, see J. C. Bramble 'Lucan', in E. J. Kenney and W. V. Clausen (eds.), *The Cambridge History of Classical Literature*, 2 vols. (Cambridge, 1982), ii. 533–57. For Lucan's deliberate reversals of Virgil, see Emanuele Narducci, 'Ideologia e tecnica allusiva nella *Pharsalia*', in H. Temporini and W. Haase (eds.), *Aufstieg und Niedergang der Römischen Welt* (Berlin and New York, 1985), II. 32. 3, 1538–64; A. Guillemin, 'L'inspiration virgilienne dans la *Pharsale*', *Revue des études latines*, 29 (1951), 214–27.

[114] *Phars.* 9. 966–9.

[115] *Phars.* 1. 138.

[116] *Phars.* 1. 135.

[117] *Phars.* 9. 973.

is usually rendered by 'every stone had its own myth'; but it is *tomb*stones
that usually have names on them: every rock is like a grave, recording a
history of the dead. In this deliberately incongruous setting Lucan
celebrates the role of the historical poet:

> O sacer et magnus vatum labor! omnia fato
> eripis et populis donas mortalibus aevum.
>   ...Pharsalia nostra
> vivet, et a nullo tenebris damnabitur aevo.[118]

Oh great and sacred labour of poets! You tear all things from destruction, and
give immortality to the mortal...Our Pharsalia will live, and will be damned to
the shadows in no age.

'Magnus' is the nickname of the unfortunate Pompey, which Lucan uses
with cruel irony throughout the poem.[119] The application of this epithet
to the poet's task, as the author pretends to immortalize Pompey's
antagonist Caesar, is grimly appropriate: the poet is as great as Pompey.
A broken epithet fits a claim to immortality which rises from the decaying
monuments of previous epic actions. The apostrophe to the immortal
power of poetry echoes in this deathly landscape with the misplaced
shrillness of an erotic giggle in a catacomb.

Nothing in this world on the edge of catastrophe, not the immortality
granted to the Homeric hero, not the immortality of the poet, can escape
death. 'In se magna ruunt' (great things charge against themselves):[120]
poets assign their predecessors to the grave, and military leaders drive a
great nation to destroy itself. The cosmos itself rushes to destruction in
Lucan's proem.[121] This apocalyptic setting has a profound effect on the
ethos of the poem. Almost all the forms of action described in the
Pharsalia lead towards destruction: republican Stoicism will eventually
lead to Cato's suicide;[122] martial frenzy repeatedly leads to suicidal
onslaughts by men who have no hope of survival.[123] And *pietas* becomes

---

[118] *Phars.* 9. 980–6.

[119] See D. C. Feeney, ' "Stat magni nominis umbra": Lucan on the Greatness of Pompeius
Maximus', *Classical Quarterly*, NS 36 (1986), 239–43.

[120] *Phars.* 1. 81. 'Ruere' can mean 'crash down'; but it is also a verb for a military charge. Lucan
exploits this range of meanings. For the topos, see E. Dutoit, 'Le Thème de "la force que se détruit
elle-même" (Hor. *Epod.* 16. 2) et ses variations chez quelques auteurs latins', *Revue des études latines*,
14 (1936), 365–73.

[121] *Phars.* 1. 72–80. For Lucan's use of the Stoic doctrine of *ekpyrosis*, see Michael Lapidge,
'Lucan's Imagery of Cosmic Destruction', *Hermes*, 107 (1979), 344–70.

[122] As is indicated by *Phars.* 4. 575–81. For a more positive view of Lucan's Stoicism, see Berthe
M. Marti, 'The Meaning of the *Pharsalia*', *American Journal of Philology*, 66 (1945), 352–76; for the
poem's underlying despair, see Otto Steen Due, 'An Essay on Lucan', *Classica et Mediaevalia*, 23
(1962), 68–132; on the vanity of heroism, see Frederick M. Ahl, *Lucan: An Introduction*, Cornell
Studies in Classical Philology, 39 (Ithaca, NY, and London, 1976), esp. 155–66.

[123] e.g. at *Phars.* 4. 516–20, 575–81, 6. 150–262;

merely a vain, retarding scruple which would prevent Caesar's troops from fighting, were it not for the eloquence of their chief:

> sed dum tela micant non vos pietatis imago
> ulla nec adversa conspecti fronte parentes
> commoveant.[124]

But while your weapons flash, let no image of compassionate duty, nor the sight of your parents facing you on the opposing lines, move you.

'Pietatis imago' is used in the *Aeneid* of a vain but powerful *frisson* of moral identity with an imperial victim.[125] This sentiment—tending a shade closer to compassion in the combative environment of the *Pharsalia*[126]—is ruthlessly exorcized by Caesar. He effectively says 'do not be like Aeneas'. Elsewhere *pietas* becomes a motive for promptly putting one's fellow countrymen out of their misery.[127] The ethos which animated the epic of Rome's growth and greatness is turned into a motive for intestinal conflict in the epic of her self-destruction. All the elements of the poem—its treatment of poetry and of heroism, the cosmic setting of Rome's decline, its very style[128]—are crushed into expressing the catastrophic paradox of a nation killing itself.

These features make Lucan's epic a dead end as a source: there is—he insists repeatedly—no further to go. All earlier epics, all earlier writers, and all previous heroes are dead. But the relentlessly terminal energy of the *Pharsalia* makes it a vital model for enacting generic self-destruction: poems which seek to break out of or to explode the idiom of their predecessors need Lucan. And this is partly why he became such an important ally in the battle against the inveiglements of romance in the later sixteenth century. No writer even seriously attempted to evoke his implosive rhetoric or madly self-thwarting heroic energies; but many used themes from the *Pharsalia* to signify and assist their desire to change the prevalent heroic idiom.

In the 1590s several writers tried to produce historical epics on the model of Lucan's *Pharsalia*, but found that martial resolve turned into

[124] *Phars.* 7. 320–2. Caesar's exhortation leads to a numbed stasis which epitomizes the self-thwarting energies of the poem: '... gelidusque in viscera sanguis | percussa pietate coit, totaeque cohortes | pila parata diu tensis tenuere lacertis' (Cold blood rushed to guts turned over by *pietas*, and whole companies long held their spears raised with tense muscles), *Phars.* 7. 467–9.

[125] *Aen.* 9. 294, 10. 824.

[126] e.g. when Caesar weeps crocodile tears over Pompey's head: 'quisquis te flere coegit | impetus, a vera longe pietate recessit' (Whatever urge makes you weep, it's a long way from real *pietas*), *Phars.* 9. 1055–6. Cf. the usage by Euryalus's mother *in extremis*, *Aen.* 9. 493–4.

[127] 'Pietas ferientibus una | Non repetisse fuit' (There was only one form of pity towards an assailant: not to let them do it again), *Phars.* 4. 565–6.

[128] See Charles Martindale, 'Paradox, Hyperbole and Literary Novelty in Lucan's *De Bello Civile*', *Bulletin of the Institute of Classical Studies*, 23 (1976), 45–54.

love under their hands. Spenser's unfulfilled promise in his invocation to Clio is typical:

> Faire Goddesse lay that furious fit aside,
> Till I of warres and bloudy *Mars* do sing,
> And Briton fields with Sarazin bloud bedyde.[129]

Many poets expressed similar, and similarly unfulfilled, desires to kill off Saracens, Spaniards, and any other enemy of England. Hugh Holland's *Pancharis: The First Booke Containing the Preparation of the Love betweene Owen Tudyr, and the Queene*[130] relates the story of Owen Tudor and Queen Margaret by way of a prologue to the Ovidian tale of Mars's love for Venus.[131] Appended to this romantic tale in elegant *terza rima* is a letter to Holland's schoolfriend Sir Robert Cotton, which expresses the poet's intention to continue the work in a more martial vein, and write 'of the two thunder-bolts of warre, the noble Percies'.[132] The epistle is modelled on Spenser's Letter to Ralegh, and bears no more relation to the work it accompanies than its predecessor. *Pancharis* remains grounded in the erotic idiom of the 1590s: its only epic source is *Aeneid* 4, the key model for lovers of pitiful passion. Queen Katherine, like Dido, nurses an internal wound, which leads to her spending a restless night 'When every creature else his ease did take'.[133]

Michael Drayton—the most copious historical poet of the period—only partially emerges from this undistinguished background. Love is a major motive in his *Mortimeriados* (1596), and often tugs the poem away from its historical sources towards love and its associated epic models, *Aeneid* 4, and Ovid's *Metamorphoses*. Drayton's magnetically attractive Queen Isabella is moved by love for Mortimer to help him escape from the Tower, whereas in all other versions he breaks free by his own energy—as in Marlowe's:

> What Mortimer? can ragged stonie walles
> Immure thy vertue that aspires to heaven?[134]

---

[129] *FQ* I. xi. 7.

[130] (London, 1603), begun *c.*1598 as its title indicates: *Long since intended to her Maiden Majestie: And now dedicated to the Invincible James.* Reprinted in *Illustrations of Old English Literature*, ed. J. Payne Collier, ii (London, 1866).

[131] Edn. cit. 144–50. For the outmodedness of *Pancharis*, see Homer Nearing, jun., *English Historical Poetry 1599–1641* (Philadelphia, 1945), 150–2.

[132] Sig. D6^{a–b}.

[133] Sig. C12^a; cf. *Aen.* 4. 522–32. 'The wound did at the first not greatly smart, | For it was inward, and there softly bled | Feeding the fire...' sig. C12^a; cf. 'At regina gravi iamdudum saucia cura | vulnus alit venis et caeco carpitur igni' (But the queen, now wounded by a grave concern, feeds the wound with her life blood, and is fretted with a secret fire), *Aen.* 4. 1–2.

[134] Marlowe, *Edward II*, ll. 1565–6; cf. *Mortimeriados*, ll. 624–778; all references to Drayton, *Works*, ed. Hebel *et al.*

Drayton's amorous Queen imitates Dido's complaint to Aeneas when she upbraids her brother for sending her home from France,[135] and the quorum of erotic allusions is filled out at the end of the poem when (again uniquely) Drayton's Mortimer is captured in the company of the Queen in a room adorned with Ovidian narrative tapestries.[136]

Drayton uses as his main formal generic indicator the pseudo-Virgilian proem to the *Aeneid*, in which the purposive author grinds relentlessly on from youthful loves to fierce wars:

> Loe now my Muse must sing of dreadfull Armes,
> And taske her selfe to tell of civill warres.[137]

As Drayton's ambitions became increasingly Lucanian, he intensified his determination to move away from love, and write of Lucan's wars worse than civil ('Bella . . . plus quam civilia'). The revised *Barons Warres* (1603) opens with a Lucanian flourish:

> The bloudie Factions and rebellious Pride
> Of a strong Nation . . .
> Me from soft Layes and tender Loves doth bring,
> Of a farre worse than Civill Warre to sing.[138]

Drayton at least tried to write of war. His determination results in some smoky battle scenes,[139] but these never manifest the grisly parodies of civic heroism which the crisis of Rome forces into life, nor do they evoke a world forced in upon itself by the weight of circumstance.

Mortimeriados does, however, explore the motives behind the civil wars. Drayton's barons are driven by a suicidal resolution, which parallels that of Spenser's Cymochles, who 'Resolu'd to put away all loathly blame, | Or dye with honour and desert of fame':[140]

> The bonds of their alegiance they have broke:
> Resolv'd with blood theyr libertie to buy,
> To live with honor, or with fame to dye.[141]

Drayton differs from his Spenserian source, because his version of a rebellious honour culture is associated, not with pagan anti-heroism, but with the old English nobility, and their desire to ensure the survival of

---

[135] ll. 1233–60; cf. *Aen.* 4. 365–87. Tillotson does not note this parallel.
[136] ll. 2311–94; cf. *Met.* 6. 103–25.
[137] ll. 253–4.
[138] St. 1. The Virgilian proem is reproduced in *Aeneidos liber primus*, ed. R. G. Austin (Oxford, 1971), 25; cf. *FQ* I. Pr. 1; *Phars.* 1. 1.
[139] e.g. ll. 400–82.
[140] *FQ* II. viii. 44.
[141] ll. 124–6.

their ancient independence from the monarch. This gives a tincture of
praise to his honour-conscious rebels. The barons are goaded into civil
war by Edward's favouring of the upstart Gaveston, and maintain that
the king is a tyrant who has denied their ancient 'liberty':

> The Barrons plead their Countries onely care,
> Exclayming on the Princes tyrannie,
> He urg'd obedience, they their libertie.[142]

Drayton never quite develops a language to describe the actions which
follow from this energetic baronial outlook; but he does use this ethos to
animate his descriptions of Mortimer:

> The temper of his nobler mooving part,
> Had that true tutch which purified his blood,
> Infusing thoughts of honor in his hart.[143]

This energetically aspiring attitude is capable of driving its hero upwards
without regard for kingship:

> Let dull-braynd slaves contend for mud and earth,
> Let blocks and stones, sweat but for blocks and stones,
> Let peasants speake of plenty and of dearth,
> Fame never lookes so lowe as on these drones,
>   Let courage manage Empiers, sit on thrones.[144]

Mortimer's wish to aspire to the throne marks a major departure from
history as written by Holinshed. In the *Chronicles* the barons are portrayed
as a miscellaneous bunch of hooligans who irresponsibly sack the Spencers'
castles and overreach themselves in objecting to the king's choice of
favourites.[145] In Drayton's interpretation of events—as in that of Marlowe,
who, with energetic literalness translated *Lucanes First Book* around 1592–
3, and who, through *Tamburlaine* in particular, helped form the emerging
violent ethos of the later 1590s—he is the aspiring malcontent whose rise
is precipitated by Edward's unjust preferment of Gaveston over the
ancient nobility.

At the end of the sixteenth century Edward's reign was frequently used
as an *exemplum* of what could happen to unjust kings. Francis Hubert
wrote a historical poem, which has few epic pretensions, on *The Historie
of Edward the Second*, which doggedly insisted that kings would most

---

[142] ll. 500–2.
[143] ll. 71–3.
[144] ll. 953–7.
[145] Raphael Holinshed, *The Third Volume of Chronicles* (London, 1587), 326, 321: 'the lords wrested
him [Edward] too much, and beyond the bounds of reason, causing him to receive to be about him
whome it pleased them to appoint.'

effectively cut off rebellious aspirations if they maintained 'An ev'n proportion Arithmaticall | Which giveth equall Justice unto all'.[146] Hubert's work was composed in about 1599, but was suppressed by the Privy Council, and remained in manuscript until pirated in 1628. This edition was so outspoken in its criticism of monarchs who preferred corrupt favourites that Hubert issued a revised text in 1629, with a protestation that he was not responsible for the earlier version.[147] Drayton's poem contains one passage on a very similar theme to that explored by this poem which was considered too critical of royal favouritism to publish in 1599. Unjust preferments have catastrophic consequences for the nation:

> A scepter's lyke a pillar of great height,
> Whereon a mighty building doth depend,
> Which when the same is over-prest with weight,
> And past his compasse, forc'd therby to bend,
> His massie roofe down to the ground doth send:
> Crushing the lesser props, and murthering all,
> Which stand within the compasse of his fall.
>
> Where vice is countenanc'd with nobilitie,
> Arte cleane excluded, ignorance held in,
> Blinding the world, with mere hipocrisie,
> Yet must be sooth'd in all their slavish sinne,
> Great malcontents to growe they then begin:
> Nursing vile wits, to make them factious tooles,
> Thus mighty men oft proove the mightiest fooles.[148]

This is the only passage in any English imitation of Lucan that catches the *Pharsalia*'s opening vision of power overburdened with its own weight and crushed into universal apocalypse: it transposes the 'in se magna ruunt' theme into an English key.[149] The fall of the monarch is precipitated by unjust preferment, by Princes (as *The Barons Warres* has it) 'Promoting whom they please, not whom they should' and letting 'men of Merit goe ungrac't'.[150]

A movement towards this form of rebellious anger is the prime force behind Lucanian writing at the turn of the century. For writers in the

---

[146] *The Poems of Sir Francis Hubert*, ed. Bernard Mellor (Hong Kong, 1961), st. 346–7.

[147] Ibid. 286–9; (London, 1629), sigs. A5^{a-b}.

[148] ll. 1639–52. Richard F. Hardin, *Michael Drayton and the Passing of Elizabethan England* (Lawrence, Kan., 1973), 43–4, regards these lines as a criticism of Essex's over-generosity with honours; but there is no reason to neglect the literal sense.

[149] *Phars.* 1. 81. See E. Dutoit, 'Le Thème', 365–73. Drayton draws on Sulpitius's gloss on Lucan's phrase: 'Translatio ab aedificiis, quae ingentia & altissima sua mole se opprimunt' (It is drawn from buildings, which crush themselves by their own huge and high mass), and translates the image back into a description of a toppling edifice. *M. Annaei Lucani, de Bello Civili... cum scholiis... Ioannis Sulpitii Verulani* (Frankfurt, 1551), fol. 7^b.

[150] *BW* iv. 62, 63.

1570s and 1580s, such as George Turbervile and James VI, Lucan was a polemical antagonist of civil war;[151] but for the next generation he became a vehicle for articulating unease at arbitrary distributions of honours, rewards, and offices. Sir Arthur Gorges's dogged translation of Lucan's *Pharsalia* has similar concerns to Drayton's historical epic. Lucan is a republican poet with no great affection for monarchy; and this has been used to suggest that Gorges, and all who wrote dedicatory poems for his version, were closet republicans.[152] Gorges, however, makes only one substantial addition to the *Pharsalia*, which strikingly overlaps with the major interests of the other late Elizabethan writers of epic poems. In the original, a wise counsellor called Achoreus makes a speech to the young king Ptolemy which is no more than a two-line summary, as Lucan attempts to evoke an age in which good political advice cannot even be heard. Gorges padded out this deliberately suppressed summary of a speech into five pages.[153] The main gist of his addition is familiar: it advises monarchs to reward virtue, remain within the law, and preserve

[151] George Turbervile probably started a translation of 'the haughtie worke of learned *Lucane*, touching the civill dissention of aspiring *Caesar*, and pitiful *Pompey*, the protector of Rome, his native Countrie' in about 1570: 'By which the civill swordes of *Rome* and mischiefes done thereby | May be a myrrour unto us, the like mishappes to flie.' *The Booke of Faulconrie or Hauking* (London, 1575), fol. ΠΑ2ᵃ; *Tragical Tales* (London, 1587), 10; see Hyder E. Rollins, 'New Facts about George Turbervile', *Modern Philology*, 15 (1917–18), 522, 527–8. Lucan was in fashion as a tragic writer who preached political unity. In the Preface to Barnaby Googe's translation of Palingenius, Melpomene commands the poet with 'Reduce to English sence she said, the lofty Lucanes verse, | The cruel chaunce and dolfull end of Cesars state rehearse', *The firste syxe bokes of the mooste christian Poet Marcellus Palingenius, called the zodiake of life* (London, 1561), sig. ¢2ᵃ⁻ᵇ. C.H. Conley, *The First English Translators of the Classics* (New Haven, Conn., 1927), 20, assumes this means Googe translated the *Pharsalia*. Thomas Hughes's *Misfortunes of Arthur*, which contains the first actual translation of Lucan into English, describes the struggle to re-establish Arthur's legitimate rule after the usurpation of Mordred. J. C. Maxwell, 'Lucan's First Translator', *Notes and Queries*, 192 (1947), 521–2, compares III. iii. 1–65 with *Phars.* 1. 195–391 and 7. 250–98. For Hughes's text, see J. W. Cunliffe (ed.), *Early English Classical Tragedies* (Oxford, 1912), 217–96. See further app. B, 'Shakespeare and Lucan', in Emrys Jones, *The Origins of Shakespeare* (Oxford, 1977), 273–7. James VI's loose paraphrase of Lucan concludes in a similar vein, 'Though subjects do conjure | For to rebell against their Prince and King' they will come 'to rewe their folie'. 'A Paraphrasticall Translation out of the Poete Lucane' (1584), ll. 25–32, *The Poems of James VI of Scotland*, ed. James Craigie, STS, 2 vols. (Edinburgh and London, 1955), i. 63. The poem paraphrases *Phars.* 5. 335–40.

[152] On Lucan's republicanism, see Charles Martindale, 'The Politician Lucan', *Greece and Rome*, NS 31 (1984), 64–79. For the insinuation that English readers of Lucan are republicans, see Hill, *Intellectual Origins*, 150. See also Gerald M. MacLean, *Time's Witness: Historical Representation in English Poetry, 1603–1660* (Madison, Wis., 1990), 26–43.

[153] *Lucans Pharsalia: containing the Civill Warres betweene Caesar and Pompey* (London, 1614), 332–7. Cf. *Phars.* 8. 480–1: 'consilii vox prima fuit, meritumque fidemque | sacraque defuncti iactavit pignora patris' (He spoke first at the council, and dwelt on merit, and faith, and the sacred oaths of a dead father). There is no similar addition in any other European translation of the poem, or in any of the editions examined. These lines have a manuscript note beside them in the Bodleian copy of Bersman's edition of Lucan: 'videtur oratio Achorei iniuria temp<?oris> defecisse: sed fingit... Arthurus Gorgus' (It seems that the speech of Achoreus is missing because of the damage of time, but Arthur Gorges has made it up), *M. Annaeus Lucani de Bello Civili, vel Pharsaliae libri decem, Gregorii Bersmani* (Leipzig, 1589), 263; Bodleian shelfmark 8°. Rawl. 179.

justice in the distribution of offices. But its final section introduces the prospect, redolent with the energy of epic poems of the 1590s, of an ambitious man spurred on by the injustice of the prince to aspire to his place:

> When kings themselves lawless grow,
> They hazard then to overthrow
> Their own estate; and teach that mind
> That is ambitiously enclind,
> How to aspire by fraud or might,
> To reave away their soveraignes right.
> He that no good deserts observes,
> The like at others hands deserves.[154]

The concluding couplet is pointed: it is not the remark of a doctrinaire republican, but indicates that Gorges is prepared to develop the prince-book commonplace that kings should reward merit by imagining what will happen if they do not. Achoreus's speech concludes with a warning to tyrants:

> *He that with blood upholds his state*
> *The most do feare, and all do hate:*
> *And he that hated is of all*
> *Is sure into mischance to fall.*[155]

The fear of tyrannical injustice and its consequences, not love of the Republic, underlies Gorges's translation. The one Lucanian moment in *Mortimeriados*, when individual drives fuse with historical circumstances to create massive destruction, occurs apropos of royal injustice; and the only figure in the poem who might have developed a rebellious energy equivalent to Lucan's Caesar—had Drayton enough courage to develop his descriptive instincts in the narrative—rises against the king because he feels wronged. Between about 1590 and 1615 Lucan assisted the emergence of honour-conscious heroes who believed they had been wronged by unjust monarchs.

In 1600 Sir John Hayward was imprisoned for a speech by the Archbishop of Canterbury in his *Life of Henrie the IIII* (dedicated to the factious Earl of Essex), allegedly 'tending to prove that deposers of kings and princes have had good success',[156] despite Hayward's defence that the speech was controverted by the Bishop of Carlisle.[157] And in 1601 the

---

[154] p. 333. I have corrected several misprints in the text.
[155] p. 336. Gorges's emphasis.
[156] *CSP Dom. 1598–1601*, 449.
[157] *The First Part of the Life and Raigne of King Henrie the IIII* (London, 1599), 62–8 and 100–10; see further Nearing, *Historical Poetry*, 35, and Margaret Dowling, 'Sir John Hayward's Troubles over his *Life of Henry IV*', *The Library*, 4th ser. 11 (1930), 212–24.

Earl of Essex led an uprising against a monarch who, he claimed, preferred corrupt counsellors (the Cecils) over men of true worth (himself)—an uprising which, it has been argued, was the last fling of the old ethos of baronial independence.[158] These events instantaneously made rebellious aristocrats risky heroes for historical poems. Partly in response to these threatening changes in the political atmosphere, *Mortimeriados* was blunted into *The Barons Warres* in 1603. The revised poem has more detailed points of similarity with the *Pharsalia* than its earlier version,[159] but far less rebellious energy. The influence of Lucan is present in the text as a swerve away from old subjects: rebellious heroes go out, and so do many elements of the uncomplicated romance idiom of the earlier version:[160] Isabella is no longer described in an erotic *blazon*, and the reminiscences of Dido are excised from her complaint to her brother.[161] When Drayton tried to be more 'Lucanian' he did not become more vehement or republican; he became more cautious. His passage about the destruction caused by royal injustice remains; but it is muted in comparison with the earlier text. The deposition scene is abruptly broken off,[162] and Drayton also consistently eradicates his earlier view of the barons as an enraged community of honour. A quarrelsome pique replaces the earlier echo of Cymochles:

> Resolv'd with Bloud their Libertie to buy,
> And in the Quarrel vow'd to live and die.[163]

The lines in which the barons oppose their liberty to Edward's tyranny were also cut, and Mortimer is no longer infused with thoughts of honour, but 'to so high a Temper wrought his Heart': he becomes a confusion of discordant elements rather than a hero driven upwards by the single motive of aspiring honour.[164] *The Barons Warres* recreates Holinshed's barons—a confused rout of proud rebels—rather than representing men whose desire to be honoured is turned against the established order with the destructive force of Lucan's Caesar.

Samuel Daniel's *Civil Wars* influenced Drayton's revisions, and was the

---

[158] See Mervyn James, 'At the Crossroads of the Political Culture: The Essex Revolt, 1601', in *Society, Politics, and Culture: Studies in Early Modern England* (Cambridge, 1986), 416–65.

[159] On Lucan and *BW*, see Anthony LaBranche, 'Drayton's *The Barons Warres* and the Rhetoric of Historical Poetry', *Journal of English and Germanic Philology*, 62 (1963), 82–95.

[160] See Nearing, *Historical Poetry*, 98–104; *Works*, v. 63–5.

[161] ll. 99–112 cut; 1233–60; cf. *BW* iii. 76.

[162] *BW* v. 9.

[163] *BW* i. 24.

[164] *BW* i. 22, iii. 40.

most sustainedly Lucanian poem of the period.[165] This work is, however, deliberately insensitized to Lucan's representation of the late Republic as a period in which all rival claims to heroism are destructive to self and society. Daniel signifies his subject-matter by closely adapting Lucan's proem,[166] and, in the early stages of his poem, uses motifs from the *Pharsalia* to mark clear poles of authorial allegiance: usurpers like Bolingbroke and the future Edward IV are associated with Caesarian imagery;[167] whereas Pompey's blasted oak is rejuvenated and aligned with Talbot, who fights for country and the *de facto* legitimate monarch.[168] The 'in se magna ruunt' topos is also used to point a moral, rather than simply as a natural law: Montague appropriates it to argue that Bolingbroke's usurpation cannot succeed.[169] The one suicidally Lucanian moment in the poem occurs when Talbot, the defender of King and Country, exhorts his men to hack their fame out of the bodies of the French. With a Lucanian perversity, their drive to dominate becomes a will to die:

> Hotly, these small but mightie-minded, Bands
> (As if ambitious now of death) doe straine
> Against innumerable armed hands.[170]

Daniel could never bring himself to provide his rebellious barons with any motive that would explain their opposition to the monarchy. His noblemen, like those of the *Barons Warres*, are confused creatures. The rebellious Percies, for example, conspire

> under pretence to right
> Such wrongs, as to their common wealth belong:
> Urg'd, either through their conscience, or despight,
> Or finding now the part they took was wrong:

---

[165] *The Complete Works in Verse and Prose*, ed. A. B. Grosart, 5 vols. (London, 1885–96), v. 63. I shall not discuss Daniel's historiography, for which, see F. J. Levy, *Tudor Historical Thought* (San Marino, Calif., 1967), 224–5; R. B. Gill, 'Moral History and Daniel's *The Civil Wars*', *Journal of English and Germanic Philology*, 76 (1977), 34–45; Pierre Spriet, 'Samuel Daniel (1563–1619): Sa vie—son œuvre', *Études anglaises*, 29 (1968), 451–547; Arthur B. Ferguson, 'The Historical Thought of Samuel Daniel: A Study in Renaissance Ambivalence', *Journal of the History of Ideas*, 32 (1971), 185–202; D. R. Woolf, 'Community, Law and State: Samuel Daniel's Historical Thought Revisited', *Journal of the History of Ideas*, 49 (1988), 61–83.

[166] *The Civil Wars*, I. 1–3 (hereafter *CW*); *Phars.* I. 1–86. All references to Daniel are from *The Complete Works*, ed. Grosart. Most of Daniel's allusions to Lucan are noted in George M. Logan, 'Daniel's *Civil Wars* and Lucan's *Pharsalia*', *Studies in English Literature*, 11 (1971), 53–68. *The Civil Wars*, ed. Laurence Mitchel (New Haven, Conn., 1958) overlooks all but the most obvious allusions to Lucan, and is extremely cursory in its discussion (p. 7) of *Phars.* as a source for *CW*.

[167] In *CW* I. 87–94 Bolingbroke is rebuked by the Genius of England as Caesar by Rome, *Phars.* I. 183–205; Caesar is compared to a Libyan lion at *Phars.* I. 205–12, and Edward at *CW* VII. 97.

[168] *CW* VI. 95; *Phars.* I. 136–43.

[169] *CW* II. 31; *Phars.* I. 81.

[170] *CW* VI. 89.

> Or else Ambition hereto did them call,
> Or others envy'd grace; or, rather, all.[171]

The Civil Wars appropriates for the monarchy those justifying explanations
of war which Drayton had applied to the barons' party: the upstart
Bolingbroke is accused of unjustly distributing 'charge and honour due
to good deserts' by the legitimate King Richard II, rather than vice
versa.[172] Like Drayton, Daniel compares a king's fall to the toppling of a
massive edifice:

> Like when some great *Colossus*, whose strong base
> Or mightie props are shrunk or sunke away,
> Fore-shewing ruine, threatning all the place
> That in the danger of his fall doth stay,
> All straight to better safetie flocke apace;
> None rest to helpe the ruine, while they may.[173]

Daniel offers no reason for the toppling of the Colossus, beyond the venal
disappearance of its underprops when the structure seems likely to fall.
There is none of Drayton's early attempt to explain the rise of his Caesar
figure as the consequence of royal injustice, and none of that conflict of self-
conflicting heroisms which drives the *Pharsalia* towards such memorable
destruction.

Yet several critics have argued that Daniel eventually came to think
that English history had a Lucanian complexity, and that accordingly he
represented the battle of Towton (which is described in Book VIII, the
latest addition to the poem[174]) as a conflict with right on neither side and
suicidal urges on both:[175]

> But, here no *Cato* with a Senate stood
> For Common-wealth: nor here were any sought
> T'emancipate the State, for publique good;
> But onely, headlong, for their faction wrought.[176]

It is often said that Daniel is the English Lucan,[177] but his despairing

---

[171] *CW* IV. 16. Alternative motives are similarly piled up at VII. 7.

[172] *CW* II. 20.

[173] Ibid. 6.

[174] Bk. VIII first appeared in the 1609 edition.

[175] Joan Rees, *Samuel Daniel: A Critical and Biographical Study* (Liverpool, 1964), 122–46; George
M. Logan, 'Daniel's *CW*' argues on the other hand that Lucan's account of the civil war is cast in
'black-and-white terms' (67) and that Daniel discarded it as a model when his own creation became
more complex.

[176] *CW* VIII. 7.

[177] 'As *Lucan* hath mournefully depainted the civil wars of *Pompey* & *Caesar*: so hath *Daniel* the
civill wars of *Edward* the second, and the Barons', Francis Meres, *Palladis Tamia* (London, 1598),
fol. 281ᵃ; Jonson's criticism is apt: 'Daniell wrott civill warres, and yet hath not one batle in all his
Book', *Works*, i. 138.

vision of an England racked by pointless, motiveless discord has little in common with the self-imploding structures of Lucan's Rome. But one can sense imaginative pressures in the poem which parallel the self-thwarting energies of Lucan. There is a latent war running throughout the *Civil Wars*; and it is a war with the appetencies and desires of the romance mode. Tasso had enlisted Lucan as an ally in his battle with pity, when he used Caesar's violation of the sacred wood to sustain his own and Rinaldo's destruction of the enchanted forest in *Gerusalemme liberata*. Lucan comes to take on a very similar significance in Daniel's poem. He is the writer one invokes in order to fight pity, and to rupture prevailing idioms. Daniel's most significant abandonment of historical accuracy occurs when he imitates the pathetic account of Pompey's meeting with his wife Cornelia in the unhistorical confrontation between the defeated Richard II and Queen Isabel.[178] The Queen fails to recognize the melancholy figure of her husband, whom she takes for 'some of ours: and we, of right, | Must pittie him, that pitties our sad plight';[179] but on realizing that this pitiful observer of the royal tragedy is the King himself, she 'gives words leave to complaine'.[180] But the Lucanian underpresence here sterilizes passion, forcing the episode towards politics, and away from love. The meeting between the royal couple is mute with a sterile pathos which issues in the best stanza of the poem:

> Thus both stood silent and confused so,
> Their eyes relating how their hearts did morne:
> Both bigge with sorrowe, and both great with wo
> In labour with what was not to be borne:
> This mightie burthen, wherewithall they goe,
> Dies undelivered, perishes unborne.[181]

Burgeoning fertility of the kind which Spenser drew from Ovid is here transformed by metaphor and pun into an abortive grief, both insupportable and incapable of utterance: amorous mutual compassion, and fertile love, have become impossible in a political marriage. The presence of Lucan forces love into perversely abortive shapes.

This episode is from the 1595 text of the *Civil Wars*. Later additions push love and compassion still further from political life. Book VI was

---

[178] *CW* ii. 66–94; *Phars.* 8. 33–108. Daniel apologizes for this episode: 'And if I have erred somewhat in the draught of the young *Q. Isabel* (wife to *Ric. 2*) in not suting her passions to her yeares...', Grosart, ii. 7. Mitchel, edn. cit. 348, errs when he claims, 'This episode is entirely Daniel's invention.'

[179] *CW* II. 76.

[180] Ibid. 81.

[181] Ibid. 93.

included in the 1599 edition,[182] but was also appended to some copies of
The First Fowre Bookes of 1595:[183] it is therefore likely to date from 1595–
6. This slightly later part of the *Civil Wars* plays on and assists the
gradual, fitful emergence of ruthless justice from the thickets of romance
which was occurring through those critical years. *Civil Wars*, Book VI,
treats the reign of Henry VI as an *exemplum* of the ill effects of excessively
clement government. At Richard Duke of York's trial, the King pleads to
'Dispense sometime with sterne severitie', and that 'Pittie draws love'.[184]
Somerset replies that to pardon York would be *crudelis misericordia*:

> Compassion, here, is crueltie my Lord;
> Pittie will cut our throates, for saving so . . .[185]

Holinshed does note 'over-much mildnesse in the King'; but Somerset
pleads only that 'so great an enemie to the king and his bloud, might
never escape punishment',[186] and York is cleared because the evidence
runs his way, rather than through the extraordinary mercy of the King.
The reasons for Daniel's reshaping of history lie within the immediate
generic context of the poem. In 1596 Spenser published Books IV to VI
of *The Faerie Queene*, in which he allegorically represented the trial of
another aspirant to the crown, Mary Queen of Scots, as the culminating
point of his privy argument against excessive Queenly compassion.
Parliament had feared that Elizabeth would succumb to *crudelis misericordia,* and spare Mary while spilling her people.[187] This episode made
its mark on the historical epic. The 1596 edition of Warner's *Albion's
England*—a poem which assimilated almost every literary fashion as it
grew—also included an account of the trial, which is in outline indebted
to Spenser. Elizabeth is represented as expressing 'Sweet Adumbrations
of her Zeale, Mercie, and Wit' in the place of the sentence requested by
Parliament.[188] Daniel's trial scene (which must also date from around
1596) follows this fashion in its representation of historical events: he,
like Spenser, was alarmed by the possible consequences of his Queen's
most distinctive virtue.

---

[182] In 1609 Bk. III of 1595 was divided in two; hence 'V' became 'VI' etc. All references are to
the 1609 numbering.

[183] James G. McManaway, 'Some Bibliographical Notes on Samuel Daniel's *Civil Wars*', *Studies
in Bibliography*, 4 (1951), 31–9, notes but does not resolve the question of the date of VI. Mitchel,
edn. cit. 28–48, lists Daniel's revisions; he is concerned largely with stylistic development, however,
and does not suggest a date for VI.

[184] *CW* VI. 60–1.

[185] Ibid. 65.

[186] Holinshed, 626, 639. Cf. Mitchel's claim that 'Nothing in the Chronicles' prompts the portrayal
of the King as pitiful, edn. cit. 357.

[187] [R. Cecil], *The Copie of a Letter to . . . The Earl of Leycester* (London, 1586), 9; see also Simonds
D'Ewes, *A Compleat Journal*, 2nd edn. (London, 1693), 210.

[188] Edn. cit. 247.

In the last Elizabethan section of the poem, Book VII, this movement away from pity continues to develop momentum. The Queen urges her husband to agree to the attainder of the rebels:

> The Queene in griefe (and in her passions hot)
> Breakes out in speech, lovingly violent:
> 'And what (saith she) my Lord, have you forgot
> To rule and be a King? Why will you thus
> Be milde to them, and cruell unto us?'[189]

Holinshed praises the King for inserting a proviso into the attainder, which provides for subsequent pardons;[190] but Daniel's Queen is made of harder stuff. The sentiments of love and compassion, which played a crucial part in the personal rule of the Virgin Queen, are squeezed out of existence by political necessity: the pitiful King Henry VI falls to the more politic Edward at the battle of Towton.

The defeat of the clement king occurs in Book VIII, Daniel's most Lucanian and his most substantial Jacobean addition to the *Civil Wars*. The battle of Towton, Daniel's *Pharsalia*, occupies the first part of VIII, and has dominated critical accounts of the whole poem, and of the book in which it occurs. But the final section of the book, which explores the aftermath of the battle, is far more revealing about Jacobean developments in the epic. Edward's victory initiates a version of Lucan's 'iusque datum sceleri' (rip-offs are made law): 'He must remunerate, prefer, advance, | His chiefest friendes . . . | . . . doo wrong, to doo men right'; he 'payes with honors, and with dignities'[191] for past services, in a manner which approaches topical satire: in the first four months of his reign James I dubbed 906 knights.[192] This subdued criticism of the Jacobean style of monarchy continues, as Lady Elizabeth Grey comes in person to the King and sues for justice:

> A wofull widdow, whom his quarrell had
> (As it had many moe) made desolate,
> Came to his Court, in mournfull habit clad,
> To sue for Justice, to relieve her state.
> And entring as a suppliant all sad;
> With gracefull sorrow, and a comely gate
> She past the Presence: where, all eyes were cast
> On her more stately presence, as she past.[193]

---

[189] *CW* VII. 37. VII appeared as 'Booke Sixt' in 1601.
[190] Holinshed, 652.
[191] *CW* VIII. 36; *Phars.* 1. 2; *CW* VIII. 47. VIII appeared in 1609.
[192] Lawrence Stone, *The Crisis of the Aristocracy 1558–1641* (Oxford, 1965), 74.
[193] *CW* VIII. 52.

Lady Elizabeth is a scrupulously purified version of Tasso's Armida and
Spenser's phantasm of Una, both of whom assail their intended protectors
with a barrage of amorous charms and equivocations, which move but do
not motivate either of the epic romance heroes Redcrosse and Goffredo.[194]
Daniel's version of the pitiful visitation, however, works a pointed reversal
of these earlier episodes. Lady Elizabeth is not out to elicit pity; she seeks
justice; and King Edward, unlike Goffredo, is overcome by desire. He
arranges a more private date, at which he propositions the beleaguered
damsel. She retorts in outrage:

> My sov'raigne Lord, it grieves me that you deeme,
> Because I in this sort for Justice sue,
> I would the same with mine own wrong redeeme,
> And by dishonour reobtaine my due:
> No: I would hate that right, which should but seeme
> To be beholding to a wanton view
> Or motive of my person, not my Cause,
> That craves but right, from Justice, and your lawes.[195]

Daniel describes at length how lust 'tyranniz'd on [Edward's] divided
hart'.[196] Warwick, the Kingmaker, meanwhile has been in France courting
a Princess for his King. He returns, and is so disgusted by the King's
passionate marriage to this lady that he leaves the court, to become 'King
of him selfe'.[197] At home, his confessor gives a lengthy disquisition on
the value of retreat from public life.[198] The poem ends, incomplete, as
the discontented Lord re-enters the public sphere.

Daniel made a cutting portrayal of the subjection of justice to passion
under personal rule from Tasso's and Spenser's unease with sentiment.
He ends his poem with a justification of retreat from such arbitrary
government. It is often said that his development from 'The Complaint
of Rosamund' to his prose *Collection of the Historie of England* (1618)
constitutes a gravitation towards Fact, which is said also to be manifested
in the revisions to the *Civil Wars*.[199] This is part of the truth. But this
progression also manifests a retreat from the arbitrary charms of pitiful
monarchs. The episode of Warwick's retreat draws on the stock of ideas
explored in Daniel's early Jacobean Epistles, which were printed with the
six-Book *Civil Wars* in *The Works* of 1602. Joan Rees has noted that the

[194] *GL* iv. 28–77; *FQ* I. i. 50–4.
[195] *CW* VIII. 73.
[196] Ibid. 76–7.
[197] Ibid. 92.
[198] Ibid. 93–101. Mitchel, edn. cit. 364, notes that this episode has no source in the Chronicles.
[199] See Nearing, *Historical Poetry*, 92; S. Clark Hulse, 'Samuel Daniel: The Poet as Literary
Historian', *Studies in English Literature*, 19 (1979), 65, and *Metamorphic Verse* (Princeton, NJ, 1981),
195–220.

Confessor's speech is similar in theme to the Epistle to Lucy Countess of Bedford on the value of retreating from the corruptions of court to enjoy personal virtue.[200] But the episode is also more obliquely akin to Daniel's Epistle to Thomas Egerton, the Lord Chancellor (1603–17). This is about Equity, a concept which was frequently entangled with regal clemency. Daniel, however, makes it quite clear that Equity and compassion have no common ground, and that the King, far from being the ultimate source of Equity, is himself subject to this supra-legal form of justice:

> ... ev'n the Scepter which might all command,
> Seeing her s'unpartiall, equall regulare,
> Was pleas'd to put it selfe into her hand,
> Whereby they both grew more admired far.[201]

Daniel's insistence, both here and at the end of the *Civil Wars*, on impersonal justice, unimpeded by the tyrannous passions of the monarch, is the Jacobean descendant of his, and indeed of Spenser's, Elizabethan unease with the Queen's compassionate government. It also reflects Daniel's concern with the retention of the customary structures of the common law, and his deep hostility to tyrannical Roman importations, which shape the imagery and argument of his *Defence of Rhyme*.[202] The *Civil Wars* closes with an imaginative renunciation, not of poetry for history, but of charismatic government for self-regiment. In an age in which the King openly preferred courtiers on the basis of their personal charms, and was fond of asserting that the monarchy was above the law,[203] this was the natural mutation for the polymorphous mode of epic romance to take. Daniel transformed the latent unease with pitiful kingship, which underlies earlier epic romances, into an outright rejection of the role of love and pity in government.

This line in the English epic, which is rootedly hostile to moments when passion permeates the law, comes to a head in the work of Thomas May (1595–1650). His career was slow to take a certain course: he dedicated historical poems on the reigns of Edward III and Henry II to Charles I,[204] but later translated the *Pharsalia*, and became official historian

---

[200] Rees, *Daniel*, 130.

[201] ll. 189–92. On Daniel's view of law, see Woolf, 'Community', 67–72. On his association with Egerton, see John Pitcher, 'Samuel Daniel's Letter to Sir Thomas Egerton', *Huntington Library Quarterly*, 47 (1984), 55–61.

[202] See the excellent piece by Richard Helgerson, 'Barbarous Tongues: The Ideology of Poetic Form in Renaissance England', in H. Dubrow and R. Strier (eds.), *The Historical Renaissance: New Essays on Tudor and Stuart Literature and Culture* (Chicago, 1988), 273–92.

[203] James VI and I, *The True Lawe of Free Monarchies* (Edinburgh, 1598), sig. C7ᵛ.

[204] *The Reigne of King Henry the Second* (London, 1633); *The Victorious Reigne of King Edward the Third* (London, 1635).

of Parliament during the Civil War.[205] Aubrey was the first of many to
suppose that May's translation of Lucan 'made him in love with the
republique',[206] and was the cause of this shift in allegiances—although
Marvell attributed the change to less elevated motives.[207] May does show
a new phase in the meaning of Lucan in England: he rejected the
conservative interpretation of the *Pharsalia* advanced by his sixteenth-
century predecessors. When Lucan argues that, if his own contemporaries
suffer tyranny, they should fight, May allows his implication to emerge:

> Post proelia natis
> Si dominum, Fortuna, dabas, et bella dedisses.
>
> To us, that since do live,
> Fates should give war, if they a tyrant give.

Arthur Gorges, by contrast, fudges, and postpones the fighting for a
generation:

> O *Fortune*! If thou needs would cast
> Our sonnes to be a tyrants thrall,
> Thou shouldst have given them warres withall.[208]

The development of May's hostility to the monarchy can be traced very
clearly in the differences between his *Continuation of Lucan* (1630) and
its Latin version, *Supplementum Lucani* (1640).[209] The earlier English work
includes two elements of Roman history which the *Pharsalia* pointedly
omits: there is a long encomium to Augustus, which represents the Civil
Wars as a *felix culpa*:

> For thee were *Marius* crimes, and *Sylla's* wrought:
> For thee was Thapsus and Pharsalia fought,
> That Rome in those dire Tragedies might see
> What horrid dangers follow'd libertie.[210]

This passage was cut from the *Supplementum* as part of a major change
of emphasis. This equivocal support ('For thee were *Marius* crimes'
retains a Lucanian cattiness) for benign dictatorship turned to a more

---

[205] See *The History of the Parliament of England* (London, 1647); *A Breviary of the History of the Parliament of England* (London, 1680).
[206] John Aubrey, *Brief Lives*, ed. Andrew Clark, 2 vols. (Oxford, 1898), ii. 56.
[207] 'Most servile wit, and mercenary pen', 'Tom May's Death', l. 40, in *The Poems and Letters of Andrew Marvell*, ed. H. M. Margoliouth, 2 vols., 3rd rev. edn. (Oxford, 1971).
[208] *Phars.* 7. 645–6; May, sig. N4^b; Gorges, 292.
[209] See the definitive study by R. T. Bruère, 'The Latin and English Versions of Thomas May's *Supplementum Lucani*', *Classical Philology*, 44 (1949), 145–63.
[210] *Continuation*, sig. H6^a.

openly anti-imperial outlook.[211] The *Supplementum* pointedly omits several similarly equivocal references to the clemency on which Caesar had prided himself.[212] The Caesar of 1630 'by his mercy winnes | . . . The peoples hearts',[213] and uses clemency as a tool of state:

> Grieving to finde what this sad conquest cost,
> He sometimes wail'd his owne slaine Souldiers then,
> Sometimes the slaughter'd foes, as Countrimen,
> And wishes some, to whom he now might show
> His mercy, had surviv'd the overthrow.[214]

Caesar's grief is motivated by a theatrical desire to *show* clemency rather than by spontaneously compassionate instincts. May does, however, defend Caesar's imperial authority immediately before his assassination, on the grounds that his 'mercy every where | So many pardon'd enemies have try'd'.[215] All these passages on imperial clemency are omitted from the *Supplementum,* in which May explicitly states: 'Nec libertatem Clementia pensat ademptam' (clemency is no substitute for lost liberty).[216] This phrase captures the deep association between a hostility to pity and a wistful love of the Republic, which runs right through the English epic romances produced by the inglorious Spensers of the Elizabethan period. Spenser's epic was vast enough to generate lines of writing which were set on opposite sides of the Civil War: *The Faerie Queene* gave rise both to the imperial peacemakers sought and praised by Waller and to the vehement hostility to imperial supremacy which emerges in the later works of May.

[211] In 1630 the people 'willingly forgive | The losse of that unsafe prerogative | Their libertie' (*Continuation*, sig. I5ᵃ) in order to ensure peace; but by 1640 they are presented as rash: 'Plebs libertatem, sola contenta salute, | Romula projecit; nec post tot praelia pacem, | Quamvis cum Domino veniat pax ista, recusat' (The people of Rome threw away their liberty, content with their safety alone; nor, after so many battles did they refuse peace, although with that peace came a tyrant), *Supplementum*, 65.

[212] For Lucan's pointed refusal to accept the myth of the Clement Caesar, see Ahl, *Lucan*, 192–7; on the antagonism between clemency and republicanism, see C. Wirszubski, *Libertas as a Political Idea at Rome* (Cambridge, 1950), 150–3.

[213] *Continuation*, sig. I6ᵇ.

[214] Ibid. sig. I2ᵇ.

[215] Ibid. sig. I7ᵃ. The conspirators also fear they shall 'Be judg'd ingrate to *Caesar's* clemency', sig. K2ᵃ.

[216] *Supplementum*, 67.

7

Inglorious Miltons

CHAPMAN'S *ILIADS*

Epic heroes in the sixteenth century very often fail to leave their ladies finally on the first attempt, as a wave of magnetic passion draws them backwards. Marlowe's Aeneas in *Dido, Queene of Carthage* needs two attempts to escape his love. When he first tries to leave he is held back by a vision of Dido, which entangles his imperial purpose in amorous delay:

> Come backe, come backe, I heare her crye a farre,
> And let me linke thy bodie to my lips,
> That tyed together by the striving tongues,
> We may as one saile into *Italye*.[1]

The pitiful, loving Aeneas died hard. Even Marlowe's apparently ruthless and martial Tamburlaine is pulled off course by a distant memory of a romance version of Aeneas. At the close of *Tamburlaine Part I*, the hero swears to destroy all the inhabitants of Damascus, the home town of Zenocrate, his love. He ruthlessly succeeds in emulating Virgil's hero when he kills Zenocrate's lover, who 'Comes now as *Turnus* against *Aeneas* did.[2] But a faint memory of a pitiful Aeneas—or of the way Virgil's hero is so nearly drawn to grant appeals to mitigate his martial ambitions when they make reference to fathers—leads Tamburlaine to overturn his oath of complete destruction, and to spare Zenocrate's father.

Works written about the Trojan War from the 1590s to the first decade and a half of the seventeenth century continue to display this bias towards the amorous. Thomas Heywood's *Troia Britanica: or, Great Britaines Troy* (1609) substitutes Ovidian love-letters between Paris and Helen for the early stages of the Trojan War, and draws on medieval sources—Caxton, Chaucer, Dictys, and Dares—for the war itself.[3] Heywood tried hard to

---

[1] *The Works of Christopher Marlowe*, ed. C. F. Tucker Brooke (Oxford, 1910), ll. 1177–80
[2] l. 2162. Tamburlaine's wish to emulate Aeneas in depriving the King of Arabia of his Lavinia is stated in ll. 2174–81.
[3] Translations of *Heroides* 16–17 occupy cantos ix–x. Canto xii relates Achilles's seduction of Deidamia, drawn from *Ars amatoria* 1. 681–707. See John S. P. Tatlock, 'The Siege of Troy in Elizabethan Literature, Especially in Shakespeare and Heywood', *PMLA* 30 (1915), 673–770.

make Achilles a wrathful Homeric hero, and claimed in a note that he had done so:

The reason why *Achilles* kept his Tent, and was not in the field when *Hector* breathed his chalenge, is not fully resolved: some thinke he was discontent about a difference betwixt the Generall *Agamemnon* and him [margin: *Homer*], who kept away perforce *Briseis*, a beauteous lady, claimed by *Achilles* as his Prise, which we rather follow in our History, then to lay his absence on his love to *Polixena*, whom he had not yet seene, and the promise which for her sake he made to *Hecuba*, to keepe himselfe and his *Mirmidons* from the battaile.[4]

But Heywood's egregious insistence on his fidelity to Homer is immediately belied by the argument to the next canto:

> *Achilles* dotes on beauteous *Polixaine*,
> And at her faire request refraines the fielde.

However hard poets of this period concentrate on eliminating love from their heroes, the desire falls short of the performance. Dares and Dictys both attribute Achilles's absence from the field to his love for Polyxena, rather than to his rage with Agamemnon, and subsequent mythographers frequently attributed the hero's death to his cupidity.[5] Sir John Harington, in the notes to his version of *Aeneid* 6, also gives considerable attention to the amours of Homer's irascible hero:

Achilles, the valyentest warryer of all the greeks, [and] though he wear amorous, and ys descrybed by homer to have lovd Bryseis, and before that to have deflowrd Deidamia daughter of King Lycomedes yet his valour being more honorable then his lust was infamows, his name ys taken, contrary to Parys in the best part as in this 6 *book*.[6]

There is little in the *Iliad* to prompt this view of Achilles as a lover. Statius's *Achilleid* relates his love for Deidamia, and prompted the later amorous revisions of the hero,[7] and Ovid made Briseis one of the wronged heroines in his *Heroides*, who exchanges regretful *œillades* with Achilles

---

⁴ *Troia Britanica: or, Great Britaines Troy* (London, 1609), 329.

⁵ Dictys Cretensis, *Ephemeridos belli Troiani*, ed. Ferdinand Meister, Teubner Texts (Leipzig, 1872), 3. 3; Dares Phrygius, *De excidio Troiae historia*, ed. Ferdinand Meister, Teubner Texts (Leipzig, 1873), p. xxvii; [Vatican Mythographers], *Scriptores rerum mythicarum Latini tres Romae nuper reperti*, ed. G. H. Bode, 2 vols. (Darmstadt, 1834), 1. 66, 143, 242; Giovanni Boccaccio, *Genealogie Deorum gentilium libri*, ed. Vincenzo Romano, 2 vols. (Bari, 1951), ii. 610. See further Katherine Callen King, *Achilles: Paradigms of the War Hero from Homer to the Middle Ages* (Berkeley and Los Angeles, 1987), 195–201. Dares and Dictys, supposed eyewitnesses at Troy, were printed in 1573, together with part of Eobanus Hessus's highly Virgilian translation of Homer, in a collection of *Belli Troiani scriptores praecipui, Dictys Cretensis, Dares Phrygius & Homerus* (Basle, 1573).

⁶ *The Sixth Book of Virgil's Aeneid, Translated and Commented on by Sir John Harington (1604)*, ed. Simon Cauchi (Oxford, 1991), 11; Berkshire Records Office MS Trumbull Add. 23, 10.

⁷ See King, *Achilles*, 171–217.

as they part.[8] But when Homer's Achilles loses Briseis he is not a lover who leaves his belle. The lady could almost be a gold tripod: 'So he spoke, and Patroclus obeyed his dear comrade and led fair-cheeked Briseis from the hut, and gave her to them to lead away. So the two of them went back beside the Achaian ships. And with them went the unwilling woman.'[9] This separation scene is described without any direct indication that the two are attached to one another.[10] Only Briseis is unwilling, and a captive who is used as currency between warlords need not love her previous master in order to be reluctant about her transfer to a new one. Achilles's conflict of motives is in the past: he has already decided in the council scene in Book I—with the admonitory help of Pallas Athene—to grant Agamemnon his war prize Briseis rather than to slay his general in rage.[11] The actual departure of his lady is ostentatiously stark, an emotional hangover from the passionate excesses of the council. But in Chapman's 1598 version of *Seaven Bookes of the Iliads* the departure *is* a moment of moral choice:

> This said, Patroclus well allow'd the patience of his frend,
> Brought Briseis forth, and to her guides her comforts did commend
> With utmost kindenesse, which his frend could not for anguish use.
> Shee wept and lookt upon her love; he sigh't and did refuse.
> O how his wisdome with his power did mightilie contend—
> His love incouraging his power and spirite, that durst descend
> As far as Hercules for her, yet wisedome all subdude,
> Wherein a high exploite he showd, and sacred fortitude.
> Briseis without her soule did move and went to th'Achive tents[12]

The final glance between the two lovers (as they have become) may be a flash of Ovid; but Chapman is uniquely interested in the unstated emotions that Homer's text may imply. Achilles's silence becomes speechless anguish, and the whole episode is glossed as a moral battle between wisdom and passion. Bartlett calls this Achilles 'a knight of Spenserian Romance',[13] but in doing so shows herself to be a victim of the Spenserian myth, that all heroes in *The Faerie Queene* are gently feelingful: the closest Spenserian analogues to this departure are remarkable more for their

---

[8] 'alter in alterius iactantes lumina vultum | quaerebant taciti, noster ubi esset amor' (each throwing glances at the face of the other, asked silently 'where is our love?'), *Heroides* 3. 11–12.

[9] *Il.* 1. 345–8.

[10] Achilles describes her as his *alochon thumarea* (delightful wife) at *Il.* 9. 336; but no affection is evident in their separation.

[11] *Il.* 1. 188–224.

[12] 1598 text: 1. 357–65. All quotations from *Chapman's Homer: The Iliad; The Odyssey and the Lesser Homerica*, ed. Allardyce Nicoll, 2 vols. (London, 1957).

[13] Phyllis B. Bartlett, 'Chapman's Revisions in his *Iliads*', *ELH* 2 (1935), 110.

abrupt inconsequentiality than for their reluctantly checked emotion.[14] Chapman's expansion of Briseis's departure is underwritten by a pitiful misprision of these familiar lines:

> At pius Aeneas, quamquam lenire dolentem
> solando cupit et dictis avertere curas,
> multa gemens magnoque animum labefactus amore
> iussa tamen divum exsequitur classemque revisit.[15]

But dutiful Aeneas, although he longed to calm her grief with consolation and to lessen her sorrows with words, groaning many things, and overcome in spirit with great love, none the less carried out the commands of the gods and went back to his fleet.

Like Aeneas, Chapman's Achilles would console his love, although he is prevented by his own anguish rather than by her fainting. 'Yet wisedome all subdude' takes the place of 'iussa tamen divum exsequitur' as the adversative clause representing the pull of duty. His decision is too equably final ('yet wisedome *all* subdude') to possess the emotional counter-thrusts of the more urgent versions of the story-type. But the passage is historically significant, since the repentant ruthfulness that tends to soften such departures in epic romance has withered to a single sigh from the hero. It reads like a deliberate, rational exorcism of romance pathos from the heroic mind.

Chapman is scrupulously careful in this delicate area: he is an extraordinarily independent translator, who, through a sequence of extensive modifications to his Homer, attempted to create a distinctive and personal language for rendering the forms of feeling and the stylistic peculiarities of his original. In his revisions to his translation he moves further and further away from the received language for interpreting classical epic, out of a determination to make Homer strange. The familiar and familiarizing emotions of 'pity' and 'ruth' are almost only used when the original has forms of *eleein* or *oiktirein*.[16] Pity is once defended as appropriate for

---

[14] e.g. 'He nought forgot, how he whilome had sworne, | In case he could that monstrous beast destroy, | Vnto his Farie Queene backe to returne: | The which he shortly did, and *Vna* left to mourne.' *FQ* I. xii. 41. Cf. *FQ* v. viii. 3.

[15] *Aen.* 4. 393–6. Spondanus, the editor on whom Chapman relied most, alludes to Aeneas and Dido in his note on the Homeric departure, and praises Achilles over Aeneas for weeping at the loss of his lady, *Homeri quae extant omnia* (Basle, 1583), 18.

[16] In references to Chapman's Homer, the first line number refers to Chapman, the second to Homer. Compare e.g. 2. 26 (Chapman; does not render *eleairei*)/27 (Homer); 5. 557/561, 611/610; 6. 91/94; 8. 305/350; 15. 11/12; 14. 331/340; 21. 72/74; 24. 22/23; 'pitie' is used once to translate *achos*, pain, 16. 20/22; additions which specifically exclude pity occur at 18. 203/236: *oxei chalkō*, 'with sharp bronze', becomes 'with unpittying steele'; 21. 119/120: *ton de*, 'him', becomes 'his unpittied corse'; Achilles's ruthless killing of Tros, 20. 408–14/464–8, is translated without any sign of disapproval: he 'had no spirit to brooke that interim | In his hote furie', 412–13.

warriors in an addition: 'Seeing him, the brave son of Menoetius had pity' becomes

> His sight in kinde Patroclus' breast to sacred pittie turnd
> And (nothing more immartiall for true ruth) thus he mourned.[17]

Chapman realizes that moments of pity need justifying in a warrior, and his expansion here is part of a consistent reading of Patroclus's character as kind and ruthful, by which the translator also explains his courteous role in the 1598 version of the departure of Briseis.[18] Chapman published *Seaven Bookes* of his *Iliad* in 1598; these were augmented to *Twelve* in 1608. The complete form, with revisions to the 1598 version, appeared in 1611.[19] Both Books 1 and 11, the chief centres of pitiful contamination, were part of the *Seaven Bookes* of 1598: these vestiges of ruth are shadows of an earlier stage of composition which Chapman, in his haste to complete the project of translating all of Homer's works, forgot to erase.[20] In general his revisions systematically excise alien traces of compassion from the 1611 version, and seek also to strip away the familiarizing intermediary of Virgil from the unfamiliar form of Homer. Achilles's heroic separation from Briseis is pared down to the crispness of its Homeric original:

> This speech usd, Patroclus did the rite
> His friend commanded and brought forth Briseis from her tent,
> Gave her the heralds, and away to th'Achives ships they went.[21]

Bald verbs (did, commanded, brought, gave, went) blankly capture the matter-of-factness of Homer's separation.

In the 1608 *Twelve Bookes*, Chapman renders Homer's other main heroic departure of a warrior from his lady in quite a different spirit, which testifies to his developing conviction that a translation of the *Iliad* should construct unusual composites of motive in order to evoke the distant mentality of the Homeric past. The moment when Hector leaves Andromache for the battlefield, despite her premonition of his death, has none of the choking of emotion which occurs in Aeneas's departure from

---

[17] 11. 728–9/814.

[18] For 'characterizing' of Homeric heroes, see Phyllis B. Bartlett, 'The Heroes of Chapman's Homer', *Review of English Studies*, 17 (1941), 257–80. She does not discuss Patroclus. Homer calls him *meilichos*, gentle (17. 671). See also A. T. Murray, edn. cit. (Cambridge, Mass., and London, 1924–5), on 19. 295, and J. Griffin, *Homer on Life and Death* (Oxford, 1980), 73.

[19] *Seaven Bookes* (London, 1598) comprised 1, 2, 7, 8, 9, 10, and 11; 1 and 2 were rewritten, and the rest revised, for the complete *Iliades* of 1611; 3–6 and 12 were added to the seven in the *Twelve Bookes* (registered 1608). See edn. cit. 1. 14–19. See Bartlett, 'Chapman's Revisions'.

[20] For Chapman's haste in recasting the *Seaven Bookes* into the 1611 text, see *Commentarius* to Book 3: 'since time (that hath ever opprest me) will not otherwise let me come to the last twelve', edn. cit. 90.

[21] 1. 348–50.

Dido: it becomes warmer and more intimate as the departure draws near.[22]
As so often in the *Iliad*, pity comes not with a protective gush of sentiment
and power, but with a recognition of shared subjection to the necessary
limits imposed on human life.[23] The episode is vastly expanded in
medieval redactions of the Troy story, in which it is often fused with the
closely parallel episode in *Iliad* 22 (when Hector is urged to leave the
battlefield by his family), and flattened into an example of pitiless
resolution. In Guido de Columnis, Hector 'earum nec movetur ad lacrimas
nec ad preces' (is unmoved by their tears and prayers);[24] and in Lydgate's
version of Guido, Andromache laments pitifully in vain to a furious
warrior:

> Have mercy lord on us or we deye!
> Have mercy eke up-on this cyte,
> Myn owne lorde! have mercy or that we
> By cruel deth passe shal echon,
> For lak of helpe, allas, whan ye ar goon![25]

But Hector is 'So indurat, and hertid as lyoun | . . . contunynge in his
rage',[26] and mercilessly leaves. A tradition deriving from Dares makes
Hector delay his departure at the insistence of Priam;[27] and this is
frequently developed into a crescendo of *miserationes* from Andromache,
Hecuba, and Priam to a pitiless hero, who eventually yields to his father's
request to stay. But medieval writers are frequently unable to represent
the motives of the hesitant warrior, or to provide any motive other
than blankness for his departure. Benoît de Sainte-Maure's Hector, like
Chaucer's Aeneas, remains enigmatically silent in response to these appeals
for pity;[28] and Caxton's hero delays his heroic departure for no clear
reason: 'But at the request of Andromeda the kinge Priant came rennynge
anon, and tooke him by the brydle and sayd to hym so manye thynges of
one and other that he made him to returne, but in no wyse he woulde
not unarme hym'.[29] We have encountered a similar vagueness about
motivation in medieval treatments of the departure of Aeneas from Dido:
this idiom cannot easily accommodate minds which are not spontaneously

---

[22] See Jasper Griffin, *Homer* (Oxford, 1980), 29–31, and pp. 19–22 above.

[23] See Colin MacLeod, *Collected Essays* (Oxford, 1983), 13.

[24] *Historia destructionis Troiae* ed. N. E. Griffin, The Mediaeval Academy of America Publications, 26 (Cambridge, Mass., 1936), 173.

[25] *Troy Book*, ed. Henry Bergen, 3 vols., EETS Extra Series, 97, 103, and 106 (London, 1906–10), iii. 5068–72.

[26] Ibid. 5102–3.

[27] Dares, 24; edn. cit. 29.

[28] *Le Roman de Troie*, ed. Léopold Constans, Societé des anciens textes français, 5 vols. (Paris, 1904–9), ll. 15263–604.

[29] *The recuile of the histories of Troie. first translated out of latin in to frenche by Raoul le fevre . . . and translated out of Frenche in to Englishe by William Caxton*, 3 vols. (London, 1553), iii. 29[b].

moved by compassion. John Heywood takes up this medieval tradition of
Hector's delay; but unlike his predecessors he does not mute Hector's
motive for remaining. His headnote to canto xiii of *Troia Britanica* makes
it clear that while 'Andromache spends many a ruthful teare | His
thoughts were fixt, they bred no soft remorse'. Hector's delay is uniquely
attributed, not to pity, but to filial piety:

> The discontented Prince at length is wonne,
> Yet will he not unarme him for them all,
> But to expresse the duty of a Sonne,
> With *Priam* and the rest he mounts the wall.[30]

Heywood's Hector is a resolute Aeneas: his 'mens immota manet' (mind
remains unmoved),[31] and he is motivated by filial *pietas*. But his *pietas*
motivates his delay, rather than his departure; he is an oddly back to
front version of *pius Aeneas*.

Chapman sets aside all these medieval accretions in his version of the
departure. But he adds a whole new repertoire of themes and emotional
concerns to Andromache's lament:

> O noblest in desire,
> Thy mind, inflam'd with others' good, will set thy selfe on fire,
> Nor pitiest thou thy sonne, nor wife, who must thy widdow be
> If now thou issue: all the field will onely rush on thee.

Husband, your martial spirit [*menos*] will destroy you, and you do not pity either
your child or your unhappy wife, who is soon to be your widow. For soon all
the Greeks will set upon you and kill you.[32]

The warning against selfless self-combustion made by Chapman's Andromache is quite different from the fear expressed in the Greek that
Hector's dominant *menos*, his martial prowess, will destroy him. And this
theme is taken up by Chapman's Hector when he tells Andromache he
must fight:

> To this great Hector said:
> 'Be well assur'd, wife, all these things in my kind cares are
>   waid:
> But what a shame and feare it is to thinke how Troy would scorne
> (Both in her husbands and her wives, whom long-traind gownes
>   adorne)
> That I should cowardly flie off! The spirit I first did breath
> Did never teach me that—much lesse since the contempt of death

---

[30] 13. 86; edn. cit., p. 350.
[31] *Aen.* 4. 449.
[32] 6. 440–3/407–10.

Was settl'd in me and my mind knew what a Worthy was,
Whose office is to leade in fight and give no danger passe
Without improvement. In this fire must Hector's triall shine.
Here must his country, father, friends be in him made divine.

Woman, I too am concerned about these things; but I have great shame of the Trojans and the Trojan wives with trailing robes if I skulk apart from the battle like a coward. Nor does my own heart [*thumos*] endure it, since I have learnt always to be valiant and to fight amid the foremost Trojans, striving to win my father's great glory and my own.[33]

Chapman's Hector is not primarily motivated by his personal sense of shame (*aidōs*), or by patriarchal honour. His 'office', his role as the agent of country, father, and friends, goads him to go out in a blaze of beatifying self-immolation. These additions to his and to Andromache's speeches show a debt to epic fashions in the early seventeenth century: they indicate that duty-bound elements of the heroic departure, a concern with the offices and obligations explored in Cicero's *De officiis*, have risen to the fore between 1598 and 1608. But they also display Chapman's chief contribution to the epic tradition: he blended, from a massive variety of sources, a highly idiosyncratic vocabulary by means of which to evoke the blazing spiritedness of a Homeric warrior. He managed—unlike any previous vernacular poet writing of the matter of Troy—to provide Hector with a convincing repertoire of arguments for his departure by exploiting this idiosyncratic idiom. Throughout the translation his heroes are inspired to blaze with a transcendent but self-destructive, irascible fury, and this self-destructive *furor* motivates his Hector to leave his wife. Very early in his translation Chapman turned the contagious animation which drives the warrior in battle (for which Homer often employs the terms *thumos* and *menos*) into blazing inspiration. In the earliest text Apollo says:

> We will direct the spirit that burns in Hector's breast.
>
> *Hektoros orsōmen krateron menos hippodamoio.*[34]

Chapman's addition of 'burns' is appropriate for a moment when the hero's spirit is being urged on by a god: *thumos* and *menos* are often linked with fire and divine inspiration when Homer describes the berserker element in his warriors.[35] But these light touches, developing a set of associations which can be found in Homer, become by 1614 a distinctive heroic idiom, which generates some of Chapman's most powerful ren-

---

[33] 6. 476–85/440–6.
[34] 7. 31/38: 'let us arouse the spirit of horse-taming Hector'.
[35] Griffin, *Life and Death*, 37.

derings. When Zeus inspires Hector to burn the Greek ships, Chapman
makes the whole scene blaze with the glow of divinely inspired heroism.
The forces for which the hero left his wife crackle through the episode:

>   he stird
> (With such addition of his spirit) the spirit Hector bore
> To burne the fleet, that of it selfe was hote enough before.
> But now he far'd like Mars himselfe, so brandishing his lance
> As through the deepe shades of a wood a raging fire should glance,
> Held up to all eyes by a hill; about his lips a fome
> Stood, as when th' Ocean is enrag'd; his eyes were overcome
> With fervour and resembl'd flames, set off by his darke browes.

He was urging Hector son of Priam against the hollow ships, who was himself eager enough. He was raging like Ares, the spear-wielder, or as when a
devouring fire rages among the mountains in the thickets of a deep wood; and
foam came out round his mouth, and his two eyes blazed beneath his dreadful
brows.[36]

Hector's blazing spirit, that 'of it selfe was hote enough before', anticipates
the flames with which he destroys the ships, and catches the contagious
fire of the simile. A distant memory of the *Aeneid* probably underlies this
metaphorical elaboration of Homer; but it is not the amorous sections of
the *Aeneid* which had coloured the early stages of the translation: Hector
here draws his burning exuberance from Virgil's Turnus, who is similarly
tinctured with metaphorical sparks from the fire which he brings to the
Trojan fleet.[37] By 1614 Chapman is reaching out towards the martial; but
in order to create his new idiom of passion he still needs support from a
Virgilian subtext, although that subtext has shifted towards the flaming
and irascible forms of martial activity explored in the later books of the
Aeneid.

    Chapman's incandescent heroes also owe much to a more mundane
source: the definitions provided in Scapula's *Lexicon* of the key terms for
describing the martial frenzy of the Homeric warrior. *Thumos* and
menos are defined respectively as 'ira, excandescentia', and 'animi ardor
quidem'.[38] 'Animi ardor' literally means 'the fire of the mind'; and
'excandescentia' derives from *excandesco*, which means to grow hot, or to
take fire. Scapula's terminology derives from a standard handbook on the
anatomy of passion, Cicero's *Tusculan Disputations*:

---

[36] 15. 549–56/603–8. Spiritual fire is absent from Spondanus: he attributes it to the flash of
armour or to torches, edn. cit. p. 290.

[37] 'haud aliter Rutulo muros et castra tuenti | ignescunt irae, duris dolor ossibus ardet' (So, flames
burn in the Rutulian Turnus, as he gazes on the walls and the camp, and resentment burns in his
bones), *Aen.* 9. 65–6.

[38] *Lexicon Graeco-Latinum* (Basle, 1580), s.v. *Menos* and *Thumos*.

ira sit libido poeniendi eius, qui videatur laesisse iniuria, *excandescentia* autem sit ira nascens et modo existens, quae *thumosis* Graece dicitur.[39]

Anger is the desire to punish someone who appears to have done one harm; *excandescentia*, however, is an anger which suddenly comes into being, which the Greeks call *thumosis*.

Chapman identified the blaze of spirit which comes on a Homeric warrior in battle with this sudden fiery spurt of anger. Yet nowhere in his translation does he express disapproval of this flaming passionateness, whereas Cicero cites Zeno, the highest Stoic authority, that all forms of perturbation (including *excandescentia*) are forms of disease, which destroy the due supremacy of right reason.[40] If, as many critics have suggested, Chapman were an orthodox Stoic,[41] his translation would not be animated by *excandescentia*, the sudden, uncontrollable burst of martial rage. His eager acceptance of this wrathful form of heroism marks an epoch, not just in the English epic, but in the whole European Renaissance of classical epic: it is an animating frenzy, akin to divine inspiration, rather than a simple passion which can fight on the side of reason like Tasso's *appetito irascibile*.

There is some precedent for Chapman's relish of heroic rage among Florentine humanists.[42] Politian's treatise *De ira* defended the short-lived flare of *excandescentia* as appropriate for a warrior:

At vero ille alter, incitatior primo, fervidiorque, mox tamen placabilior motus animi, qui a Graecis *Thumos*: a nostris vero excandescentia appellatur, in iis plerumque eminere videtur qui ingenuo sunt animo, & liberali: idemque & misericordes, & placabiles prae caeteris sunt, qui ad excandescentiam propensiores ...Hic ille est impetus, qui (ut Homerus ait) bellatorum animis robur iniicit.[43]

---

[39] *Tusculan Disputations*, trans. J. E. King, Loeb Classical Library, rev. edn. (London and Cambridge, Mass., 1945), 4. 21.

[40] Ibid. 4. 11. Cf. 'Deinde nihil habet ira in se utile nec acuit animum ad res bellicas. Numquam enim virtus vitio adiuvanda est se contenta' (So anger has nothing useful in it, nor does it sharpen the mind to martial actions. For virtue is never content to be assisted by a vice), Seneca, *De ira* 1. 9, *Moral Essays*, trans. John W. Basore, 3 vols., Loeb Classical Library (London and Cambridge, Mass., 1928), 128.

[41] See e.g. Bartlett, 'The Heroes of Chapman's Homer'; Roy W. Battenhouse, 'Chapman and the Nature of Man', *ELH* 12 (1945), 87–107; Donald Smalley, 'The Ethical Bias of Chapman's Homer', *Studies in Philology*, 36 (1939), 169–91. For a more sophisticated account of the relations between Stoicism and anger, see Gordon Braden, *Renaissance Tragedy and the Senecan Tradition: Anger's Privilege* (New Haven, Conn., and London, 1985), 5–27.

[42] See Edgar Wind, *Pagan Mysteries in the Renaissance*, rev. edn. (Oxford, 1980), 68–9. Wind misleadingly implies that the elevation of rage occurred under the influence of Seneca's *De ira*, a work which is aimed throughout at the eradication of the passion. The terminology alone of these writers is drawn from classical Stoicism.

[43] Angelus Politianus, *Omnium operum (quae quidem extare novimus)*, 2 vols. (Paris, 1519), ii. fol. 55^b.

But that other motion of the spirit, which is more urgent at first, and more vehement, but which soon becomes milder, which the Greeks call *thumos*, and we call *excandescentia*, appears to be more apparent in those who are of an honest and outgoing nature. Those who are more prone to *excandescentia* are on the whole more pitiful, and more readily calmed down. This is that impetus which (as Homer says) adds strength to the spirits of warrior.

Politian (1454–94) shared many of Chapman's interests: he translated Epictetus, one of the authors from whom Chapman drew most,[44] and initially owed his fame to his translation of the *Iliad*, on which he worked 1470–6. Ficino referred to him as 'Homericum illum adolescentem' (that Homeric young man) on the strength of his translation of Books 2–5 into Latin hexameters.[45] This work is highly Virgilian, shows little sympathy for Homer's martial spirit, and remained in manuscript until the nineteenth century.[46] Chapman cannot have used it; but he almost certainly did possess Politian's *Omnium operum tomus*,[47] in which the treatise *De ira* is immediately followed by a short discourse *In Homerum* (a commonplace interpretation of Homer as a mine of *exempla* for citizens.)[48] This juxtaposition of topics may well have set Chapman's mind alight. Through absorbing Politian's thought on anger, Chapman became able to apprehend and relish the martial ethos for which Politian himself was unable to find any sympathy in his version of Homer.

The inspired blaze under the influence of which Chapman's Hector leaves Andromache, and the incandescent fury which possesses his warriors in battle, are relatively easy to defend, since they are forces which propel heroes to their martial tasks. But the *Iliad* contains another form of anger, which was regularly distinguished in terminology and causation from the rage of the warrior, and which moralists and poets found far harder either to justify or sympathetically to evoke. The professed subject of the whole poem is 'the wrath of Achilles', a long-standing, passive rage into which the hero falls as a result of the confiscation of Briseis. The first word of the *Iliad*, *mēnis*, 'anger', was glossed by Scapula as 'ira permanens', and

[44] See F. L. Schoell, *Études sur l'humanisme continental en Angleterre à la fin de la renaissance* (Paris, 1926), 99–131.

[45] Saverio Orlando, '*Ars vertendi*: La giovanile versione dell'*Iliade* di Angelo Poliziano', *Giornale storico della letteratura italiana*, 143 (1966), 2.

[46] Ibid. 4–5, 23. Franck L. Schoell, 'George Chapman and the Italian Neo-Latinists of the Quattrocento', *Modern Philology*, 13 (1915), 217, suggests that Chapman may have 'consulted' Politian's *Iliad*. A collation of the texts reveals no signs of influence. Reprinted in A. Mai, *Spicilegium Romanum*, 10 vols. (Rome, 1839), ii. 1–100.

[47] The Epistle to Chapman's *Odysseys* is partially translated from Politian's *Ambra*, *Opera*, ii. fols. 86ᵃ–89ᵃ (Schoell, 'Chapman and the Neo-Latinists', 219). Chapman's interest in Politian was at its height 1610–14 (ibid. 217), while he was moving away from Virgil's influence.

[48] *Opera*, ii. fols. 56ᵃ–61ᵇ. See Emilio Bigi, 'Il Poliziano critico', *La rassegna della letteratura italiana*, 58 (1954), 367.

this long-lasting anger was regularly contrasted with *excandescentia*, the short blaze of martial fury. Politian, who defended *excandescentia*, roundly condemned rankling anger as the 'foulest enemy of the human spirit'.[49] Cicero translates the passage when the hero says: 'My heart boils with savage fury from its very depths, when I recall how all my deserved rewards of praise were stripped from me', and goes on to call rankling, resentful anger a kind of disease. 'Wise men', he adds, 'are never inflamed, never swell with rage'.[50] Cicero's attack on anger is quoted with approval by Spondanus in his commentary on the passage in Book 9 when Achilles swells with rage;[51] but Chapman emphatically did not follow his commentator in his rendering of this tumescent rage. He explicitly defends the rage which Cicero condemns:

> But still, as often as I thinke how rudely I was usd
> And like a stranger for all rites fit for our good refusd,
> My heart doth swell against the man that durst be so profane
> To violate his sacred place—not for my private bane,
> But since wrackt vertue's generall lawes he shameless did infringe,
> For whose sake I will loose the reines and give mine anger swinge
> Without my wisedome's least impeach.

But my heart swells with wrath when I think of how the son of Atreus has made me look foolish among the Argives, as though I were some stranger without privileges.[52]

Elsewhere in the translation, Chapman inserts a number of little asides which justify and defend the wrath of Achilles, almost all of which depend on the idea that the hero's rankling anger stems from his ruler's failure to accord honour its due reward. In Book 1, Achilles claims that Agamemnon is helped by the Greeks 'whose deserts thou never dost employ | With honour nor with care'; whereas the Greek says, 'you take no notice or heed of this'.[53] Agamemnon is 'ravishing my right' rather than 'taking his fill of goods and wealth'.[54] And, later, when Achilles receives the heralds, Chapman adds the justifying lines:

> I am scusde to keepe my aide in wane,
> Since they mine honour.'[55]

---

[49] *Opera*, ii. fols. 55[a-b].
[50] *Il.* 9. 646–8; *Tusculan Disputations* 3. 18–19.
[51] Spondanus, 172.
[52] 9. 612–18/646–8.
[53] 1. 162–3/160.
[54] 1. 173/171.
[55] 1. 340–1; not in Homer.

Achilles's 'just wrath'[56] like that of the baronial heroes of historical epics, is the anger of one whose King has failed to grant public honour to merit.

A full account of the relation between anger and honour is given in *A Table of Humane Passions, with their Causes and Effects*, by N. Coëffeteau (1574–1623), a book for which Chapman was to write a dedicatory poem.[57] This treatise is based on Aquinas's *Prima secundae*; but, unlike its model, it argues for the primacy of the irascible over the concupiscible element in the mind.[58] Tasso had followed Aquinas in according prime place to the concupiscible passions, since these are susceptible of religious ennoblement; and this belief underlay many of the romance interludes in his poem.[59] The changes in epic heroism through the sixteenth century were intimately associated with shifting emphases in moral psychology: Chapman's move towards irascible heroism is part of a general European tendency. Coëffeteau also connects anger with honour, and often plunders Homer's *Iliad* for *exempla* of different types of wrath. He makes the usual distinction between *excandescentia* and *ira permanens*, and attributes the latter to Achilles.[60] Calchas's remarks on the smouldering durability of royal anger are invoked in an argument about the origins of wrath:

> ...men of authority and command, will have such as are subject to their governement, honour them with service. And if their inferiours faile to yeeld them the honor which they think is due unto them, they cannot endure this injury, but fall into a rage; which makes them to seeke all occasions to punish this contempt. And therefore it was truly said, That the indignation of a King is great and fearefull; for when as a great king is incensed against any one that is not of his quality, although he temper and moderate his *choler* for a time, yet hee smothers it in his brest, and is never satisfied untill hee hath made him feele the effects of his power, that durst presume to offend him.[61]

The *Table of Humane Passions* makes the *Iliad* into an encyclopaedia of wraths, among which the anger of the dishonoured is central.[62] Neostoic handbooks on the passions of the soul provide an emotional language in which to probe the stress-lines in the social framework of the Greek

---

[56] 9. 620; not in Homer; cf. 16. 191/202: 'Through all the time that my just anger raign'd...' from 'All through my raging...'

[57] Trans. Edward Grimeston (London, 1621), 547–632. See further Anthony Levi, *French Moralists: The Theory of the Passions 1585–1649* (Oxford, 1964), 74–111 *et passim*.

[58] Levi, *French Moralists*, 145.

[59] *Discorsi*, ed. L. Poma (Bari, 1964), 106.

[60] '*Aristotle* tearmes these men sharpe, bitter, and secret: such was the *choler of Achilles*, which the death of so many brave princes slaine at the seige of *Troy*, during his despight, could hardly mollifie.' *Human Passions*, 573.

[61] Ibid. 569–70; cf. *Il.* 1. 80–3: 'For a king is mightier, whenever he is angry with an inferior. For if he swallows his anger for that one day, he still holds resentment in his heart, until he vents it.'

[62] *Human Passions*, 567–9.

camp: the King fumes because he considers himself dishonoured by a subordinate, and the subordinate because he has been reviled by the King. But Chapman's interpretation of the quarrel-scene is a little ahead of its time: Coëffeteau's treatise was not published until 1620, and Chapman's *Iliad* was complete by 1611. And no one simply influenced by French Neostoicism could have defended prolonged righteous anger against a monarch. Coëffeteau rounds off his section on anger with an exhortation to 'avoyde and flie from it', and remarks that 'wee dare not bee angry... against kings, and great personages that have wronged us'.[63]

A more immediate context may well underlie Chapman's remarkable valorization of irascible heroism. English Prince books and treatises on the nature of true nobility, with their distinctive stress on the Prince as a just distributor of rewards, swung towards anger at the end of the sixteenth century. James I's *Basilicon Doron* advises Chapman's patron Prince Henry that 'where you find a notable injurie, spare not to give course to the torrents of your wrath'.[64] James Cleland's *Heropaideia, or the Institution of a Young Noble Man* (also directed to Prince Henry) starts with a commonplace account of the *virtus vera nobilitas* theme, but then explores the discontent that results from unjust advancement:

Whosoever intrudes him selfe, and creepes into this rancke [nobility] otherwise [than by merit], whether by monie, or a friend at court, I maie justly mainetaine that his title of honour redounds in a double dishonour to him. First for surprising his Prince unawares, by seeking a title that suits not, neither can agree with him; whereby hee brings his Majesties prudencie into question for giving equal honours to unequall deserts. Which provoked *Achilles* his choller against *Agamemnon*; and now a daies maketh manie to contemne and vilipend that, which hath beene formerlie so highlie accompted of, besides the ruine of manie common wealths.[65]

It is not quite clear if 'that which hath beene formerlie so highlie accompted of' is the office concerned, the monarch, or his prudence; but the gist of the passage is clear. Achilles's anger derives from the experience of having deserts but no honour, which was becoming a major part of English courtly life, and which threatened the prestige of the monarchy and the order of the commonwealth.

Cleland is not alone in this concern. Henry Crosse's *Vertues Commonwealth: or the High Way to Honour*, which was written very late in the reign of Elizabeth, opens with a conventional account of the cardinal

[63] Ibid. 574, 555–6.
[64] Ed. James Craigie, STS, 2 vols. (Edinburgh and London, 1944–50), i. 152.
[65] James Cleland, *Heropaideia, or the Institution of a Young Noble Man* (Oxford, 1607), 7–8.

virtues.[66] There follows a long lament for the licentiousness of the times, in which Crosse dwells with considerable fear on the prospects for civil life when virtue fails to be granted its due:[67] revolts and dissidence are the likely consequences. Ambitious men 'revolt from obedience, and eyther fall into dishonest shifts at home, or bad achievements abroad: thrusting their weapons into the bowels of their mothers, eyther by open practises, or secret conspiracies'.[68] The tradition of writing which in its English form stemmed from Elyot's *Governour* aimed to identify kingship and morality, and it sought to do this by making royal recognition of virtue the key to noble status.[69] When this system of centralized distribution of honour functioned smoothly (or was believed to be functioning smoothly) a subject could in theory never harbour justifiable resentment against a Prince, since the monarch would justly distribute rewards and punishment according to deserts. But a breakdown in this system of due rewards raised the possibility, not only of resentment against a Prince, but of the *justified* resentment of one who has been denied his due. It is this dishonoured rage that Chapman finds in Achilles, the hero who receives 'mangl'd law for merites absolute'.[70]

The close of the sixteenth century marked an epoch in English political attitudes, when a snubbed subject could say: 'What, cannot Princes err? Cannot subjects receive wrong? Is an earthly power or authority infinite? Pardon me, pardon me, my good Lord, I can never subscribe to these principles... As for me I have received wrong, and feel it. My cause is good, I know it.'[71] The Essex rebellion lies behind Crosse's fear that revolt and disobedience result from a breakdown in the just distribution of honours. This treasonable palace *coup* of 1601 is likely to have been on the mind of a writer who published a work on the state of the nation in 1603. Chapman's *Iliads* was begun under the patronage of Essex, and Gabriel Harvey, in a marginal note in his copy of Quintilian, made probably the first of many comparisons between Achilles and the rebellious Earl.[72] Essex's outburst occurred after the Queen dismissed his suggestion

---

[66] Henry Crosse, *Vertues Commonwealth: or the High Way to Honour* (London, 1603). The early sections draw directly on Elyot's *Governour* in several places. Cf. sig. C2ᵃ: 'Now lastly followeth Temperance, a sad and a sober Matron, a provident guide and wise Nurse...'; and Elyot: 'foloweth Temperaunce, as a sad and discrete matrone and reverent governesse...', ed. Croft (London, 1880), ii. 325.

[67] *Vertues Commonwealth*, sig. I4ᵃ.

[68] Ibid. sig. K2ᵇ–K3ᵃ.

[69] See Mervyn James, 'English Politics and the Concept of Honour', in *Society, Politics and Culture* (Cambridge, 1986), 308–415.

[70] 19. 171.

[71] Essex to Egerton, quoted in G. B. Harrison, *The Life and Death of Robert Devereux Earl of Essex* (London, 1937), 200–1.

[72] The comparison occurs in a list of parallels between Elizabethan and classical figures: 'Sub regina Elizabetha, Smithus Cineas; Cecilius Nestor; Baconus, Scaevola; Essexius, Achilles', *Marginalia,*

that George Carew be made governor of Ireland in 1598. Essex turned his back on her. She boxed his ears; he put his hand on his sword. Not Pallas Athene, but the Lord Admiral restrained him from violence against his monarch. This event late in 1598 is unlikely to have played a direct part in the conception of the *Seaven Bookes*; but the example of Essex shows how, late in the sixteenth century, a subject could have a sufficient sense of his own right to reproduce something of Achilles's just rage. Essex's stance at his trial in 1601 had much in common with the ethical autonomy of the feudal baron, who violently confronted 'unworthy ministers or even monarchs'.[73] Chapman's Achilles also draws on an aristocratic independence:

> Fearefull and vile I might be thought if the exactions laid
> By all meanes on me I should beare. Others command to this:
> Thou shalt not me—or, if thou dost, farre my free spirit is
> From serving thy command.

Yes, and I'll be called a coward and a nobody if I yield to you in everything, whatever you command. Make these orders to others, but give me none; for I am certain I shall not obey you any more.[74]

'Spirit' is a potent term in Chapman. Here it gives a sanctioning energy to Achilles's refusal to obey—the energy of the 'free' warrior, whose obedience is 'owing as long as [his master] showed himself a "good" lord—that is, while he protected, was just, rewarded, and took counsel'.[75]

One might expect this rejection of obedience to come from the 1598 text, before the rebellious 'free' nobility of Essex was disgraced, and while Drayton was exploring Marlovian heroism in *Mortimeriados*. In fact it comes from the version of 1611, when Chapman was shifting to the patronage of Prince Henry. The 1598 version was more cautious:

---

ed. G. C. Moore Smith (Stratford-upon-Avon, 1913), 122. See further Richard S. Ide, *Possessed with Greatness: The Heroic Tragedies of Shakespeare and Chapman* (London, 1980), pp. xiv, 3. Detailed parallels between the *Seaven Bookes* and the life of Essex are proposed by John Channing Briggs, 'Chapman's *Seaven Bookes of the Iliades*: Mirror for Essex', *Studies in English Literature*, 21 (1981), 59–73.

[73] Mervyn James, 'At the Crossroads of the Political Culture: The Essex revolt, 1601', in *Society, Politics and Culture*, 455. On Essex's cultivated stance of aristocratic independence, see also Richard C. McCoy, *The Rites of Knighthood: The Literature and Politics of Elizabethan Chivalry* (Berkeley and Los Angeles, 1989), 79–102.

[74] 1. 290–3/293–6.

[75] James, 'English Politics and Honour', 330. When Achilles refuses restitution for Briseis in Book 9 a marginal note reads: 'The free and most ingenuous spirit of Achilles'; edn. cit. i. 191. The text mentions the 'freeness' of his mind twice at this point: 'the life that my free breast infolds' is an addition, and 'What fits the freenesse of my mind my speech shall make displaid' is a revealingly mistaken rendering of *autar egōn ereō hōs moi dokei einai arista* (but I will say what seems best [*ariston*] to me), in which Chapman has instinctively associated *aristos* with something like 'aristocratic', and 'aristocratic' with freeness, or *franchise*; 9. 389–91/401–5, 302–3/314.

> Thou mightst esteeme me base
> And cowardlie to let thee use thy will in my disgrace;
> To beare such burthens never were my strength and spirites combinde,
> But to reforme their insolence, and that thy soule should finde
> Were it not hurt of common good more than mine own delight.[76]

In 1598 Chapman muted the rebellious violence of Homer's 'Command others, but not me; for I will obey no more',[77] by adding an un-Homeric concern for the public good to his Achilles. A similar fear that a warrior could do massive harm by open disobedience lies behind another addition in the 1598 text to Achilles's most violently insulting speech:

> tis more safe, with contumelious breath,
> To show thy manhood gainst a man that contradicts thy lust
> And with thy covetous valour take his spoiles with force unjust,
> Because thou knowest a man of fame will take wrong ere he be
> A generall mischiefe.

It is a lot better to take for yourself the prize of honour of whoever speaks against you throughout the wide camp of the Achaians.[78]

Essex was presumably meant to hear that line about the willingness of men of fame to bear wrongs; and he may also have been meant to catch a modification to Nestor's remarks on civil war, which suggests that a single man with a sense of his own 'right' could harm the general good by contentious strife:

> A hater of societie, unjust, unhousde is he
> Loves civill warre, and for his right does all men injurie.
> I call that our intestine warre, where still growes the offence
> Sprung twixt our king and *Thetis* son.

A man who loves dreadful war among his own people is without kin, lawless and homeless.[79]

The 1598 version of the *Iliads* contains several indications that the centralized honour system, with the monarch at its head rewarding 'right', was in danger of breaking down. Chapman's additions on the need for 'men of fame' to consider 'the common good' show an anxious desire to cap any possibility of an aristocratic rebellion.

While Daniel and Drayton were revising their historical epics to remove

---

[76] 1598, 1. 302–6.

[77] 1. 295–6.

[78] 1598, 1. 233–7/229–30. Cf. 1611, 1. 228: 'Tis safer far, in th'open host, to dare an injurie | To any crosser of thy lust.'

[79] Edn. cit. Textual Notes 1. 600/9. 63–4. Cf. 1611, 9. 63–4: 'A hater of societie, unjust and wilde is he | That loves intestine warre, being stuffed with manless crueltie.' Cf. Spondanus, who says the dispute 'quasi bellum est civile' (is like a civil war), 152.

references to the rebel earl, together with all vestiges of sympathy for nobles who rose against unjust rulers, Chapman was doing the opposite. His Achilles, in versions after 1598, has that martial independence and righteousness which the majority of historical poets, after the Essex rebellion, excised from their epics. It is as though Chapman picked up from his friend Drayton the elements which a Jacobean historical poet could not dare to introduce into his work and assembled them in the safely distant world of ancient Greece: the final version of his *Iliads* absorbs the residual momentum of the Essex rebellion, and fuses it with a smouldering irascibility.

Such rebellious energy is a vital element in any translation of the poem. The earliest English version of Homer has no such insurgent fire to it. Arthur Hall of Grantham translated Hugues Salel's *Dix livres* of the *Iliad* in 1581. Between the two translators, and the odd conservative footnote plucked from Eobanus Hessus's Virgilian version of the 1560s, the *Iliad* loses any trace of spirited wrath. Ulysses's speech to the Greek council, in which he argues for the utility of a single ruler, causes Hall to make a departure from his original, which suggests why Achilles left him cold:

> Pas n'est raison que tous ayons honneurs,
> Tous soyons Roys, tous soyons Gouverneurs
> Toute Police est plus recommandée,
> Quand elle n'est que par ung seul guydée
> Donc, soit ung Roy (lequel Juppiter donne)
> Tresobey, en tout ce qu'il ordonne.

> Eche one of honor maye not be a king and Ruler straight,
> For worthy *Fame* and great renoume are things that are of waight,
> If they be Marshalled by one: wherfore in every case
> Let us obey that king, whome *Jove* hath set here in his place.[80]

If this were an entirely accurate translation it would have to mean 'Not everyone through their honour [of honour] can be a king: fame and renown are only valuable if possessed by [marshalled by] one.' But it simply cannot mean this: 'marshalled' must mean 'distributed', in order for Hall's sentence to hang together. The justification of monarchy that Hall puts forward is that the distribution of good report is only of value if performed by one man. This marks his *Iliad* as part of a widespread cultural project. Mervyn James has argued that early Tudor monarchs aimed to centralize the potentially rebellious 'honour system', a network

[80] Salel (Paris, 1555), fols. 34^b–35^a; Hall (London, 1581), 25. Cf. *Il.* 2. 204–6: 'Multiple rule is not good: let there be one lord, one king, to whom the son of crooked-counselling Chronos has given the sceptre and the power of judgement, so that he may take counsel for his people.'

of baronial values that emphasized the independence of aristocratic subjects. The insistence in conduct books that no form of gentility was truly gentle unless sanctioned by the monarch was a crucial element in a general attempt to restrain the actions of the nobility.[81] Hall's Homer participates in the creation of this vision of a society regulated by a king who acted as 'the fount of honour'.

Hall was no fiery radical. He was tried by Parliament in 1581 for publishing *A Letter sent by F.A.*, which in its second part, *An Admonition by the Father of F.A.*, argues that the first Parliament did not occur until the reign of Henry III, and even then had no legislative power.[82] This was thought 'to deface the Authority of the Laws and Proceeding in the Parliament, and so to impair the Ancient Orders touching the Government of the Realm and Rights of this House and the form of making Laws, whereby the Subjects of the Realm are governed.'[83] Hall's *Letter* emphasizes the inability of Parliament to make laws without Royal assent,[84] and the 'gracious, liberall, and continual favour of the Princes of this land'[85] in allowing the Commons to participate in legislation. These facts help to explain why Hall's translation can find no sympathy for Agamemnon's rebellious subordinate. His conviction that political authority and status originate solely in the monarch effectively stifles the wrath of Achilles. To represent the uneasy equipoise of Homeric society—in which Agamemnon is first among equals rather than a single sovereign[86]—requires an ethical language charged with rebellious energy, a language which allows a powerful inferior to have a strong claim against the supremacy of a superior. Chapman, alone among Homeric imitators in the sixteenth and seventeenth centuries, made that language.

[81] For the Tudor 'nationalization' of the honour system, see James, 'English Politics and Honour', 328.

[82] Reprinted in *Miscellanea Antiqua Anglicana*, no ed. (London, 1816), 63, Item 3. See H. G. Wright, *The Life and Works of Arthur Hall of Grantham* (Manchester, 1919), 24–34. G. R. Elton, 'Arthur Hall, Lord Burghley and the Antiquity of Parliament', in Hugh Lloyd-Jones *et al.* (eds.), *History and Imagination: Essays in Honour of H. R. Trevor-Roper* (London, 1981), 88–103, defends Hall against the Commons' charges.

[83] Simonds D'Ewes, *A Compleat Journal*, 2nd edn. (London, 1693), 295; Hall responded insolently, ibid. 296.

[84] *A Letter*, 81.

[85] Ibid. 79.

[86] M. I. Finley, *The World of Odysseus*, 2nd edn. (London, 1977), 84. See also A. M. Snodgrass, *The Dark Age of Greece: An Archaeological Survey of the Eleventh to the Eighth Centuries BC* (Edinburgh, 1971), 389.

CHAPMAN'S *ODYSSEYS*: PARADISE LOST

Ben Jonson saw the epic hero as ideally seeking to return home, to the praise and conversation of his friends:

> Roe (and my joy to name) th'art now, to goe
> Countries, and climes, manners, and men to know,
> T'extract, and choose the best of all these knowne,
> And those to turne to bloud, and make thine owne:
> May windes as soft as breath of kissing friends,
> Attend thee hence; and there, may all thy ends,
> As the beginnings here, prove purely sweet,
> And perfect in a circle alwayes meet.
> So, when we, blest with thy returne, shall see
> Thy selfe, with thy first thoughts, brought home by thee,
> We each to other may this voyce enspire:
> This is that good ÆNEAS, past through fire,
> Through seas, stormes, tempests: and imbarqu'd for hell,
> Came back untouch'd. This man hath travail'd well.[87]

Jonson might almost as well have said that his Aeneas had not travailed, or travelled at all. The weight of this description lies solidly at home, in an environment of familiarity, friendship, and praise: for all his wish that Roe digest foreign *mores* into his own substance, Jonson emphatically states that the hero is to return 'untouch'd', equipped with his 'first thoughts', rather than be radically changed by contact with the foreign. The journey is not to be a break with the present, let alone a mission to found a new empire in hitherto unknown spaces: it is ultimately to 'meet' in a circle. The line 'And perfect in a circle always meet' carries the delicate equipoise of the poem: it catches both Jonson's desire for Sir William's return and, through the use of that so sociable verb 'meet', also hints at a hope that Roe will encounter a circle of friends abroad to match those he has left. It would be entirely characteristic of Jonson's concern with the perfection of the circle, and entirely correspondent with his love of the sociable, for him to be sensitive to the emergence of *OED* sense 21 of 'circle': 'A number of persons united by acquaintance, common sentiments, interests', which *OED* dates to 1646. Abroad, Roe will encounter an extension of that circle of friends, who, when he returns, will mingle their voices in praise of their unaltered Aeneas. He will move into the strange and dangerous area of a romance voyage in order to retain and enrich what is familiar; and he will return to familiar voices united in praise.

[87] *Works*, ed. C. H. Herford and P. Simpson, 11 vols. (Oxford, 1925–52), viii. 80–1.

Brilliant and entirely distinctive as it is, Jonson's poem does highlight
an acute limitation in the English epic before Milton. Journeys seldom
go anywhere. Heroes rarely encounter the fundamentally alien, and when
they do so the meeting is often attenuated into a process of self-discovery,
self-regulation, or the eradication of sensual delusions. There are few
Odysseys into strange and magical realms in English sixteenth-century
romances, and this limits the whole tradition. In *The Faerie Queene*,
encounters with the magically unfamiliar tend to be associated with
the delusions of appetite, passion, idolatry, or opinion: disguised hags,
phantasms, and seductively lovely ladies occupy the spaces beyond its
heroes' immediate purposes; and very often, like the siren voices which
tempt Guyon from his Odyssey to the Bowre of Bliss, such alluring
creatures are little more than extensions of the hero's own delusive desires,
which are to be stunned by the temperate self-control of the hero.

This is in keeping with the prevailing Renaissance interpretations of
the *Odyssey*, which show more interest in the ethical qualities required of
Odysseus in order to overcome the hardships which he endures than in
the dislocating spaces beyond the bounds of the civilized through which
he travels. Odysseus—who, like Roe, saw many cities and came to know
the minds and manners of many men—was generally held to exemplify
prudence, fortitude (the endurance of material hardships), and temperance.[88] He was frequently regarded as a man who subdued his passions
and overcame the storms and temptations of life, while his companions
were metamorphosed into swine for their cupidity and greed. Like
Spenser's Guyon, his main virtue lay in resisting the demands of appetite.

Chapman's debt to this exegetical tradition is large, and has been
thoroughly explored by writers on his *Odysseys*.[89] The *Odyssey* is for him
about 'the mind's inward, constant and unconquered Empire, unbroken,
unaltered with any most insolent and tyrannous infliction', where the
Iliad expresses 'the Bodie's fervour and fashion of outward fortitude'.[90]
He frequently stresses the unbridled 'appetites' of Penelope's suitors, and,
with similar regularity, emphasizes the intemperate desires of the sailors
in contrast with the piety and fortitude of Odysseus.[91] Yet the translation
is flexibly accommodating of elements which do not quite fit in with

---

[88] For the allegorical background, see Don Cameron Allen, *Mysteriously Meant: The Rediscovery
of Pagan Symbolism and Allegorical Interpretation in the Renaissance* (Baltimore and London, 1970),
83–105; esp. 90 ff.; W. B. Stanford, *The Ulysses Theme: A Study in the Adaptability of a Traditional
Hero*, 2nd edn. (Oxford, 1963), 119–84; see also Horace, *Epistulae* 1. 2. 17–26. The Latin version
printed in Spondanus regularly translates *polumētis* (many-wiled) as 'prudens'.

[89] See Donald Smalley, 'The Ethical Bias of Chapman's Homer', 190; George DeF. Lord, *Homeric
Renaissance: The 'Odyssey' of George Chapman* (London, 1956), 33–77, discusses how Chapman
develops the traditional allegories.

[90] *Chapman's Homer*, ed. Nicoll, ii. 4.

[91] Lord, *Homeric Renaissance*, 61.

Chapman's officially presented interpretation. The newly adopted heroic couplets move with an enjambed fluidity which feels often more like blank than rhymed verse:

> Two nights yet, and daies,
> He spent in wrestling with the sable seas,
> In which space often did his heart propose
> Death to his eyes. But when Aurora rose
> And threw the third light from her orient haire,
> The winds grew calme and cleare was all the aire,
> Not one breath stirring.[92]

This moves more easily than the *Iliads*—up, that is, until two firm stopping points: 'Death to his eyes.' and 'Not one breath stirring.' Both phrases cut off their lines with a deathly caesura, and are attracted to each other by internal rhyme on 'death' and 'breath'. The stillness of their content reinforces their association. The resulting effect is of pessimistic cheer or gloomy optimism: the stillness of death that Odysseus expects is replaced by another stillness, that of calm seas. This looks like a relief, but 'not one *breath* stirring' reminds us that Odysseus is alone out at sea—and the breathlessness of death still lurks in the admonitory rhyme.

Chapman knew that he was translating a poem in which the hero spends the bulk of his active career in numbing misery and danger of death. The best he can hope for is passing cheer from hosts who recognize an obligation to offer *xenia* (the gifts offered to a travelling stranger). Circe eventually offers a solidly nutritive form of comfort to the exiles, and urges them to cheer themselves up by eating:

I myself know both the woes you have suffered on the teeming sea and all those harms done you by hostile men on land. But come on, and eat food and drink wine until you get the kind of *thumos* in your hearts that you had at first when you left your native land of rugged Ithaca. But now you are worn out and spiritless, always thinking of your weary wanderings, and your hearts are never happy, since you have suffered so much.

> I know my selfe what woes by sea and shore
> And men unjust have plagu'd enough before
> Your injur'd vertues: here then, feast as long,
> And be as cheerfull, till ye grow as strong
> As when ye first forsooke your Countrie earth.
> Ye now fare all like exiles, not a mirth
> Flasht in amongst ye but is quencht againe

---

[92] 'Then for two nights and days he was driven about over the swollen waves, and very often his heart feared death. But when Dawn with lovely hair brought the third day the wind stopped and there was breezeless calm.' 5. 504–10/388–92.

> With still-renewd teares—though the beaten vaine
> Of your distresses should (me thinke) be now
> Benumb with sufferance.[93]

Chapman recognizes how intensely mournful it is to be an exile with such
clarity that he changes Circe's homely appeal to end sorrow by eating
into a statement that sorrow must bludgeon away the capacity to feel,
and so end itself. Sparks of mirth—fire was the prevailing element in his
Iliads—are quenched by the predominant element of this poem: salt
water. It is not quite Homer, but it shows that Chapman recognizes the
painful and inescapable self-absorption of exile.

Absence from home in Homer's *Odyssey* leads to confrontations with
an inhumanity which often takes the form of failure hospitably to give
xenia. The passage quoted above gives an inkling of Chapman's equivalent
for this idea. He expands Circe's quite brief allusion to 'the wrongs that
hostile men have done you' (*hos' anarsioi andres edēlēsant'*) into 'And men
unjust have plagu'd enough before | Your injur'd vertues'. The altered
emphasis suggests that Chapman conceives the world beyond civility not
so much as a place which shows its otherness by godless contempt for
strangers, but as a zone of injustice where there is no respect for virtue:
it is a place (as Jonson, too, delicately insinuates by the chorus of adulation
that greets Roe *when he returns*) away from praise.

In Homer's *Odyssey*, the episode at the Phaeacian court is a crucial
moment, when the qualities of something like pity, and the more mech-
anical civility indicated by accepting suppliants show themselves in the
people Odysseus meets. The emergence of these qualities directly contribute to the hero's return home.[94] The same episode is an important
locus for the Chapmanian equivalents for these qualities. In the Greek,
Athene warns Odysseus not to speak to anyone among the Phaeacian
populace, since they are not as susceptible to charm as their king's
daughter:[95] 'the men here can't abide strangers, nor do they give a warm
welcome to men who come from elsewhere'. This becomes:

> The men
> That here inhabite do not entertain
> With ready kindnesse strangers, of what worth
> Or state soever, nor have taken forth
> Lessons of civill usage or respect
> To men beyond them.[96]

---

[93] 10. 456–65/576–85.

[94] See above, pp. 26–9.

[95] Finley notes the ambivalence in the Phaeacians' attitude to strangers, *World of Odysseus*, 100–1.

[96] 7. 32–3/40–5. Spondanus accurately paraphrases: 'notat Phaeacas inhospitalitatis' (he notes the
inhospitality of the Phaeacians), 90.

This is not exactly contempt of virtue; it is more like disregard of rank. The language points to an association of superior rank and superior merit, tinged with a sense of the difficulty of recognizing such qualities in strangers: 'worth' and 'men beyond them' suggest that these are the sort of unjust men whom Circe talked of, who plague injured virtue by neglecting to be polite to alien superiors. But when Odysseus comes to the king's household, matters are rather different. Homer's Phaeacia is a distant paradisiac state, well ruled, and well placed, far from *barbaroi* like the Cyclopes. The garden of Alcinous and the continual festivities that go on in the land make it the first earthly paradise in the Western epic.[97] There are signs that Chapman too regarded the court at least as a distant ideal state. Queen Arete is (reasonably enough, given her name) allegorized as virtue (*aretē*), and called 'The all-lov'd Arete'.[98] The king is a paradigm monarch, in keeping with this universal love for virtue: 'O past all men here | Cleare, not in powre but in desert as clere.'[99]

The recognition of merit among the Phaeacians is very important for Chapman's Odysseus. Homer's hero gets home by winning Nausicaa over with tickling flattery, and by exploiting her *philoxenia*, her friendliness to strangers. In the English, Odysseus's account to her parents of what she did for him presents a new version of what it means to make contact with civilization:

> Like a Deitie
> She shin'd above them, and I praid to her:
> And she in disposition did prefer
> Noblesse and wisdome, no more low than might
> Become the goodnesse of a Goddesse' height.

Then I saw your daughter's handmaids on the shore at play, and she was amongst them, as lovely as the goddesses. I supplicated her, and she did not at all fail to understand.[100]

An earlier translator in the romance tradition might have made Nausicaa pity Odysseus's sufferings; but here the English equivalent for the Homeric virtue of *philoxenia*, the quality most crucial to Odysseus's return, is

---

[97] See A. Bartlett Giamatti, *The Earthly Paradise and the Renaissance Epic* (Princeton, NJ, 1966), 34–6.

[98] 7. 330/231 (Homer has just 'Arete'). She 'stands for the fundamental principles of civilized behaviour', Lord, *Homeric Renaissance*, 98.

[99] 8. 523–4/382: 'Great Alcinous, most conspicuous among men.' 'Clere' is used in a Latinate sense which the context, but not the *OED*, sanctions: 'claris', or famous; or it may be used in sense 15 'unspotted, innocent'. Chapman translates Divus ('Spondanus'): 'Alcinoe rex, omnium *clarissime* populorum', p. 109. The mention of 'desert' is his own.

[100] 7. 404–8/290–3. Dolce praises Nausicaa for her 'cortesia' in his allegory, and makes her recognize simply noble birth rather than nobility and wisdom in the text: 'tu dimostri ne l'aspetto | Non esser vil, ma nato nobilmente' (Your demeanour shows that you are not lowly, but nobly born), *L'Ulisse, tratto dell'Odissea d'Homero* (Venice, 1573), 59.

Nausicaa's ability to read the hero's worth in his appearance. The change
to the Greek here marks a point of contact with the earliest English
translator of Homer (if we are to believe his own word) from Greek.
Thomas Elyot uses another moment from the Phaeacian episode in the
Governour to illustrate the quality of 'Majestie', the radiant emanation of
worth and rank. Odysseus, he writes,

beinge all naked, savynge a mantell sente to hym by the kynges doughter, without
other apparaile or servant, represented suche a wonderfull majestie in his
countenance and speche, that the kynge of the countray, named Alcinous, in that
extreme calamitie, wisshed that Ulisses wold take his doughter Nausicaa to wyfe
... The people also wondringe at his majestie, honoured hym with sondrye
presentes.

Elyot then translates *Odyssey* 11. 362–7:

> Whan I the consider, Ulysses, I perceive
> Thou doest nat dissemble to me in thy speche
> As other have done, whiche craftely can deceive,
> Untruely reportinge where they list to preche
> Of thinges never done; such falshode they do teche.
> But in thy wordes there is a righte good grace,
> And that thy mynde is good, it sheweth in thy face.[101]

The final couplet is the only point at which Elyot modifies the meaning
of the original in order to make it say what he wants it to say. He is
intent on seeing the phrase 'But you have grace of words and a wise
mind' as a recognition of radiant virtuous nobility, rather than as just a
wary denial of disbelief in Odysseus's story. He may owe this detail to
Raphael Volaterranus's Latin translation, in which Alcinous says 'Tibi
vero & forma verborum & *mens bona* inesse videtur' (You seem to have
both elegance of speech and a good mind);[102] but, whatever its origin,
Elyot's became the standard interpretation of Odysseus's rescue. In
Sidney's *New Arcadia*, Musidorus is accepted by Kalander because of his
radiant virtue, when he, like Odysseus, emerges naked from the sea and
is presented to the Arcadian gentry: ' "I am no herald to inquire of men's
pedigrees. It sufficeth me if I know their virtues, which, if this young
man's face be not a false witness, do better apparel his mind than you
have done his body." '[103] This version of how a stranger gains recognition
in an alien culture is also found in Fanshawe's *Lusiads*, when the Christian

---

[101] Ed. Croft, ii. 13–14. For Elyot's role in restoring Odysseus to favour in England, see Stanford,
Ulysses Theme, 160–4, 296–303.
[102] *Odissea Homeri* (Rome, 1510), sig. I1^b. David G. Hale, 'Sir Thomas Elyot and "Noble
Homere" ', *Acta*, 5 (1978), 121–31, assumes rather than proves that Elyot translated from the Greek.
[103] *The New Arcadia*, ed. Victor Skretkowicz (Oxford, 1987), 12–13.

King of Melinda (who is compared to Alcinous) hospitably receives the Portuguese after their ordeals among the Muslims:

> For such you *worths* are, and your *deeds* have been,
> To make you over all the *world* esteem'd.
> And *They* who injur'd *you*, We will be bold,
> Know not what price *Vertue* and *Honor* hold.[104]

It is not the formal rite of supplication, or the less formal bonds of sympathy, but their radiant merit that enables these Renaissance heroes to win recognition abroad: praise and recognition of worth makes their identity, and makes them feel at home, while they linger abroad.

When the Homeric Nausicaa meets Odysseus and replies to his flattering speech she is struck (as the Phaeacians tend to be) by his eloquence, and concludes that if he can speak that well he cannot be a total scoundrel:

Stranger, since you seem neither a scoundrel nor a fool, and it is Olympian Zeus himself who gives good fortune to men, whether they're good or evil, as he feels like it, so he seems to have given this misfortune to you, and you must in any case endure it.

> She answerd: 'Stranger! I discerne in thee
> Nor Sloth nor Folly raignes; and yet I see
> Th'art poore and wretched. In which I conclude
> That Industry nor wisedome make endude
> Men with those gifts that make them best to th'eie:
> Jove onely orders man's felicitie.
> To good and bad his pleasure fashions still
> The whole proportion of their good and ill.
> And he perhaps hath formd this plight in thee,
> Of which thou must be patient, as he, free.'[105]

The English Nausicaa does display something of the extraordinary ethical intuition on which Odysseus complimented her. She can perceive quality through wretchedness, and tell that he is industrious and wise, despite his having none of the trimmings of a successful life. Yet her meditation on why his virtues have not brought him any luck leads into a major source of the melancholy in Chapman's *Odysseys*: 'That Industry nor

---

[104] Luiz de Camoens, *The Lusiads*, trans. Sir Richard Fanshawe, ed. Geoffrey Bullough (London, 1963), ii. 86. Alludes to Alcinous at ii. 82. Fanshawe is close to Camoens: 'Their virtues and exploits are such that the world may rightly hold them in high esteem, only the ignoble mind could treat them ill.' *The Lusiads*, trans. W. C. Atkinson (Harmondsworth, 1952), 71.

[105] 6. 187–90/283–92. Spondanus's note (p. 87) gives some of Chapman's philosophical tone to her comments.

wisedome make endude | Men with those gifts that make them best to th'eie', that there is no surety of material well-being in virtue.[106]

In the *Iliads* Agamemnon's local act of injustice when he failed properly to reward Achilles justified the warrior's rage. Here the whole lie of the world is against the success of virtue: even Zeus does not necessarily reward wisdom. The *Odyssey* repeatedly resists human attempts to control affairs by force rather than by manipulative tricksiness, and a good dose of divinely assisted luck. Chapman's translation puts forward a near-equivalent vision of the world as hostile to virtue, and inscrutable to human attempts to understand its workings. There is a substantial addition to a passage where Odysseus says plaintively to Athene that it is hard to recognize her:

> 'Goddesse,' said he, 'unjust men and unwise,
> That author injuries and vanities,
> By vanities and wrongs should rather be
> Bound to this ill-abearing destiny
> Than just and wise men. What delight hath heaven,
> That lives unhurt it selfe, to suffer given
> Up to all domage those poore few that strive
> To imitate it and like the Deities live?'[107]

As Chapman put it in the roughly contemporary *Revenge of Bussy D'ambois* (1613) 'no vertuous labour | Ends ought rewarded.'[108] The isolated act of injustice that fires the *Iliads* has become universal: Odysseus (who has been told he has more to suffer) briefly grumbles against an opposing world in which an 'ill-abearing destiny' is unwilling to reward virtuous behaviour.

This near-universal hostility to virtue (except in the distant never-never land of Phaeacia) derives partly from the different interests of the *Odyssey* as against the *Iliad*.[109] But the translation also exploits Jacobean nostalgia for the days of Elizabeth.[110] Telemachus self-deprecatingly puts the rule of virtue in the past:

---

[106] 'Chapman's insistence on the incompatibility of virtue and prosperity forces a virtual equation between the wise man and the unfortunate man.' Richard S. Ide, 'Exemplary Heroism in Chapman's *Odysseys*', *Studies in English Literature*, 22 (1982), 129.

[107] 13. 452–9/312–13: 'It is difficult for a mortal to know you when he meets you, however wise he is, for you take on whatever form you like.'

[108] 1. 1. 33–4; *The Plays of George Chapman: The Tragedies*, ed. Allan Holaday (Cambridge, 1987).

[109] Millar McLure, *George Chapman: A Critical Study* (Toronto, 1966), 192, attributes it to 'the growing piety of Chapman's temper, the disillusion with heroics'.

[110] Anne Barton, 'Harking Back to Elizabeth: Ben Jonson and Caroline Nostalgia', *ELH* 48 (1981), 713–15, notes that Chapman incurred the censor's disapproval for an excessively enthusiastic encomium of Elizabeth in *The Conspiracy of Byron* (1608), III. ii.

An ascent so hie
My thoughts affect not: dead is he that held
Desert of virtue to have so exceld.[111]

Alcinous is one meritorious king; but he lives in a distant paradise. Odysseus is another; but he is presumed dead. This mistranslation connects with the tendency, which was widespread among the Spenserian poets in the Jacobean period,[112] to look backwards to a Golden Age of virtue now lost. Works like W.H.'s *Englands Sorrowe or, a Farewell to Essex* (London, 1606) lamented the passing of a generation of virtuous nobility who were now sadly in the past,[113] and William Browne of Tavistock in his Epistle appended to the Second Part of *Poly-Olbion*, celebrated Drayton as the sole remaining trace of Elizabethan virtue:

We have a *Muse* in this mortalitie
Of Vertue yet survives; All met not Death,
When wee intoomb'd our deare *Elizabeth*.[114]

Fulke Greville's *Dedication to Sir Philip Sidney* is believed to derive from exactly the same period as Chapman's *Odysseys*: 1612–14.[115] Greville too looks back to the Elizabethan period and laments the 'differences between the real and large complexions of those active times and the narrow salves of this effeminate age'. He also represents Sidney as a 'true model of worth' from the past.[116] He remembers a period in which the recognition of worth in strangers was the determining attribute of monarchy when he describes his meeting with William of Nassau:

His uppermost garment was a gown, yet such as (I dare confidently affirm) a mean-born student in our Inns of Court would not have been well-pleased to walk the streets in; ... his company about him the burgesses of that beer-brewing town, and he so fellow-like encompassed with them as (had I not known his face) no exterior sign of degree or reservedness could have discovered the inequality of his worth or estate from that multitude. Notwithstanding, I no sooner came to his presence, but it pleased him to take knowledge of me; and even upon that (as if it had been a signal to make a change) his respect of a stranger instantly begat respect to himself in all about him—an outward passage of inward greatness, which, in a popular state, I thought worth the observing,

---

[111] 1. 610–12/396: 'One of these [other kings] will keep this place, since godlike Odysseus is dead.'

[112] Joan Grundy, *The Spenserian Poets: A Study in Elizabethan and Jacobean Poetry* (London, 1969), 128–42.

[113] The author is probably William Herbert of Glamorgan. For the milieu of this compilation, see Michael Brennan, *Literary Patronage in the English Renaissance: The Pembroke Family* (London, 1988), 116–17.

[114] Drayton, *Works*, ed. J. W. Hebel *et al.*, 5 vols. (Oxford, 1931–41), iv. 393; ll. 2–4.

[115] *The Prose Works*, ed. John Gouws (Oxford, 1986), pp. xxi–xxiv.

[116] Ibid. 7, 21; also 3 and 20.

because there no pedigree but worth could possibly make a man prince and no-prince in a moment, at his own pleasure.[117]

Greville's admiration is twofold, both for 'the respect of a stranger', and for the constitutional framework which attaches importance to this virtue rather than to the external trappings of rank. In 'a popular state' *virtus est vera nobilitas*: the meritorious king recognizes merit in others. Chapman's *Odysseys* was (like that other epic of retrospective melancholy, *Poly-Olbion*) conceived under the patronage of Prince Henry, and it contains hints that Telemachus was to have been judiciously tailored into an elegant compliment to the Prince as the deserving heir to the throne.[118] At the start of the translation the Prince is recurrently 'inspired' by Athene with virtuous indignation against the swinish disorder of the suitors. Chapman evidently associated Telemachus's epithet *pepnumenos* with *pneuma*, and consequently made his Prince breathe divine hostility to corruption.[119] During Telemachus's tour round the courts of the returned Greek warriors, the Homeric concern for identity and paternity is often overlaid with the familiar humanist topos of children emulating their ancestral virtue—a topos frequently reiterated in works associated with Henry.[120] Had the Prince lived, it is possible that Chapman would have done more to portray Telemachus as the inspired heir to the throne attempting to re-establish the lost supremacy of virtue. He does, however, become a potential ideal ruler when Anticlea tells Odysseus

> That none possest
> My famous kingdome's Throne, but th'interest
> My sonne had in it still he held in peace—
> A Court kept like a Prince, and his increase
> Spent in his subjects' good, administring lawes
> With justice and the generall applause
> A king should merit, and all calld him king.

---

[117] Greville, *Prose Works*, 13–14. Cf. Fairfax's addition of regal virtues, rather than splendid ornaments, to Tasso's humbly dressed Goffredo, *GL* ii. 60.

[118] For Henry's patronage of Chapman, see Leila Parsons, 'Prince Henry (1584–1612) as a Patron of Literature', *Modern Language Review*, 47 (1952), 503–7; Elkin Calhoun Wilson, *Prince Henry and English Literature* (Ithaca, NY, 1946), 74–5, 104–5; Jean Jacquot, *George Chapman (1559–1634): Sa vie, sa poésie, son théâtre, sa pensée*, Annales de l'Université de Lyon, NS 3: 19 (Paris, 1951), 43–7; Roy Strong, *Henry, Prince of Wales and England's Lost Renaissance* (London, 1986), 180. See also *Euthymiae Raptus*, ll. 86–90, 1207–15, for Chapman's own version. The *Odysseys* was published in 1614–15 and Henry died in November 1612; but several passages suggest composition with the Prince in mind.

[119] 1. 527/345 and 1. 562/367. Cf. 1. 490/324, 1. 593/384. Divus/Spondanus translates the word by 'prudens'. Chapman follows Scapula's definition, which associates the epithet with breathing, '*pneumai* idem quod *pnumi*, spiro, unde *pepnumenos*, spirans', and fuses it with his interest in the connection of virtue and inspiration.

[120] 1. 344/222, 2. 428–31/278–80, 4. 276–8/206. See also the marginal note to 1. 325: 'Pallas thus enforcing her question to stirre up the son the more to the father's worthiness.'

The son's rule during the exile of the virtuous ruler is bountiful and just and merits the name of king. 'A court kept like a Prince' may evoke a memory of the contrast between the extravagant court of James and the much-publicized temperate sobriety of his son's.[121] The Greek is more concerned with solid nutriment: Telemachus is rewarded by his subjects for dealing justice by invitations to dinner: 'No one possesses your honour, but Telemachus rules your holding in peace and feasts at such shared banquets as are appropriate for a man who deals justice to share, for all men invite him.'[122] Chapman misunderstands *pantes gar kaleousi* ('all invite him'): *kaleō* can mean 'to name', but here it rather means 'to summon, invite', rather than 'all calld him king'. He wants to see this description of the Prince's rule as corresponding to the familiar ideal of the benign monarch who wins public acclaim for his generosity—with perhaps an original intention to bring a glow to his patron's cheek at the suggestion that a Prince could merit the name of king. Even this glimpse of a benign, meritorious ruler is past. By the time Odysseus is told of his son's success Telemachus no longer controls his household. By the time Chapman published his translation Henry was dead, and with him his hopes of secure patronage. The regret for a past ideal expressed in the *Odysseys* is intimately linked with the increasingly elegiac tone of the Spenserian view of Jacobean culture. The two work sadly together to portray life as a vale of tears.

Lament for the past is a recurrent feature of Homer's *Odyssey*; but there is no meditation on the psychology of regret in it so prolonged as an addition which Chapman makes after Demodocus has sung about the Trojan horse and the fall of Troy:

> This the divine Expressor did so give
> Both act and passion that he made it live,
> And to Ulysses' facts did breathe a fire
> So deadly quickning that it did inspire
> Old death with life, and rendred life so sweet
> And passionate that all there felt it fleet—
> Which made him pitie his owne crueltie,
> And put into that ruth so pure an eie
> Of humane frailtie, that to see a man

---

[121] W[illiam] H[aydon], *The True Picture and Relation of Prince Henry* (Leiden, 1634), 9, relates how James I, seeing the immaculate order of his son's household, 'was forced to say, that he had never seen the like before all his lifetime, and that he could never doe so much in his owne house'. Sir Charles Cornwallis, *A Discourse of the most Illustrious Prince, Henry, Late Prince of Wales* (written 1626, published 1641), repr. in *The Harleian Miscellany*, 10 vols. (London, 1808–13), iv. 333–40, praises the Prince for the government of his household (335, 336); also for moderation: 'Plenty and magnificence were the things in his house he especially affected; but not without such a temper as might agree with the rules of frugality and moderation', 335.

[122] 11. 233–9/184–7.

> Could so revive from Death, yet no way can
> Defend from death, his owne quicke powres it made
> Feele there death's horrors, and he felt life fade.
> In teares his feeling braine swet: for in things
> That move past utterance, teares ope all their springs.
> Nor are there in the Powres that all life beares
> More true interpreters of all than teares.[123]

This is Chapman at his most obscure. The gist of the passage is stated at the opening: the lively expression of death ('deadly quickning') gives to those who listen a sudden *frisson*, in which they realize with a terrifying vividness what death is.[124] This sudden understanding of death comes with a passionate love of life, and leads Odysseus to feel a pitying regret for killing people in the past. The most obscure lines, 'that to see a man | Could so revive from Death, yet no way can | Defend from death...' also allude to the paradox of a 'living' creation of death: Demodocus ('a man') 'revives' the final moments of the living warriors in song, but cannot avert their end by the vividness of his re-creation; he just continues to represent their final moments with such realism that Odysseus feels as if he is himself dying. Chapman attempts a complex description of the sympathy aroused by an evocation of death so vivid that you can feel it yourself. It is well-motivated complexity, since (as so often with Chapman's changes to his original) he is elaborating the effect of a Homeric simile:

The famous minstrel sang this song. But Odysseus's heart was melted. Tears flowed from his eyes and wet his cheeks. And as a woman howls and flings herself about her dear husband, who has fallen in front of his city and his people in attempting to ward off the pitiless day from his city and his children; and when she sees him dying and gasping for breath, she clings to him and shrieks aloud, while the enemy behind her hit her back and shoulders with their spears, and lead her away to captivity to endure labour and suffering, her cheeks wasted with pitiable mourning: so did pitiful tears fall from the eyes of Odysseus.[125]

The simile is founded on the Greek concept of sympathetic pity, which in part depends on a recognition that one shares humanity with the people one sees suffering, and may consequently oneself be at some point in a state as painful as theirs.[126] Chapman's groping glossing does not have

---

[123] 8. 708–23. Discussed by Bartlett, 'The Heroes', 274, and by Lord, *Homeric Renaissance*, 102–3.

[124] Chapman's note on 'deadly quickning' is helpful: 'In that the slaughters he made were exprest so lively.'

[125] 8. 521–31.

[126] See Chapter 1 above and MacLeod, *Collected Essays*, 10–11, for an analysis of this simile: pity arises from seeing that 'human life, whatever else it may contain, includes shared suffering and inevitable death, and that human destinies are the gift of gods who do not always work with human justice ... Such understanding is, in fact, the cognitive and rational element in compassion.' ibid. 14.

the extraordinary eloquence of the Homeric simile, but his addition shows
that he felt it necessary to explain the cause of the regretful pity which
it describes: Odysseus pitied his victims because the poet made death so
vivid that he felt he was dying himself. It is not a bad shot at explaining
the forms of feeling at work in his original; and it is almost unique as a
serious attempt at redrawing the contours of Homeric compassion in the
Renaissance. The translator of Achilles Tatius's *The History of Clitophon
and Leucippe* made a hopeless botch of a passage on Greek compassion in
1597: 'as he spoke, Clinias wept as the Trojan women wept for Patroclus;
he remembered Charicles',[127] becomes: 'While that *Menelaus* did recount
these strange misfortunes; not much unlike to the hard chance of *Patroclus*,
Clinias, being put into remembrance of his beloved *Charicles*, could not
chuse but weepe.'[128] Thomas Underdowne caught the note of independent
suffering more accurately in his translation of Heliodorus, however: 'and
therewithall he wept. So did the straungers also under cover of his
calamitie, but in deede for the remembraunce of their own mishappes'.[129]
Chapman goes beyond the heroic ethos of the sixteenth-century
romanzieri—Bacelli, for example, makes Odysseus gush with tears of
pity[130]—and attempts to reproduce not just the outlines of his original,
but to create an equivalent for its forms of thought.

Yet Chapman's addition is not purely Homeric. There is also a hint of
a Virgilian subtext, which filters and forms his response to the *Odyssey*.
When Aeneas sees the picture of the Trojan wars in Dido's Temple of
Juno,

> constitit et lacrimans 'quis iam locus,' inquit, 'Achate,
> quae regio in terris nostri non plena laboris?
> en Priamus. sunt hic etiam sua praemia laudi,
> sunt lacrimae rerum et mentem mortalia tangunt.
> solve metus; feret haec aliquam tibi fama salutem.'[131]

He stopped, and weeping said, 'What place, Achates, what region of the earth is
not full of reminders of our labours? Look, here is Priam. Even here too are the
rewards of praise; even here tears fall for human affairs, and mortality touches
the heart. Drive fear away: this fame will bring you a degree of immortality.'

---

[127] Trans. S. Gaselee, Loeb Classical Library (Cambridge, Mass., and London, 1969), 2. 34,
recalling *Il.* 19. 302.

[128] *The History of Clitophon and Leucippe (London, 1597)*, trans. W. B[urton], The English
Experience, 837 (Amsterdam, 1977), 42.

[129] Heliodorus, *An Aethiopian History*, trans. Thomas Underdowne, ed. Charles Whibley, Tudor
Translations, 5 (London, 1895), 28.

[130] 'So did pitiful tears fall from the eyes of Odysseus' becomes 'Così dolente Ulisse il volto e 'l
petto | Bagnava per le lagrime che folte, | Giù da gl'occhi stillavan' (So the grieving Odysseus bathed
his face and breast with tears which trickled down from his eyes), *L'Odissea d'Homero tradotta in
volgare Fiorentino* (Florence, 1582), 238.

[131] *Aen.* 1. 459–63.

The similarity of the two scenes, both of which involve a hero confronting his past history and weeping, makes it likely that the last two couplets of Chapman's version of Homer are a free paraphrase—a sort of bad quarto translation from memory—of 'sunt lacrimae rerum et mentem mortalia tangunt':

> In teares his feeling braine swet: for in things
> That move past utterance, teares ope all their springs.
> Nor are there in the Powres that all life beares
> More true interpreters of all than teares.

This melancholy image of life, where tears are the 'true interpreters of all', approaches, as no other translation does, the uncertain melancholy of 'sunt lacrimae rerum'. But it lacks the compensatory glory and permanence of fame with which Aeneas tries to brace his wilting resolve. Chapman's meditation on the tearfulness of life follows an intricate analysis of art, not as a preserver of life or fame, but as the medium through which one obtains a vivid sense of death and of personal fragility. Virgilian tears of regret are not accompanied by a Virgilian satisfaction that heroic and virtuous deeds will receive their due recognition.

The translation develops a heroic idiom which corresponds to this visionary sadness. Chapman develops those elements in classical heroism concerned with how grim it is to be good. Underlying the translation is a transformation of 'pius Aeneas' which is new to the English epic. His Odysseus is a pious man who moves unrewarded through a hostile world, receiving a fate that he does not deserve. As Athene says,

> But that Ithacus
> (Thus never meriting) should suffer thus
> I deeply suffer. His more pious mind
> Divides him from these fortunes. Though unkind
> Is Pietie to him, giving him a fate
> More suffering than the most infortunate . . .[132]

He suffers 'thus never meriting': his piety, a religious version of Aeneas's painful dutifulness, is no consolation, nor does it give him any reward of glory. Henry Peacham's *Compleat Gentleman* (1622), which stands at the end of the tradition inaugurated by Elyot's *Governour*, deplores the way that 'vertue in our declining and worser daies, generally findeth no

---

[132] 1. 79–84/48–50: 'But my heart is torn for wise Odysseus, the unlucky man, who far from his friends has been long suffering woes in an island surrounded by the sea.' Spondanus's note (p. 5) may have influenced Chapman: 'Ulisses vero pius & religiosus inique & sine ulla causa tot laboribus exerceatur' (Ulysses is a *pius* and religious man, who was put through so many labours without any reason).

regard',[133] and also includes a long section on the *Aeneid*, which emphasizes the sadness, and the resistant virtues of constancy and fortitude, which dominate Chapman's hero:

forasmuch as griefe and perpetuall care, are inseparable companions of all great and noble atchievements, he gives him *Achates quasi achis ates*, his faithful companion? What immooved constancy, when no teares or entreaty of *Eliza* could cause him stay? What *Piety*, *Pity*, Fortitude beyond his companions.[134]

Piety still rubs shoulders with pity in the catalogue of heroic virtues; but Aeneas has become the exemplar of constancy in adverse, necessarily hostile circumstances. The outraged honour of Achilles when he is denied his due has metamorphosed into a sad view of virtue's place in the scheme of things. It is only recognized in the civilized but distant paradise of the Phaeacians, and occasionally voices a complaint against the injustice of the world; but its element is tears, the 'true interpreters of all'. The paradise in which virtue rules and attains public glory is lost.

DEATH BY ANATOMY: EPIC AFTER CHAPMAN

Chapman's *Odysseys* follows—and to an extent anticipates—the major developments of the English epic in the seventeenth century.[135] Its emphasis on 'the mind's inward, constant and unconquered Empire' in response to the injustice of external circumstances, rather than on 'the outward fashion of fortitude', is typical of early seventeenth-century epic. The end of Daniel's *Civil Wars*, which shows Warwick retreating from an arbitrary and passionate monarchy to be 'King of himself',[136] shows a similar retreat from civic concerns to inner self-regulation. The resistant and retiring forms of heroism portrayed by the biblical epic poets who followed the writers discussed in the last two chapters are also anticipated in the patience and heroic fortitude of Chapman's hero. Sylvester's translation of Du Bartas, for example, contains several satiric additions which describe the corruptions of English life, and this rottenness in the state (as in the French original) leads the poet to advocate retreat into a

---

[133] *The Compleat Gentleman* (London, 1622), 82. For parallels, see D. T. Starnes, 'Elyot's *Governour* and Peacham's *Compleat Gentleman*', *Modern Language Review*, 22 (1927), 319–22.

[134] *Compleat Gentleman*, 83.

[135] On which, see Douglas Bush, *English Literature in the Earlier Seventeenth Century 1600–1660*, 2nd edn. (Oxford, 1962), 368–76.

[136] *CW* VIII. 92. Daniel presented a treatise on *The Prayse of Private Life* (c.1605) to Margaret Clifford which advocates a similar retreat from court life to a realm of personal virtue, and has been attributed to his friend and fellow epic poet Sir John Harington. See McLure, *Chapman*, 44–6 and 327–78.

private realm of independent virtue.[137] This set the tone for a wave of
early seventeenth-century epics which adopt as their ethical model the
self-regulatory heroism of *The Faerie Queene* Book II, rather than the
more active and impassioned virtues displayed in III or V. Among the
baroque curlicues of Giles Fletcher's *Christs Victorie and Triumph* (1610)
it is possible to discern an identification of Christ's heroism with self-
reliant resistance to temptation. Fletcher's Christ resists Panglory in a
way that amalgamates Guyon's rejection of Philotime and his hostile
response to Acrasia. Unlike the ever-fallible Guyon, however, Fletcher's
hero is perfectly insensitive to the passions which creep so close to the
Spenserian hero.[138] His one concession to his assumed humanity is his
desire for Mercy, a religious refinement of the romance element of *The
Faerie Queene* with which one could imagine Fletcher quite happily
dispensing, were it not for the fact that Christ is so notoriously merciful.[139]

Giles's brother Phineas shows a similar penchant for self-regulatory
heroism. In *The Purple Island* (1633) he develops the psycho-physiological
allegory of Alma's castle—again turning to Book II of *The Faerie Queene*
as his major model—and treats virtue as inhering in the due regimen of
the inner faculties, rather than in the active passions of anger or amours.[140]
Thumos—Chapman's blaze of martial inspiration—is no source of energy,
or of inspiration. It becomes violent vengefulness:

> *Thumos* the fourth, a dire, revengefull swain;
> Whose soul was made of flames, whose flesh of fire:
> Wrath in his heart, hate, rage and furie reigne;
> Fierce was his look, when clad in sparkling tire;
> But when dead palenesse in his cheek took seisure,
> And all the bloud in's boyling heart did treasure,
> Then in his wilde revenge kept he nor mean, nor measure.
>
> Look as when waters wall'd with brazen wreath
> Are sieg'd with crackling flames, their common foe;
> The angrie seas 'gin foam and hotly breathe,
> They swell, rise, rave, and still more furious grow;

---

[137] See Guillaume de Salluste, Sieur Du Bartas, *The Divine Weeks and Works*, trans. Joshua
Sylvester, ed. Susan Snyder, 2 vols. (Oxford, 1979), i. 20–31, for Henry's patronage and the satirical
additions. See Week 1 Day 2, 889–958; Day 3, 497–528, for lines on the corruption of justice. For
his advocacy of retreat from public life, see Day 3, 1057–72.

[138] *Christs Victorie on Earth*, 57–60: 'Thus sought the dire Enchauntress in his minde | Her guilefull
bayt to have embosomed, | But he her charmes dispersed into winde, | And her of insolence
admonished, | And all her optique glasses shattered.' Giles and Phineas Fletcher, *Poetical Works*, ed.
F. S. Boas, 2 vols. (Cambridge, 1908–9). Cf. *FQ* II. vii. 44–50, where Guyon rejects Philotime on the
grounds that he already has a lady, and *FQ* II. xii. 57, where Guyon breaks Excesse's cup. Spenser's
hero, unlike Fletcher's 'gan secret pleasaunce to embrace', II. xii. 65.

[139] *Christs Victorie in Heaven*, 41–85.

[140] See Grundy, *The Spenserian Poets*, 186–7. *FQ* II. ix. 22, the description of Alma's castle, also
attracted Kenhelm Digby's first learned commentary on the poem, *Var.* ii. 472–8.

> Nor can be held, but forc't with fires below,
> Tossing their waves, break out and all o'reflow:
> So boyl'd his rising bloud, and dasht his angry brow.[141]

Part of this ferment derives from *Aeneid* 7, in which Turnus, whipped
into a frenzy by Allecto, is compared to a seething cauldron;[142] but the
stanza containing the simile is lifted almost verbatim from Fletcher's
earlier brief epic *The Locustae, or Apollyonists* (1627),[143] in which the Pope
is inspired to boil with fury under diabolic influence. Fletcher assigns the
aspiring honour and 'haughty rage' of pagan heroism to diabolical Catholics
and to the ruler of Hell. The source of such equivocal power in Chapman
and the earlier English Lucanians is banished to the underworld. The
moral ideal of *The Apollyonists*, as of *The Purple Island*, is again not the
outward fashion of fortitude, but the rational inward ordering of the
mind. The theme of government again shrinks to self-regimen:

> Would'st thou live honoured? Clip ambitious wing,
> To reasons yoke thy furious passions bring.
> Thrice noble is the man, who of himselfe is King.[144]

He laments—as does Peacham—the 'abused honour' of Spenser, and
looks back to an age

> When th' highest flying Muse still highest climbes;
> And vertues rise keeps down all rising crimes.
> Happy, thrice happy age! happy, thrice happy times![145]

Fletcher's response to this present universal antagonism to merit is not
combative anger, but pastoral retreat, in which kingship is again attenuated
to a metaphor for self-government: 'so in my little house my lesser heart
shall reigne'.[146]

The Spenserian poets show the fundamental changes forced on the
epic when the public realm of counsel and virtuous aspiration to rule was
closed by the erratic patronage of the Stuarts. They may reflect, or seek
to establish, a prevailing idiom of social discontent; but it is very likely

---

[141] *The Purple Island*, vii. 55–6.

[142] *Aen.* 7. 462–6: 'magno veluti cum flamma sonore | virgea suggeritur costis undantis aëni | exsultantque aestu latices, furit intus aquai | fumidus atque alte spumis exuberat amnis, | nec iam se capit unda, volat vapor ater ad auras' (As when burning, crackling firewood is placed below the ribs of a bubbling cauldron, and the liquid dances with delight at the heat; the turmoil of waters rages within, and raises in a foaming torrent. The waters can control themselves no longer. Black smoke rises into the sky).

[143] *Apollyonists*, iv. 5.

[144] Ibid. iii. 10.

[145] Ibid. i. 16; Spenser is treated as an example of abused merit, i. 19–21; Henry Peacham, *The Truth of Our Times* (London, 1638), 37–8.

[146] *Apollyonists*, i. 29.

that the chief reason for this shift in the nature of epic, and in the elements of *The Faerie Queene* which were seen to be important, lay in humble material quarters. Epics become physically smaller in the period of their retreat into a concern with internal regimen, and grander productions like Drayton's *Poly-Olbion* are not welcomed by fashion-conscious printers. Spenser, Fairfax, and Harington had all dedicated substantial and well-produced volumes to the Queen; Chapman's Homer is almost the last epic folio before Dryden's *Aeneid*, and his royal patron was dead by the time the *Whole Works* was published in 1616. After Chapman, epic poetry lost much of its traditionally close relation to political authority: Gorges's badly printed *Pharsalia*, and the austere quartos of the Fletchers found less regal patrons than their predecessors. Slatyer's *Palae-Albion* (1621) managed to be both big and bad, but it looked to the neglected Drayton as a spiritual patron, and its discerning public never demanded a reprint. The authors of such modest and provincial works (the Fletchers emerged from the Fens) might be expected to explore personal, rather than political regimen. And they might be expected grudgingly to imply that the arena of politics is a dangerous and misleading distraction from the true heroism of patience and heroic fortitude. They had little choice: when Princes will not pay for, or make any pretence of listening to, epic poems there is little point in retaining Spenser's fiction that personal passions have a direct application to political life: the alternative is to invert the Spenserian model, and to appropriate government as a metaphor for self-regulation. It was only by claiming to be able to rule their own minds that the Spenserian poets could persuade themselves that their poems played any part in the government of the country.

The retreat of the epic poem into obscurity continued without check under Charles I. Most epic energies in the Caroline period went into a revival of prose romance, and with it the left-overs of the cult of Gloriana.[147] The reign of Charles did not produce a published original verse epic animated by Spenser's martial and political virtues. R<alph> K<nevett>'s *Supplement of the Faerie Queene* (1635),[148] is filled with heroes who embody newly circumspect attributes. There is little room among them for a potentially rebellious martial rage, or for those assaults on monarchy which emerge through pulses of violent energy from the works

---

[147] This vast area requires a separate study, but has been well served recently. See Paul Salzman, *English Prose Fiction 1558–1700: A Critical History* (Oxford, 1985), 123–210; Annabel Patterson, *Censorship and Interpretation* (Madison, Wis., 1984), 159–202; Lois Potter, *Secret Rites and Secret Writing: Royalist Literature, 1641–1660* (Cambridge, 1989), 72–80.

[148] Cambridge University Library MS Ee. 3. 53. For Knevett's authorship, see C. B. Millican, 'Ralph Knevett, Author of the *Supplement* to Spenser's *Faerie Queene*', *Review of English Studies*, 14 (1938), 44–52.

of Sidney and Spenser. Wisdom and Prudence accompany the more outgoing virtues of Fortitude and Liberalitie as the titular virtues of Knevett's knights; but the latter qualities are not to be found in the present, but when

> under Gloriane the Parragon
> Of honour, and heroicke action
> Those that by bloudy Tyrants were opprest,
> Found freedome if they sought it at her throne.[149]

Knevett helps to create the prevailing flavour of loss which colours epic writing in the later seventeenth century: it is as though he wishes to remind his readers to turn again to the more vigorous works of earlier epic poets, but would not himself wish to risk emulating their manner. He represents the association of romance with the correction of tyranny— a vital feature of Rous's and Harington's Elizabethan epics—as a quality in epic which has passed, together with the benign, active virtue of Gloriana's reign.

In the majority of Civil War epics, passions are not simply reified into the constituents of the mind, as they are in Fairfax's Tasso. They become associated with particular causes, and are set at war with each other.[150] The prime representative of this political polarization of epic is Cowley's Lucanian *Civil War* (*c*.1642–5). This work undertakes as part of its Royalist propaganda to damn anger in hell. It strips all vestiges of Marlovian heroism from the rebel Mortimer and his barons. The hero of Drayton's *Mortimeriados* sits with Isabel fuming in Cowley's hell, where flames burn out irascible and concupiscible passions alike:

> Her Mortimer close by forever mourns.
> Their scorching lusts, and all their hot desires,
> Are now extinguisht quite by greater fires.[151]

Meanwhile, the diabolic spirits who inspire the Roundheads release 'the rebell Passions' from their unruly ministers.[152] Passions no longer equip

---

[149] VIII. i. 7; cf. IX. i. 3: 'Nor was this vertue Liberality, | In any countrey of more high regard, | Then in the land of Gloriana high, | Who wont was to requite with high reward, | Achievements brave, and enterprises hard.'

[150] See Jonathan Sawday, ' "Mysteriously Divided": Civil War, Madness and the Divided Self', in Thomas Healy and Jonathan Sawday (eds.), *Literature and the English Civil War* (Cambridge, 1990), 127–43. This essay tends to attribute features of the epic which run right back to Tasso to the specific context of the civil war.

[151] *The Civil War*, ed. Allan Pritchard, University of Toronto Department of English Studies and Texts, 20 (Toronto and Buffalo, 1973), ii. 472–4; cf. ii. 457–8: 'There thowsand stubborne Barons fetterd ly, | And curse their old vaine noyse of Liberty'. On *The Civil War*, see Gerald M. MacLean, *Time's Witness* (Madison, Wis., 1990), 177–211.

[152] iii. 17–18.

heroes with the impetus required to create new versions of the events related in classical epic; they are used as tokens of rebellion, and become tools in the author's propaganda war. Each camp of passions, which blur and overlap so fruitfully in Spenser, takes on a clear political allegiance in Cowley. While anger is associated with hell and rebellion, pity takes on increasingly Royalist colours. It has been suggested that the works of May and Waller are animated by the ideal of a clement Augustan ruler, and this view is strongly supported by the way that the pitiful element in the shattered Spenserian synthesis is often associated in their works with royalist epic heroes.[153] Cowley's *Civil War* shares this bias. He imitates the pathetic death of Pallas in the demise of Cavendish:

> Like some fair *Flower*, which *Morne* saw freshly gay,
> In the fields generall ruine mowne away.
> The *Hyacinth*, or purple *Violet*,
> Just languishing, his colour *Light* just set.
> Ill mixt it lies amidst th'ignoble *Grasse*;
> The country *daughters* sigh as by'it they passe.[154]

Falkland—another victim of what Cowley erroneously hoped would be the unfolding of an imperial history—is eulogized as 'More civill, then Romance ere fancied yet; | Above the noblest draughts of Sidneys Wit'.[155] Cavalier warriors become the pitifully mortal reincarnations of Virgil's imperial victims, killed by an uncontrolled and devilish *furor*.

Cowley (in all probability) plagiarized the description of hell in the *Civil Wars* for his later epic *Davideis* (*c.*1650[156]). The later poem shows a growing void at the heart of the genre. It is extremely cautious in attributing any passion to anyone. Indeed, it gives the impression that Cowley had so effectively branded the motives of action with ideological significance in his earlier unpublished and incomplete *Civil Wars* that he became uneasy in attributing any motive at all to any of his characters. Even his ideal King David—who, after all, must have needed some martial impetus to enable him to overcome Goliath—has little signs of the heroic rage which Tasso, Spenser, and Chapman had in various forms deployed to drive their heroes. David does at one point feel 'Anger and brave disdain' in his combat with his gigantic adversary;[157]

---

[153] See further Howard Erskine-Hill, *The Augustan Idea in English Literature* (London, 1983), 198–205, and pp. 179–80 above.

[154] ii. 151–6; cf. *Aen.* 11. 67–70.

[155] iii. 597–8.

[156] Composed *c.*1650–4. See Frank Kermode, 'The Date of Cowley's *Davideis*', *Review of English Studies*, 25 (1949), 154–8. *Davideis*, i. 71–100, *The English Writings*, ed. A. R. Waller, 2 vols. (Cambridge, 1905), i. 244, draws its description of Hell from *The Civil War*, ii. 365–96 (noted by Pritchard, 157).

[157] Waller, i. 335. Cf. 'pious rage', i. 392.

but his true victory is over self, insurgent passions, and adverse circumstances:

> The *Prince* alone stood mild and patient by,
> So bright his sufferings, so triumphant show'd,
> Less to the *best* then *worst* of fates he ow'd.
> A victory now he o're *himself* might boast;
> He *Conquer'd* now that *Conqu'eror* of an *Host*.[158]

Victories over oneself earlier in the tradition of epic romance grow from
writerly struggles to transcend a way of reading past texts. Struggles of
characters to conquer themselves in, say, *Gerusalemme liberata*, grow from
the author's tense and unstable struggle to set a modern motive aside for
what he perceives to be a closer approximation of an ancient and alien
one. Here, the king's victory is brought about by a kind of cowardly non-
engagement: Cowley cannot bear to associate his hero with any precise
set of emotional priorities. As a result he avoids the problems of
anachronism, the fears of misappropriation, and that living sense of the
dangers of miswriting past epic, which had kept the tradition energetically
alive through the sixteenth century.

There is perhaps only one moment when Cowley engaged with the
problems of writing and motivating a modern epic, and it is in a poem
which uses the imagery and energies of the epic romance tradition, not
to write epic, but to invent and praise a new form of heroism. In his ode
'To the Royal Society', Cowley lauds the rebellious energy required to
liberate the boy Philosophy from his incarceration in the labyrinthine,
delusion-filled house of error, in language which flows with the unabsorbed
energy of the Civil War. Francis Bacon becomes the heroic destroyer of
Authority:

> He broke that Monstrous God which stood
> In midst of th'Orchard, and the whole did claim,
> Which with a useless Sith of Wood,
> And something else not worth a name,
> (Both vast for shew, yet neither fit
> Or to Defend, or to Beget;
> Ridiculous and senseless Terrors!) made
> Children and superstitious men afraid.
> The Orchard's open now, and free;
> *Bacon* has broke the Scare-crow Deitie;
> Come, enter, all that will,
> Behold the rip'ned Fruit, come gather now your Fill.[159]

---

[158] Ibid. 392.
[159] Ibid. 449.

None of Cowley's Civil War epic writings quite dare to engage with Lucan's *Pharsalia*, or to tap its self-mutilating energy. Cowley never managed to write about the Civil War in a way that was not polarized and narrowly polemical; but here, in the aftermath of conflict, in an ode about science, he manages to capture a Lucanian self-destruction, and to tie that in with an anxiety about the effect of transvaluing past forms of heroism. His scientific hero has the irreligious violence of Lucan's Caesar, tinged with the self-mutilating energies of Tasso's Rinaldo: both destroy the delusions of the haunted wood.[160] Cowley's scientific hero acquires the radical power to ruin the great work of time in his liberation of Philosophy. And the activities of this updated hero issue in a powerful form of sacrilege. He opens the Garden of Eden, and offers the fruit of knowledge to all. This leaves Cowley anxiously protesting against the sacrilegious violence of his own invention, who is a rebellious liberator of something that might be good or bad to the ultimate degree:

> Yet still methinks, we fain would be
> Catching at the forbidden Tree ...

This non-epic poem dramatizes the final self-destruction of the romance tradition. That tradition had fought, from *Orlando furioso* onwards, with its own understanding of classical epic: the demons and delusions and desires released by its revisions of classical epic became its own chief adversary. With Cowley these delusions finally died. His ode 'To the Royal Society' shows, at least, that he worried about this imaginative sacrilege, and saw it as a violation of something sacred.

Davenant's *Gondibert* (1651) shows few signs of this healthy guilt. It further anatomizes the polarized heroic idiom inherited from Cowley, and continues to push the epic away from the glories of desire towards the scientific. Davenant was praised by Cowley for drawing the epic from the thickets of faerie-land into the open plains of human manners, and by Waller for exploring 'humane Passions, such as with us dwell'.[161] *Gondibert* is founded on a careful distinction between the amorous sympathies of the loyal Gondibert and the aspiring, honour-conscious, and malign faction of Oswald.[162] The poem betrays its daily scrutiny by Thomas Hobbes,[163] both in its scrupulously analytic treatment of heroic passion

---

[160] *Phars.* 3. 432–6; *GL* xviii. 25–38.

[161] *Gondibert*, ed. David F. Gladish (Oxford, 1971), 269–71. Cf. the similarly anatomized heroic idiom of Samuel Sheppard, *The Faerie King fashioning Love and Honour [c.1650]*, ed. P. J. Klemp (Salzburg, 1984). This work remained in manuscript (Bodleian MS Rawl. Poet. 28). It is sadly true when Sheppard says 'How Tortoise like I march', III. vi. 1.

[162] '...the Characters of men (whose passions are to be eschew'd) I have deriv'd from the distempers of Love, or Ambition: for Love and Ambition are to often the raging Feavers of great mindes', edn. cit. 13. Cf. I. iii. 25–40.

[163] Davenant thanks Hobbes for his 'daylie examination' of the poem, ibid. 3.

and in its redirection of desire towards scientific rather than civic goals. For Gondibert does not aspire to rule, but falls for the retiring charms of Birtha, the daughter of the scientist Astragon. The hero explicitly denies that his love is adulterated by the slightest hint of political aspiration for the princess Rhodalind:

> Think not Ambition can my duty sway;
> I look on *Rhodalind* with Subjects Eies,
> Whom he that conquers, must in right obay.
>
> And though I humanly have heretofore
> All beauty lik'd, I never lov'd till now;
> Nor think a Crown can raise his valew more,
> To whom already Heav'n does Love allow.[164]

He renounces this old civic form of desire: his love is simply love. None the less, his King repeatedly solicits Gondibert to take his daughter, and with her his throne, which, he generously declares, the hero has merited by his superhuman virtue.[165] This pressure from the meritocratic element of the English epic is, however, conspicuously deadened. The civic dimension of *The Faerie Queene* is strangled and stifled and repeatedly denied, with an insistence that indicates that Davenant regarded it as the most dangerous fraughtage of the epic tradition. Gondibert will not rule. He will not even aspire to do so. The King eventually visits the hero in Astragon's scientific retreat, in order once more to overcome his unaccountable lack of an ambitious desire for his daughter.[166] Gondibert does not desert his love for empire, as the civic heroes of earlier epic romances had (eventually) left their Didos: he greets the centre of political authority with amorous reluctance when it comes to *him*.[167] His true lover Birtha— who is, again conspicuously, *not* a princess—is concealed in one of the many closets which encrust Davenant's labyrinthine halls of the great, while the hero equivocally stalls the King's demand that he marry Rhodalind.[168] Both the King and the eavesdropping Birtha have the guiding ideas of Spenserian civic heroism so deeply ingrained in their minds that they cannot even understand Davenant's new kind of hero when he denies that he has any designs on government. Indeed, they are so predisposed to believe that all heroic minds aspire to rule that they interpret his speech as an acceptance of Rhodalind, the one with delight,

---

[164] II. viii. 26–7.

[165] 'Vertue's claim exceeds the right of blood', III. iv. 10; 'Whose merit may aspire to *Rhodalind*', II. viii. 55; cf. IV. iv. 6: 'Thy dang'rous worth is grown above reward.'

[166] III. iii. 23–iv. 16.

[167] 'Now *Gondibert* advanc'd, but with delay; | As fetter'd by his love; for he would fain | Dissembled weakness might procure his stay, | Here where his Soul does as in Heav'n remain', III. iii. 50.

[168] III. iv. 21–35.

the other with despair. But Gondibert does not desert Birtha so easily, and gallantly plights her his troth to quell her fears.[169] He renounces the throne for the autotelic emotion of love; only those who judge him by alien standards believe that he is motivated by ambition.

Gondibert is, as Cowley suggests, founded on a conscious design to pull the epic out of Faerie-land. But this does not mean just a shift in location or subject-matter. It means that it deliberately and repeatedly affirms the Spenserian synthesis of love and a quest for glory to be a pernicious mistake. There is a politics in its departure from earlier epic romance; and that politics lies in its attempt rigidly to separate romantic love for the daughter of a scientist from aspiring love for a princess. In *Gondibert* the spectrum of political emotions is reduced to a blurry fringe which surrounds the hero in the distorted perceptions of others. It has been argued that Caroline poets seek political reform through their treatments of love, and that there is no evidence of a 'cultural rift, or of retreat from social engagement after the demise of Shakespeare and Jonson'.[170] This claim is not in any simple way true of *Gondibert*: it labours with suspicious energy to detach love from politics, and to disentangle desire for a woman from a meritocratic desire to rule. It labours to make the main subject of epic to be *only* manners. Spenser's unstable, synthetic, and civic ethos of love and the search for Glory split apart in the early seventeenth century, and subsequent poets tended to align the early Spenserians' equivocal affection for wrathful pursuit of Glory with diabolic rebellion, whilst they laboured to invent a form of love increasingly independent of civic goals. The synthetic motive of ambitious love is explicitly renounced in *Gondibert* for a more retiring form of scientific desire, and was never reconstituted.

Dryden's translation of the *Aeneid* is the resting-place for much of the material explored here, and shows at once the success and the dangers of Davenant's project. Dryden's Turnus, his Mezentius, and his Rutuli are frequently goaded into an irascibility, and a disdain, which is absent from the original, while Aeneas droops at times with a misplaced pity.[171] A

---

[169] III. iv. 36–54.

[170] Kevin Sharpe, *Criticism and Compliment: The Politics of Literature in the England of Charles I* (Cambridge, 1987), 52 *et passim*; on *Gondibert*, see 101–8. Many of the features which Sharpe regards as distinctive to the writing of the period are greatly attenuated versions of Elizabethan techniques of insinuation. Cf. Potter, *Secret Rites*, 93–100.

[171] *Aen.* 9. 66/74–5: 'ignescunt irae, duris dolor ossibus ardet' becomes 'Thus ranges eager *Turnus* o're the Plain, | Sharp with Desire, and furious with Disdain.'; *Aen.* 10. 732–3/1030–1: 'fugientem haud est dignatus Oroden | sternere...' becomes 'Then with Disdain the haughty Victor view'd | *Orodes* flying, nor the wretch pursu'd.'; *Aen.* 10. 762/1081–2: 'At vero ingentem quatiens Mezentius hastam | turbidus ingreditur campo' becomes 'Once more the proud *Mezentius*, with Disdain, | Brandish'd his Spear, and rush'd into the Plain.' Dryden defends Aeneas's supposed pitiful amorousness in the *Dedication*, *Poems*, ed. J. Kinsley (Oxford, 1958), 1022–30. Dryden used Caro's translation, which imports many of these details. See Robert Fitzgerald, 'Dryden's *Aeneid*', *Arion*, 2: 3 (1963), 17–31. For the improbable claim that Dryden 'greatly underplays Virgil's pathos', see Mark

Fairfacian response to Spenser runs through almost every line of the poem, and persists right through to its final moment. The translation ends with a familiar opposition of passions. Dryden adopts the analytic scheme of the romance tradition; he draws attention to the compassion which so many earlier writers had felt in Aeneas's hesitation over his opponent, and picks out Turnus's pagan disdain in a gory pun:

> In deep Suspence the *Trojan* seem'd to stand;
> And just prepar'd to strike repress'd his Hand.
> He rowl'd his Eyes, and ev'ry Moment felt
> His manly Soul with more Compassion melt.
>
>   .   .   .   .
>
> He rais'd his Arm aloft; and at the Word,
> Deep in his Bosom drove the shining Sword.
> The streaming Blood distain'd his arms around:
> And the disdainful Soul came rushing through the Wound.[172]

The final alexandrine acknowledges Dryden's debt to romance with a bow to the long last line of the Spenserian stanza. But the polarization of ideals which began with Tasso had run its course, and left to the next generation of poets an epic tradition that was exhausted by anatomy. Sixteenth- and early seventeenth-century epic writers had to work hard to invent a modern equivalent for the conceptual idiom of classical epic, and laboured both to unpick the idioms of earlier imitators and to create in the process a role for epic in their society. They improvised a modern heroic idiom, often while they composed. A sense that they had got epic wrong frequently led them to revise and extend their poems: Ariosto, Tasso, Drayton, Daniel, Sidney, and Spenser all attempted to overcome the prevalent romance view of the *Aeneid* by revising their epic works, by fracturing and rewriting Virgilian episodes to accommodate rival interpretations, or by continuing their poems in a more ruthless idiom. They had to break away from a part of themselves in order to feel that they could write like authors of the past. And by developing the civic aspect of classical epic they sought to explore and modify the structures of power and of emotion which sustained their society. It was this effort of assimilation which kept the epic tradition alive. Once a stable, polarized idiom for the portrayal of heroic passions was established, few writers could engage their imaginations with the genre in any other form than the mock heroic. Only Milton managed to break free of this idiom.

O'Connor, 'John Dryden, Gavin Douglas, and Virgil', in Harold Love (ed.), *Restoration Literature: Critical Approaches* (London, 1972), 251. See also L. Proudfoot, *Dryden's 'Æneid' and its Seventeenth-Century Predecessors* (Manchester, 1960), 135.

[172] *Aen.* 12. 938–52/1360–77.

8

Milton

EARLY MILTON: WANDERING MUSES LOST

Dryden thought that *Paradise Lost* was something like a romance. He remarked that '*Milton* hath acknowledg'd to me, that *Spencer* was his original',[1] and excluded *Paradise Lost* from his list of true epics on the grounds that the poem is a contorted romance, in which the villain beats the elfin knight into errancy. He dismisses the claims of Pulci, Boiardo, and Ariosto to be 'the descendants of *Virgil* in a right line', and continues:

> *Spencer* has a better plea for his *Fairy-Queen*, had his action been finish'd, or had been one. And *Milton*, if the Devil had not been his Heroe instead of *Adam*, if the Gyant had not foil'd the Knight, and driven him out of his strong hold, to wander through the World with his Lady Errant.[2]

Envy probably helped to form this view of the poem. Dryden had just finished his own attempt at the *Aeneid*, which was trapped within the rigidities of the English romance idiom, and had also tried (with palpable lack of success) to transform *Paradise Lost* into a replica of heroic drama in *The State of Innocence and the Fall of Man*. It would have calmed his nerves to think that Milton's poem was wrecked by the same forces which had enslaved his own epic ambition.

But envy can speak true. Milton knew earlier English epic romances intimately. He boasted—in Italian, as if to show he had no need of a crib—that he had read Harington's *Orlando furioso* twice, and may have imparted some of his enthusiasm for Fairfax to his pupil and nephew Edward Phillips.[3] He also gives the odd sign of reading the genre for its political content, citing Berni's version of *Orlando innamorato* to the effect that 'a king, if he wishes to do his duty, is not truly a king but a

---

[1] *Poems*, ed. J. Kinsley (Oxford, 1958), p. 1445.

[2] Ibid. 1010.

[3] Milton quotes something very like Harington's translation in *Of Reformation*, *The Complete Prose Works*, ed. Don M. Wolfe (hereafter *CPW*), 8 vols. (New Haven, Conn., 1953–82), i. 560 and 811. See *The Works of John Milton*, ed. F. A. Patterson, 20 vols. (New York, 1931–40), xviii. 330–6, for his marginalia. Edward Phillips called Fairfax 'one of the most judicious, elegant and haply in his time, most approved of *English* Translators, both for his choice of so worthily extoll'd a Heroic Poet as *Torquato Tasso*; as for the exactness of his version', *Theatrum Poetarum, or a Compleat Collection of the Poets* (London, 1675), 34.

steward of the people'.[4] The tentative and uncertain advocacy of elective, meritocratic monarchy which runs through works such as Harington's *Orlando furioso* finds full and frank expression in Milton: from his *Commonplace Book* onwards, he advocates the familiar ideal of reason's due supremacy in both personal and political spheres, and the parallel notion that merit—in his case frequently identified with divine election[5]— should rule over undeserving heredity. Yet for all Milton's evident predilection for English romance, his juvenilia do not include drafts of a proposed romance (say, *The Paradise Queene; or, The Faerie Lost*). Why?

His earliest published remarks on his poetic ambitions in *The Reason of Church Government* (1642) do gravitate towards the chivalric:

Time serves not now, and perhaps I might seem too profuse to give any certain account of what the mind at home in the spacious circuits of her musing hath liberty to propose to her self, though of highest hope, and hardest attempting, whether that Epick form whereof the two poems of *Homer*, and those other two of *Virgil* and *Tasso* are a diffuse, and the book of *Job* a brief model: or whether the rules of *Aristotle* herein are strictly to be kept, or nature to be follow'd, which in them that know art, and use judgement is no transgression, but an enriching of art. And lastly what K[ing] or Knight before the Conquest might be chosen in whom to lay the pattern of a Christian heroe.[6]

This reads like a deceptively bullying list of agenda for a meeting: 'Item 1: Decide to write an epic. Item 2: Decide on neoclassical or romance form for this epic. Item 3: Decide to write an epic romance about Arthur.' Each stage of Milton's private musings moves with a drifting certainty towards the next stage of his deliberations, and the whole process seems to point towards an Arthurian romance. Yet a hard look at other passages in Milton's early writings where he actually envisages the subject-matter of earlier romance narratives—love, pitiful digressions, warriors leaving or not leaving ladies, heroes succumbing to love—indicates that Milton had little affection for the materials of romance. In *The Reason of Church Government* he alludes not to the prototypically romancish departure of Hector from Andromache, but to the closely related moment when Hector is begged not to enter the battlefield by his family. Homeric compassion leaves not a trace on Milton's view of the scene. And not civic virtue, nor martial *furor* keeps Hector fighting; but shame is the spur:

Hence we may read in the *Iliad* where *Hector* being wisht to retire from the

---

[4] *CPW* i. 439.

[5] Of Nobility he writes 'From the spirit of God it must be derived, not from forefathers or man made laws', *CPW* i. 605.

[6] *CPW* i. 812–13. On Milton's projected Arthuriad, see also *Epitaphium Damonis*, ll. 161–79; *Mansus*, ll. 78–84. All quotations and references to the poems are from *The Poems of John Milton*, ed. John Carey and Alastair Fowler (London, 1968).

battel, many of his forces being routed, makes answer that he durst not for shame, lest the Trojan Knights and Dames should think he did ignobly...But there is yet a more ingenuous and noble degree of honest shame, or call it if you will an esteem, whereby men bear an inward reverence towards their own persons. And if the love of God as a fire sent down from Heaven to be ever kept alive upon the altar of our hearts, be the first principle of all godly and vertuous actions in men, this pious and just honouring of our selves is the second, and may be thought of as the radical moisture and fountain head, whence every laudable and worthy enterprise issues forth.[7]

Milton avoids the sentimental revision of Homer, and sidesteps the galloping rush of 'piety' towards 'pity' by yoking it with justice. But the qualities with which he replaces these tender passions are alien to romance narrative forms. This 'self-pious regard'[8] is an introjection of *pietas*, a combined love of God and regard of self—a sort of piety within thee, happier far. Self-respect and divine inspiration could be used to extenuate deeds which seem on the face of it inhumane or perverse, but they are not motives which are naturally associated with particular forms of behaviour. 'I acted through pity' tells us something about the kind of action a speaker has performed, and about what he or she might do next. But to say 'I did it out of self-respect', or 'I acted through divine inspiration' reveals nothing about what the speaker actually has done. The imputation of these motives to Homer does not lead one to expect that Milton would ever read unreflective compassion into the Homeric poems, or produce a narrative which flowed from pitiful episode to pitiful episode.

Both passages from *The Reason of Church Government* imply that, from very early in his career, Milton was cultivating a scrupulous blindness to the pitiful inner character of romance. His earliest public statement about the higher poetic kinds reinforces these suspicions. In 1628 he interrupted the vacation exercise at Christ's (a sort of Latin end-of-term review: Milton's early allusions to epic are almost all as deliberately untimely as *Paradise Lost* itself) to prophesy great things for the vernacular Muse:

> Then sing of secret things that came to pass
> When beldam Nature in her cradle was;
> And last of kings and queens and heroes old,
> Such as the wise Demodocus once told
> In solemn songs at king Alcinous' feast,
> While sad Ulysses' soul and all the rest
> Are held with his melodious harmony

[7] *CPW* i. 840–1; cf *Il.* 6. 440–6, 22. 38–130.
[8] *CPW* i. 842.

In willing chains and sweet captivity.
But fie my wandering Muse how thou dost stray![9]

What draws his Muse off course is not so much the subject-matter of romance (the summary line about kings and queens is scarcely magnetizing), but the delicious effects of a poetic narrative. And the lines describing those effects have little to do with the Homeric passage to which they allude. The tales which Homer's Demodocus tells to Odysseus are about Odysseus, rather than of 'kings and queens and heroes old'; and this direct tie with the subject-matter, rather than the independent power of the poet, makes the hero weep like a woman in a city he has himself sacked. It is the most powerful example in Homer of the way sympathy can break through into the emotion of others. Milton gives his Demodocus knights and ladies, but he shows no interest in the sympathetic magic by which Homer's bard has such a magnetic effect on his audience. Nor does his Muse really range with the breezy digressiveness of Ariosto's: it is only that final rebuke, in which he calls his Muse wandering, that makes it look as though the sympathetic fluency of the mode is important to him.

Milton's rebuke to his wandering Muse is an early instance of his habitual tendency (which persists until its *ne plus ultra* in *Paradise Regain'd*) to establish the fact that he has instincts, desires, and ambitions by saying he will *not* indulge them. 'The Passion' stops before the event of its title with an anxious note protesting that the poet knew he was too young to represent God dying. His whole first collection of *Poems* (1645) oscillates between unsteady bursts of poetic or amorous exuberance and a restraint so strong as to give the impression that an enormously powerful instinct is being stunned. The volume is designed to appear bulimic: bursts of indulgent digression and violent resistance rapidly succeed each other.[10] And the eroticism of romance is one of the luscious visions that the collection glances at, and which it energizes by repeatedly resisting. The Latin elegies are put in a sequence which creates a contained power through the counterpoint of indulgence and restraint. 'Elegia Quinta', which describes a great burst of poetic energy, blooming with the spring, scampers off for a moment into the Ovidian vitality of Spenser's *Mutabilitie Cantos*, where desire and flight fill the landscape with a protracted game of hide-and-seek:

Atque aliquam cupidus praedatur Oreada Faunus,
  Consulit in trepidos dum sibi nympha pedes,

---

[9] 'At a Vacation Exercise in the College', ll. 45–53.
[10] For an alternative account of the structure of the 1645 volume, see Louis Martz, *Milton: Poet of Exile*, 2nd edn. (New Haven, Conn., and London, 1986), 31–59.

> Iamque latet, latitansque cupit male tecta videri,
>   Et fugit, et fugiens pervelit ipsa capi.[11]

And randy Faunus lasciviously pursues some Oread, while the nymph relies on her trembling feet: and now hides, and hiding, poorly covered, she wants to be seen: and flies, and flying wishes to be caught.

For all the timeless participles with which they are described, these Spenserian-Ovidian pleasures are short-lived. The next Elegy terminates them abruptly. 'Elegia Sexta' praises food and (especially) drink as the fuel of small poems; but the epic poet should stick to water:

> Sic dapis exiguus, sic rivi potor Homerus
>   Dulichium vexit per freta longa virum,
> Et per monstrificam Perseiae Phoebados aulam,
>   Et vada femineis insidiosa sonis,
> Perque tuas rex ime domos, ubi sanguine nigro
>   Dicitur umbrarum detinuisse greges.[12]

So Homer, sparing of food and drinking river water, led Ulysses through broad seas, and through the halls of Circe, where men were made monsters, and through the shallows made treacherous by Siren voices, and through your halls, king of the underworld, where he is said to have detained the hoards of souls with a libation of black blood.

It is easy to miss the oddest feature of this passage. It is not the temperance of *Odysseus* which gets him away from Circe (as in most Renaissance allegories of the poem); the sparse appetite of *Homer* himself leads ('vexit') the hero through his obstacle course. For Milton it is a poet's abstemiousness, an abstemiousness which sits very oddly beside the indulgences described in the previous elegy, that enables heroes to avoid the opportunities for errancy provided by Circes and Sirens. The movement from the sumptuous vitality of 'Elegia Quinta' to the total sparseness of poetic lifestyle advocated in 'Elegia Sexta' evokes a congenial feature of Milton's life. He had binges:

once in three Weeks or a Month, he would drop into the Society of some Young Sparks of his Acquaintance...the *Beau's* of those Times, but nothing near so bad as those now-a-days; with these Gentlemen he would so far make bold with his Body, as now and then to keep a Gawdy-day.[13]

Edward Phillips, Milton's nephew and pupil, evidently suffered from Milton's exemplary abstemiousness. This passage follows hard on a list of the massive range of reading Milton required of his pupils. But no

---

[11] 'Elegia Quinta. In Adventum Veris', ll. 127–30.
[12] 'Elegia Sexta', ll. 71–6.
[13] Helen Darbishire (ed.), *The Early Lives of Milton* (London, 1932), 62.

revenge could have been sweeter than the mischievous dryness of 'he would so far make bold with his Body, as now and then ...', which makes Milton's body sound like a rusty Morris Minor kept in the garage for a breathtaking spin at 30 miles per hour every other Sunday. But, for all its respectfully concealed mischief, Phillips's anecdote replicates the fretful movement from indulgent sensuousness to savage restraint of the *Poems* volume. The unstable resistance to the allurements of romance which had entangled the heroes of Spenser and Tasso has become a personal matter, and has become intertwined with the power and authority of the poet himself.

In *Poems* (1645) Milton develops canny methods of stealing the energy of romance without implicating himself in its indulgences. In 'L'Allegro' a landscape full of romance ladies is just out of sight of the eye:

> Towers, and battlements it sees
> Bosomed high in tufted trees,
> Where perhaps some beauty lies,
> The cynosure of neighbouring eyes.[14]

This imaginary damsel becomes a fixed object of adoration, not for the dwindling pronoun of the poet's, or l'Allegro's eye—if that is indeed what 'it' is—but for *neighbouring* eyes. Romance is there—a Lady of Shalott tucked away in the privy reaches of imagination—but is there for other people. Unlike in the *Elegies* there is no need for any violent denial of these distant desires, since here the conditional syntax does the job of dissociating them from Milton instead. In 'Il Penseroso' there is a similarly wary attitude to earlier marvellous tales in Milton's invocation to Night:

> Or call up him that left half-told
> The story of Cambuscan bold,
> Of Camball, and of Algarsife,
> And who had Canace to wife,
> That owned the virtuous ring and glass,
> And of the wondrous horse of brass,
> On which the Tartar king did ride;
> And if aught else, great bards beside,
> In sage and solemn tunes have sung,
> Of tourneys and of trophies hung;
> Of forests, and enchantments drear,
> Where more is meant than meets the ear.[15]

The mazy syntax of melancholy loosens the sense of this extract, but the

---

[14] ll. 77–80.
[15] ll. 109–20.

whole passage from which it is drawn subsides into 'Night, if you can do these things, then see me often'. The prolonged paratactic description of romance stories leads through Chaucer's unfinished 'Squire's Tale'—which both Spenser and John Lane, a friend of Milton's father,[16] had attempted in various ways to complete—to a version of Spenserian allegory 'where more is meant than meets the ear'. The dreamy amble of the syntax shrinks the digressive movement of Spenserian narrative technique, with its drifts towards a withheld meaning, into the tiny compass of a sentence. In the process, Milton only summarizes the extant portion of the 'Squire's Tale', rather than venturing his own version. And the issue of the passage is not the completion of an endless romance, or even the direction of a heroic life, but the choice of a timbre of existence for the poet himself. It suggests that Milton's elusive Angelica, his goal that flees him as he pursues, is the desirable and unattainable fact of becoming a poet writing a romance which is not quite a romance.

THE GENESIS OF SATAN

These early writings—some of which were composed as much as forty years before *Paradise Lost* appeared—suggest that, if Milton had written a romance before 1645, it would have been a romance without romance motives, a plot shaped more by resistance to than indulgence in the amorous and digressive forms of earlier Renaissance epic. And this constructive avoidance of the established content for an epic does imply that Milton had, very early in his career, grasped the chief dynamic which kept the epic tradition moving along: he, like all the major writers of Renaissance epic, was shrinking away from the established motives of his predecessors. The history of Renaissance epic related so far follows a consistent shape. A group of writers construct a rigid scheme for inter-preting and motivating classical models, which is then developed, qualified, and perhaps broken down by later imitators and translators of those originals. Novelty in this tradition consists, not in a showdown with a literary parent, but in scattered sniping at the pervasive and commonplace consequences of an earlier author's way of reading the past. Spenser and Tasso niggle away at the pitiful indulgences of Ariosto: they curtail his amorous readings of Virgil by introducing bursts of rage into the minds

---

[16] See W. R. Parker, *Milton: A Biography*, 2 vols. (Oxford, 1968), 678, 715–16; and John Lane, *The Squire's Tale*, ed. F. J. Furnivall, Chaucer Society (London, 1888). Spenser's relations with the 'Squire's Tale' are discussed in Jonathan Goldberg, *Endlesse Worke: Spenser and the Structures of Discourse* (Baltimore and London, 1981), 35–64. On conclusions to the 'Squire's Tale', see J. A. Burrow, 'Poems without Endings', *Studies in the Age of Chaucer*, 13 (1991), 17–37.

of their heroes, or by breaking off episodes which seem too pitifully indulgent to suit with their more austere designs. It is by these destructive means that they create new approximations of the classical prototypes which lie beneath their poems.

Paradise Lost is the last and most powerfully destructive contributor to this history. And it responds more fully than is often recognized to the chief features, and chief weaknesses, of epic writing in seventeenth-century England. No self-respecting writer of epic, nor any heroic dramatist for that matter, in the later seventeenth century could fail to make a tidy antithesis between Disdain and Pity, Love and Honour, or to create a hero who swung between the two within a scene, a couplet, or a single line. The tradition of epic romance in this sclerotic form invited either parody—as when Butler in *Hudibras* turns martial exploits into no more than an excuse subsequently to spare the abject victim of one's might, and so oscillate between the passions of rage and pity[17]—or radical restructuring. It is from these imprisoning simplicities that Milton attempts to break free in *Paradise Lost*.[18]

The main agent for this destructive form of creation is Satan. In Book VI of *Paradise Lost* Milton's devil denies he has any origin, and claims to be 'self-begot, self-raised'.[19] But there were a lot of Satans around in minor seventeenth-century English epics, most of which descend ultimately from Tasso's association of the irascible with the adversarial. In the years leading up to the Civil War, the increasingly polarized idiom of epic poetry provided congenial materials for polemic. Whatever a writer did not like would turn up in hell associated with Turnus, anger, and the Devil. Raging devils became a commonplace of seventeenth-century epic. In *The Locustae* of Phineas Fletcher, in Crashaw's spirited translation of Marino's *Sospetto d'Herode*, and in the *Psyche* of Crashaw's Cambridge

[17] 'The ancient *Hero's* were illustrious | For b'ing benigne, and not blustrous, | ... And did in fight but cut work out | T'employ their Curtesies about', Samuel Butler, *Hudibras*, ed. John Wilders (Oxford, 1967), I. iii. 879–84. The squire's association of mercy with power also points to Butler's awareness of earlier English epic: 'To save, where you have pow'r to kill, | Argues your Pow'r above your Will', I. ii. 1049–50.

[18] This chapter is heavily indebted to the following studies of Milton's relations to his classical sources: Davis P. Harding, *The Club of Hercules: Studies in the Classical Background of Paradise Lost* (Urbana, Ill., 1962); John M. Steadman, *Milton and the Renaissance Hero* (Oxford, 1967); Francis C. Blessington, *'Paradise Lost' and the Classical Epic* (Boston, London, and Henley, 1979); Richard DuRocher, *Milton and Ovid* (Ithaca, NY, and London, 1985); Charles Martindale, *John Milton and the Transformation of Ancient Epic* (London and Sydney, 1986). These works underestimate the role of earlier Renaissance and English epic in determining how Milton read the classics. In this area I have found Judith A. Kates, *Tasso and Milton: The Problem of a Christian Epic* (London and Lewisburg, Pa., 1983) very helpful. John Guillory, *Poetic Authority: Spenser, Milton, and Literary History* (New York, 1983), is the most stimulating study of literary relations between Milton and Spenser, although Maureen Quilligan, *Milton's Spenser: The Politics of Reading* (Ithaca, NY, and London, 1983) has its moments.

[19] *PL* v. 860.

contemporary and friend Joseph Beaumont there is an angry Satan, with overtones of Turnus, who sets the story in motion.[20] These undistinguished poems, written by people who were at Cambridge between 1600 and 1643 (call them the Cambridge Satanists),[21] created Milton's immediate literary milieu. They construct a nexus of ideas—an association between Popery, Satan, and irascibility, and a tendency to attribute the start of their narratives to these forces—similar to that which Milton employed in his juvenile brief epic *In Quintum Novembris*, written while its author was at Cambridge in the 1620s.

The Satan of *Paradise Lost* may have begun life as a cliché from this school. There is a high likelihood that Milton did *not* begin *Paradise Lost* by sonorously dictating 'Of man's first disobedience . . .'.[22] Edward Phillips provides a hazy but atmospheric account of the poem's growth. Milton, he claims, wrote in bursts during the winter (as though the great burst of poetic and vernal energy that Milton described in 'Elegia Quinta' was supplanted by a wintry solace when he began his vernacular epic): a sad tale's best for winter. He also says that Milton recited to him the opening lines of Satan's soliloquy from the top of Mount Niphates 'several years before the Poem was begun'.[23] The lines were then intended to begin a tragedy on the Fall. Phillips quotes IV. 32–41, which concludes with Satan's own story of how his rebellion began:

[20] In Crashaw's Marino, Satan is 'the wrathfull King, and while he reignes | His Scepter and himselfe both he disdaines', st. 9, in *Poems*, ed. A. R. Waller, Cambridge English Classics (Cambridge, 1904). Satan here too, as in Fletcher's *Locustae*, works Herod into a boiling, cauldronlike frenzy in st. 61, which again imitates the way Allecto arouses Turnus. See above, pp. 234–5. On Marino's influence on Milton, see 'Digamma', 'On the Original of Milton's Satan', *Blackwood's*, 1 (1817), 140. Beaumont's *Psyche, or Loves Mysterie* (London, 1648) begins with a diabolic council, where Satan speaks with considerable bravura (canto i). The description of Eden in canto vi, with its luxurious Eve and its exuberant treatment of her temptation, has strong affinities with *Paradise Lost*. Beelzebub's inspiration of the Serpent again borrows the cauldron simile from Virgil's Turnus, 6. 226–7; cf. *Aen.* 7. 462–6. See also the account of the Fall and Hell in Edward Benlowes, *Theophila* (London, 1652), canto ii. 15–53. This English background has been neglected in accounts of Satan's relation to classical prototypes. See e.g. Robert M. Boltwood, 'Turnus and Satan as Epic "Villains"', *Classical Journal*, 47 (1952), 183–6. On the diabolization of romance, see George Williamson, 'Milton the Anti-Romantic', *Modern Philology*, 60 (1962), 13–21.

[21] Cowley was at Trinity, 1637–43, where he is likely to have begun *Davideis*, which contains versions of the hell depicted in *The Civil Wars*; Phineas Fletcher was at King's 1600–16; his friend Benlowes (to whom *The Purple Island* is dedicated) was at St John's from 1620; Crashaw was at Pembroke Hall from 1631 until 1637, when he became a fellow of Peterhouse, where he remained until his expulsion by Parliament in 1643; Crashaw's friend Beaumont was at Peterhouse from 1631 until he too was expelled in 1643–4 for his Royalist sympathies. This group of poets is sufficiently close to be called a school. All, with the exception of the older Fletcher, were Royalists, many with Catholic sympathies.

[22] Various attempts have been made to determine how *Paradise Lost* was written, and most have been damagingly speculative. See e.g. Allan H. Gilbert, *On the Composition of Paradise Lost* (Chapel Hill, NC, 1947); Grant McColley, *Paradise Lost: An Account of its Growth and Major Origins* (Chicago, 1940). Cf. the pragmatic approach adopted in G. K. Hunter, *Paradise Lost*, Unwin Critical Library (London, 1980), esp. ch. 3.

[23] Darbishire, *Early Lives*, 72–3.

> O thou that with surpassing glory crowned,
> Look'st from thy sole dominion like the God
> Of this new world; at whose sight all the stars
> Hide their diminished heads; to thee I call,
> But with no friendly voice, and add thy name
> O sun, to tell thee how I hate thy beams
> That bring to my remembrance from what state
> I fell, how glorious once above thy sphere;
> Till pride and worse ambition threw me down
> Warring in heaven against heaven's matchless king.

Phillips is not likely to have got the wrong end of the stick entirely.[24] It is very probable that Satan as he was originally conceived is on display in the soliloquy on Niphates' top: he is, after all, considering his own beginnings, as a villain might well do at the start of a play as cumbersome as *Adam Unparadiz'd* promised to be. He is also describing his fall, for the first time in the poem as we have it, in simply moralized terms: 'pride and worse ambition' are words which prigs, angels, and biblical commentators would use of Satan, rather than those with which he usually describes himself. As the speech continues (beyond the lines which Phillips quotes, so this may have been composed later) Satan considers the origins of his rebellion, using a language which constructs a basic currency of emotion. The idiom of this speech is unmistakably that of earlier disdainful pagan villains:

> What could be less than to afford him praise,
> The easiest recompense, and pay him thanks,
> How due! Yet all his good proved ill in me,
> And wrought but malice; lifted up so high
> I sdeigned subjection, and thought one step higher
> Would set me highest, and in a moment quit
> The debt immense of endless gratitude,
> So burdensome still paying, still to owe;
> Forgetful what from him I still received,
> And understood not that a grateful mind
> By owing owes not, but still pays, at once
> Indebted and discharged; what burden then?[25]

[24] His story is supported by the final draft of Milton's proposed play in the Trinity Manuscript, which, after a prologue, has Satan bemoaning his plight. Late 17th-cent. scholars were becoming increasingly aware of the fitful ways epic poets may have composed: L. Küstero cites Suidas saying of Homer: 'scripsit vero Iliadem non simul, nec ea serie, qua hodie juncta est, sed ipse quidem singulas rhapsodias composuit, & exhibuit eas in urbibus' (He wrote the *Iliad* not all at once, nor in that order in which it is now put together, but he composed it in individual rhapsodies, and performed those in cities), *Historia critica Homeri* (Frankfurt, 1696), 78. See the accounts of this speech in Guillory, *Poetic Authority*, 115–18; and Hunter, *Paradise Lost*, 86–90.

[25] *PL* IV. 46–57.

This is a loveless pagan cabined in the language of payment and reward. The jingle of money (afford, recompense, pay, due, debt, paying, owe, received, owing, owes, pays, indebted) dominates all areas of experience.[26] At the end of this extract Satan tries to describe how he lacked a loving obligation to the being who gave him his life; but this sense of indebtedness is not translated into any language beyond that of mechanically exact debt and requital. He

> understood not that a grateful mind
> By owing owes not, but still pays, at once
> Indebted and discharged...[27]

This ought to be a description of love, or at least the realization that an obligation to one who loves you is not an obligation if they know that you feel it in the right way. But, just at the moment when Satan is trying to transcend the idea of ignominious financial obligation, he reverts to the language of debt—though 'redeem', the word that marks the intersection between 'buying back' and God's deliverance of man, is, pointedly, one of the few financial terms which he does not use. The effect is of a mind stuck in a groove, able to see what it lacks, but unable to find a language to express it. This Satan is reaching out to the emotion which *The Faerie Queene* labours to construct: a grateful love independent of servitude. Guyon says to Arthur when rescued at II. viii. 55–6 from Pyrochles:

> What may suffise, to be for meede repayd
> Of so great graces, as ye haue me shewd,
> But to be euer bound

This first phase of his relation to his saviour is a political tie which invites expression in economic terms ('meede repayd'). But Arthur interrupts him, and rebuts the idea that a giver must be bound to receive reward for his gift:

> what need
> Good turnes be counted, as a seruile bond,
> To bind their doers, to receiue their meede?

When Spenser is least congested by the need to accommodate the violences of history he represents mercy as no more than a phase in the development of a mutual love which renounces all bonds. The Satan on Mount Niphates, however, is stuck, like Pyrochles, in an archaic mental system that regards being saved or raised up as an obligation which creates

---

[26] See Hunter, *Paradise Lost*, 80.

[27] There might be an avaricious trace of Macbeth's disingenuous protestation to Duncan here: 'The service and the loyalty I owe, | In doing, pays itself', *Macbeth*, I. iv. 21.

grounds for disdain, resistance, and rebellion. Pyrochles, 'subiect to the victours law' is inwardly gnawed by 'vile disdaine and rancour': Satan, raised up by God, shares the language of pagan villains in the romance tradition. Like them, his response to subjection is *sdegno*. Like them, he cannot reach the idea which Spenser failingly sought throughout *The Faerie Queene*: that love even between unequal people need not grind the inferior down.

The disdainful paralysis charted in this soliloquy would be the natural point for Milton to begin thinking about Satan, since many of his contemporary epic writers were identifying the Devil with pagan irascibility and disdain. But Milton is remarkable in that, after a brief period when he thought he might begin a play with this sort of Satan, he then put this disdainful, self-reproaching creature towards the middle of his epic. The soliloquy from Book IV as it is now placed has often struck critics as a turning-point in Satan: as Empson notes, it is the first moment that he recognizes that God is omnipotent and so decides that all he can do is be really good at being bad.[28] For a reader who works through the plot as it now stands, the soliloquy marks the moment when something simply Satanic, adversarial, emerges from the chaos of Satan's earlier miscellany of actions.

In creating Satan, Milton thought himself behind the pre-formed idiom of the Cambridge Satanists, and sought to give his hero a prehistory full of options, alternatives, and confusions, before his final hardening into a disdainful rejection of loving gratitude. There are signs that, as the plans for what became *Paradise Lost* grew, so did Milton's ambitions to cover the whole of time. This does not (or does not only) indicate that Milton had a madly ambitious urge to write the ultimate epic, which would compress all time into itself; it testifies to a restless and immensely powerful desire to think himself into a time *before* good and evil, in which the one could grow from the other, or even be, for a brief, fragile moment, seen as the other. The poem in the form we have it traces Satan's story right back to the first moment of his rebellion, when wickedness began. There is little sign that Milton attempted anything so ambitious in his early meditations on plays on the Fall, in which, as far as one can tell, Satan was intended to be simply Satanic right from the start. The final draft tragedy in the Trinity Manuscript (called *Adam Unparadiz'd*) does, however, open out some room for a pre-Satanic past for its irascible hero, and simultaneously with this development something energetic twitches into life:

[28] See William Empson, *Milton's God* (London, 1965), 64: 'he has become an entirely new character'. See also Barbara Kiefer Lewalski, *Paradise Lost and the Rhetoric of Literary Forms* (Princeton, NJ, 1985), 99–101.

Lucifer appeares after his overthrow, bemoans himself, seeks revenge on man
the Chorus prepare resistance at his first approach at last after discourse of
enmity on either side he departs wherat the chorus sings of the battell, & victorie
in heavn against him & his accomplices.[29]

Satan almost starts a fight in the present, but then scuttles off to leave
the chorus to continue the battle in the displaced form of a narrative
about his past. As *Paradise Lost* grew, Satan acquired at once more past
and more energy; and the poem in its final form takes this dynamic as
far as it could go: it recedes right back to the nodal moment when the
disdainful hostility of Satan first began to emerge, when a good angel
began to become a devil.

The first event in the chronological range covered by *Paradise Lost* is
God's elevation of the Son. This is the moment which prompts Satan's
rebellion, and which marks the origin of both wickedness and history.
Milton's decision to pursue Satan's story back to this point of origin was
remarkable, and the moment he created to explain the origin of evil
required enormous imaginative power. It required him to think about
how goodness might cease to be good; but it also, at a more mundane
level, required him to invent a near-canonical fiction. The fall of Lucifer
is one of the most mysterious events in Christian history: the Bible says
that he fell, but does not tell how, or clearly relate why. Theologians have
tried to fill in the gap with speculation, but it is hard to find any who
anticipated Milton in making God's decision to elevate his Son to the
rank of King the original cause of all our woe.[30] And, as though guilty
about his fiction, Milton buried it deep in the inset narrative of Raphael
to Adam in Book V.[31] Raphael's inset story of the origins of Satan has
something of the creative danger which frequently accompanies the
narrative form of a flashback in earlier epic: it presents a shocking

---

[29] John Milton, *Poems Reproduced in Facsimile from the Manuscript in Trinity College Cambridge*
(Menston/Ilkley, Yorks., 1970), 38.

[30] 'Some murmur because the scripture does not in various passages give a distinct and regular
exposition of Satan's fall, its cause, mode, date, and nature. But as these thing are of no consequence
to us, it was better, if not entirely to pass them in silence, at least only to touch lightly upon them.'
Calvin, *The Institutes of Christian Religion*, trans. H. Beveridge, 2 vols. (London, 1957), i. 52.
Augustine says that 'With the proud disdain of a tyrant [Satan] chose to rejoice over his subjects
rather than to be a subject himself; and so he fell from the spiritual paradise', *City of God* 14. 11;
cf. 11. 13, 12. 1. This offers no specific moment from which to date, and by means of which to
narrate, the start of wickedness. Hieronimus Zanchius approvingly cites the view that, soon after the
creation, God anounced his intention of incarnating his Son in Man and thereby elevating Man to a
state above the Angels. This prompted the angelic rebellion. Hieronimus Zanchius, *Operum Theo-
logicorum Tomus*, 8 vols. (Geneva, 1613), iii. *De Operibus Dei*, iv. 2, pp. 169–72. Milton separates the
elevation of the Son from the proclamation that he will be incarnated. This is presumably to avoid
the apparent perversity of a God who causes the fall of the angels by creating the means to reverse
the effects of the Fall of man. See also C. A. Patrides, *Milton and the Christian Tradition* (Oxford,
1966), 91–120, for a survey of contemporary opinion.

[31] See O. B. Hardison, jun., '*In Medias Res in Paradise Lost*', *Milton Studies*, 17 (1983), 27–41.

theological novelty, a moment when good angels are on the verge of becoming bad, and when Milton is of necessity inventing theological events. The pivotal moment occurs when God says:

> Hear all ye angels, progeny of light,
> Thrones, dominations, princedoms, virtues, powers,
> Hear my decree, which unrevoked shall stand.
> This day I have begot whom I declare
> My only Son, and on this holy hill
> Him have anointed, whom ye now behold
> At my right hand; your head I him appoint;
> And by my self have sworn to him shall bow
> All knees in heaven, and shall confess him Lord:
> Under his great vicegerent reign abide
> United as one individual soul
> For ever happy: him who disobeys
> Me disobeys, breaks union, and that day
> Cast out from God and blessed vision, falls
> Into utter darkness, deep engulfed, his place
> Ordained without redemption, without end.[32]

This God asserts power, and offers no equable, loving parity with his creations. He almost creates resentful disdain by a naked assertion of authority: he *orders* his angels to 'abide...For ever happy' (can even angels be *commanded* to be happy?), and emphasizes (for no immediately apparent reason) his solitary authority in 'And *by my self* have sworn to him shall bow | All knees in heaven'. This makes it rather unnecessarily clear that those who will be doing the bowing have no part in the decision to bow. He ends his proud baptismal speech with what is the first mention of hell in the chronological sequence of *Paradise Lost*. It is a speech which invites either utter obedience or rebellion.[33] And one could read it as profoundly nepotistic. It might sound as though God is begetting his Son, elevating him to vicegerency simply because he is his Son, and then ordering his subjects to obey this jumped-up babe. Critics have laboured hard to save Milton from the charge that he is heretically representing a moment when God decrees the existence of the Son here, and regularly note that 'begot' is the term used by Milton to describe the elevation of

---

[32] *PL* v. 600–15.

[33] See Empson, *Milton's God*, 103. Cf. David Quint, *Origin and Originality in Renaissance Literature: Versions of the Source* (New Haven, Conn., and London, 1983), 208: 'For Satan, the proclamation of the Son is merely God's self-authorizing fiction.'

the Son to kingly status in Psalm 2.[34] But one would hardly expect a theological fiction about the aetiology of evil to be contentedly orthodox. And even if the event represented in this original moment is regarded as being purely the elevation of the Son to some sort of quasi-regal status, rather than his creation, Milton is still not quite orthodox. The elevation of the Son is usually thought to have occurred after the crucifixion, rather than before the Fall.[35] All but the erudite or orthodox might have some grounds to assume from God's language that we are witnessing the moment when he decrees the existence of the Son, and arbitrarily decides to elect him king. This God speaks in the same key as Homer's Agamemnon when he insists on seizing Briseis: he asserts an apparent injustice as a means of expressing authority.

But God's speech does not only allude to the rigours of Psalm 2. The other biblical allusions from which it grows would provide a well-read and faithful audience with faint indications that this moment which prompts the emergence of evil, for all its apparent arbitrariness, heralds something loving. The autocratic phrase 'By my self have sworn' alludes to the moment when God blesses Abraham for offering to sacrifice his son Isaac:[36] '*By myself have I sworn*, saith the LORD, for because thou hast done this thing, and hast not withheld thy son, thine only son: That in blessing I will bless thee.' *This* is not autocratic. The allusion to Jewish

---

[34] This has been much debated. Psalm 2: (*AV*): 6–7 'Yet have I set my king upon my holy hill of Zion. I will declare the decree: the LORD hath said unto me, Thou art my Son; this day have I begotten thee.' In the *De Doctrina* Milton glosses 'this day I have begotten thee', as meaning 'this day I have made you king', which takes account of the context in the Psalm. So, according to Fowler, the passage contains 'no obtrusive evidence' of Milton's Arianism (the heretical belief that the Son was generated by the Father, rather than being consubstantial and coeternal with him). Rather, it shows God making his Son King. This is a pleasingly antiseptic view of the passage, but it squashes the juice out of it: why should God use that awkward word 'begot'? See Arthur Sewell, *A Study in Milton's Christian Doctrine* (Oxford, 1939), 90, for a more literal (indeed over-literal) reading of the passage. See also Hugh MacCallum, *Milton and the Sons of God: The Divine Image in Milton's Epic Poetry* (Toronto, Buffalo, and London, 1986), 79–87; Gordon Campbell, 'The Son of God in *De Doctrina Christiana* and *Paradise Lost*', *Modern Language Review*, 75 (1980), 507–14. On Milton's Arianism, see William B. Hunter *et al.*, *Bright Essence: Studies in Milton's Theology* (Salt Lake City, 1971), 29–70. William B. Hunter, 'Milton on the Exaltation of the Son: The War in Heaven and *Paradise Lost*', *ELH* 36 (1969), 215–31, labours hard to save Milton from Arianism, so hard that the war in heaven becomes a vast metaphor for the resurrection. For a recent and powerful argument that Milton was an Arian in the *De Doctrina*, see M. Bauman, *Milton's Arianism* (New York and Berne, 1987), reviewed by Roy Flannagan, *Milton Quarterly*, 21 (1987), 113–17.

[35] See Marvin P. Hoogland, *Calvin's Perspective on the Elevation of Christ* (Amsterdam, 1966). Fowler tries to evade this difficulty by saying, 'Milton believed events in eternity to have sequence but no measure'. This is a gloss on 'There is certainly no reason why we should conform to the popular belief that motion and time, which is the measure of motion, could not, according to our concepts of "before" and "after", have existed before this world was made', *De Doct.*, *CPW* vi. 313–14. I am not sure how this explains away Milton's anachrony, since it shows precisely that he thought sequence possible before time.

[36] Genesis 22: 16–17. Fowler cites Gen. 22: 16 'By myself have I sworn, saith the Lord', without quoting the rest of the verse.

history obliquely mollifies God's harsh words by reminding the reader of Abraham's sacrifice, an Old Testament story which was often read as a typological anticipation of the New: the ram who is miraculously provided as surrogate Isaac is a type of Christ. The prospect of divine mercy, a love which sacrifices itself and then blesses the beneficiary of its sacrifice, is, though, no more than a faint allusion. The angels who make up God's audience could scarcely be expected to spot it. The Bible is not yet written, and divine history has not yet begun. An angel in the back row, who had not read the Bible and who was not too well up in divine hierarchies, could assume, if, like Satan, he were not prepared to trust God, that this is an act of monumentally assertive nepotism.

Only Abdiel, the zealous angel who refuses to rebel with Satan, looks beyond the apparent autocracy of the elevation to a higher, more genial purpose. Only he catches the faint suggestion of perfect fusion between angels and their creator, which lies in God's phrase 'United as one individual soul':

> Yet by experience taught we know how good,
> And of our good, and of our dignity
> How provident he is, how far from thought
> To make us less, bent rather to exalt
> Our happy state under one head more near
> United.[37]

This is a distant, tentatively worded anticipation of the incarnation: God elevates his Son to Godhead in order to raise his angels towards his level. 'Under one head more near | United' implies both that the Son is a sort of superangel elected from the ranks, a head 'more near' than God, and that the angels will themselves be 'more near united' with each other under him. We hear beneath the language of political unity the sympathetic proximity between creator and creation which is brought about by incarnation, by a creator lowering himself into the nature of his creation. This intimates the eventual emergence of a form of romance sympathy more elevated than any encountered before in the history of epic, in which a multitude of different beings blend to become one individual force, through the voluntary self-humiliation of their creator. Such a form of sympathetic authority, in which a power chooses to take on the condition of an inferior, would effectively stun the rebellious urges of a Satan, and could purge sympathetic love of its contamination with power and servitude: it would establish a substantial identity between ruler and ruled, which could ultimately create a kind of power-free love: all choose to be the same, all choose lovingly to be one. And that identity between

[37] *PL* v. 826–31.

ruler and ruled would depend upon the superior's lowering himself to
the level of the inferior. The elevation of the Son, on Abdiel's reading, is
not an act of power, but an act of self-humiliation.

Readers of the poem are biased towards Abdiel's view of the elevation,
both by what they might know of the Bible, and by what they have
already seen of God in *Paradise Lost*. The elevation of the Son in Book
V should inspire a sense of *déjà vu*, since we have in a sense already
experienced it. Milton provides two closely related but carefully distinct
versions of the moment when God makes the Son his vicegerent. This
pairing creates a carefully engineered overlap of responses, which yokes
together a sneaking sense of arbitrary injustice with an underlying
impression that God means to be more benign than he appears to the
lovelessly combative Satan.[38] Earlier in the poem, though later in time,
the Son offers to die for man and is elevated by his Father:

> So heavenly love shall outdo hellish hate
> Giving to death, and dying to redeem,
> So dearly to redeem what hellish hate
> So easily destroyed, and still destroys
> In those who, when they may, accept not grace.
> Nor shalt thou by descending to assume
> Man's nature, lessen or degrade thine own.
> Because thou hast, though throned in highest bliss
> Equal to God, and equally enjoying
> Godlike fruition, quitted all to save
> A world from utter loss, and hast been found
> By merit more than birthright Son of God,
> Found worthiest to be so by being good,
> Far more than great or high; because in thee
> Love hath abounded more than glory abounds,
> Therefore thy humiliation shall exalt
> With thee thy manhood also to this throne,
> Here shalt thou sit incarnate, here shalt reign
> Both God and man, Son both of God and man,
> Anointed universal king, all power
> I give thee, reign for ever, and assume
> Thy merits; under thee as head supreme
> Thrones, princedoms, powers, dominions I reduce.[39]

[38] On the connections between the two episodes, see Edmund Creeth, 'The "Begetting" and the
Exaltation of the Son', *Modern Language Notes*, 76 (1961), 696–700; Dennis Richard Danielson,
Milton's Good God: A Study in Literary Theodicy (Cambridge, 1982), 219–24.
[39] *PL* III. 298–320.

Even Empson recognizes that this is God's best moment.[40] It shows Abdiel's kind of God, who humiliates himself in order to exalt the condition of his creations to a higher state. 'Redeem', the word which stuck in Satan's throat on Mount Niphates, here eradicates any trace of moneyish dealings: it is hard to feel a bottom line rising through words like 'dearly' or 'loss', words which Satan would taint with gilt. The passage lovingly transfigures the apparent arbitrariness of God's earlier speech, and shows that Abdiel was right to suspect some higher, sympathetic purpose in the elevation of the Son. We read this speech first in Book III, and so hear its cadences behind the account of the elevation in Book V. This strong relation between the two speeches—between the apparent arbitrariness of God's first words and the subsequent revelation that they portended grace—has both significant theological overtones and a powerful relation to the literary idiom with and against which Milton worked.

To take the theological overtones first, in the *De Doctrina* Milton tended towards the Arminian belief that God does not predestine his Elect in a purely arbitrary fashion, but offers grace to all those who will believe in him; he then uses his foreknowledge to determine whether each person would choose to be faithful. He accordingly saves or damns people for their future free choice of faith or otherwise, rather than freely and arbitrarily electing or condemning people as an expression of the absolute power of his decrees.[41] God's choice of his Elect from eternity may look arbitrary, but in Milton's form of Arminianism it does eventually turn out to be justly related to their faith. God's earlier and apparently arbitrary decree that the Son should become King is given a similar retrospective justification.[42] The election of the Son was founded on his extraordinary future merit. This merit was foreknown both by God, and, through the disruption of 'real' time sequence, the readers of the poem. We see God's reasons for the elevation before his arbitrary act. We see sympathy and meritocracy before arbitrary election. And, unless we are Empson, or have the misfortune to be Satan, we get the story in a shape which makes God's actions intelligible: when we come to read the origin of Satan's rebellion in Book V, God's apparently arbitrary elevation of the Son is overlaid with the genial sympathy which causes the elevation in Book III, a genial sympathy fused with a respect for merit. God seems, by this

---

[40] Empson, *Milton's God*, 137. This is surely Empson's worst moment, since if one is prepared to acknowledge a modicum of goodness in God when he foretells the incarnation, then one has accepted that the main point of a Christian God is a good one.

[41] On Milton's Arminianism, see Danielson, *Milton's Good God*, 58–91.

[42] Maurice Kelley, *This Great Argument: A Study of Milton's 'De Doctrina' as a Gloss on 'Paradise Lost'* (Princeton, NJ, 1941), 19, makes this point in a way too crude to be true: '*Paradise Lost* expresses the Arminian dogma of the *De Doctrina* ...' See further *CPW* vi. 74–86.

manipulation of time sequence, justified in his earlier elevation of the Son.

God's concern with the Son's merit points to the wider literary dimension of this speech. It is vitally connected with the ambitions and endeavours of earlier English epic romances. *The Faerie Queene* labours to weld love and honour into a single force, and to find an arena before the main human narrative in which to fuse together the apparently distinct concepts of justice and mercy, in order to elide them in some higher form of being. The originating moment of Satan's story is driven by a similar urge to bring about the coalescence of sympathy with the strict apportionment of due rewards in an area that marks the beginning of time. God's insistence that the Son *deserves* to be the Son is a radical extension of the classical republicanism which had such a vital formative influence on the nature of the English epic tradition, and from which Milton enthusiastically recorded extracts in his *Commonplace Book*.[43] Elections to office, even to the office of Universal King, should be founded on merit more than birthright. But here merit does not consist in power or aggressive *virtus*, being 'great or high': it consists in a love sufficient to take on the nature of another being. The extraordinary swaying line 'Love hath abounded more than glory abounds' holds in its rocking movement not a simple, Drydenesque, opposition between Love and Glory, but a new imbalanced coalescence between the two. The words which have to be stressed when reading the line (as in the biblical passage from which Milton probably caught the cadence[44]) are 'abounded... abounds'. The passions, love, and (especially) glory, the stuff of a neoclassical antithesis, are necessarily swallowed. The Son's glory and his merit—terms which are traditionally associated with a pagan system of just apportionment of rewards to virtue—consist in his loving willingness to forgo his own nature, and sympathetically to take on the nature of another.

The chronological origin of Satan is a moment which collapses together the simple antitheses of love and glory. But it does not offer a permanent

---

[43] e.g *CPW* i. 421, quoting Machiavelli: 'A commonwealth is preferable to a monarchy: "... because in the former virtue is honoured most of the time and is not feared as in the kingdom".' Ibid. 433–4: 'It is best, if a King expects to entrust his kingdom to his son after him, that he should so appoint his son that he will believe that his father establishes the succession of the realm, not on the basis of his coming of age, but on the basis of his deserts, and that he is to receive his father's authority, not as inherited spoils, but as the reward of worth.' This passage continues in a way that makes God's elevation of the Son seem by human standards impolitic: 'therefore, that the king should rather decide in his own mind and in secret than publicly proclaim whom he expects to leave as an heir to the realm, and leave the succession, as it were, in doubt'. See further the illuminating but scrappy essay by Merritt Y. Hughes, 'Merit in *Paradise Lost*', *HLQ* 31 (1967), 3–18.

[44] Romans 5: 20: 'Moreover the law entered, that the offence might abound. But where sin abounded, grace did much more abound.'

fusion of disparate notions in some private, secluded, Spenserian place of impersonal myths. The elevation of the Son creates a coincidence of apparently antagonistic ideas which not everyone is equipped to understand fully, and which not everyone wants to understand. The entire action of *Paradise Lost* begins with a question of interpretation: is the elevation of the Son, like Agamemnon's theft of Briseis, an act of arbitrary tyranny? Or is it the first, faltering step by an unimaginably distant and completely just creator to move closer to his creations, and thereby to fuse justice into a kind of sympathy so complete that it involves the judge's taking on the nature of those he judges? Milton constructs an origin of wickedness which is both these things at once. We are made to see both versions of the episode, both the apparent injustice and the latent mercy fused with merit. The historical origins of Satan in *Paradise Lost* are entangled in a much wider literary project: an effort to create an idiom in which love and honour, justice and mercy, pagan and Christian modes of perceiving overlap, and blend ambiguously into one another.

THE ROMANCE OF HELL

These are, of course, the beginnings of Satan only in rather a specialized sense. But his first actions in the narrative sequence of the poem also show Milton's desire to transcend rigid oppositions between passions, and with them the inhibiting idiom of modern epic. Satan's emergence from hell is extremely unlikely to have been conceived until after Milton had given up the idea of writing a play, since it would have taxed the most sophisticated stage to represent flaming marl, darkness visible, or the shapeless shape of Death. Hell—with the repeated anticipations of Eve which cling to Sin, and the shadowy traces of the Trinity which lurk in Satan, Sin, and Death—is designed to seem strangely familiar, a secondary world which we have the misfortune to see before its original, a world driven by the nervous energy of tired repetition. Hell is a secondary world playing at being primary, a sort of prequel to heaven, created after it, but coming before it. And Satan's journey from hell is a version of a romance narrative, a toil to reach an elusive goal, which it is tempting to identify with the miscellaneous but purposive wanderings of the *Odyssey* or the *Aeneid*.[45] His story has all the episodic delays and entanglements of his prototypes: fascinating women, magical creatures, battles, and desires all stand in the way of his purpose. But Satan's main problem is that he has no purpose, beyond some vaguely defined sense that he should do

---

[45] See Lewalski, *PL and Rhetoric*, 65–71.

something. Throughout his passage through hell, Satan is continually striving to acquire and act on the kind of coherent motive which seems to have begun to emerge by the time he delivers the soliloquy with which he opens Book IV, in which he disdainfully proclaims evil to be his good. But, throughout the early stages of his quest, he is a creature of potentialities, of ruptures in motive, and of raw incoherences. He crawls, sinks, swims, and flails his way through Chaos as though he is neither flesh nor fowl, and, from his first moments in the poem, he is a creature of a splendidly unfixed essence, who occupies a space before the constraining categories of good and evil, passion or motive. At the end of Book I he first formulates the plan to assail earth and man in a speech which is vehement in impetus, but fuzzy in detail. He does not know what he wants from earth, but war he does want:

> Thither [earth], if but to pry, shall be perhaps
> Our first eruption, thither or elsewhere:
> For this infernal pit shall never hold
> Celestial spirits in bondage, nor the abyss
> Long under darkness cover. But these thoughts
> Full counsel must mature: peace is despaired,
> For who can think submission? War then, war
> Open or understood must be resolved.
>   He spake: and to confirm his words, out flew
> Millions of flaming swords, drawn from the thighs
> Of mighty cherubim; the sudden blaze
> Far round illumined hell; highly they raged
> Against the highest, and fierce with grasped arms
> Clashed on their sounding shields the din of war,
> Hurling defiance toward the vault of heaven.[46]

The cumulative frenzy of war presented here—swords fly, then blaze, then crash on shields—creates powerful expectations. The next paragraph ought to begin with a description, say, of loins being girded for a new assault on heaven, or at the very least with a council of war. Nothing prepares for the way it does begin:

> There stood a hill not far whose grisly top
> Belched fire and rolling smoke; the rest entire
> Shone with a glossy scurf, undoubted sign
> That in his womb was hid metallic ore,
> The work of sulphur.[47]

This could initially be taken as some species of simile. The mountain spews smoke, and, like the devils, threatens eruption (a word Satan uses

---

[46] *PL* I. 655–69.   [47] *PL* I. 670–4.

to describe their proposed escape from hell a few lines before). But with the mention of ore the hill begins to look like a source for the raw materials of war, from which the fallen angels could multiply their 'millions of flaming swords' to billions. What no one could expect is that these frenzied warriors are going to build themselves a tiny model of a palace by means of a diabolical precursor of injection moulding. The building of Pandemonium is conspicuously unnecessary: all Homeric and Virgilian heroes manage to hold perfectly good councils without having to build palaces in which to stage them.[48] And the construction work— which appears spontaneous, unplanned, and universal among the devils— cuts off the anticipated movement from fury to war. It is a conspicuously unnecessary ornamental disruption of rage, which is deliberately made to feel like a late addition, an unnecessary interpolation by a baroque editor which falls between wrath and action, disrupting the narrative flow.

It establishes, however, the main characteristic of Satan's Odyssey: whenever it seems to be acquiring a motive, a mischievously digressive narrator chops off his story and intersperses it with unseasonable trans- itions. Spenser uses the romance technique of abruptly terminating stories before their natural endings in order to break the hold of Ariosto's passionate pity over the narrative form. In Milton's hell these digressions and hiatuses in the narrative sequence tend to occur whenever it looks as though Satan and his crew are winding themselves up into a state of clearly formed motive passion—and in particular whenever it appears that they are about to act through martial rage.[49] Spenser also often used anger to disrupt the unfolding of romance tales from pathetic episodes, when Arthur, say, with a blaze of rage, overcomes an appeal for pity. *Paradise Lost* sets about fragmenting the motive power of anger, by indulging in sudden shifts of scene or subject which are as redolent with suggestion as the jolts and sudden transitions of Homeric narrative.

The first interruption of Satan's irascible urges, the Great Consult, has often been regarded as having Homeric overtones. It descends ultimately from the Council of the Greeks in Book 2 of the *Iliad*, in which Aga- memnon tricksily tests the resolve of his forces by pretending he wants to go home. But it also has faint, though highly suggestive, structural reminiscences of the later consult in *Iliad* 9 and 10 when the Greeks, like the fallen angels, are at their most desperate.[50] In Book 9, Agamemnon

---

[48] Aeneas does pause with Dido to build palaces, but the precedent is not auspicious, since this is a digression explicitly contrary to divine wishes. See also Mason Hammond, '*Concilia Deorum* from Homer through Milton', *Studies in Philology*, 30 (1933), 1–16.

[49] See Martindale, *Milton and Ancient Epic*, 99–100.

[50] Lewalski, *PL and Rhetoric*, 86, and Blessington, *PL and Classical Epic*, 1–2, relate it to the Council in *Iliad* 2. 50–397. Martindale, *Milton and Ancient Epic*, 53–106, argues strongly that Homer

despairingly calls a nocturnal council (and he summons it, like Satan, with tears and sighs[51]), in which the Greeks eventually decide to send out Ulysses and Diomedes on an ill-defined mission either to spy on the Trojans or to pick off a few stragglers. This is answered by a Trojan Council (as the diabolic consult is answered by the heavenly council in Book III) in which the scout Dolon is sent out on a similarly vague mission. This faint reminiscence holds up fascinating possibilities for the relations of *Paradise Lost* to the romance tradition. *Iliad* 10, often called the 'Doloneia', is the most futile and entirely digressive episode in the poem. It has been regarded since the scholiast as a post-Homeric interpolation, since it is entirely separable from the rest of the poem in narrative content, and describes a gory, macabre, and twilit battlefield which has little in common with the rest of the poem in style. The scholiast's doubts about the authenticity of the episode were available to the learned from the 1520s.[52] But whether spurious or simply digressive, the 'Doloneia' has a huge history, which much of this book has explored: Nisus and Euryalus, Cloridano and Medoro, Timias and Belphoebe are all romance shades of Ulysses and Diomedes. The 'Doloneia' is *the* original of many of the epic romance interludes discussed in this book: it is the chaos, void of motive, which subsequent writers attempted to assimilate into the ethos of their poems. The faint but formative glow of this crepuscular episode in the darkness visible of Milton's hell illuminates the structural and imitative significance of the consult, and of its surrounding action: this is at once a primary epic and a spurious digression, a pseudo-quest, a purposeless twilit interlude. Satan goes on a goalless, motiveless, pseudo-Homeric quest neither to return home, like Odysseus, nor to found an empire like Aeneas, but to go and, well, scout around and mess things up a bit.

The original Homeric outlines of the nocturnal meeting of the Greeks are almost entirely lost under the sumptuously modern ornamentation of the Great Consult, which overlays the sparseness of Homer with layers of rich and entirely unnecessary colour. The closest analogues for these accidental embellishments in Western epic occur in a poem remarkable for its *bad*, spuriously imperial modernity. In the first Book of Giangiorgio Trissino's *Italia liberata da Gotthi*, the Christian Emperor Giustiniano is

---

is of more importance to Milton than had previously been recognized, but on p. 5 remarks only that 'such councils are a conventional feature of epic'. On which, see Douglas Bush, 'Virgil and Milton', *Classical Journal*, 47 (1952), 178–82.

[51] *PL* I. 619–21; *Il.* 9. 13–15.

[52] See *Interpretationes et antiquae, et perquam utiles in Homeri Iliada, nec non in Odyssea*, ed. F. Asulanus (Venice, 1521). The 'Doloneia' is one of the episodes which L. Küstero, loc. cit. n. 24 above, singles out in his discussion of the episodic structure of the *Iliad*.

inspired by a divine dream to seek to regain Italy from the Goths. He calls a council to ratify his Christian imperialism, at which he is placed high on a throne of royal state in the middle of a sumptuously opulent chamber:

> E sopra lei pendeva un'alta ombrella
> D'oro, ed di grosse perle adorna ...[53]

Above him hung a high canopy [*ombrella*] of gold, studded with fat pearls ...

This detail is mischievously picked up in Milton's

> Or where the gorgeous East with richest hand
> Showers on her kings barbaric pearl and gold.[54]

Giustiniano's protective canopy of pearl and gold becomes a shower which pours down on his antitype (and eventually it metamorphoses into the shower of grains which Pope's Public pours on her Curlls in the *Dunciad*). Milton's Satan, like Trissino's Emperor, speaks first at the Council to justify his supremacy as both a divinely chosen and a deserving ruler. Both leaders seek 'to claim our just inheritance of old', to regain a lost land which they consider their right, and both are answered at length by four counsellors. Trissino's first speaker has something of the trick of Belial to him:

> Io non dirò, che 'l far la guerra a i Gotthi
> Non é cosa cortese, e manco è giusta,
> Ma che fia piena d'infiniti mali.

I am not suggesting that the war with the Goths is not a courteous action, nor that it is not just, but that it would be full of infinite evils.

This is not quite the contorted cowardliness of 'I should be much for open war, O peers ...', but it is a stage on the way there, a preliminary genuflection which could be transformed by a vehement antagonist of empire into a stream of grovelling qualifications.

By placing such a protracted ornamental consult between the devils' anger and their action, Milton makes a sly sideswipe at Trissino's wandering, incompetent, ceaselessly and pointlessly elaborative romance. But he also directs a powerful buffet against the politics of modern, decadently digressive forms: the only practical consequences of the

---

[53] For the council scene, see *La Italia liberata da Gotthi* (Rome, 1547), fols. 5ᵃ–15ᵇ; passages cited are on fols. 6ᵃ; 8ᵃ. As it was a familiar whipping-boy in literary theory of the period, Milton would certainly have known the *Italia liberata*; and as one of the worst and also the most imperialist epics of the sixteenth century, it would be surprising if he did not despise it. See e.g. Tasso, *Discourses on the Heroic Poem*, ed. and trans. Mariella Cavalchini and Irene Samuel (Oxford, 1973), 52, 55; Tasso describes him as 'dead to the light', 66.

[54] *PL* II. 3–4.

building of Pandemonium are to dissipate the devils' martial energies, and *silently* to confirm Satan's *de facto* supremacy. While the devils smelt, Satan becomes their ruler. The ability of romances to change the subject at a crucial moment becomes the object of considerable suspicion. And so does the unitary purpose imposed on the epic plot by single, imperial heroes such as Trissino's Emperor Giustiniano. The council scene in *Italia liberata* lays vestigial conflicts of character over dull inevitability: the last two speakers both support their divinely favoured Emperor, who will inevitably have his way, council or no council. In *Paradise Lost*, however, the consult does not blandly accumulate the support of Satan's minions for his plans: it re-enacts the nosedive of martial energies which led to the construction of Pandemonium. Moloch cries for war, continuing the impetus which led to the construction of the palace; but this impetus is progressively deadened, first through the tricksy Belial, and then by Mammon's wish to spend eternity in constructing an opulent parody of heaven. The consult moves away from the war which their Emperor wishes on the devils towards endless, pointless replication of Pandemoniums, the breeding of digression from sumptuous imperial digression. It is only Beelzebub who, like a good committee man, reminds the devils of the martial impetus which, 600 lines before, had led to the building of Pandemonium and to the consult. He belatedly imposes Satan's wishes on a council which is ostentatiously *not* ratifying the will of its Emperor as Trissino's zombie-like nodders had done. When the building is over and the digressive impulses of the consult are finally concluded, its decision is substantially the one Satan propounded about 650 lines before.

After 650 lines of unnecessary epic business, a prolonged architectural diversion from the purpose of the story, which has only succeeded in making an Emperor out of a military ruler, Satan sets off on a vaguely defined mission to earth. And war? Well, that has been forgotten. This is a romance without motivating love, in which blusters of motivating rage issue in nothing but the distracting ornaments of romance poems, and in which unifying motives are established by trickery rather than passion or imperial designs.

Some of the devils, after the consult, aimlessly vent their martial energies in rending up trees; others wander off in mazes intricate, the familiar spaces of romance, now rendered metaphorical and attenuated into speculation:

> Others apart sat on a hill retired,
> In thoughts more elevate, and reasoned high
> Of providence, foreknowledge, will and fate,

Fixed fate, free will, foreknowledge absolute,
And found no end, in wandering mazes lost.[55]

Satan, meanwhile, sets out on a more literal form of wandering, in which
hell continues to spawn an unsavoury composite of the raw Homeric
elements of romance narrative, spiced with a rank flavour of the wearily
modern. The first episode in his objectless quest to earth occurs when he
nearly fights Death at hell's gate. Deeds of potentially epic violence are
once more on the edge of occurring, as Satan flares up to an enormous
confrontation:

> and now great deeds
> Had been achieved, whereof all hell had rung...[56]

But Satan is again saved from the sweat of battle by an untimely
interruption, as Sin rises up and cries

> O Father, what intends thy hand, she cried,
> Against thy only son?

Then she goes on to describe her parentage and incestuous birth-pangs.
Sin, spawned of Errour in *The Faerie Queene* Book I, is the most
wearisomely derivative figure in *Paradise Lost*. And she pushes Satan's
story into a shape which suggests both the furthest reaches of antiquity
and the most tired forms of narrative cliché. She breaks the flow of the
martial narrative, and makes it recoil away from war, towards an erotic
past:

> Thy self in me thy perfect image viewing
> Becamest enamoured, and such joy thou took'st
> With me in secret, that my womb conceived
> A growing burden ...
>
> . . . .
>
> ...Pensive here I sat
> Alone, but long I sat not, till my womb
> Pregnant by thee, and now excessive grown
> Prodigious motion felt and rueful throes.[57]

This is the oldest, most wearily sad story in the book, a story of rape and
violently painful metamorphosis. But Milton enfolds within a tired tale a
bewildering amalgam of potential motives. In epic romance, fights are
generally prevented by pity or love; in classical epic, a narrative about a
shared past might create a sense of kinship between two antagonists, such

---

[55] *PL* II. 557–61.
[56] Ibid. 722–3.
[57] Ibid. 764–80.

as Glaucus and Diomedes, which could make them stick their spears in
the ground rather than into each other. The fight between Satan and
Death is interrupted by a twisted form of this early epic predecessor of
romance sentiments. Underneath the interrupted battle lies another distant
trace of a Roman proto-romance sentiment, too: a family sympathy:

> O Father, what intends thy hand, she cried,
> Against thy only son?[58]

Sin's story establishes the grounds for a sympathetic tie between Satan
and Death which blends over into the *pietas* of the *Aeneid*—a term which
is forced towards 'pity' by the peculiar energy of Virgilian relations
between fathers and sons. The figure of Sin—who is at once the archaic
Scylla from the *Odyssey* and the modern Errour from *The Faerie Queene*—
splices together an unsavoury erotic parody of love with a form of *ur-*
romance sympathy. Hell—itself probably a belated beginning, at once
early and late in the design of *Paradise Lost*—is constructed by combining
the grotesque superficies of a romance narrative with an unstable under-
presence of antiquity. Neither part of the synthesis is ever seen simply
without the other. Prototype and distant descendant of romance blur
drunkenly together in a way that disables our sense of which comes first.
And no one motive—indeed no clear motive at all—is given to the hero
who interrupts his fight in order to hear a woman (of sorts) claim that he
is about to kill his son. Sin gives Satan a decently pious and heroic excuse
to stop fighting; but she ends on a less rarefied note by reminding her
father and husband—at once her creator who merits dutiful love, and
her romance lover—that he cannot possibly defeat Death. Milton is
judiciously silent about what leads Satan to abandon the battle:

> She finished, and the subtle fiend his lore
> Soon learned, now milder, and thus answered smooth.
> Dear Daughter, since thou claim'st me for thy sire,
> And my fair son here show'st me, the dear pledge
> Of dalliance had with thee in heaven . . .[59]

This splices a mass of possible motives together without allowing any to
predominate. Fear (or, to be charitable, prudence) must be there somewhere in the speed with which Satan learns his lore and abandons his
martial purpose. There could be a trace of romance sentiment for Sin
too, since Satan speciously conflates earlier epic *pietas* with language that
is suspiciously redolent of romance: 'dalliance' is what Redcrosse does
with Duessa. Although his story follows a romance contour—supplication

---

[58] *PL* II. 727–8. See p. 19 above.
[59] Ibid. 815–19.

leads to an ended fight—his motives probably do not. In the early stage
of his story, Satan is continually entangled between something which is
not quite a modern, pitiful heroism, and some dim archetype of classical
piety. He is a hero surrounded by a cloud of motive possibilities, which
blurs the neat distinctions initiated by Tasso between an irascible pagan
past and a pitiful Christian present. Satan operates in space before such
clear motive certainties, a space before the despairingly fixed categories
of emotion which underlay the soliloquy with which Milton began him.

Satan's poise between the new and old continues for a space after his
soliloquy at the start of Book IV, however, as he only gradually crystallizes
into something simply adversarial. In Eden his story reaches its most
frustrating stage: he teeters on the edge of some great assault, but never
moves from his desires or stated intentions to the corresponding deeds.
Throughout his wanderings through Eden, Satan enacts the frustrations
of a Ruggiero before an unattainable Angelica, whilst experiencing only
numbed versions of romance emotions. When he sees and does not assault
Adam and Eve he describes himself as pitiful, both in the subjective and
objective senses:

> yet no purposed foe
> To you whom I could pity thus forlorn
> Though I unpitied: league with you I seek,
> And mutual amity so strait, so close,
> That I with you must dwell, or you with me
> Henceforth ...[60]

Envy and sympathy are extraordinarily close to one another: the one
benignly sees kinship between sufferer and observer and says, 'I can see
myself in you'. Envy does not see but *seeks* kinship between the envier
and his object by trying to make the envied share the misery of the envier.
If envy is at all wholesome it is because both the envious person and the
sympathetic person are seeking to break down the solitude of experience,
that state of isolation in which there is an unbridgeable gap between your
mode of existence and someone else's. What makes envy nasty is that it
involves wrecking someone in order to make them as miserable as you.
But Milton could not have made Satan appear distractingly heroic if he
had not seen this kinship between the two emotions. It is a wholesome
form of envy, a mirror image of sympathy, which breaks through Satan's
sour adulation over Adam and Eve, and raises this speech above simple
sneering at his victims. His envy is heavily masked as a near-Homeric
form of sympathy which, like its ancestor, emerges through hospitality:
he wishes to share his state of being and his roof with them. He proceeds

[60] *PL* IV. 373–8.

in a vein which continues unsettlingly to evoke heroic sentiment in fragmented form:

> And should I at your harmless innocence
> Melt, as I do, yet public reason just,
> Honour and empire with revenge enlarged,
> By conquering this new world, compels me now
> To do what else though damned I should abhor.[61]

This speech derives from Renaissance writers' attempts to fill Aeneas's silent departure from Dido, and his silent hesitation over Turnus, with a conflict between pity and empire. Satan, however, masks and involutes this simple opposition of motives. He begins 'should I', avoiding the direct attribution of pity to himself, and, once his hypothetical pity has crystallized into a verb which is not in the conditional mood ('as I do'), he rapidly ousts this softer form of feeling for its traditional antagonists, 'public reason just' and 'honour'. These epic motives in turn rapidly collapse into 'empire with revenge enlarged'. Scattered fragments of epic romance language for describing mixed emotions cling to his actions, and drag him away from access to the ancestor of compassion.

And romance motives again appear to shape his story. A new Aeneas would pause over Adam and Eve and then, in a rush of imperial rigour, would stab them. But no such assault follows Satan's impotently gabbled imperial delay, despite his mendaciously sinew-stiffening 'compels me *now* | To do . . .'. Just as his story begins to crystallize into an imperial form, he sportively bounces off into another sub-Ovidian digression. Satan does not kill: he just metamorphoses himself a beast or two:

> as one who chose his ground
> Whence rushing he might surest seize them both
> Griped in each paw.[62]

This hypothetical pounce of martial assertiveness, like all the others in these opening books, falls flat, tripping over its conditional form. Satan does not spring at his enemies, but instead crawls around paradise until he ends up in a final ignominious metamorphosis: squat like a toad beside the ear of Eve.

Romances based on classical sources often begin to imitate a passage from one of their models and then break off to insert a variety of padding between the beginning of the episode and its end. This is usually to delay something violent or terminal which is alien to their idiom. This way of fragmenting classical epic is fundamental to epic romance, and runs right

---

[61] *PL* IV. 388–392.
[62] Ibid. 406–8.

through Ariosto, Tasso, and Spenser's poems; it is also fundamental to Satan's story. At the end of Book IV he is discovered squirting sedition into the ear of Eve by a squadron of angels. He begins once more the cumbersome preliminary limberings which had preceded his failed battle with Death, and is hemmed in with a volley of allusions to the final encounter between Aeneas and Turnus. These allusions consummate the pressure towards a martial, imperial encounter which has been building up throughout Book IV.

Or rather they fail to consummate it. When the toad-like Devil is assailed by the angelic squadron he once again prepares to fight with a volley of conditional verbs ('now dreadful deeds | *Might have* ensued . . .'). Then, like Turnus, he sees God's scales weighing his chances in the sky. Whereupon he flees from replicating his prototype:

> The fiend looked up and knew
> His mounted scale aloft: nor more; but fled
> Murmuring, and with him fled the shades of night.[63]

This description of Satan's bunk is an allusion to the death of Turnus, whose spirit 'fugit indignata sub umbras' (flees crossly to the shades), 'Murmuring' is a good version of 'indignata': this difficult epithet is uniformly understood in Renaissance translations of Turnus's last stand to mean 'disdainful' or 'indignant'. 'Murmuring' drifts under this impulse towards *OED* 2: 'To complain or repine in low muttered tones'.[64] But whether complaining or muttering, sadly for Satan, the enemy of the Roman Empire who flees with the shades of night is not Turnus nor, as he would wish, Adam and Eve. It is himself. He has changed sides, turned from a pausing Aeneas to a conquered Turnus in the 600 lines between his imperial delay over his human opponents and the end of Book IV—and all without a battle.

But Satan's story is a kind of romance, and romances characteristically spare their imperial victims. Satan does not die. He just flees. This structure, like the whole of his story, has the formal characteristics of a romance, since the villain is spared after a delay, and lives to continue the tale. But, again like the rest of Satan's story, it has none of the emotions which in earlier epic romances cause such continual deferment of an ending. The angelic forces do not pity him. Compassion has become a distant notion, which appears to have an influence on the shape of the narrative, but which, throughout the early Books of *Paradise Lost*, does not directly figure in the motives which shape it. These early Books are

---

[63] Ibid. 1013–15.
[64] Martindale argues that it shows the vocal Satan winded and wordless, *Milton and Ancient Epic*, 102. See p. 128 above, and *Aen.* 12. 952.

a kind of anti-romance, which is driven along by checked and frustrated battles, rather than by interrupted amours, and from which all but the dregs of motivating pity have been evacuated.

Milton's evacuation of motive from his romance plot is a vital part of the meaning of *Paradise Lost*. The reasons for it, and its significance, lie deep in the English tradition of epic. Elizabethan romance, stripped of its civic concern for meritocracy, provided an ethos for the imperial ambition of much later seventeenth-century proto-Augustan panegyric, in which the imperial associations of pity make it an instrument of praise. A King's clemency, his pitiful love of his subjects, and his tearful willingness to share their ills all form important elements in the Royalist panegyrics and epic productions of Waller and Dryden. A romance version of Aeneas underlies the depiction of Charles II's response to the Fire of London in *Annus Mirabilis*, when Dryden describes the 'pious tears which down his cheeks did show'r'.[65] Shaping *Absalom and Achitophel*, too, is an opposition between the rebels, 'Made drunk with honour, and Debauch'd with Praise', and the clement monarch 'Enclin'd to Mercy, and averse from blood'.[66] These antitheses are the lineal descendants of Fairfax's Tasso, and its over-clarification of Spenser's heroic idiom. Split up, packaged into an idiom for rhythmically exploring the opposition of prevailing passions, the English epic was in the process of becoming a rigid vehicle for praising pitiful, quasi-imperial monarchs, and for distinguishing them from irascible, aspiring rebels. Milton's political antipathy to absolute monarchy led him to assail an idiom which was being tidily assimilated to a Royalist purpose. The romance of hell has the *form* of a romance. But this form is dispossessed of its motivating passions: just rage, clemency, and imperial destiny all fail to determine the shape of events. Powerful antipathy to these imperial sentiments led Milton to create a ruined romance without imperial motives.

In the process he makes an entirely new kind of epic narrative, which is just the kind of oblique but energetic transformation of romance towards which his earlier poems had pointed. The course of the plot gives the impression that compassion is a condition within which the action of *Paradise Lost* takes place, that it is a necessary law which shapes events, but which does not need to be felt by the protagonists in order to do so. Compassion is not redescribed, divinely elevated, or explicitly liberated from its servitude to Restoration panegyric and heroic verse. Instead a new form of compassion is implicitly emergent from the structure of the narrative. *Paradise Lost*, as critics are fond of remarking, makes its readers

---

[65] l. 958.
[66] ll. 312, 326. David complains at ll. 943 ff. that 'now so far my Clemency they slight, | Th'Offenders question my Forgiving Right.'

complicit in the origins of their corruption. Satan's delays, in a story to which we are tied by our binding kinship with Adam and Eve, do not just slow the plot down: they are desperately what we want. Satan's pauses, and the unseasonable interruptions to his plot, are not *caused* by romance pity; but they are filled with an implied compassion which wills a delay in the Fall of Adam and Eve, a fate which we, with necessary sympathy, share with them. And Milton allows that we might, just possibly, be colluding with God in our desire that the plot of *Paradise Lost* will be as endless as that of *The Faerie Queene*. Implicitly, wordlessly, the form of the poem allows us to believe that this is not Satan's story, but a tale with pauses imposed upon it by some external force—a narrator or a divinity. In a tantalizingly oblique fashion the form of the poem gestures towards a unity of feeling between God and the reader: both share in, and might will delays in, the prehistory of mankind.

FALLING IN LOVE

Paradise Lost is often berated for its eagerness to worry an answer from almost every unanswerable question. But the poem is almost too careful never to make this privy resonance between God and man explicit. *Paradise Lost* avoids the highest and most universally significant version of the romance plot with scrupulous care. The sympathetic union of God with man, which it would be tempting for a writer of Christian epic to see as the highest form of fellow-feeling, is introduced only obliquely through the form of *Paradise Lost*, or through the extraordinary intuition of Abdiel that some higher purpose underlies God's apparently arbitrary elevation of the Son. The Son does descend to pity and clothe Adam and Eve after the Fall,[67] but Milton remains almost entirely silent about the central incident which expresses the pitiful mortality of God: the crucifixion, God dying for and in the flesh of man, has a remarkably small role in his writing. *Paradise Regain'd* represents Jesus refusing temptation—and with it the digressive plot structure of romance[68]—rather than feeling human nature in death; 'The Passion' breaks off with nervy protestations of the young poet's inability to represent such a massive event. The crucifixion is the ultimate moment on which to centre a transvaluation of pity into divinely incarnate sympathy: it manifests both an extreme of active pity, since it represents God pitying man

[67] *PL* x. 209–28.
[68] See Annabel Patterson, '*Paradise Regained*: a Last Chance at True Romance', *Milton Studies*, 17 (1983), 187–208.

enough to die for him, and an unsurpassable form of passive pity, as God
himself becomes the object of pity. It begs to be treated as, and in neo-
Latin epic frequently became, the archetype of all romance, a moment
which locates the ultimate form of heroism in a passive, pitiful piety.
Descriptions of the event in neo-Latin epic frequently draw out the
compassion latent in classical epic. In Vida's *Christiad*, Christ's death is
the ultimate sympathetic transformation of *pietas*:

> Tantane te pietas miserantem incommoda nostra,
> Tantus adegit amor, coeli o lux clara sereni,
> Vera Dei suboles, verus Deus aethere missus,
> Tam gravi haec velles perpessuque aspera ferre.[69]

Such great piety, such great love, leads you, pitying our hardships, O true
offspring of God, O true God sent from heaven, O clear light of a peaceful sky,
to wish to bear these hardships with such great patience.

And, hearing of the crucifixion, both Vida's Mary and the heroine of
Sannazaro's *De partu Virginis* complain long and piteously, before they
merge into that Virgilian prototype of a suffering romance heroine,
Euryalus's mother. Her cry, 'figite me, si qua est pietas', the only time a
potentially Christian 'pity' seems fully to emerge from Virgil's piety,
accompanies the crucifixion:

> Quando nulla mihi superant solatia vitae,
> Atque meo major nusquam dolor: addite me
> Huic etiam, si qua est pietas, et figite trunco.[70]

When no comforts of life are left to me, and when there is no grief greater than
mine, grant me this too—if there is any pity—and stab my body through.

But in *Paradise Lost*, which systematically avoids the motive structures of
its contemporaries, and cautiously shuffles compassion to its periphery,
the only person who directly mentions this pivotal moment of sympathetic
union between man and his creator is the Angel Michael, and he only
devotes a dozen or so lines to it in his potted history of mankind, in the
course of which, with 'But to the cross he nails thy enemies',[71] he all but
allegorizes the physicality of the act away. There is little room in *Paradise
Lost* for a moment which has such potential for pure and naked pity,

[69] Text from *The Christiad: A Poem in Six Books*, trans. J. Cranwell (Cambridge, 1768), v. 284–7.
[70] Ibid. 328–10. Cf. the complaint of the virgin before the cross in Sannazaro, *Opera* (Venice,
1535), fol. 9ᵃ: 'Quem misera exorem? quo tristia pectora vertam? | Cui querar? o tandem dirae me
perdite dextrae: | Me potius (si qua est pietas) immanibus armis | Obruite: in me omnes offundite
pectoris iras' (To whom should I, miserable, plead? Where should I turn my sad breast? To whom
should I complain? Oh at least kill me with your terrible right hand. Kill me rather—if there is any
pity—with your deadly weapons: pour all the anger of your breast on me). Cf. *Aen.* 9. 493–4, and
p. 46 above.
[71] *PL* XII. 415.

which might so easily become a celebration of the passions released by powerlessness.

Sympathy, though, in a displaced and multitudinous form, is the central, animating idea behind, and the chief structural force in *Paradise Lost*. The difficulty is recognizing it. Milton is eager to avoid any trace of simple, imperial passion, with all the servitude and inequality that is implicit in the relation of pitying. Rather than following his contemporaries in elevating pity into an expression of the human or divine power to save, he luxuriates in the varied and complex forms of identity between sufferers and sympathizer into which compassion could mutate, and into which it had mutated in the epic tradition before him. Like Homer, Milton is aware that a sense of shared mortality can be an elevating, unifying emotion, which could draw two beings, not to relish the disparity between their relative powers, but to acknowledge their kinship with each other. But like Homer too, he recognizes that a desire to make others share one's grief could lead to the vehement destructiveness of Achilles in his final *aristeia*, or to the vengeful envy which underlies Satan's offer of hospitality to Adam and Eve. It is principally through this negative version of sympathy, its envious, destructive double, that Milton explores what it might mean for one being to share the nature of another. He habitually represents a valued idea or emotion through an opposite with which it is kin: for him, to see heaven it is necessary to look through hell. Paradoxically, the sympathetic union of God with man, towards which *Paradise Lost* points, is most fully represented in the poem through deviant and diabolic types. The word 'sympathy' occurs only three times in the poem, and on two occasions it is used of creatures from hell, in the exhaustedly bleached closing leg of the poem. When Satan, returned triumphant from his imperial mission, is changed to a serpent as he crows over his conquest of Adam and Eve, his cronies share his snaky metamorphosis:

> horror on them fell,
> And horrid sympathy; for what they saw,
> They felt themselves now changing ...[72]

The force which induces this change is not the inner drive of passion which impels the endings of Ovid's tales into strange shapes, but it is collusively aware of such feelings: the devils are metamorphosed by 'horrid sympathy'. This phrase tries very hard to mean that horror creates a fellow-feeling for the horrid condition of Satan, which draws the devils to share their leader's shape. But, for the devils, this 'horrid sympathy'

[72] *PL* x. 539–41.

is the consequence not the cause of their change: they are *made* to take
on the form of another being. Satan's Odyssey was forced into a romance
shape by powers which were not his own; this 'horrid sympathy', similarly,
is an imposed condition of existence rather than a spontaneously emergent
sense of kinship with other beings. This form of involuntary 'sympathy',
which draws like to like in spite of themselves, first emerges in the poem
just before the devils' incarnation as snakes, when Sin and Death, with
wolfish snufflings, sense that the fallen world is united with them by its
mortality. Milton calls this blood-lust 'sympathy':

> Methinks I feel new strength within me rise,
> Wings growing, and dominion given me large
> Beyond this deep; whatever draws me on,
> Or sympathy, or some connatural force
> Powerful at greatest distance to unite
> With secret amity things of like kind
> By secretest conveyance.[73]

This is a hideously etiolated version of Homeric fellow-feeling. Mortality
leads to a kind of felt kinship, but this form of kinship is founded entirely
on the destruction, and on the shared mortality, of both parties. Sin's
sympathy for mankind here amounts to no more than the quasi-mechanical
affinity between material objects which draws iron to a magnet.

The drive towards likeness is, however, intimately kin with all that is
good in the poem. In *Paradise Lost* all creatures ideally tend towards
fusion with another being. Angelic love is 'union of pure with pure |
Desiring', a feeling of oneness which shrinks the body to a yearning.
Elsewhere Milton attaches peculiar importance to the desire—which
clings to his descriptions of both human and divine love—to fuse with
the nature of another. In the more Pauline sections of the *De Doctrina*
the goal of religious experience is to become one flesh with Christ, and
in the *Doctrine and Discipline of Divorce* the Platonic myth of the
hermaphroditic union of the sexes is used to describe ideal marital union.[74]
In *Paradise Lost* almost every character seeks—from God's attempt to
make his angels 'under one head more near united', through Adam's
original desire not to be alone in the world, to Satan's envious desire to
make man feel like him—some form of union with another. But this
desire has deviant forms implicit in it. Milton's shrewdest and most
agonizingly hard conceptual insight is that egoism is all but inseparable

---

[73] *PL* x. 243–9.
[74] *CPW* vi. 498–501; on Eros and Anteros see *CPW* ii. 254–5—a passage which has suggestive
conections with the description in *Areopagitica* of good and evil 'as two twins cleaving together',
CPW ii. 514. On angelic love, see *PL* viii. 627–8.

from sympathy. The effort to become one flesh with another being could become sinister: if it were to take the form of imposing one's own condition on another, sympathy would become an act of violent envy, or an assertion of power; and if it were to dissolve all bounds between self and other, it could entail either a kind of domination, or a denial of one's own independence and liberty. The recognition that sympathy is permanently deliquescing into undesirable forms lies at the core of *Paradise Lost*, and is the determining force behind many of its most original moments. Indeed, the very origin of Satan derives from the doubleness of sympathy: the elevation of the Son is at once apparently domineering and actually loving, at once apparently an effort by God to control, and actually an effort to become closer to his creations. It is the terrible proximity of love and envious domination that enables the world of the devils to move so intimately close to the world of God and man, and makes echoes rebound between heaven, hell, and Eden.

Deviant forms of sympathy play a vital part in the human drama of *Paradise Lost*. Adam and Eve lie between God and Satan, and their different understandings of what it might mean to feel identity with the other are poised with delicate and dangerous precision between a divine urge towards voluntary oneness and a Satanic wish to appropriate the other to one's self. Through Adam and Eve, *Paradise Lost* explores different forms of love, and each of the two human characters is shown, from their very beginnings, to be inclining towards a different understanding of what it means to be united with another being. Adam, created single, complains to God that he is 'In unity defective, which requires | Collateral love, and dearest amity'.[75] When Eve relates her origins, while Satan is frisking around Eden in beastly shapes, her tale also shows the pull of instinctive sympathy for another being. But it has disturbing literary underpresences. She tells how she saw a lovely being in a lake:

> As I bent down to look, just opposite,
> A shape within the watery gleam appeared
> Bending to look on me, I started back,
> It started back, but pleased I soon returned,
> Pleased it returned as soon with answering looks
> Of sympathy and love; there I had fixed
> Mine eyes till now, and pined with vain desire,
> Had not a voice thus warned me, What thou seest,
> What there thou seest fair creature is thyself,
> With thee it came and goes: but follow me,
> And I will bring thee where no shadow stays
> Thy coming, and thy soft embraces, he

---

[75] *PL* VIII. 425–6.

Whose image thou art, him thou shall enjoy
Inseparably thine, to him shalt bear
Multitudes like thyself, and thence be called
Mother of human race.[76]

The main source for this narrative is of course the story of Narcissus from the *Metamorphoses*, the youth who pines from self-love into nothingness, and from nothing to a flower. But, while Satan roves around in aimless metamorphic forms, Eve transforms Ovid into something more purposive. What here becomes the voice of God is, in the *Metamorphoses*, a vain authorial interjection which does nothing to prevent Narcissus's self-loving pinings:

credule, quid frustra simulacra fugacia captas?
quod petis, est nusquam; quod amas, avertere, perdes!
ista repercussae, quam cernis, imaginis umbra est:
nil habet ista sui; tecum venitque manetque;
tecum discedet, si tu discedere possis![77]

Foolish boy, why do you clutch in vain at a flitting shadow? What you seek is nowhere. Look away from what you love and you will lose it. What you see is the shadow of a reflected form with no substance of its own. With you it comes and went. And with you it will go away—should you be able to go away.

Milton makes Ovid's own authorial voice divine, and he makes it have a practical effect on the outcome of the story, by substituting imperatives for abuse. Ovid's outcry becomes an exhortation to breed, which has an immediate impact: it stops Eve imitating the deadly broodlessness of Narcissus. The divine version of Ovid's voice leads her towards reproduction rather than metamorphosis. In Eve's creation (as in Spenser's tale of Chrysogone, which also occupies an unspecified, creative time before the main narrative) Ovid becomes the force which leads to generative love, the force which unovids Ovid.[78]

But Milton's tale of Eve does not desert the difficulties of human love for the abstractedly mythical fecundity which Spenser generates from the *Metamorphoses*. *The Faerie Queene* is desperately ingenious in the methods by which it approaches the problems of power implicit in sexual love, but its repertoire of narrative materials in which to refashion these problems is acutely limiting. Spenser's main way of exploring relations between love and domination is to show battles between men and women. This

[76] *PL* iv. 460–75.
[77] *Met.* 3. 432–36.
[78] See further DuRocher, *Milton and Ovid*, 85–93; Lewalski, *PL and Rhetoric*, 71–6; Martindale, *Milton and Ancient Epic*, 153–96.

combative vehicle inevitably contaminates its tenor with violence and power: 'fierce warres' do not enable Spenser to represent literally the mutual yielding of faithful lovers. His alternative allegorical vehicle, a world of myth displaced from the literal level of the narrative, is too distant from the literal content of its allegory to accommodate more than a residuum of human uncertainties. Milton engages with the links between love and authority which Spenser had wrought into the epic tradition; but sympathetic love and its complex relations with power and egoism are confronted directly, without the distracting intermediary of allegory. There is no martial overlay to these issues; nor is there any convenient escape from the tangles of human emotion into a world of myth.

Milton's refusal to shrink from the problems implicit in sympathetic unity enables him to draw Eve innocently close to the idiom of hell before she falls. Her instinctive love of her own image unsettlingly echoes that earlier sub-Ovidian digression: Satan's encounter with Sin. Eve shares a sinister trace of the incestuous delight which leads Satan to breed with his own daughter. Sin relates to Satan how 'Thy self in me thy perfect image viewing | Becamest enamoured', and reveals that she is generated from a corrupt version of the central drive of the poem: Satan seeks to become one flesh in a grisly, literalized way with the incestuous object of his love. Sympathy and incest are close kin, since both long more for sameness than for difference. But when Eve innocently looks at and loves herself, her self-attraction cannot be founded simply on an identity which she perceives between her image and herself, since at about four minutes old she could scarcely know what she looks like. She is struck by a far less misdirected version of the main motive of *Paradise Lost* than this: 'sympathy and love'. 'Sympathy' is a significant Miltonic addition to the emotions which Ovid's Narcissus feels for his image. It is the only time in *Paradise Lost* that the word is used outside hell, and the usage reinforces a dangerous kinship between Eve, Sin, and sympathy. Eve's creation intimates that, from nearly the beginning of time, a desire for identity with another being could come dangerously close to eradicating that other altogether. Even the voice of God implies that a sense of near-identity is an inescapable aspect of love: Adam is beguilingly presented to Eve as a further extension of self-directed desire: he is her 'image'.

Adam's narrative about Eve's creation (which he relates to Raphael in Book VIII) places a similarly delicate emphasis on the difficulty of acknowledging the difference of another person, whilst recognizing that person's similarity to oneself. But here the emergent defect of love is not egoism, but something more like possessiveness. Adam shows an urge to absorb the independent existence of the other into a version of himself:

                                              I now see
         Bone of my bone, flesh of my flesh, my self
         Before me; woman is her name, of man
         Extracted; for this cause he shall forego
         Father and mother, and to his wife adhere;
         And they shall be one flesh, one heart, one soul.[79]

Much of this is from Genesis, and much of it too is replicated in a
spiritualized form in the Solemnization of Matrimony in the Book of
Common Prayer, where the union of lovers' flesh is regarded as a
prefiguration of the mystical union of all Christians in Christ. But Adam
makes a significant addition to the biblical texts on which he draws: 'my
self', which ends his string of possessive pronouns with delighted identity,
is not in Genesis or the marriage service. A sense of similarity here blends
with uncomfortable closeness into possession: it obliterates the autonomy
of Adam's love in a manner which is likely to prompt—and eventually
does prompt in Eve's Fall—a desire to become just a bit more equal.

   In order to provide a motive for the Fall without making it look as
though Adam and Eve were created prone to sin, Milton had to create
emotions which could appear unfallen, and yet have the potential for
corruption within them. The sympathetic loves of Adam and Eve present
just this potential: they express the central drive of the poem towards
voluntary union, but, at the same time, hint at ways in which that central
drive could go horribly wrong, how it could slide towards egoism, or a
sense of emulous superiority. To admit love into the world admits the
possibility of a perfect union; but, if that love is a voluntary fusion of
creatures who are not of precisely the same rank or nature, it introduces
also the possibility of pride, of domination, of aspiration, of a fall.

   Some deviant form of sympathy would naturally have presented itself
to Milton as a means of explaining the Fall of Adam. For a mid-
seventeenth-century epic poet, pity and love (in the diabolic form given
to them in epic tradition since Tasso) would immediately seem to be the
sort of emotions which might pull a man down. In his massive epic on
the progress of the soul and the life of Christ, *Psyche, or Loves Mysterie*
(1648), Joseph Beaumont represented the Fall of Adam as the consequence
of pity:

         Fair in his bosome written was the Law,
         And reverent Terror kept his Soul in awe.

         In awe a while it kept it: But at last

---

   [79] *PL* VIII. 494–9. Cf. Gen. 2: 23–4; Mark 10: 7–8. For a full account of this area of *Paradise Lost*,
see James Grantham Turner, *One Flesh: Paradisal Marriage and Sexual Relations in the Age of Milton*
(Oxford, 1987).

> Commiseration of his *Spous's* case
> Grew to such strength in his too-tender Breast
> That Pitty to himselfe it did displace.
> *Eve* sate so neer to his Uxorious Heart,
> That rather he with Heav'n, then Her will part.[80]

This Adam is an Aeneas who stays with his Dido through pity, and an impious form of love. He has taken a heavy fall into the idiom of romance even before his decision to eat the apple. Milton's Adam has a family resemblance to this romance hero; but his features have been delicately rearranged. He falls for subtly regenerate reasons, reasons which grow from the main sources of what is good in the poem. God is on the brink of becoming one flesh with man; and it is from a sense of the practical consequences of being one flesh with Eve that Adam falls:

> Should God create another Eve, and I
> Another rib afford, yet loss of thee
> Would never from my heart; no no, I feel
> The link of nature draw me: flesh of flesh,
> Bone of my bone thou art, and from thy state
> Mine never shall be parted, bliss or woe.[81]

Adam again prefigures the Solemnization of Matrimony. Without quite saying that he will be with Eve in sickness and in health, he makes it clear enough that he does not just fall: he falls in love. The pressure of events has forced a few of his intrusively possessive pronouns from his earlier description of Eve: she is 'flesh of flesh', not 'flesh of *my* flesh'. The conjugal sympathy expressed in the whole passage is quite distinct from the kind of passionate defect which Beaumont found in Adam. It reveals something like a sense of necessary kinship with Eve. This emotion is easy to regard too harshly: C. S. Lewis said 'Adam fell by uxoriousness', taking his cue from the equally unflattering description offered by Milton of Adam 'fondly overcome with female charm'.[82] But neither of these moralized explanations fit Adam's version of events. As he ends his next speech:

> So forcible within my heart I feel
> The bond of nature draw me to my own,
> My own in thee, for what thou art is mine;

---

[80] vi. 260–1.

[81] *PL* ix. 911–16.

[82] C. S. Lewis, *A Preface to Paradise Lost* (Oxford, 1942), 122. *PL* ix. 999. The stridency of Milton's tone here is offset by numerology: this explicit statement of mortal fallibility occurs in the 999th line of the ninth book. Nine is the number of the incorruptible body. See Alastair Fowler, *Spenser and the Numbers of Time* (London, 1964), 273.

Our state cannot be severed, we are one,
One flesh; to lose thee were to lose my self.[83]

Both this and the previous outburst recall the love which Adam first felt
for Eve, that primal form of love which absorbed the identity of the
other. But new concerns emerge through this speech, which overgo his
virginal rapture. 'The bond of nature' could almost be a legal tie that
pulls Adam to his 'own' possession; but the verb 'draw' implies there is
a sympathetic magic at work, a kind of magnetism which pulls like to
like, rather than an owner to his property. 'What thou art is mine' is also
powerfully different in force from 'you are mine': it suggests something
like 'your *condition* is mine', that 'from thy state | Mine never shall be
parted'. This is not a statement of fact, since the fallen Eve is in a
completely different state from the unfallen Adam. It is rather a description
of impulsive union which involves choice: he feels drawn by kinship to
take on her state of being.

This is an elevating moment in the history of Adam's love: a wish to
possess has given way to a desire to be linked with a sufferer, even at the
price of sharing her pain, and her mortal nature. Adam, like Hector
when he leaves Andromache, acknowledges that he shares a nature and
constraining circumstances with his wife.[84] But his sense of kinship with
Eve differs in two crucial and heroic respects from its Homeric prototype.
Adam, like the true hero of a romance, does not leave his wife: he chooses
to stay with her, and to wander through the world with her. And he does
not, like Hector, simply *accept* that his condition and that of his wife are
similar; he *chooses* to share Eve's state of existence. The Fall is brought
about by the precursor—even the precondition—of the sympathy which
runs from the Homeric poems through the innumerable forms of their
successors: a moment when a man chooses to accept the mortal nature of
his lady.

It is tempting to read the Fall of Adam as the ultimate transfiguration
of the attitudes which sustain the Homeric poems: Adam's decision to
fall enables the existence of a sympathy founded on a shared mortal
nature, and so enables the whole history of epic romance, with its multiple
versions and revisions of that sympathy, to begin. This would fit in with
a very seductive view of Milton as a powerful conqueror of the past, who
effectively destroyed the epic by laying claim to the earliest, primal

---

[83] *PL* IX. 955–9.

[84] See Ch. I, above. There is a faint trace of Andromache's horrified response to the death of
Hector in Adam's greeting of the fallen Eve. *Il.* 22. 466–72 and *PL* IX. 886–95. This might imply a
deeper analogy with the sympathetic relation between Hector and Andromache. See the interesting
study by Martin Mueller, '*Paradise Lost* and the *Iliad*', *Classical Literature Studies*, 6 (1969), 292–
316.

grounds for a heroic action: by choosing to write of the earliest moments of human history, he predates his predecessors, and all possible successors, and so makes the epic vanish into its own origins. In the process he ensures the priority, and the superiority, of his Christian epic over its predecessors: his hero makes possible the pitiful deeds of generations of Hectors, Aeneases, and Rinaldos. This view of Milton as the heroic dominator of the past is, however, at odds with many of the most intimate and pervasive concerns of *Paradise Lost*: the poem dwells repeatedly on the duties and bonds which link creations to their creators. It exhibits a profound unease with any claim, like that of Satan, to be 'self-begot', without debt to or acknowledgement of prior beings. Milton is also very wary about any claim to absorb the independence of another without his or her prior consent. This, again, is a Satanic trick. The story of Adam and Eve hesitantly develops a kind of love which is founded on similarity between people who are made in the same image, but which acknowledges the differences between, and the independence of, those two beings. Their story is circumscribed with the kinds of egoism and appropriation which can so easily emerge from such a human love. The dangers and difficulties of the human story in *Paradise Lost* reflect on a wider problem which underlies the whole work. How can a new narrative, and a new heroic ethos, be both like, and different from, a past work, without either replicating that earlier work, or forcibly transforming it into the image of the present?

Adam's fall shows the intensity and seriousness with which Milton addressed this problem. He does not simply overgo Homer by transforming sympathy into a purely voluntary choice of mortal union with a sufferer. His hero retains a pitiful uncertainty about the nature of his feeling for Eve. Faint tinctures of desire, of a wish to control and own, and a sense of *necessary*, rather than voluntary, kinship with a being who is his flesh discolour Adam's free choice of death with his wife. The mortal hero's sympathy for Eve is closely, and dangerously, analogous to the involuntary, murderously appetitive sense of shared mortality which Sin and Death feel for the fallen man. *Paradise Lost* exhibits a scrupulous modesty in its claims either to overgo the classical past, or to present a revival of the values of that past. A complete transcendence of Homeric sympathy into a purely voluntary union with the mortal nature of another being is something of which no human character in the poem proves capable: Adam, *before* he falls, already shares the nature of Eve, and is bound by the 'bond of nature' before he chooses to fall. Only God, who differs in kind from the creatures whom he pities, can choose with complete freedom to share their nature and fate: only he can completely transform the shape of sympathy—and even he prompts a rebellion by the fears of domination which his desire for transcendent union with his creations inspires. A perfectly successful form of such sympathetic union between different beings is a prerogative which, throughout the poem, remains divine, and which, throughout the poem, is postponed to a future date. Milton—who is so often regarded as the epitome of demonic self-confidence—cautiously avoids directly representing the final trans-figuration of romance into redemptive sympathy.

Paradise Lost is, though, as Dryden suspected, intimately connected with the changing attitudes and forms of feeling which run through the history of epic romance. It pursues, and seeks to transcend, the argument of sympathy to which the works discussed in this book had contributed. Perhaps its greatest moments arise, however, from its generous acknow-ledgements of failure. Like a true romance, it never quite gets to where it is going. The aspects of the poem explored in this chapter move in two main directions: one leads backwards to the lineaments of classical epic, and the forms of emotion explored in Virgil and Homer; the other points forwards to a new transformation of sympathy. Through Satan's story the poem develops a powerfully regressive impetus: it moves back towards the shape of Homeric compassion, and creates a spectral version of that deadly sympathetic realism with which warriors in the *Iliad* confront the mortality that they share with their enemies. Yet this movement towards the past falls just tantalizingly short of its goal. Satan's motives retain traces of pitiful romance forms of heroism, which distort their lineaments. Like the heroes of Ariosto, he remains imprisoned by a crippling incapacity to realize his desires in action, and is ensnared in a digressive plot over which he has no control. These debts to the romance tradition prevent Satan from fully re-creating the motives of his pagan prototypes, and stop him from becoming fully one with a heroic Aeneas: he acquires dubious vestiges of Odysseus, of Turnus, and of Virgil's hero, but he never completely re-creates their motives. He remains tragically isolated from them, as he ends isolated from all of the rest of the world—apart from a chorus of hissing devils who share his snaky form.

The other movement of the poem is a contrasting parallel to Satan's heroically unfulfilled regressive quest for the past, and might be called a progressive tendency. This strand in *Paradise Lost* points forward to an ideal voluntary union of mankind with mankind, and of God with man, when 'God shall be all in all'.[85] Here too Milton scrupulously holds off from his goal, and recognizes that his poem is entangled in the past. Adam cannot fully avoid a pitiful susceptibility to his lady: his residual romance attachment for Eve just prevents his fall from manifesting a

[85] *PL* III. 341.

perfectly voluntary decision to be one flesh with his wife. The delicious tentativeness with which the poem finally glances aside from the voluntary union of God with mankind, and of mankind with each other, is another apect of its modesty, and perhaps its finest. *Paradise Lost* does not simply overwrite the past. It does not explode, transume, or transcend past writing, as though it could lay aside the generations of writers who had made an interpretive shape for the epic. The poem feels its way tentatively through the methods and ideas of its modern predecessors towards the shape of past writing, and beyond that shape it intimates that there will ultimately be a kind of sympathy greater than anything hitherto imagined within the epic tradition. It creates a utopian pressure towards an ideal future, in which an ideally creative poet would revolutionize the form of epic; but it remains aware of its necessary debts to the language and narrative forms which it has inherited, and which hold it back from fully achieving that perfect transformation of the genre.

In this respect, *Paradise Lost* consummates the tentatively revisionary attitude to past literature which is displayed in Renaissance epic from its earliest stages. It progressively approximates towards the writing of the past and its forms of heroism, by undoing, and by fragmenting, the writing habits of the present. It is driven by twin urges both to communicate with, and to depart from, the writing of the past. The poem intimates that one can try to imagine towards past epic, and that one can at least *seek* a transcendent release from the limitations of past forms of heroism; but it also implies that one can never quite arrive at the motive structures of past authors; and that one cannot escape fully from the idiom of the writers who have transmitted the work of those past authors into the present.

These features also mark the poem's continuity with the wistful skirtings around romance themes in which Milton's earlier poems abound. At the end of *Comus*, the Attendant Spirit sings a song in which he looks forward to an ideal space beyond the limits of the masque. He describes a place where Iris

> drenches with Elysian dew
> (List mortals if your ears be true)
> Beds of hyacinth, and roses,
> Where young Adonis oft reposes,
> Waxing well of his deep wound
> In slumber soft, and on the ground
> Sadly sits the Assyrian queen;
> But far above in spangled sheen
> Celestial Cupid her famed son advanced,
> Holds his dear Psyche sweet entranced

> After her wandering labours long,
> Till free consent the gods among
> Make her his eternal bride,
> And from her fair unspotted side
> Two blissful twins are to be born,
> Youth and Joy; so Jove hath sworn.[86]

The mythic characters here grow from the Garden of Adonis, the main location in which Spenser attempted to transform the continual pursuits of the romance narrative into endless, processual love. Yet in *Comus* these Spenserian delights are not directly revealed, nor are they forced backwards into a mythic time before the main narrative; they are described as ever more about to be. We never witness the Spirit's arrival at this ideal place; and the birth of Youth and Joy is doubly deferred, since even after the future free consent of the gods they still are only '*to be* born'. The transformation of a romance tale of wandering into an ideal union of lovers is postponed to the future, and is carefully related to a paradisal location which belongs to an earlier poet. *Paradise Lost* springs from the same imagination, an imagination which pushes towards the future, whilst recognizing an overwhelming debt to the past: its revolutionary vision of romance is evoked as something just beyond the edges of its vision, just beyond us.

But in one respect *Paradise Lost* does mark a major break with the past. It seeks to outgrow and transform the heroic idiom of earlier Renaissance epic. As we have seen, the poem shares this ambition, and many of the methods used to achieve it, with its chief predecessors in the romance tradition. The sudden digressions of Tasso and Spenser, which those poets had used to fashion their new motives for epic romance, enable Milton in his turn to create the broken-backed rage which drives Satan so powerfully nowhere. But *Paradise Lost* goes further in the process of disrupting the interpretive forms of its immediate predecessors than any other Renaissance epic. In its pressure towards a prototypical version of classical heroism, and in its oblique intimations that the sympathy of God for man shapes the plot of the world, the poem pays a high price. It utterly fragments the simple, passionate motives which had sustained generations of epic romances. After Milton, heroes who wavered between pity and disdain would appear to be hopeless anachronisms, and their authors would feel themselves to be the victims of an interpretive tradition, rather than its masters. Milton created a new and bewilderingly vast space for the epic. He moved the genre away from the wars of antagonistic

---

[86] *A Masque Presented at Ludlow Castle (Comus)*, ll. 995–1010. Cf. *FQ* III. vi. 46–50.

passions, which had preoccupied his immediate predecessors, towards a concern with obligations to, and differences from, past writing. This legacy no later epic poet was strong enough to sustain.

Select Bibliography

PRIMARY PRINTED SOURCES

ACHILLES TATIUS, *Clitophon and Leucippe*, ed. and trans. S. Gaselee, Loeb Classical Library (Cambridge, Mass., and London, 1969).

—— *The History of Clitophon and Leucippe*, trans. W. B[urton] (London, 1597); repr. The English Experience, 837 (Amsterdam, 1977).

APOLLONIUS RHODIUS, *Argonautica*, ed. and trans. R. C. Seaton, Loeb Classical Library (Cambridge, Mass., and London, 1912).

ARIOSTO, LODOVICO, *Orlando furioso*, ed. Emilio Bigi, 2 vols. (Milan, 1982).

—— *Orlando furioso di messer Ludovico Ariosto . . . nuovamente da lui proprio corretto d'altri Canti Nuovi ampliato* (Ferrara, 1532).

—— *Orlando furioso ornato di varie figure. Con alcune stanze et Cinque Canti d'un nuovo Libro . . . Con alcune Allegorie . . .* (Venice, 1548).

—— *Orlando furioso, tutto ricorretto, et di nuove figure adornato. Con le annotationi . . . di Girolamo Ruscelli, la Vita dell'Autore descritta dal Signor Giovambattista Pigna* (Venice, 1565).

—— *Orlando furioso con gli Argomenti in ottava rima di M. Lodovico Dolce, e con le Allegorie a ciascun canto di Thomaso Porcacchi* (Venice, 1570).

—— *Orlando furioso di M. Lodovico Ariosto, nuovamente adornato di figure di Rame da Girolamo Porro . . . [con] una allegoria universale sopra tutta L'opera dell'Ariosto fatta da Giuseppe Bononome* (Venice, 1584).

—— *Ludovico Ariosto's Orlando furioso translated into English Heroical Verse by Sir John Harington (1591)*, ed. Robert McNulty (Oxford, 1972).

—— *Two Tales Translated out of Ariosto, The one in dispraise of Men, the other in disgrace of Women. With certaine other Italian Stanzas and Proverbs*, trans. R[obert] T[ofte] (London, 1597).

AUGUSTUS CAESAR, *Res gestae Divi Augusti*, ed. P. A. Brunt and J. M. Moore (Oxford, 1967).

BEAUMONT, JOSEPH, *Psyche, or Loves Mysterie* (London, 1648).

BENI, PAOLO, *Comparatione di Homero, Virgilio e Torquato* (Padua, 1607).

BENLOWES, EDWARD, *Theophila* (London, 1652).

BENOÎT DE SAINT-MAURE, *Le Roman de Troie*, ed. Léopold Constans, Société des anciens textes français, 5 vols. (Paris, 1904–9).

BERNARDUS SILVESTRIS, *The Commentary on the First Six Books of the 'Aeneid' of Virgil*, ed. J.W. and E. F. Jones (Lincoln, Nebr., and London, 1977).

BOCCACCIO, GIOVANNI, *Genealogie Deorum gentilium libri*, ed. Vincenzo Romano, 2 vols. (Bari, 1951).

—— *Tutte le opere*, ed. V. Branca, 12 vols. (Milan, 1964–   ), esp. vol. ii, *Tesiede* and *Filostrato*.

BOIARDO, MATTEO MARIA, *Orlando innamorato*, ed. Giuseppe Anceschi, 2 vols. (Milan, 1978).

—— *Orlando innamorato del Signor Matteo Maria Boiardo . . . nuovamente riformato per M. Lodovico Domenichi* (Venice, 1553).

—— *Orlando innamorato nuovamente composto da M. Francesco Berni Fiorentino* (Venice, 1541).

—— *Orlando Inamorato. The three first Bookes . . . Done into English Heroical Verse by R[obert] T[ofte]* (London, 1598).

BUTLER, SAMUEL, *Hudibras*, ed. John Wilders (Oxford, 1967).

CALEPINUS, AMBROSIUS, *Dictionarium* (Venice, 1571).

CAMOENS, LUIZ DE, *The Lusiads*, trans. W. C. Atkinson (Harmondsworth, Middx., 1952).

—— *The Lusiads*, trans. Sir Richard Fanshawe, ed. Geoffrey Bullough (London, 1963).

CASTIGLIONE, BALDASSARE, *The Booke of the Courtier*, trans. Thomas Hoby, Tudor Translations, 23 (London, 1900).

CAXTON, WILLIAM, *The recuile of the histories of Troie*, 3 vols. (London, 1553).

La Chanson de Roland, ed. F. Whitehead, Blackwell's French Texts, 2nd edn. (Oxford, 1946).

CHAPMAN, GEORGE, *The Poems*, ed. Phyllis Brooks Bartlett, Modern Language Association of America General Series, 12 (New York, 1941).

CHARRON, PIERRE DE LA, *Of Wisdome*, trans. Samson Lennard (London, n.d. [?1606]).

CHAUCER, GEOFFREY, *The Riverside Chaucer*, ed. L. D. Benson and F. N. Robinson, 3rd edn. (Boston, 1987).

CLELAND, JAMES, *Heropaideia, or the Institution of a Young Noble Man* (Oxford, 1607).

COËFFETEAU, N., *A Table of Humane Passions, with their causes and effects*, trans. Edward Grimeston (London, 1621).

COMES, NATALES, *Mythologiae, sive explicationum fabularum libri decem* (Paris, 1583).

COOPER, THOMAS, *Thesaurus Linguae Romanae & Britannicae* (London, 1565).

COWELL, JOHN, *The Interpreter* (Cambridge, 1607).

COWLEY, ABRAHAM, *The English Writings*, ed. A. R. Waller, 2 vols. (Cambridge, 1905).

—— *The Civil War*, ed. Allan Pritchard, University of Toronto Department of English Studies and Texts, 20 (Toronto and Buffalo, 1973).

CRASHAW, RICHARD, *Poems*, ed. A. R. Waller, Cambridge English Classics (Cambridge, 1904).

CUNLIFFE, J.W. (ed.), *Early English Classical Tragedies* (Oxford, 1912).

DANIEL, SAMUEL, *The Complete Works in Verse and Prose*, ed. A.B. Grosart, 5 vols. (London, 1885–96).

—— *Tethys Festival, or the Queenes Wake. Celebrated at Whitehall, the fifth day of June 1610* (London, 1610).

—— *The Civil Wars*, ed. Laurence Mitchel (New Haven, Conn., 1958).

DANTE ALIGHIERI, *The Divine Comedy*, ed. and trans. C. S. Singleton, Bollingen Series, 80, 3 vols. (Princeton, NJ, 1970–5).

DARES PHRYGIUS, *De excidio Troiae historia*, ed. Ferdinand Meister, Teubner Texts (Leipzig, 1873).

DAVENANT, SIR WILLIAM, *Gondibert*, ed. David F. Gladish (Oxford, 1971).

DENHAM, SIR JOHN, *Poetical Works*, ed. T. H. Banks (New Haven, Conn., 1928).

D'EWES, SIMONDS, *A Compleat Journal of ... the House of Lords and House of Commons throughout the Whole Reign of Elizabeth*, 2nd edn. (London, 1693).

DICTYS CRETENSIS, *Belli Troiani scriptores praecipui, Dictys Cretensis, Dares Phrygius & Homerus* (Basle, 1573).

——*Ephemeridos belli Troiani*, ed. Ferdinand Meister, Teubner Texts (Leipzig, 1872).

DOLCE, LODOVICO, *L'Achille et l'Enea di M. Lodovico Dolce. Dove egli tessendo l'historia della Illiade d'Homero a quella dell'Eneide di Virgilio* (Venice, 1571).

DRAYTON, MICHAEL, *The Works*, ed. J. William Hebel, Kathleen Tillotson and B. H. Newdigate, 5 vols. (Oxford, 1931–41).

DRYDEN, JOHN, *The Poems*, ed. James Kinsley, 4 vols. (Oxford, 1958).

DU BARTAS, GUILLAUME DE SALUSTE, *The Works*, ed. U. T. Holmes, jun., J. C. Lyons, and R. W. Linker, 3 vols. (Chapel Hill, NC, 1935–40).

——*The Divine Weeks and Works*, trans. Joshua Sylvester, ed. Susan Snyder, 2 vols. (Oxford, 1979).

DU VAIR, GUILLAME, *The Morall Philosophie of the Stoicks*, trans. T[homas] I[ames] (London, 1598).

ELYOT, SIR THOMAS, *The Boke Named the Governour*, ed. H. H. S. Croft, 2 vols. (London, 1880).

Eneas, Roman du XIIe siècle, ed. J.-J. Salverda de Grave, Classiques français du moyen âge, 2 vols. (Paris, 1983–5).

ERASMUS, DESIDERIUS, *Proverbiorum Chiliadas* (Basle, 1515).

——*The Colloquies*, trans. Craig R. Thompson (Chicago and London, 1965).

——*The Education of a Christian Prince*, ed. Lester K. Born, Records of Civilization, Sources and Studies, 27 (New York, 1936).

Excidium Troiae, ed. E. B. Atwood and V. K. Whitaker, Mediaeval Academy of America Publications, 44 (Cambridge, Mass., 1944).

The Fairfax Correspondence, ed. George W. Johnson, 2 vols. (London, 1848).

FLETCHER, GILES and PHINEAS, *Poetical Works*, ed. F. S. Boas, 2 vols. (Cambridge, 1908–9).

FORNARI, SIMON, *La spositione di M. Simon Fornari sopra l'Orlando furioso di M. Ludovico Ariosto*, 2 vols. (Florence, 1549).

FRANKLIN, JULIAN H. (ed.), *Constitutionalism and Resistance in the Sixteenth Century, Three Treatises by Hotman, Beza, and Mornay* (New York, 1969).

FULGENTIUS, *Opera*, ed. R. Helm, Teubner Texts (Stuttgart, 1970).

——*Fulgentius the Mythographer*, ed. and trans. L. G. Whitbread (Columbus, Ohio, 1971).

GIRALDI CINTHIO, GIOVANNIBATTISTA, *Dell'Hercole* (Modena, 1558).

——*Discorsi ... intorno al comporre de i Romanzi, delle Comedie, e delle Tragedie* (Venice, 1554).

——*On Romances: Being a Translation of the 'Discorsi intorno al comporre dei romanzi'*, ed. and trans. H. L. Snuggs (Lexington, Ky., 1968).

——*Didone Tragedia* (Venice, 1583).

GOOGE, BARNABY, *The firste syxe bokes of the mooste christian Poet Marcellus Palingenius, called the zodiake of life* (London, 1561).

GORGES, SIR ARTHUR, *The Poems*, ed. H. E. Sandison (Oxford, 1953).

GREVILLE, FULKE, First Lord Brooke, *Poems and Dramas*, ed. Geoffrey Bullough, 2 vols. (Edinburgh and London, 1939).

——*The Prose Works*, ed. John Gouws (Oxford, 1986).

GUIDO DE COLUMNIS, *Historia destructionis Troiae*, ed. N. E. Griffin, Mediaeval Academy of America Publications, 26 (Cambridge, Mass., 1936).

HAKE, EDWARD, *Epieikeia: A Dialogue on Equity in Three Parts*, ed. D. E. C. Yale, Yale Law Library Publications, 13 (New Haven, Conn., 1953).

[HALL, ARTHUR], *A Letter Sent by F.A.*, in *Miscellanea Antiqua Anglicana*, no ed. (London, 1816).

HARINGTON, JOHN, OF STEPNEY, *John Harington of Stepney, Tudor Gentleman. His Life and Works*, ed. Ruth Hughey (Columbus, Ohio, 1971).

HARINGTON, SIR JOHN, *A Short View of the State of Ireland*, ed. W. D. Macray, Anecdota Bodleiana, 2 (Oxford and London, 1879).

——*A New Discourse of a Stale Subject, called the Metamorphosis of A-Jax*, ed. E. S. Donno (London, 1962).

——*The Letters and Epigrams*, ed. N. E. McClure (Philadelphia, 1930).

HARRINGTON, JAMES, *The Political Works of James Harrington*, ed. J. G. A. Pocock (Cambridge, 1977).

HARVEY, GABRIEL, *Marginalia*, ed. G. C. Moore Smith (Stratford-upon-Avon, 1913).

HAYWARD, JOHN, *The First Part of the Life and Raigne of King Henrie the IIII* (London, 1599).

HELIODORUS, *An Aethiopian History ... Englished by Thomas Underdowne anno 1587*, ed. Charles Whibley, Tudor Translations, 5 (London, 1895).

HEYWOOD, THOMAS, *Troia Britanica: or, Great Britaines Troy* (London, 1609).

HOLINSHED, RAPHAEL, *The Third Volume of Chronicles* (London, 1587).

HOLLAND, HUGH, *Pancharis: the first Booke. Containing the Preparation of the Love betweene Owen Tudyr, and the Queene, long since intended to her maiden Majestie, And now dedicated to the invincible James* (London, 1603).

HOMER, *The Iliad*, trans. A. T. Murray, Loeb Classical Library, 2 vols. (Cambridge, Mass., and London, 1924–5).

——*The Odyssey*, trans. A. T. Murray, Loeb Classical Library, 2 vols. (Cambridge, Mass., and London, 1919).

——*The Iliad: A Commentary*, ed. G. S. Kirk, J. B. Hainsworth, R. Jenks, M. W. Edwards, and N. J. Richards, 6 vols. (Cambridge, 1985–   ).

——*The Iliad Book XXIV*, ed. C. W. MacLeod (Cambridge, 1982).

——*A Commentary on Homer's Odyssey*, ed. A. Heubeck, S. West, and J. B. Hainsworth, 3 vols. (Oxford, 1988–92).

HOMER, *Poetarum omnium seculorum longe principis Homeri omnia quae quidem extant omnia* (Basle, 1551).

—— *Homeri Opera Graeco-Latina, quae quidem nunc extant, omnia* (Basle, 1561).

—— *Homeri quae extant omnia. Ilias, Odysseu, Batrachomyomachia, Hymni,* ed. Johannus Spondanus (Basle, 1583).

—— *Homeri Iliados, de rebus ad Troiam gestis, Libri XXIIII. nuper latino carmine elegantissime redditi, Helio Hobano Hesso* (Basle, ?1550).

—— *Iliadus Homeri,* trans. Angelus Polizianus in A. Mai (ed.), *Spicilegium Romanum,* 10 vols. (Rome, 1839), ii. 1–100.

—— *Homeri poetarum omnium principis, Ilias, hoc est de bello Troiano libri XXIIII. Per Lauren. Vallam* (Cologne, 1537).

—— *Les dix premiers livres de l'Iliade d'Homere, prince des poetes, tradictz en vers François, par M. Hugues Salel* (Paris, 1555).

—— *Les XXIIII. livres de l'Iliade d'Homere, prince des poëtes grecs traduicts dy grec en vers françois. Les XI premiers par M. Hugues Salel ... et les XIII derniers par Amadis Jamyn* (Paris, 1580).

—— *Odissea Homeri,* trans. Raphael Volaterranus (Rome, 1510).

—— *L'Odissea d'Homero tradotta in volgare Fiorentino,* trans. Girolamo Bacelli (Florence, 1582).

—— *L'Ulisse, tratto dell'Odissea d'Homero,* trans. L. Dolce (Venice, 1573).

—— *Ten Books of Homers Iliades translated out of French by A[rthur] H[all]* (London, 1581).

—— *Seaven Bookes of the Iliades of Homere, Prince of Poets, Translated according to the Greeke, in judgement of his best commentaries,* trans. George Chapman (London, 1598).

—— *Homer Prince of Poets translated according to the Greeke in Twelve Bookes of his Iliads,* trans. George Chapman (London, [1608?]).

—— *The Iliads of Homer, Prince of Poets,* trans. George Chapman (London, [1611?]).

—— *Homer's Odysseys,* trans. George Chapman (London, [1614?]).

—— *The Whole Works of Homer, Prince of Poets, Translated according to the Greeke,* trans. George Chapman (London, [1616?]).

—— *Chapman's Homer: The Iliad, The Odyssey and the Lesser Homerica,* ed. Allardyce Nicoll, 2 vols. (London, 1957).

HOWARD, HENRY, EARL OF SURREY, *Poems,* ed. Emrys Jones, Clarendon Medieval and Tudor Series (Oxford, 1964).

HUBERT, SIR FRANCIS, *The Poems,* ed. Bernard Mellor (Hong Kong, 1961).

—— *The Historie of Edward the Second ... Together with the fatall down-fall of his two unfortunate Favorites Gaveston and Spencer* (London, 1629).

JAMES VI AND I, *The Poems,* ed. James Craigie, Scottish Text Society, 2 vols. (Edinburgh and London, 1955).

—— *Basilicon Doron,* ed. James Craigie, Scottish Text Society, 2 vols. (Edinburgh and London, 1944–50).

—— *The True Law of Free Monarchies* (Edinburgh, 1598).

JONSON, BEN, *Works,* ed. C. H. Herford and P. Simpson, 11 vols. (Oxford, 1925–52).

Lactantius, *Opera Omnia*, ed. S. Brandt and G. Laubmann, in *Corpus Scriptorum Ecclesiasticorum Latinorum*, 19 (Prague, 1890).

Lambarde, William, *Archion, or a Commentary upon the High Courts of Justice in England* (London, 1635).

Landino, Christophero, *Quaestiones Camaldulenses* (Venice, ?1505).

La Primaudaye, Pierre de, *The French Academie, wherein is discoursed the institution of maners*, trans. T[homas] B[owes] (London, 1589).

Lipsius, Justus, *Two Bookes of Constancie*, trans. Sir John Stradling, ed. Rudolph Kirk and Clayton Morris Hall, Rutgers University Studies in English, 2 (New Brunswick, 1939).

Lucan, *The Civil War (Pharsalia)*, trans. J. D. Duff, Loeb Classical Library (Cambridge, Mass., and London, 1928).

——*Pharsalia diligentissime per G. Versellanum recognita. Cum commentariis Ioannis Sulpitii Verulani . . . Philippi Beroaldi . . . Iodoci Badii Ascensii* ([Paris], 1514).

——*Pharsalia libri X. scholiis per margines illustrati . . . his quoque Henrichi Glareani . . . annotationes novissime iam accedunt* (Basle, 1550).

——*De Bello Civili, libri decem, cum scholiis, integris quidem Ioannis Sulpitii Verulani, certis autem locis etiam Omniboni, una cum Annotationibus . . . Iacobi Micylli* (Frankfurt, 1551).

——*Pharsalia Libri X. cum Lamberti Hortensii . . . explanationibus* (Basle, 1578).

——*De Bello Civili, vel Pharsaliae libri decem, Gregorii Bersmani* (Leipzig, 1589).

——*Delle guerre civili*, trans. Giulio Morigi (Ravenna, 1587).

——*Lucans First Booke Translated line for line, by Chr. Marlowe* (London, 1600).

——*Lucans Pharsalia: containing the Civill Warres betweene Caesar and Pompey. Written in Latin Heroicall Verse by M. Annaeus Lucanus. Translated into English Verse by Sir Arthur Gorges Knight* (London, 1614).

——*Lucan's Pharsalia: or the Civill Warres of Rome, betweene Pompey the great, and Julius Caesar, the Whole ten Bookes Englished, by Thomas May, Esquire* (London, 1627).

——*Supplementum Lucani Libri VII Authore Tho. May Anglo* (Lyons, 1640).

——*A Continuation of Lucan's Historicall Poem till the death of Julius Caesar by T[homas] M[ay]* (London, 1630).

Lydgate, John, *Troy Book*, ed. Henry Bergen, 3 vols., EETS Extra Series, 97, 103, and 106 (London, 1906–10).

Macrobius, *The Saturnalia*, trans. P. V. Davies (New York and London, 1969).

Marlowe, Christopher, *The Works*, ed. C. F. Tucker Brooke (Oxford, 1910).

——*The Complete Works of Christopher Marlowe*, vol. i, ed. Roma Gill (Oxford, 1987).

May, Thomas, *The Reigne of King Henry the Second, written in Seaven Bookes. By his Majesties Command* (London, 1633).

——*The Victorious Reigne of King Edward the Third* (London, 1635).

——*The History of the Parliament of England* (London, 1647).

——*A Breviary of the History of the Parliament of England* (London, 1680).

MILTON, JOHN, *The Poems*, ed. John Carey and Alastair Fowler (London, 1968).
—— *Poems both English and Latin* (London, 1645).
—— *The Complete Prose Works*, ed. Don M. Wolfe, 8 vols. (New Haven, Conn., and London, 1953–82).
—— *The Works of John Milton*, ed. F. A. Patterson, 20 vols. (New York, 1931–40).
—— *The Early Lives of Milton*, ed. Helen Darbishire (London, 1932).
—— *Poems Reproduced in Facsimile from the Manuscript in Trinity College Cambridge* (Menston/Ilkley, Yorks., 1970).
MULCASTER, RICHARD, *Positions, wherein those primitive circumstances be examined, which are necessarie for the training up of Children* (London, 1581).
NENNA DA BARI, *Il Nennio, nel quale si ragiona di nobilità* (Venice, 1542).
—— *Nennio, or a Treatise of Nobilitie: wherein is discoursed what true Nobilitie is, with such qualities as are required in a perfect Gentleman* (London, 1595).
NICHOLS, JOHN, *The Progresses and Public Processions of Queen Elizabeth*, 2nd edn., 3 vols. (London, 1823).
OROSIUS, *Historiarum adversum Paganos libri VII*, ed. C. Zangemeister, in *Corpus Scriptorum Ecclesiasticorum Latinorum*, 5 (Prague, 1882).
OVID, *Metamorphoses*, ed. Frank Justus Miller, Loeb Classical Library, 2 vols. (Cambridge, Mass., and London, 1916).
—— *Fabularum Ovidii Interpretatio, Ethica, Physica, et Historica, tradita in Academia Regiomontana a Georgio Sabino* (Cambridge, 1584).
—— *Metamorphoses: The Arthur Golding Translation, 1567*, ed. J. F. Nims (New York and London, 1965).
PATRIZIO, FRANCISCO, *Enneas de regno, & regis institutione* (Paris, 1519).
PEACHAM, HENRY, *The Compleat Gentleman* (London, 1622).
—— *The Truth of Our Times* (London, 1638).
PERKINS, WILLIAM, *The Workes*, 2 vols. (Cambridge, 1608–9).
PETRARCA, FRANCESCO, *Petrarch's Lyric Poems: The 'Rime Sparse' and Other Lyrics*, ed. and trans. Robert M. Durling (Cambridge, Mass., 1976).
PHILLIPS, EDWARD, *Theatrum Poetarum, or a Compleat Collection of the Poets* (London, 1675).
PIGNA, GIOVANNI BATTISTA, *I Romanzi* (Venice, 1554).
PLATO, *Omnia Divini Platonis Opera tralatione Marsilii Ficini* (Basle, 1532).
POLITIANUS, ANGELUS [ANGELO POLIZIANO], *Omnium operum (quae quidem extare novimus) tomus prior [posteriorque]*, 2 vols. (Paris, 1519).
POPE, ALEXANDER, *The Twickenham Edition of the Poems of Alexander Pope*, ed. John Butt, 11 vols. (New Haven, Conn., and London, 1961–7).
PORTA, MALATESTA, *Il Rossi: o vero del parere sopra alcune obiettioni, fatte dall'Infarinato Academico della Crusca. Intorno alla Gierusalemme liberata* (Rimini, 1589).
—— *Il Beffa, o vero della favola dell'Eneide, dialogo* (Rimini, 1604).
PUTTENHAM, GEORGE, *The Arte of English Poesie*, ed. Gladys Doidge Wilcock and Alice Walker (Cambridge, 1936).

RONSARD, PIERRE DE, *Œuvres complètes*, ed. Paul Laumonier, Société des textes français modernes, 20 vols. (Paris, 1931–75).

ROUS, FRANCIS, *Thule, or Vertues Historie* (London, 1598).

—— *Thule, or Vertues Historie*, Spenser Society, 23 (London, 1878).

—— *The Bounds and Bonds of Publique Obedience* (London, 1649).

SANNAZARO, JACOPO, *Opera* (Venice, 1535).

SCALIGER, JULIUS CAESAR, *Poetices libri septem* ([Lyons], 1561).

SCAPULA, JOHANNUS, *Lexicon Graeco-Latinum Novum* (Basle, 1580).

SERVIUS, *Servii Grammatici qui feruntur in Vergilii Carmina Commentarii*, ed. G. Thilo and H. Hagen, 2 vols. (Leipzig, 1878–83).

SHEPPARD, SAMUEL, *The Faerie King fashioning Love and Honour [c.1650]*, ed. P. J. Klemp (Salzburg, 1984).

SIDNEY, SIR PHILIP, *The Works*, ed. A. Feuillerat, 4 vols. (Cambridge, 1912–26).

—— *The Countess of Pembroke's Arcadia (The Old Arcadia)*, ed. Jean Robertson (Oxford, 1973).

—— *The Countess of Pembroke's Arcadia (The New Arcadia)*, ed. Victor Skretkowicz (Oxford, 1987).

—— *An Apology for Poetry*, ed. Geoffrey Shepherd, 2nd edn. (Manchester, 1973).

SLATYER, WILLIAM, *The History of Great Britain [Palae Albion]* (London, 1621).

SMITH, G. GREGORY, (ed.), *Elizabethan Critical Essays*, 2 vols. (Oxford, 1904).

SPENSER, EDMUND, *The Works of Edmund Spenser: A Variorum Edition*, ed. Edwin Greenlaw, Charles Grosvenor Osgood, Frederick Morgan Padelford, and Ray Heffner, 10 vols. (Baltimore, 1932–49).

—— *The Faerie Queene*, ed. A. C. Hamilton (London, 1977).

—— *The Minor Poems*, ed. E. de Selincourt (Oxford, 1910).

—— *The Poetical Works of Spenser*, ed. E. de Selincourt (Oxford, 1912).

STARKEY, THOMAS, *A Dialogue between Reginald Pole and Thomas Lupset*, ed. K. M. Burton (London, 1948).

STATIUS, *Statius*, trans. J. H. Mozley, Loeb Classical Library, 2 vols. (Cambridge, Mass., and London, 1928).

—— *Thebais cum Lactantii Commentariis* (Venice, 1494).

—— *La Thebaide di Statio ridotta in ottava rima del Erasmo di Valvasone* (Venice, 1570).

STEWART OF BALDYNNEIS, JOHN, *Poems*, ed. Thomas Crockett, Scottish Text Society, vol. ii only (Edinburgh, 1913).

TASSO, TORQUATO, *Gerusalemme liberata*, ed. Lanfranco Caretti, 2nd edn. (Turin, 1980).

—— *Le prose diverse*, ed. Cesare Guasti, 2 vols. (Florence, 1875).

—— *Le lettere*, ed. Cesare Guasti, 5 vols. (Naples, 1852–5).

—— *Apologia in difesa della Gierusalemme liberata, a gli Accademici della Crusca* (Ferrara, 1586).

—— *Discorsi dell'arte poetica e del poema eroico*, ed. Luigi Poma (Bari, 1964).

TASSO, TORQUATO, *Discourses on the Heroic Poem*, ed. and trans. Mariella Cavalchini and Irene Samuel (Oxford, 1973).

—— *Godfrey of Bulloigne, or the Recoverie of Hierusalem*, trans. R[ichard] C[arew] (London, [1594]).

—— *Godfrey of Bulloigne, or the Recoverie of Hierusalem*, trans. R[ichard] C[arew], ed. Werner von Koppenfels, Gerstenberg English Reprints, 7 (Hildesheim, 1980).

—— *Godfrey of Bulloigne, or The Recoverie of Jerusalem. Done into English Heroical Verse, by Edward Fairfax Gent.* (London, 1600).

—— *Godfrey of Bulloigne: A Critical Edition of Edward Fairfax's Translation of Tasso's 'Gerusalemme liberata', together with Fairfax's Original Poems*, ed. Kathleen M. Lea and T. M. Gang (Oxford, 1981).

TRISSINO, GIANGIORGIO, *La Italia liberata da Gotthi*, 3 vols. (Rome, 1547).

TURBERVILE, GEORGE, *The Booke of Faulconrie or Hauking, for the onely delight and plesure of all Noblemen and Gentlemen* (London, 1575).

[VATICAN MYTHOGRAPHERS], *Scriptores rerum mythicarum Latini tres Romae nuper reperti*, ed. G. H. Bode, 2 vols. (Darmstadt, 1834).

VIDA, GIROLAMO, *The Christiad: A Poem in Six Books*, text with a translation by J. Cranwell (Cambridge, 1768).

VIRGIL, *The Aeneid*, ed. and trans. H. R. Fairclough, Loeb Classical Library, 2 vols. (Cambridge, Mass., and London, 1935).

—— *P. Vergili Maronis Opera*, ed. R. A. B. Mynors (Oxford, 1969).

—— *P. Vergili Maronis, Aeneidos liber primus*, ed. R. G. Austin (Oxford, 1971).

—— *P. Vergili Maronis, Aeneidos liber secundus*, ed. R. G. Austin (Oxford, 1964).

—— *P. Vergili Maronis, Aeneidos liber quartus*, ed. R. G. Austin (Oxford, 1955).

—— *P. Vergili Maronis, Aeneidos liber quartus*, ed. Arthur Stanley Pease (Cambridge, Mass., 1935).

—— *P. Vergili Maronis, Aeneidos liber sextus*, ed. R. G. Austin (Oxford, 1977).

—— *Virgil Aeneid VI*, ed. F. Fletcher (Oxford, 1941).

—— *Ciris: A Poem Attributed to Virgil*, ed. R. O. A. M. Lyne (Cambridge, 1978).

—— *Publii Virgilii Maronis Opera cum quinque vulgatis commentariis* (Strasburg, 1502).

—— *Vergilius cum commentariis. Opera Vergiliana: . . . docte et familiariter exposita a Servio, Donato, Mancinello, Probo, Augustino Datho, Domitio Calderino, et Jodoco Badio Ascensio* (Venice, 1519).

—— *Publii Virgilii Maronis Poetae Mantuani, universum poema: cum . . . Servii Honorati Mauri, Grammatici, & Badii Ascensii interpretatione* (Venice, 1572).

—— *Publii Virgilii Maronis opera*, ed. Pomonius Sabinus (Basle, 1586).

—— *Eneydos*, trans. William Caxton, ed. W. T. Culley and F. J. Furnivall, EETS Extra Series, 57 (London, 1890).

—— *Eneydos*, trans. Gavin Douglas, ed. D. C. Coldwell, Scottish Text Society, 4 vols. (Edinburgh and London, 1957–64).

—— *The Nyne fyrst Bookes of the Eneidos of Virgil converted into Englishe vearse by Thomas Phaer* (London, 1562).

—— *The .xiii. Bookes of Aeneidos . . . translated into English verse to the first thirdpart of the tenth Booke, by Thomas Phaer Esquire, and the residue finished ... by Thomas Twyne* (London, 1584).

——— *The First Four Bookes of Virgils Aeneis, translated into English Heroicall Verse by Richard Stanyhurst* (London, 1583).

——— *The Sixth Book of Virgil's Aeneid Translated and Commented on by Sir John Harington (1604)*, ed. Simon Cauchi (Oxford, 1991).

——— *L'Enea di M. Lodovico Dolce* (Venice, 1558).

——— *L' Eneida in Toscano del ... signor cavalier Cerretani* (Florence, 1560).

——— *L'opere di Vergilio...Novamente da diversi eccellentissimi auttori tradotte in versi sciolti*, trans. Alessandro Sansedoni *et al.* (Venice, 1573).

——— *L'Eneide di Virgilio, del commendatore Annibal Caro* (Venice, 1581).

WALLER, EDMUND, *A Panegyrick to my Lord Protector* (London, 1655).

——— *Poems Written upon Several Occasions*, 3rd edn. (London, 1668).

WARNER, WILLIAM, *Albions England ... whereunto is also added an Epitome of the whole Historie of England* (London, 1612).

SECONDARY SOURCES

AGNES, ROBERTO, 'La *Gerusalemme liberata* e il poema del secondo cinquecento', *Lettere italiane*, 16 (1964), 117–43.

AHL, FREDERICK M., *Lucan: An Introduction*, Cornell Studies in Classical Philology, 39 (Ithaca, NY, and London, 1976).

ANDERSON, D. M., 'The Trial of the Princes in the *Arcadia*, Book V', *Review of English Studies*, NS 8 (1957), 409–12.

ANDERSON, W. B., 'Sum pius Aeneas', *Classical Review*, 44 (1930), 3–4.

ANDERSON, WILLIAM S., 'Virgil's Second *Iliad*', Transactions and Proceedings of the American Philological Association, 88 (1957), 17–30.

AUERBACH, ERICH, *Mimesis: The Representation of Reality in Western Literature*, trans. Willard R. Trask (Princeton, NJ, 1953).

——— *Literary Language and its Public in Late Latin Antiquity and in the Middle Ages*, trans. R. Manheim (London, 1965).

BAKHTIN, M. M., *The Dialogic Imagination: Four Essays*, trans. C. Emerson and M. Holquist (Austin, Tex., and London, 1981).

BALDASSARI, GUIDO, *Il sonno di Zeus: Sperimentazione narrativa del poema rinascimentale e tradizione omerica* (Rome, 1982).

BARTLETT, PHYLLIS B., 'Chapman's Revisions in his *Iliads*', ELH 2 (1935), 92–119.

——— 'The Heroes of Chapman's Homer', *Review of English Studies*, 17 (1941), 257–80.

——— 'Stylistic Devices in Chapman's *Iliads*', *PMLA* 57 (1942), 661–75.

BATTENHOUSE, ROY W., 'Chapman and the Nature of Man', *ELH* 12 (1945), 87–107.

BAWCUTT, PRISCILLA, *Gavin Douglas* (Edinburgh, 1976).

BELL, CHARLES G., 'A History of Fairfax Criticism', *PMLA* 62 (1947), 644–57.

—— 'Edward Fairfax, a Natural Son', *Modern Language Notes*, 62 (1947), 24–7.

—— 'Fairfax's Tasso', *Comparative Literature*, 6 (1954), 26–52.

BENEDETTI, ANNA, *L''Orlando furioso' nella vita intellettuale del popolo inglese* (Florence, 1914).

BENNETT, JOSEPHINE WATERS, *The Evolution of 'The Faerie Queene'* (Chicago, 1942).

—— 'Genre, Milieu and the "Epic-Romance"', *English Institute Essays* (1951), 95–125.

BERGER, HARRY, JUN., *Revisionary Play: Studies in the Spenserian Dynamics* (Berkeley and Los Angeles, 1988).

BEYE, C. R., *Epic and Romance in the 'Argonautica' of Apollonius Rhodius* (Carbondale, Ill., 1982).

BLANCHARD, HAROLD H., 'Imitations from Tasso in *The Faerie Queene*', *Studies in Philology*, 22 (1925), 198–221.

BLESSINGTON, FRANCIS C., *'Paradise Lost' and the Classical Epic* (Boston, London, and Henley, 1979).

BLISSETT, WILLIAM, 'Lucan's Caesar and the Elizabethan Villain', *Studies in Philology*, 53 (1956), 553–75.

—— 'Caesar and Satan', *Journal of the History of Ideas*, 18 (1957), 221–32

BLOOM, HAROLD, *The Anxiety of Influence* (Oxford, 1973).

—— *A Map of Misreading* (Oxford, 1975).

BOLTWOOD, ROBERT M., 'Turnus and Satan as Epic "Villains"', *Classical Journal*, 47 (1952), 183–6.

BONO, BARBARA J., *Literary Transvaluation: From Vergilian Epic to Shakespearean Comedy* (Berkeley and Los Angeles, 1984).

BOWRA, C. M., *From Virgil to Milton* (London, 1963).

—— *Homer* (London, 1972).

BRADEN, GORDON, *Renaissance Tragedy and the Senecan Tradition: Anger's Privilege* (New Haven, Conn., and London, 1985).

BRAMBLE, J. C., 'Lucan', in E. J. Kenney and W. V. Clausen (eds.), *The Cambridge History of Classical Literature* (Cambridge, 1982), ii. 533–57.

BRAND, C. P., *Torquato Tasso: A Study of the Poet and of his Contribution to English Literature* (Cambridge, 1965).

—— 'Ludovico Ariosto—Poet and Poem in the Italian Renaissance', *Forum for Modern Language Studies*, 4 (1968), 87–101.

—— 'Tasso, Spenser, and the *Orlando furioso*', in Julius A. Molinaro (ed.), *Petrarch to Pirandello: Studies in Honour of Beatrice Corrigan* (Toronto and Buffalo, 1973), 95–110.

—— *Ludovico Ariosto: A Preface to the 'Orlando furioso'*, Writers of Italy, 1 (Edinburgh, 1974).

BRIGGS, JOHN CHANNING, 'Chapman's *Seaven Bookes of the Iliades*: Mirror for Essex', *Studies in English Literature*, 21 (1981), 59–73.

BRIGGS, W. D., 'Political Ideas in Sidney's *Arcadia*', *Studies in Philology*, 28 (1931), 137–61.

BRISSON, J.-P., 'Le "pieux Énée"!', *Latomus*, 31 (1972), 379–412.

BROWER, REUBEN A., *Hero and Saint: Shakespeare and the Graeco-Roman Heroic Tradition* (Oxford, 1971).

BRUÈRE, R. T., 'The Latin and English Versions of Thomas May's *Supplementum Lucani*', *Classical Philology*, 44 (1949), 145–63.

BURROW, COLIN, 'Original Fictions: Metamorphoses in *The Faerie Queene*', in Charles Martindale (ed.), *Ovid Renewed: Ovidian Influences on Literature and Art from the Middle Ages to the Twentieth Century* (Cambridge, 1988), 99–119.

BUSH, DOUGLAS, *English Literature in the Earlier Seventeenth Century 1600–1660*, 2nd edn. (Oxford, 1962).

CAMERON, ALICE, *The Influence of Ariosto's Epic and Lyric Poetry on Ronsard and his Group*, Johns Hopkins Studies in Romance Literatures and Language, 15 (Baltimore, 1930).

CAMPBELL, LILY B., *Divine Poetry and Drama in Sixteenth Century England* (Cambridge, 1961).

CANNY, NICHOLAS P., *The Elizabethan Conquest of Ireland: A Pattern Established 1565–76* (Hassocks, Sussex, 1976).

——'Edmund Spenser and the Development of an Anglo-Irish Identity', *Yearbook of English Studies*, 13 (1983), 1–19.

CARETTI, LANFRANCO, *Ariosto e Tasso* (Turin, 1961).

CARNE-ROSSE, D. S., 'The One and the Many: A Reading of *Orlando furioso*, Cantos 1 and 8', *Arion*, 5: 2 (1966), 195–234.

CARRINGTON, SAMUEL M., 'Amadis Jamyn, Translator of Homer', in Frieda S. Brown (ed.), *French Renaissance Studies in Honor of Isidore Silver, Kentucky Romance Quarterly*, 21, Suppl. 2 (1974), 123–36.

CASPARI, FRITZ, *Humanism and the Social Order in Tudor England* (Chicago, 1954).

CASTELLI, ALBERTO, *La 'Gerusalemme liberata' nella Inghilterra di Spenser* (Milan, 1936).

CATTANEO, GIULIO, 'Varietà e unità nella *Gerusalemme liberata*', in Carlo Ballerini (ed.), *Atti del convegno di Nimega sul Tasso* (Bologna, 1978), 15–34.

CAVE, TERENCE, *Recognitions: A Study in Poetics* (Oxford, 1988).

CHARLESWORTH, M. P., 'The Virtues of a Roman Emperor: Propaganda and the Creation of Belief', *Proceedings of the British Academy*, 23 (1937), 105–33.

CHERNAIK, W. L., *The Poetry of Limitation: A Study of Edmund Waller* (New Haven, Conn., and London, 1968).

CIORĂNESCU, A., *Les imitations de l'Arioste de Philippe Desportes* (Paris, 1936).

——*L'Arioste en France des origines à la fin du XVIII siècle*, 2 vols. (Paris, 1939).

CONLEY, C. H., *The First English Translators of the Classics* (New Haven, Conn., 1927).

CORMIER, RAYMOND J., *One Heart One Mind: The Rebirth of Virgil's Hero in Medieval French Romance*, Romance Monographs, 3 (Oxford, Miss., 1973).

CRAIG, D. H., *Sir John Harington* (Boston, 1985).

CREETH, EDMUND, 'The "Begetting" and the Exaltation of the Son', *Modern Language Notes*, 76 (1961), 696–700.

CROCE, BENEDETTO, *Ariosto, Shakespeare e Corneille*, 4th edn. (Bari, 1950).

CROFT, P. J., 'Sir John Harington's Manuscript of Sir Philip Sidney's *Arcadia*', in Stephen Parks and P. J. Croft (eds.), *Literary Autographs: Papers Read at the Clark Library Seminar 26 April 1980* (Los Angeles, 1983), 39–75.

CUCCARO, VINCENT, *The Humanism of Ludovico Ariosto, from the 'Satire' to the 'Furioso'* (Ravenna, 1981).

DANIELSON, DENNIS RICHARD, *Milton's Good God: A Study in Literary Theodicy* (Cambridge, 1982).

DEARING, BRUCE, 'Gavin Douglas' *Eneados:* A Reinterpretation', *PMLA* 67 (1952), 845–62.

DE BLASI, GIORGIO, 'L'Ariosto e le passioni: Studio sul motivo poetico fondamentale dell'Orlando furioso', Giornale storico della letteratura Italiana, 129 (1952), 318–62; 130 (1953), 178–203.

DERLA, LUIGI, 'Sull'allegoria della *Gerusalemme liberata*', *Italianistica*, 7 (1978), 473–88.

DIFFLEY, P. B., *Paolo Beni: A Biographical and Critical Study*, Oxford Modern Languages and Literature Monographs (Oxford, 1988).

DIPPLE, ELIZABETH, ' "Unjust Justice": In the *Old Arcadia*', *Studies in English Literature*, 10 (1970), 83–101.

DODGE, R. E. N., 'Spenser's Imitations from Ariosto', *PMLA* 12 (1897), 151–204.

—— 'The Text of the *Gerusalemme liberata* in the versions of Carew and Fairfax', *PMLA* 44 (1929), 681–95.

DONALDSON, IAN, 'Jonson and Anger', *The Yearbook of English Studies*, 14 (1984), 56–71.

DONATO, EUGENIO, ' "Per Selve e Boscherecci Labirinti": Desire and Narrative Structure in Ariosto's *Orlando furioso*', in Patricia Parker and David Quint (eds.), *Literary Theory/ Renaissance Texts* (Baltimore and London, 1986), 33–62.

DOWLING, MARGARET, 'Sir John Hayward's Troubles over his *Life of Henry IV*', *The Library*, NS 4: 11 (1930), 214–24.

DRONKE, PETER, 'Dido's Lament', in *Festschrift Franco Munari* (Hildesheim, 1986), 364–90.

DuBOIS, PAGE, *History, Rhetorical Description and the Epic from Homer to Spenser* (Cambridge, 1982).

DUE, OTTO STEEN, 'An Essay on Lucan', *Classica et Mediaevalia*, 23 (1962), 68–132.

DUNHAM, WILLIAM H., JUN., 'Regal Power and the Rule of Law', *Journal of British Studies*, 3: 2 (1964), 24–56.

DUNSEATH, T. K., *Spenser's Allegory of Justice in Book Five of 'The Faerie Queene'* (Princeton, NJ, 1968).

DURLING, ROBERT, 'The Bower of Bliss and Armida's Palace', *Comparative Literature*, 6 (1954), 335–47.

—— *The Figure of the Poet in Renaissance Epic* (Cambridge, Mass., 1965).

DUROCHER, RICHARD J., *Milton and Ovid* (Ithaca, NY, and London, 1985).

DUTOIT, E., 'Le Thème de "la force que se détruit elle-même" (Hor., *Epod.* 16, 2) et ses variations chez quelques auteurs latins', *Revue des études latines*, 14 (1936), 365–73.

EDMOND, MARY, *Rare Sir William Davenant*, Revels Plays Companion Library (Manchester, 1987).

EGAN, RORY B., 'Euryalus' Mother and *Aeneid* 9–12', in Carl Deroux (ed.), *Studies in Latin Literature and Roman History II, Collection Latomus*, 168 (1980), 157–76.

ELTON, G. R., 'Arthur Hall, Lord Burghley and the Antiquity of Parliament', in Hugh Lloyd-Jones, V. Pearl, and B. Worden (eds.), *History and Imagination: Essays in Honour of H. R. Trevor-Roper* (London, 1981), 88–103.

EMPSON, WILLIAM, *Milton's God* (London, 1965).

ENGLISH, H.M., JUN., 'Spenser's Accommodation of Allegory to History in the Story of Timias and Belphoebe', *Journal of English and Germanic Philology*, 59 (1960), 417–29.

ERSKINE-HILL, HOWARD, *The Augustan Idea in English Literature* (London, 1983).

FAY, H. C., 'Chapman's Materials for his Translation of Homer', *Review of English Studies*, NS 2 (1951), 121–8.

—— 'Poetry, Pedantry, and Life in Chapman's *Iliads*', *Review of English Studies*, NS 4 (1953), 13–25.

FÉCHEROLLE, PAUL, 'La Pietas dans l'Énéide', *Études classiques*, 2 (1933), 167–81.

FEENEY, D. C., 'The Taciturnity of Aeneas', *Classical Quarterly*, NS 33 (1983), 204–19.

—— 'Epic Hero and Epic Fable', *Comparative Literature*, 38 (1986), 137–58

—— '"Stat magni nominis umbra", Lucan on the Greatness of Pompeius Maximus', *Classical Quarterly*, NS 36 (1986), 239–43.

—— *The Gods in Epic* (Oxford, 1991).

FENIK, BERNARD, *Typical Battle Scenes in the 'Iliad': Studies in the Narrative Technique of Homeric Battle Description, Hermes*, 21 (Weisbaden, 1968).

FERGUSON, ARTHUR B., *The Articulate Citizen and the English Renaissance* (Durham, NC, 1965).

—— 'The Historical Thought of Samuel Daniel: A Study in Renaissance Ambivalence', *Journal of the History of Ideas*, 32 (1971), 185–202.

FERGUSON, MARGARET W., *Trials of Desire: Renaissance Defenses of Poetry* (New Haven, Conn., and London, 1983).

FICHTER, ANDREW, *Poets Historical: Dynastic Epic in the Renaissance* (New Haven, Conn., and London, 1982).

FINK, ZERA S., *The Classical Republicans: An Essay on the Recovery of an Ancient Pattern of Thought in Seventeenth-Century England*, Northwestern University Studies in the Humanities, 9 (Evanston, Ill., 1945).

FINLEY, M. I., *The World of Odysseus*, 2nd edn. (London, 1977).

FIRETTO, GAETANO, *Torquato Tasso e la controriforma* (Palermo and Milan, 1939).

FITZGERALD, ROBERT, 'Dryden's *Aeneid*', *Arion*, 2: 3 (1963), 17–31.

FRIEND, ALBERT C., 'Chaucer's Version of the *Aeneid*', *Speculum*, 28 (1953), 317–23.

FROST, WILLIAM, 'Translating Virgil, Douglas to Dryden: Some General Considerations', in Maynard Mack and George DeForest Lord (eds.), *Poetic Traditions of the English Renaissance* (New Haven, Conn., and London, 1982), 271–86.

FYLER, JOHN M., *Chaucer and Ovid* (New Haven, Conn., and London, 1979).

GADAMER, HANS-GEORG, *Truth and Method*, 2nd edn. (London, 1979).

GANG, T.M., 'The Quarrel between Edward Fairfax and his Brother', *Notes and Queries*, 214 (1969), 28–33.

GARDNER, EDMUND G., *Dukes and Poets in Ferrara: A Study in the Poetry, Religion and Politics of the Fifteenth and Sixteenth Centuries* (London, 1904).

GEERTZ, CLIFFORD, 'Centers, Kings, and Charisma: Reflections on the Symbolics of Power', in J. Ben-David and T.N. Clark (eds.), *Culture and its Creators: Essays in Honor of Edward Shils* (Chicago and London, 1977), 150–71.

GENETTE, GÉRARD, *Narrative Discourse*, trans. J.E. Lewin (Oxford, 1980).

GIAMATTI, A. BARTLETT, *The Earthly Paradise and the Renaissance Epic* (Princeton, NJ, 1966).

GIBALDI, JOSEPH, 'The Fortunes of Ariosto in England and America', in Aldo Scaglione (ed.), *Ariosto 1974 in America* (Ravenna, 1974), 135–77.

GILBERT, ALLAN H., *On the Composition of Paradise Lost* (Chapel Hill, NC, 1947).

—— 'Spenser's Imitations from Ariosto: Supplementary', *PMLA* 34 (1919), 225–32.

GILL, R.B., 'Marlowe, Lucan, and Sulpitius', *Review of English Studies*, NS 24 (1973), 401–13.

—— 'Moral History and Daniel's *The Civil Wars*', *Journal of English and Germanic Philology*, 76 (1977), 34–45.

—— 'Marlowe's Virgil: *Dido Queen of Carthage*', *Review of English Studies*, NS 28 (1977), 141–55.

GODSHALK, W.L., 'Marlowe's *Dido Queen of Carthage*', *ELH* 38 (1971), 1–18.

GOLDBERG, JONATHAN, *Endlesse Worke: Spenser and the Structures of Discourse* (Baltimore and London, 1981).

—— *James I and the Politics of Literature* (Baltimore and London, 1983).

GOULD, JOHN, 'Hiketeia', *Journal of Hellenic Studies*, 93 (1973), 74–103.

GRANSDEN, K.W., *Virgil's Iliad: An Essay on Epic Narrative* (Cambridge, 1984).

GRAZIANI, RENÉ, 'Elizabeth at Isis Church', *PMLA* 79: 1 (1964), 376–89.

GREENBLATT, STEPHEN J., 'Sidney's *Arcadia* and the Mixed Mode', *Studies in Philology*, 70 (1978), 269–78.

—— *Renaissance Self-Fashioning: From More to Shakespeare* (Chicago, 1980).

GREENE, THOMAS M., *The Descent from Heaven: A Study in Epic Continuity* (New Haven, Conn., and London, 1963).

—— *The Light in Troy: Imitation and Discovery in Renaissance Poetry* (New Haven, Conn., and London, 1982).

GREG, W. W., 'An Elizabethan Printer and his Copy', *The Library*, NS 4: 2 (1923), 102–18.

GRIFFIN, JASPER, 'The Epic Cycle and the Uniqueness of Homer', *Journal of Hellenic Studies*, 97 (1977), 39–53.

—— *Homer on Life and Death* (Oxford, 1980).

—— *Homer* (Oxford, 1980).

—— *Virgil* (Oxford, 1986).

GRIMBLE, IAN, *The Harington Family* (London, 1957).

GRUNDY, JOAN, *The Spenserian Poets: A Study in Elizabethan and Jacobean Poetry* (London, 1969).

GUILLEMIN, A., 'L'inspiration virgilienne dans la *Pharsale*', *Revue des études latines*, 29 (1951), 214–27.

GUILLORY, JOHN, *Poetic Authority: Spenser, Milton, and Literary History* (New York, 1983).

GUNDERSHEIMER, WERNER L., *Ferrara: The Style of a Renaissance Despotism* (Princeton, NJ, 1973).

HAINSWORTH, J. B., *The Flexibility of the Homeric Formula* (Oxford, 1968).

—— *The Idea of Epic* (Berkeley and Los Angeles, 1991).

HALE, DAVID, 'Sir Thomas Elyot and "Noble Homere"', *Acta*, 5 (1978), 121–31.

HALL, LOUIS BREWER, 'Caxton's "Eneydos" and the Redactions of Virgil', *Medieval Studies*, 22 (1960), 136–47.

—— 'Chaucer and the Dido-and-Aeneas Story', *Medieval Studies*, 25 (1963), 148–59.

HAMMOND, MASON, '*Concilia Deorum* from Homer through Milton', *Studies in Philology*, 30 (1933), 1–16.

HARDIN, RICHARD F., *Michael Drayton and the Passing of Elizabethan England* (Lawrence, Kan., 1973).

HARDING, DAVIS P., *The Club of Hercules: Studies in the Classical Background of Paradise Lost* (Urbana, Ill., 1962).

HARDISON, O. B., JUN., '*In Medias Res* in *Paradise Lost*', *Milton Studies*, 17 (1983), 27–41.

HARRISON, G. B., *The Life and Death of Robert Devereux Earl of Essex* (London, 1937).

HARRIT, HÉLÈNE J., 'Hugues Salel, Poet and Translator', *Modern Philology*, 16 (1919), 595–605.

HELGERSON, RICHARD, 'Barbarous Tongues: The Ideology of Poetic Forms in Renaissance England', in Heather Dubrow and Richard Strier (eds.), *The Historical Renaissance: New Essays on Tudor and Stuart Literature and Culture* (Chicago, 1988), 273–93.

HENDERSON, JOHN, 'Lucan/The Word at War', in A. J. Boyle (ed.), *The Imperial Muse: Ramus Essays on Roman Literature of the Empire to Juvenal through Ovid* (Victoria, 1988), 122–64.

HENRY, JAMES, *Aeneidea, or Critical, Exegetical, and Aesthetical Remarks in the Aeneis*, 4 vols. (London, 1873–89).

HEXTER, J. H., 'Power, Struggle, Parliament, and Liberty in Early Stuart England', *Journal of Modern History*, 50 (1978), 1–50.

HILL, CHRISTOPHER, *Intellectual Origins of the English Revolution* (Oxford, 1965).

HIRST, DEREK, 'Unanimity in the Commons, Aristocratic Intrigues, and the Origins of the English Civil War', *Journal of Modern History*, 50 (1978), 51–71.

HOUGH, GRAHAM, *A Preface to 'The Faerie Queene'* (London, 1962).

HUGHES, MERRITT Y., *Virgil and Spenser* (Cambridge, Mass., 1929).

—— 'Virgilian Allegory and *The Faerie Queene*', *PMLA* 44 (1929), 696–705.

HULSE, S. CLARK, 'Samuel Daniel: The Poet as Literary Historian', *Studies in English Literature*, 19 (1979), 55–69.

—— *Metamorphic Verse: The Elizabethan Minor Epic* (Princeton, NJ, 1981).

HUME, ANTHEA, *Edmund Spenser: Protestant Poet* (Cambridge, 1984).

HUNTER, G. K., *Paradise Lost*, Unwin Critical Library (London, 1980).

HUNTER, WILLIAM B., 'Milton on the Exaltation of the Son: The War in Heaven and *Paradise Lost*', *ELH* 36 (1969), 215–31.

—— Adamson, J. H., and Patrides, C. A., *Bright Essence: Studies in Milton's Theology* (Salt Lake City, 1971).

HUXLEY, G. L., *Greek Epic Poetry from Eumelus to Panyassis* (London, 1969).

IDE, RICHARD S., *Possessed with Greatness: The Heroic Tragedies of Shakespeare and Chapman* (London, 1980).

—— 'Exemplary Heroism in Chapman's *Odysseys*', Studies in English Literature, 22 (1982), 121–36.

ISER, WOLFGANG, *The Act of Reading: A Theory of Aesthetic Response* (Baltimore and London, 1978).

ISLER, ALAN D., 'Heroic Poetry and Sidney's Two *Arcadias*', *PMLA* 83 (1968), 368–79.

JACQUOT, JEAN, *George Chapman (1559–1634): Sa vie, sa poésie, son théâtre, sa pensée*, Annales de l'université de Lyon, NS 3: 19 (Paris, 1951).

JAMES, MERVYN, *Society, Politics, and Culture: Studies in Early Modern England* (Cambridge, 1986).

JAUSS, HANS ROBERT, *Toward an Aesthetic of Reception*, trans. Timothy Bahti (Minneapolis, 1982).

JAVITCH, DANIEL, 'Rescuing Ovid from the Allegorizers: The Liberation of Angelica, *Furioso* X', in Aldo Scaglione (ed.), *Ariosto 1974 in America* (Ravenna, 1974), 85–98.

—— *Poetry and Courtliness in Renaissance England* (Princeton, NJ, 1978).

—— 'Cantus Interruptus in the *Orlando furioso*', *Modern Language Notes*, 95 (1980), 66–81.

—— 'The *Orlando furioso* and Ovid's Revision of the *Aeneid*', *Modern Language Notes*, 99 (1984), 1023–36.

—— *Proclaiming a Classic: The Canonization of Orlando furioso* (Princeton, NJ, 1991).

JENNI, ADOLFO, 'Appunti sul Tasso', *Studi Tassiani*, 17 (1967), 5–27.

JOHNSON, W. R., 'Aeneas and the Ironies of *Pietas*', *Classical Journal*, 60 (1965), 360–4.

—— *Momentary Monsters: Lucan and his Heroes*, Cornell Studies in Classical Philology, 47 (Ithaca, NY, and London, 1987).

KATES, JUDITH A., *Tasso and Milton: The Problem of a Christian Epic* (London and Lewisburg, Pa., 1983).

KEEN, MAURICE, *Chivalry* (New Haven, Conn., and London, 1984).

KELSO, RUTH, *The Doctrine of the English Gentleman in the Sixteenth Century*, University of Illinois Studies in Language and Literature, 14 (Urbana, Ill., 1929).

KER, W. P., *Epic and Romance: Essays on Medieval Literature* (London, 1922).

KERMODE, FRANK, 'The Date of Cowley's *Davideis*', *Review of English Studies*, 25 (1949), 154–8.

—— *Shakespeare, Spenser, Donne* (London, 1971).

—— *The Classic* (London, 1975).

KING, JOHN N., *English Reformation Literature: The Tudor Origins of the Protestant Tradition* (Princeton, NJ, 1982).

KING, KATHERINE C., *Achilles: Paradigms of the War Hero from Homer to the Middle Ages* (Berkeley and Los Angeles, 1987).

KINNEY, ARTHUR F., 'Sir Philip Sidney and the Uses of History', in Heather Dubrow and Richard Strier (eds.), *The Historical Renaissance: New Essays on Tudor and Stuart Literature and Culture* (Chicago and London, 1988), 293–314.

KIRK, G.S., *The Songs of Homer* (Cambridge, 1962).

—— *Homer and the Epic* (Cambridge, 1965).

KNIGHT, W. NICHOLAS, 'The Narrative Unity of Book V of *The Faerie Queene*: "That Part of Justice which is Equity"', *Review of English Studies*, NS 21 (1970), 267–94.

KOEPPEL, E., 'Die Englischen Tasso-Übersetzungen des 16. Jahrhunderts', *Anglia*, 11 (1889), 333–62.

KOSTIC, VESELIN, *Spenser's Sources in Italian Poetry: A Study in Comparative Literature*, Faculty of Philology of the University of Belgrade Monographs, 30 (Belgrade, 1969).

KOUWENHOUVEN, JAN KAREL, *Apparent Narrative as Thematic Metaphor: The Organization of 'The Faerie Queene'* (Oxford, 1983).

LaBRANCHE, ANTHONY, 'Drayton's *The Barons Warres* and the Rhetoric of Historical Poetry', *Journal of English and Germanic Philology*, 62 (1963), 82–95.

LAPIDGE, MICHAEL, 'Lucan's Imagery of Cosmic Destruction', *Hermes*, 107 (1979), 344–70.

LATHROP, HENRY BURROWES, *Translations from the Classics into English from Caxton to Chapman 1477–1620*, University of Wisconsin Studies in Language and Literature, 35 (Madison, Wis., 1933).

LEA, KATHLEEN M., 'Harington's *Folly*', in *Elizabethan and Jacobean Studies Presented to Frank Percy Wilson* [ed. H. Davis and Helen Gardner] (Oxford, 1959), 42–58.

LEE, JUDITH, 'The English Ariosto: The Elizabethan Poet and the Marvellous', *Studies in Philology*, 80 (1983), 277–99.

LEE, M. OWEN, *Fathers and Sons in Virgil's 'Aeneid'* (Albany, NY, 1979).

LEHMBERG, STANFORD E., *Sir Thomas Elyot: Tudor Humanist* (Austin, Tex., 1960).

——'English Humanists, the Reformation, and the Problem of Counsel', *Archiv für Reformationsgeschichte*, 52 (1961), 74–91.

LESLIE, MICHAEL, *Spenser's 'Fierce Warres and Faithful Loves': Martial and Chivalric Symbolism in 'The Faerie Queene'* (Cambridge, 1983).

LEVACK, BRIAN P., *The Civil Lawyers in England 1603–1641* (Oxford, 1973).

LEVI, ANTHONY, *French Moralists: The Theory of the Passions 1585–1649* (Oxford, 1964).

LEVY, F. J., *Tudor Historical Thought* (San Marino, Calif., 1967).

LEWALSKI, BARBARA KIEFER, *Paradise Lost and the Rhetoric of Literary Forms* (Princeton, NJ, 1985).

LEWIS, C. S., *The Allegory of Love* (Oxford, 1936).

——*A Preface to Paradise Lost* (Oxford, 1942).

——*English Literature in the Sixteenth Century Excluding Drama* (Oxford, 1954).

LINTOTT, A. W., 'Lucan and the History of the Civil War', *Classical Quarterly*, NS 21 (1971), 488–505.

LOGAN, GEORGE M., 'Daniel's *Civil Wars* and Lucan's *Pharsalia*', *Studies in English Literature*, 11 (1971), 53–68.

LORD, GEORGE DeF., *Homeric Renaissance: The 'Odyssey' of George Chapman* (London, 1956).

LYNE, R. O. A. M., 'Virgil and the Politics of War', *Classical Quarterly*, 33 (1983), 188–203.

——*Further Voices in Vergil's Aeneid* (Oxford, 1987).

MACCALLUM, HUGH, *Milton and the Sons of God: The Divine Image in Milton's Epic Poetry* (Toronto, Buffalo, and London, 1986).

MCCOLLEY, GRANT, *Paradise Lost: An Account of its Growth and Major Origins* (Chicago, 1940).

MCCONICA, JAMES KELSEY, *English Humanists and Reformation Politics under Henry VIII and Edward VI* (Oxford, 1965).

MCCOY, RICHARD C., *Sir Philip Sidney: Rebellion in Arcadia* (Hassocks, Sussex, 1979).

——*The Rites of Knighthood: The Literature and Politics of Elizabethan Chivalry* (Berkeley and Los Angeles, 1989).

MCDIARMID, HUGH, 'Notes on the Poems of John Stewart of Baldynneis', *Review of English Studies*, 24 (1948), 12–18.

McIlwain, C. H., 'The English Common Law, Barrier against Absolutism', *American Historical Review*, 49 (1943), 23–31.

MacLean, Gerald M., *Time's Witness: Historical Representations in English Poetry, 1603–1660* (Madison, Wis., 1990).

MacLeod, Colin, *Collected Essays* (Oxford, 1983).

McLure, Millar, *George Chapman: A Critical Study* (Toronto, 1966).

McManaway, James G., 'Some Bibliographical Notes on Samuel Daniel's *Civil Wars*', *Studies in Bibliography*, 4 (1951), 31–9.

McMurphy, Susannah Jane, *Spenser's Use of Ariosto for Allegory*, University of Washington Publications in Language and Literature, 2 (Seattle, 1924).

McNamee, Maurice B., *Honor and the Epic Hero: A Study of the Shifting Concept of Magnanimity in Philosophy and Epic Poetry* (New York, 1960).

Mann, Jill, *Geoffrey Chaucer* (Hemel Hempstead, 1991).

Marichal, Robert, 'La première édition de la traduction de l'*Iliade* par Hugues Salel', *Humanisme et Renaissance*, 1 (1934), 156–60.

[Markham, Clements R.], 'Genealogy of the Fairfaxes', *The Herald and Genealogist*, 6 (1871), 385–407; corrected, ibid. 7 (1873), 145–60.

Marsh, David, 'Ruggiero and Leone: Revision and Resolution in Ariosto's *Orlando furioso*', *Modern Language Notes*, 96 (1981), 144–51.

Marston, Jerrilyn Greene, 'Gentry Honour and Royalism in Early Stuart England', *Journal of British Studies*, 13 (1973), 21–43.

Marti, Berthe M., 'The Meaning of the *Pharsalia*', *American Journal of Philology*, 66 (1945), 352–76.

Martindale, Charles, 'Paradox, Hyperbole and Literary Novelty in Lucan's *De Bello Civile*', *Bulletin of the Institute of Classical Studies*, 23 (1976), 45–54.

——*John Milton and the Transformation of Ancient Epic* (London and Sydney, 1986).

—— 'The Politician Lucan', *Greece and Rome*, NS 31 (1984), 64–79.

Martz, Louis, *Milton: Poet of Exile*, 2nd edn. (New Haven, Conn., and London, 1986).

Mason, R. A., 'Rex Stoicus: George Buchanan, James VI and the Scottish Polity', in J. Dwyer, R. A. Mason, and A. Murdoch (eds.), *New Perspectives on the Politics and Culture of Early Modern Scotland* (Edinburgh, 1982), 9–33.

Masters, Jamie, *Poetry and Civil War in Lucan's Bellum Civile* (Cambridge, 1992).

Mauss, Marcel, *The Gift: Forms and Functions of Exchange in Archaic Societies*, trans. I. Cunnison (London, 1954).

Maxwell, J. C., 'Lucan's First Translator', *Notes and Queries*, 192 (1947), 521–2.

Millican, C. B., 'Ralph Knevett, Author of the *Supplement* to Spenser's *Faerie Queene*', *Review of English Studies*, 14 (1938), 44–52.

Minesi, Emanuela, 'Indagine critico-testuale e bibliografica sulle *Prose diverse* di T. Tasso', *Studi Tassiani*, 32 (1984), 123–46; 33 (1985), 125–42.

MITCHELL, R. J., *John Tiptoft (1427–1470)* (London, 1938).

MONSARRAT, GILLES, *Les thèmes stoïciens dans la littérature de la renaissance anglaise* (Lille, 1975).

MORETTI, WALTER, 'La storia di Cloridano e Medoro: Un esempio della umanizzazione ariotesca delle idealità erioche e cavalleresche', *Convivium*, 37 (1969), 543–51.

—— *Cortesia e furore nel rinascimento italiano* (Bologna, 1970).

—— *L'ultimo Ariosto* (Bologna, 1977).

—— *Torquato Tasso* (Rome and Bari, 1973).

MUELLER, MARTIN, '*Paradise Lost* and the *Iliad*', Classical Literature Studies, 6 (1969), 292–316.

—— *The Iliad* (London, 1984).

MULTINEDDU, SALVATORE, *Le fonti della 'Gerusalemme liberata'* (Turin, 1895).

MURRIN, MICHAEL, *The Allegorical Epic: Essays in its Rise and Decline* (Chicago and London, 1980).

NAGLER, MICHAEL M., *Spontaneity and Tradition: A Study in the Oral Art of Homer* (Berkeley and Los Angeles, 1974).

NARDUCCI, EMANUELE, 'Ideologia e tecnica allusiva nella *Pharsalia*', in H. Temporini and W. Haase (eds.), *Aufstieg und Niedergang der Römischen Welt* (Berlin and New York, 1985), II. 32. 3, 1538–64.

NEARING, HOMER, JUN., *English Historical Poetry 1599–1641* (Philadelphia, 1945).

NELSON, T. G. A., 'Sir John Harington and the Renaissance Debate over Allegory', *Studies in Philology*, 82 (1985), 359–79.

NEWDIGATE, B. H., *Michael Drayton and his Circle*, 2nd edn. (Oxford, 1961).

NEWMAN, JOHN KEVIN, *The Classical Epic Tradition* (Madison, Wis., 1986).

NOHRNBERG, JAMES, *The Analogy of 'The Faerie Queene'* (Princeton, NJ, 1976).

NORBROOK, DAVID, *Poetry and Politics in the English Renaissance* (London, 1984).

NORTHROP, DOUGLAS A., 'Spenser's Defence of Elizabeth', *University of Toronto Quarterly*, 38 (1968–9), 277–94.

—— 'Mercilla's Court as Parliament', *Huntington Library Quarterly*, 36 (1972), 153–8.

O'CONNELL, MICHAEL, *Mirror and Veil: The Historical Dimension of Spenser's Faerie Queene* (Chapel Hill, NC, 1977).

ORLANDO, SAVERIO, '*Ars vertendi*: La giovanile versione dell'*Iliade* di Angelo Poliziano', *Giornale storico della letteratura italiana*, 143 (1966), 1–24.

ORME, NICHOLAS, *From Childhood to Chivalry: The Education of the English Kings and Aristocracy 1066–1530* (London, 1984).

OTIS, BROOKS, *Virgil: A Study in Civilized Poetry* (Oxford, 1964).

—— *Ovid as an Epic Poet*, 2nd edn. (Cambridge, 1970).

OWEN, W. J. B., 'The Structure of *The Faerie Queene*', *PMLA* 68 (1953), 1079–1100.

—— 'Narrative Logic and Imitation in *The Faerie Queene*', *Comparative Literature*, 7 (1955), 324–37.

PALMA, GIUSEPPE DALLA, 'Dal secondo al terzo *Furioso*: Mutamenti di struttura e movimenti ideologici', in Cesare Segre (ed.), *Ludovico Ariosto: Lingua, stile e tradizione. Atti del congresso organizzato dai communi di Reggio Emilia e Ferrara 12–16 ottobre 1974* (Milan, 1976), 95–105.

PALMER, HENRIETTA R., *List of English Editions and Translations of Greek and Latin Classics printed before 1641* (London, 1911).

PALOCK, BARBARA, *Eros, Imitation, and the Epic Tradition* (Ithaca, NY, and London, 1990).

PARKER, PATRICIA A., *Inescapable Romance: Studies in the Poetics of a Mode* (Princeton, NJ, 1979).

PARKER, W. R., *Milton: A Biography*, 2 vols. (Oxford, 1968).

PARRY, ADAM, 'The Two Voices of Virgil's *Aeneid*', *Arion*, 2: 4 (1963), 66–80.

—— *The Making of Homeric Verse* (Oxford, 1971).

PARRY, HUGH, 'Ovid's *Metamorphoses*: Violence in a Pastoral Landscape', *Transactions and Proceedings of the American Philological Association*, 95 (1964), 268–82.

PARSONS, LEILA, 'Prince Henry (1584–1612) as a Patron of Literature', *Modern Language Review*, 47 (1952), 503–7.

PATRIDES, C.A., *Milton and the Christian Tradition* (Oxford, 1966).

PATTERSON, ANNABEL, '*Paradise Regained*: A Last Chance at True Romance', *Milton Studies*, 17 (1983), 187–208.

—— *Censorship and Interpretation: The Conditions of Writing and Reading in Early Modern England* (Madison, Wis., 1984).

PETROCCHI, GIORGIO, 'Virgilio e la poetica del Tasso', *Giornale italiano di filologia*, NS 2: 23 (1971), 1–12.

PHILLIPS, JAMES E., 'George Buchanan and the Sidney Circle', *Huntington Library Quarterly*, 12 (1948), 23–55.

—— *Images of a Queen: Mary Stuart in Sixteenth-Century Literature* (Berkeley and Los Angeles, 1964).

—— 'Renaissance Concepts of Justice and the Structure of *The Faerie Queene* Book V', *Huntington Library Quarterly*, 33 (1969–70), 103–20.

PHINNEY, EDWARD, JUN., 'Continental Humanists and Chapman's *Iliads*', *Studies in the Renaissance*, 12 (1965), 218–26.

PITCHER, JOHN, 'Samuel Daniel's Letter to Sir Thomas Egerton', *Huntington Library Quarterly*, 47 (1984), 55–61.

POCOCK, J.G.A., *The Machiavellian Moment: Florentine Political Thought and the Atlantic Republican Tradition* (Princeton, NJ, 1975).

—— *The Ancient Constitution and the Feudal Law: A Study in English Historical Thought in the Seventeenth Century*, rev. edn. (Cambridge, 1957, 1987).

PÖSCHL, VIKTOR, *The Art of Virgil: Image and Symbol in the Aeneid*, trans. Gerda Seligson (Ann Arbor, Mich., 1962).

POTTER, LOIS, *Secret Rites and Secret Writing: Royalist Literature, 1641–1660* (Cambridge, 1989).

PRALL, STUART E., 'The Development of Equity in Tudor England', *American Journal of Legal History*, 8 (1964), 1–19.

PRAZ, MARIO, *The Flaming Heart: Essays on Crashaw, Machiavelli, and Other Studies in the Relations between Italian and English Literature* (New York, 1958).

PRESCOTT, ANNE LAKE, *French Poets and the English Renaissance* (New Haven, Conn., and London, 1978).

PURSGLOVE, GLYN, 'Robert Tofte, Elizabethan Translator of Boiardo', in J. Salmons and W. Moretti (eds.), *The Renaissance in Ferrara and its European Horizons* (Cardiff and Ravenna, 1984), 111–22.

PURVES, JOHN, 'The *Abbregement of Roland Furious* by John Stewart of Baldynneis, and the Early Knowledge of Ariosto in England', *Italian Studies*, 3 (1946–8), 65–82.

PUTNAM, MICHAEL C.J., *The Poetry of the Aeneid: Four Studies in Imaginative Unity and Design* (Cambridge, Mass., 1965).

—— '*Pius* Aeneas and the Metamorphosis of Lausus', *Arethusa*, 14 (1981), 139–56.

QUILLIGAN, MAUREEN, *Milton's Spenser: The Politics of Reading* (Ithaca, NY, and London, 1983).

QUINT, DAVID, *Origin and Originality in Renaissance Literature: Versions of the Source* (New Haven, Conn., and London, 1983).

—— 'Epic and Empire', *Comparative Literature*, 41 (1989), 1–32.

RAJNA, PIO, *Le fonti dell'Orlando furioso: Ricerche e studi* (Florence, 1876).

REES, JOAN, *Samuel Daniel: A Critical and Biographical Study* (Liverpool, 1964).

REINHOLD, MEYER, 'The Unhero Aeneas', *Classica et Mediaevalia*, 27 (1966), 195–207.

RICE, EUGENE F., JUN., *The Renaissance Idea of Wisdom*, Harvard Historical Monographs, 37 (Cambridge, Mass., 1958).

RICH, TOWNSEND, *Harington and Ariosto: A Study in Elizabethan Verse Translation*, Yale Studies in English, 92 (New Haven, Conn., 1940).

ROBERTS-BAYTOP, ADRIANNE, *Dido, Queen of Infinite Literary Variety: The English Renaissance Borrowings and Influences*, Salzburg Studies in English Literature, English and Renaissance Studies, 25 (Salzburg, 1974).

ROCHE, THOMAS P., JUN., *The Kindly Flame: A Study of the Third and Fourth Books of Spenser's Faerie Queene* (Princeton, NJ, 1964).

ROLLINS, HYDER E., 'New Facts about George Turbervile', *Modern Philology*, 15 (1917–18), 513–38.

ROSE, MARK, *Heroic Love: Studies in Sidney and Spenser* (Cambridge, Mass., 1968).

RUTHERFORD, R.B., 'Tragic Form and Feeling in the *Iliad*', *Journal of Hellenic Studies*, 102 (1982), 145–60.

SACCONE, EDUARDO, *Il 'soggetto' del 'Furioso' e altri saggi tra quatri e cinquecento* (Naples, 1974).

—— 'Prospettive sull'ultimo Ariosto', *Modern Language Notes*, 98 (1983), 55–69.

SALMONS, J., and MORETTI, W. (eds.), *The Renaissance in Ferrara and its European Horizons* (Cardiff and Ravenna, 1984).

SAMMUT, ALFONSO, *La fortuna dell'Ariosto nell'Inghilterra elisabettiana* (Milan, 1971).

SANCTIS, FRANCESCO DE, *Storia della letteratura italiana*, ed. Benedetto Croce, rev. A. Parente (Milan, 1912).

SANDISON, HELEN ESTABROOK, 'Arthur Gorges, Spenser's Alcyon and Ralegh's Friend', *PMLA* 43 (1928), 645–74.

SAVOIA, FRANCESCA, 'Notes on the Metaphor of the Body in the *Gerusalemme liberata*', in Luisa Del Giudice (ed.), *Western Jerusalem: University of California Studies on Tasso* (New York, 1984), 57–70.

SAWDAY, JONATHAN, ' "Mysteriously Divided": Civil War, Madness and the Divided Self', in Thomas Healy and Jonathan Sawday (eds.), *Literature and the English Civil War* (Cambridge, 1990), 127–43.

SAYCE, R.A., *The French Biblical Epic in the Seventeenth Century* (Oxford, 1955).

SCHEIN, SETH L., *The Mortal Hero: An Introduction to Homer's Iliad* (Berkeley and London, 1984).

SCHMITZ, GÖTZ, *The Fall of Women in Early English Narrative Verse* (Cambridge, 1990).

SCHOELL, FRANCK L., 'George Chapman and the Italian Neo-Latinists of the Quattrocento', *Modern Philology*, 13 (1915), 215–38.

——*Études sur l'humanisme continental en Angleterre à la fin de la renaissance*, Bibliothèque de la revue de littérature comparée, 29 (Paris, 1926).

SCHOEMBS, JACOB, *Ariosts* Orlando furioso *in der Englischen Literatur des Zeitalters der Elizabeth*, Strasburg Doctoral Thesis, (Soden a.T., 1898).

SCHOLES, ROBERT, *Structuralism in Literature* (New Haven, Conn., and London, 1974).

SCHUNK, ROBIN R., *The Homeric Scholia and the 'Aeneid': A Study of the Influence of Ancient Homeric Literary Criticism on Vergil* (Ann Arbor, Mich., 1974).

SEGAL, CHARLES P., 'Myth and Philosophy in the *Metamorphoses*: Ovid's Augustanism and the Augustan Conclusion of Book XV', *American Journal of Philology*, 90 (1969), 278–90.

——*Landscape in Ovid's 'Metamorphoses'*, Hermes, 23 (Wiesbaden, 1969).

SEWELL, ARTHUR, *A Study in Milton's Christian Doctrine* (Oxford, 1939).

SHANKMAN, STEVEN, *Pope's 'Iliad': Homer in the Age of Passion* (Princeton, NJ, 1983).

SILVER, ISIDORE, *Ronsard and the Hellenic Renaissance in France*, i. Ronsard *and the Greek Epic* (St Louis, 1961).

SIMEONE, L., 'L'elezione di Obizzio d'Este a Signore di Ferrara', *Archivio storico italiano*, 93 (1935), 165–88.

SIMON, JOAN, *Education and Society in Tudor England* (Cambridge, 1967).

SIMON, JOCELYN, 'Dr Cowell', *Cambridge Law Journal*, 26 (1968), 260–72.

SIMPSON, PERCY, 'Ben Jonson on Chapman', *The Times Literary Supplement*, 3 March (1932), 155.

SINGERMAN, JEROME E., *Under Clouds of Poesy: Poetry and Truth in French* and English Reworkings of the 'Aeneid', *1160–1513* (New York and London, 1986).

SKINNER, QUENTIN, *The Foundations of Modern Political Thought*, 2 vols. (Cambridge, 1978).

SMALLEY, DONALD, 'The Ethical Bias of Chapman's *Homer*', *Studies in Philology*, 36 (1939), 169–91.

SMITH, HALLETT, *Elizabethan Poetry: A Study in Convention, Meaning and Expression* (Cambridge, Mass., 1952).

SNODGRASS, A. M., *The Dark Age of Greece: An Archaeological Survey of the Eleventh to the Eighth Centuries BC* (Edinburgh, 1971).

SNOW, VERNON F., 'Essex and the Aristocratic Opposition to the Early Stuarts', *Journal of Modern History*, 32 (1960), 224–33.

—— *Essex the Rebel: The Life of Robert Devereux, the Third Earl of Essex* (Lincoln, Nebr., 1970).

SOMMERVILLE, J. P., *Politics and Ideology in England, 1603–1640* (London, 1986).

SPENS, JANET, 'Chapman's Ethical Thought', *Essays and Studies*, 11 (1925), 145–69.

SPRIET, PIERRE, 'Samuel Daniel (1563–1619): Sa vie—son œuvre', *Études anglaises*, 29 (1968).

STAHL, HANS-PETER, 'Aeneas—an "Unheroic" Hero?', *Arethusa*, 14 (1981), 157–77.

STANFORD, W. B., *The Ulysses Theme: A Study in the Adaptability of a Traditional Hero*, 2nd edn. (Oxford, 1963).

STEADMAN, JOHN M., *Milton and the Renaissance Hero* (Oxford, 1967).

—— 'Achilles and Renaissance Epic: Moral Criticism and Literary Tradition', in Horst Meller and Hans-Joachim Zimmerman (eds.), *Lebende Antike: Symposion für Rudolf Sühnel* (Berlin, 1967), 139–54.

—— *The Walls of Paradise: Essays on Milton's Poetics* (Baton Rouge, La., and London, 1985).

STERN, VIRGINIA F., *Gabriel Harvey: His Life, Marginalia, and Library* (Oxford, 1979).

STEWART, DOUGLAS J., *The Disguised Guest: Rank, Role and Identity in the Odyssey* (Lewisburg, Pa., and London, 1976).

STIRLING, BRENTS, 'Daniel's *Philotas* and the Essex Case', *Modern Language Quarterly*, 3 (1942), 583–94.

STONE, LAWRENCE, *The Crisis of the Aristocracy 1558–1641* (Oxford, 1965).

STRONG, ROY, *Henry, Prince of Wales and England's Lost Renaissance* (London, 1986).

TATLOCK, JOHN S. P., 'The Siege of Troy in Elizabethan Literature, Especially in Shakespeare and Heywood', *PMLA* 30 (1915), 673–770.

THOMPSON, LYNETTE, and BRUÈRE, R. T., 'Lucan's Use of Virgilian Reminiscence', *Classical Philology*, 63 (1968), 1–21.

—— —— 'The Virgilian Background of Lucan's Fourth Book', *Classical Philology*, 65 (1970), 152–72.

THORNTON, AGATHE, *Homer's Iliad: Its Composition and the Motif of Supplication*, Hypomnemata, 81 (Göttingen, 1984).

TILLYARD, E. M. W., *The English Epic and its Background* (London, 1954).

TODD, MARGO, *Christian Humanism and the Puritan Social Order* (Cambridge, 1987).

TODOROV, TZVETAN, *The Poetics of Prose*, trans. R. Howard (Oxford, 1977).

TREVOR-ROPER, H. R., 'George Buchanan and the Ancient Constitution', *English Historical Review*, Suppl. 3 (1966).

TURNER, JAMES GRANTHAM, *One Flesh: Paradisal Marriage and Sexual Relations in the Age of Milton* (Oxford, 1987).

TUVE, ROSAMUND, *Allegorical Imagery: Some Medieval Books and their Posterity* (Princeton, NJ, 1966).

VESEY, DAVID, *Statius and the Thebaid* (Cambridge, 1973).

VICARIO, ANNAGIULIA ANGELONE DELLO, *Il richiamo di Virgilio nella poesia italiana (momenti significativi)* (Naples, 1981).

VICKERS, BRIAN, 'Epideictic and Epic in the Renaissance', *New Literary History*, 14 (1983), 497–538.

VOGT, GEORGE McGILL, 'Gleanings for the History of a Sentiment: *Generositas Virtus, non Sanguis*', *Journal of English and Germanic Philology*, 24 (1925), 102–24.

WAITH, EUGENE M., *The Herculean Hero in Marlowe, Chapman, Shakespeare and Dryden* (London, 1962).

—— *Ideas of Greatness: Heroic Drama in England* (London, 1971).

WALLERSTEIN, RUTH C., 'The Development of the Rhetoric and Metre of the Heroic Couplet, Especially in 1625–1645', *PMLA* 50 (1935), 166–209.

WALZER, MICHAEL, *The Revolution of the Saints: A Study in the Origins of Radical Politics* (London, 1966).

WEINBERG, BERNARD, *A History of Literary Criticism in the Renaissance*, 2 vols. (Chicago, 1961).

WELLS, ROBIN HEADLAM, *Spenser's 'Faerie Queene' and the Cult of Elizabeth* (London, 1983).

WELLS, WILLIAM (ed.), 'Spenser Allusions in the Sixteenth and Seventeenth Centuries', *Studies in Philology*, Supplements 68 (1971) and 69 (1972).

WIGGINS, PETER DE SA, 'The *Furioso*'s Third Protagonist', *Modern Language Notes*, 98 (1983), 30–54.

—— *Figures in Ariosto's Tapestry: Character and Design in the 'Orlando furioso'* (Baltimore and London, 1986).

—— 'Spenser's Anxiety', *Modern Language Notes*, 103 (1988), 75–86.

WILCOX, JOEL F., 'Ficino's Commentary on Plato's *Ion* and Chapman's Inspired Poet in the *Odyssey*', *Philological Quarterly*, 64 (1985), 195–209.

WILKINSON, L. P., *Ovid Recalled* (Cambridge, 1955).

WILLIAMS, R. D., 'The Purpose of the *Aeneid*', Antichthon, 1 (1967), 29–41.

WILLIAMSON, GEORGE, 'Milton the Anti-Romantic', *Modern Philology*, 60 (1962), 13–21.

WILLIAMSON, J. W., *The Myth of the Conqueror: Prince Henry Stuart: A Study in Seventeenth-Century Personation* (New York, 1978).

WILSON, ELKIN CALHOUN, *England's Eliza*, Harvard Studies in English, 20 (Cambridge, Mass., 1939).

——*Prince Henry and English Literature* (Ithaca, NY, 1946).

WINNIFRITH, TOM, MURRAY, P., and GRANSDEN, K. W. (eds.), *Aspects of the Epic* (London, 1983).

WIRSZUBSKI, C., *Libertas as a Political Idea at Rome during the Late Republic and Early Principate* (Cambridge, 1950).

WOOLF, D. R., 'Community, Law and State: Samuel Daniel's Historical Thought Revisited', *Journal of the History of Ideas*, 49 (1988), 61–83.

WORDEN, BLAIR, 'Classical Republicanism and the Puritan Revolution', in Hugh Lloyd-Jones, V. Pearl, and B. Worden (eds.), *History and Imagination: Essays in Honour of H. R. Trevor-Roper* (London, 1981), 182–200.

——'Fulke Greville, Friend to Sir Philip Sidney', *The London Review of Books*, 8: 12 (July 1986), 19–22.

WRIGHT, H. G., *The Life and Works of Arthur Hall of Grantham*, Publications of the University of Manchester, English Series, 9 (Manchester, 1919).

WRIGHT, JOHN, *Essays on the Iliad: Selected Modern Criticism* (Bloomington, Ind., and London, 1978).

Index

Sub-headings for 'actions', for 'epic parallels', and for 'other parallels' are followed by entries in chronological, rather than alphabetical, order. This is so a reader can readily follow who does what when. In entries for major texts a list of *passages discussed* follows after the main alphabetical listings.